TRADER CLARK

Six decades of racing lore

by John H. Clark

1991
THOROUGHBRED PUBLICATIONS, INC.
LEXINGTON, KENTUCKY

Copyright © 1991 by Thoroughbred Publications, Inc.

All rights reserved. No part of this book may be reproduced or transmitted in any form or by any means, electronic or mechanical, including photocopying, recording, or by any information storage and retrieval system, without written permission from the publisher.

Articles in this book appeared in *The Thoroughbred Record* from 1980-'82 and *Thoroughbred Times* from 1987-'90.

Published by Thoroughbred Publications, Inc., 801 Corporate Drive, Lexington, Kentucky 40503

Manufactured in the United States of America

ISBN 1-879850-00-1

Contents

Foreword .... *i*

Chapter 1
Getting Started in Tradin' 1

Chapter 2
Colonel Phil T. Chinn 14

Chapter 3
From Keene to Keeneland 27

Chapter 4
Giants of the Bluegrass 50

Chapter 5
Plain Ben and Jimmy 70

Chapter 6
Rascals and Writers, Hardboots and Hangouts 87

Chapter 7
Legends of the Sport 109

Chapter 8
Breeding, Buying, and Selling 132

Chapter 9
The Senor and Other Masters of the Turf 160

Chapter 10
Life Is a Gamble 185

Chapter 11
Around the Circuits 202

Chapter 12
Clients and Other Owners 227

Chapter 13
Horsemen and Friends 264

Chapter 14
Jockeys I've Known 291

Index 325

Acknowledgements

This book was compiled from a collection of articles that was published originally under the title "Clark's Chronicles." "Clark's Chronicles" first appeared in the April 23, 1980, issue of *The Thoroughbred Record*, under the direction of editor Dan Farley. "Clark's Chronicles" appeared in the *Record* until 1982. John Clark resumed writing "Clark's Chronicles" in 1987 in the *Thoroughbred Times*, under editor Mark Simon, and excerpts in this book appeared in print in the *Times* from 1987 to '90.

In the decade "Clark's Chronicles" was published, literally dozens of people worked on the articles—editing, researching, and proofreading.

In publishing the collection under the title *Trader Clark*, special mention needs to be made for the contribution of book editor Don Clippinger, who took hundreds of separate stories written over a ten-year period and wove them into a cohesive work that reads as if the book were written in a single sitting.

Patty Lankford was responsible for researching and verifying facts for the book, in addition to proofreading the manuscript. Others who helped research and proofread were Anne Scott, Jan Jennemann, and David Dink.

Doris Waren provided considerable research on the original articles, and Dr. Alex Harthill was the inspiration for many of the story ideas.

Susanna Thurston and Christie Hardy designed the book and the layout. Bob Bunting illustrated and designed the cover.

Foreword

John Clark walks into the office with a cigar hanging out of his mouth and looking like he's just mucked out some stalls. His cigar is unlit, as is usually the case, and the end of it looks like it's been chewed on for hours.

While John Clark does smoke, more often than not the cigars are used merely as a prop to his story telling. He sits back in his chair and begins, "Did I ever tell you about ..." and then launches into one tale that quickly leads to another. If you have all day to listen, he will have all day to tell tales. Throughout the storytelling, the cigar is used for emphasis, produced at just the right time, as he stabs the air or points at his listener with it.

The key ingredient to all John's stories is humor. To tell a tale that didn't make light of himself or his subject just isn't worth telling.

The other primary ingredient of John's stories is people. People, first and foremost. He rarely tells stories about horses, only about the people who owned them, or bred them, or trained them, or foaled them, or rubbed them, or bought them, or sold them. "This is a people sport," he often says.

The stories he tells are always entertaining, and the listener cannot help but sit in amazement over the range of people and stories John knows— knows them like they just happened on the way to the office. Here was someone who seemingly knew everyone who has participated in the sport in the last 50 years. His stories encompass the breadth of the industry, from the biggest names in the business to exercise riders and grooms. To John, there is no class distinction. Each and every one is an integral part of the game, and each has his own story.

ii   Trader Clark

The word "story" is used loosely here, because fact and fiction in racing, as the years pass, are often hard to distinguish. And, for all purposes, it matters not. The stories John tells are treasures of the Turf, a permanent part of the lore of racing. Many of the stories are known only to John because he was there, an active participant. Which is another way of saying that only he can testify as to the veracity of the tale.

His first-hand involvement with owners, breeders, and trainers was made possible because he was a "horse trader," a term that today has evolved into bloodstock agent.

John was called "Trader Clark" because, when he was starting to make a name for himself in the early 1940s, there happened to be another John Clark—John C. Clark—and a distinction had to be made between the two, as if the two would ever be confused: John C. Clark was president of Hialeah Park and a member of the Jockey Club.

But, more significantly, he was called "Trader" because that's what he did. An honest name for an honest man. He dealt in volume because he liked to turn over horses at small profits. "I operated by the theory that I never bought a horse too quickly, feeling that if I was patient I would get him at my price and be able to resell him quickly at a profit, and I never sold a horse for the absolute most I ever could get for him. This way I could get in and out of the market quickly, making a lot of trades. I would be in there 20 times while someone else was in there just once."

The name Trader followed him around the races for a decade, until he became an adviser to Captain Harry F. Guggenheim, owner of the powerful Cain Hoy Stable and one of the leading owner-breeders in the country in the 1950s and '60s. When he went to work for Guggenheim, Dr. Eslie Asbury, one of John's best friends and clients, told him one day that he should drop the name Trader, because it was not a dignified appellation for a man working for Guggenheim. The name was soon abandoned, for over three decades, only to resurface because of his work on this book. "I'm proud," he says, "of the name 'Trader.' Because many of the stories I wrote about I learned while I was Trader Clark."

Before one gets the wrong impression, it should be noted that John H. Clark was not and is not just a trader. As the great writer Joe Palmer once wrote of him in the New York *Herald-Tribune*: "Suffice it to say he does 'this thing and that' in the business to make a damn fine living."

Born July 23, 1919, John started out in the game early, in his pre-teens, showing horses and earning some money, and then used his growing knowledge of horses and people to get a job as a reporter for the Lexington *Herald* and *Leader*. Though he had no formal training in writing or reporting, this did not deter him from asking for—and getting—the job. This was accomplished by boldly walking into the office of the publisher of the newspaper, Fred Wachs, and telling him that he would like to be a Turf writer. He was 15 years old.

Okay, Wachs said, he could have the job, but he was to be paid only when his stories were printed. Rather than sit around an office, John went to find the stories—at the farms, on the backstretch, and in the track kitchen.

He made enough contacts, and impressed enough people with his knowledge, that he was able to get into what he always wanted to do—tradin' horses. He hung out his own shingle, in the Hernando building in downtown Lexington, which also happened to be the site where the legendary Colonel Phil T. Chinn operated.

This was not coincidental: John wanted to learn from the best. He learned his lessons well. He went on to become an adviser to some of the leading owners and breeders in the business, which in turn put him in the position of being able to give back to the sport something in return.

He advised such important owner-breeders as John D. Hertz, Captain Guggenheim, and Elizabeth Arden; was publicity director for Keeneland; helped reconstitute the then-dormant Thoroughbred Breeders of Kentucky to help fight unfavorable legislation that was being considered in Washington, D.C., and was elected its president; was regional vice president of the Kentucky division of the Horsemen's Benevolent and Protective Association; trained horses; owned stakes winners; and has been an integral part of the American polo scene—for over ten years, he was chairman of the rules committee of the U.S. Polo Association, and was rated at two goals at age 60.

In recent years, John has spent considerable time as an expert witness on legal cases in the Thoroughbred industry. In typical style, he is quick to point out that the side he's represented has never lost a case.

John still lives on his farm directly across from Keeneland Racecourse next to Bluegrass Field. At the age of 71, he still rides polo ponies and breaks them at his farm.

The great sports writer Red Smith once said that racing was his favorite sport because it had more interesting stories—and characters—than any other. Everyone familiar with racing knows that to be true.

In the pages that follow, John Clark brings to life—and saves for posterity—many of the characters this sport has produced.

Upon completion of the book, there is a good chance that the reader will come to the conclusion that one of the most memorable characters contained in this book is John H. Clark himself.

Mark Simon, Editor
Thoroughbred Times
March 21, 1991

Chapter 1
Getting Started in Tradin'

To steal a line from the old Jimmy Stewart movie, it *has* been a wonderful life. I do not believe that I could have asked for anything more, and I did not need an angel second-class named Clarence to tell me that. Almost before I knew how to read, I knew what I wanted to do with my life. I wanted to work with horses. I knew that with an iron-clad assurance since I started my activities in our wonderful game at the old trotting track located near my family's home in south Lexington. The year was 1925. I was six years old.

Fortune never smiled more kindly on a kid from an impoverished family who had a great love for horses and an insatiable thirst for knowledge of them. Almost from the first day I was able to read, I studied the history of our game back to before the turn of the century. I also closely followed current events in the horse industry as it sunk into some pretty nasty times during the Great Depression. In addition, I poured over statistical records on Standardbreds and Thoroughbreds.

I made up my mind when I was seven or eight years old that I wanted to be a horse trader, that I would become Trader Clark. In addition to the harness track, my childhood hangout was the Old Tattersalls sales barn on South Broadway, where numerous Saddlehorse dealers stabled and trained their horses. I rode everything that passed for a horse, and I was often called upon to demonstrate the gentleness of horses the traders there were offering for sale to out-of-town buyers in quest of a safe mount for their children or their wives. When a sale was made, I would be given $5 or $10 or $20 to take home to my mother.

Trader Clark.

My mother, who was not at all horse-oriented, started getting suspicious. One day when I returned with a crisp C-note, the first time I had ever seen a picture of Benjamin Franklin outside of a school book, she said: "I'm going to check this out, and if Mr. Walter Baker didn't give it to you as you say, you're in for a good paddling. I'm not going to allow you to steal." Thank goodness for Walter Baker. He verified the gratuity and added: "Little Johnny deserved even more—I made more than $2,000 on that sale."

By age 12, I had won my first time out in a child's riding class at a local horse show, and was getting paid handsomely for driving trotters and pacers in workouts at The Red Mile, and I won an amateur race in my first drive in competition at age 14.

In my early teens, I considered myself very well-informed, not just with my "book knowledge" but my practical experience. In addition to my work with the Saddlebreds and the Standardbreds, I had walked hots, groomed, and galloped Thoroughbreds (which I did until nearly my 70th birthday). I was a cocky kid. Polite—"Yes sir," "No sir," "Thank you sir"—but still a little too brash. George Kerler, in a profile on me in the Lexington *Leader* a few years later, noted: "Johnny has an attractive immodesty."

My experience and my reading put me in good stead to start the Turf writing phase of my horse career with by-line stories in the Lexington *Leader* at the age of 15. My first big break came in 1934 when I rode my bicycle to the *Leader* building and appeared in the outer office of the crusty and tyrannical publisher, Fred B. Wachs. I told his friendly secretary, Miss Adams, that I would like to talk to him about becoming the newspaper's Turf writer. In a few minutes, I was sitting before Wachs.

"How old are you, Johnny, and who do you know in the horse business?" Wachs asked. I answered each question with confidence, the last of which was: "And I guess you want a by-line?" "Certainly," I replied. After Wachs had laughed out loud for what seemed an eternity, repeating "a 15-year-old by-line Turf writer" several times, he stopped and said seriously: "You're hired, you'll get $3 a column. Be sure of your facts. Someone in the sports department will help you with your composition."

I was on my way. Within five years I would be writing weekly Sunday features for the *Leader*, the Cincinnati *Enquirer*, and the Louisville *Courier-Journal*. The money I made from my writing for these newspapers and from contributing notes, mostly oddities, to Clem McCarthy for his daily syndicated column on racing provided me with the funds to complete high school and two years of college. They also helped buy a very, very used car that got me to the farms, Churchill Downs, and old Latonia.

My second big break during those early years was establishing a lifelong friendship with Joe Estes, then editor of *The Blood-Horse* and the most brilliant writer and researcher of my time. He taught me what statistics to compile and how to interpret them. He was 30 years ahead of his time.

My by-lines also gave me recognition that I would need in my horse business activities later on. Because, as much as I love to write about the wonderful people and athletes in the Thoroughbred business, it was always my "road game." Trading horses got "into my blood" and never left. As Joe Palmer once wrote of me in his New York *Herald-Tribune* column: "Suffice it to say he does 'this thing and that' in the business to make a damn fine living."

A Choice Location

Back in 1940, at age 20, I decided to strike out on my own as a sales agent. Sheer fate—I had little wisdom then, if I indeed have any now—told me to take office space in the Hernando Building in Lexington. The building was located between two hotels, one door removed from the train station. Among the office lessees were Phillip Thompson Chinn, W. Arnold Hanger, Horatio P. Mason, and the Kentucky State Racing Commission.

I guess Lady Luck told me to play for the fallout. I would be in the hub of the horse business—and the rent was right, $25 a month for a one-room office, janitorial service included. The fallout indeed came quickly. I wrote a very formal letter to Senator Johnson N. Camden, chairman of the racing commission, noting that he was a far better judge of pedigree than I, but that with my limited knowledge of Thoroughbred breeding and conformation, the mare on which I had a listing was reasonably priced at $2,500. He bought her two days later. I made a big $250 commission. I was on my way.

Training and Tradin'

Not getting enough listings to sell or orders to buy, I borrowed heavily through a banker friend and started horse tradin' on my own. Unbroken yearlings that went through the September sales at Keeneland were cheap in those days. In training as two-year-olds, if they were sound and could run a bit, you could expect a 300% return on an investment. Also, you could buy a well-bred filly off the racetrack, fatten her up, and get about 200% profit by selling her as a broodmare prospect. I went both ways, and did well.

At first, I sent my two-year-olds to other trainers, selling them after they had worked well or raced decently a time or two. By 1950, I was taking a string of two-year-olds to Hialeah, training them myself, and selling them. I got off to a flying start. Cold Heart, with apprentice jockey Steve DiMauro riding, won her first start as a two-year-old. She cost me $2,000, and I sold her for $15,000. She won four races and was a close second at Saratoga Race Course in the 1952 Schuylerville Stakes. Ted Atkinson won first time out for me with Sotto Voce. I had paid $5,600 for her and sold her for $25,000.

A hands-on trainer.

I could not sell Chalk Talk at my price, and trainer Red Ness won the 1957 Narragansett Nursery Stakes with her for me. Mabe Cee went unsold, too, even after she won her first start, but by August she had won seven races for me, placed in a stakes, and I sold her at auction in Saratoga for $25,000. She only cost $1,000 as a yearling.

I often reinvested profits from sales. I bought Winning Count, announced as wind-broken, for $800 in September of 1953 at a Belmont Park auction, tied down his tongue, and won with him in his first lifetime start 30 days later. The following April, he was second for me in the Arkansas Derby, and I sold him for my biggest price ever for a racehorse to W. Cal Partee.

I have held a trainer's license in nearly every racing state east of the Mississippi River, and I have enjoyed training—but never fully. Because of the absolute-insurer rule, which I agree is necessary for the integrity of racing, I have always felt ill at ease until 48 hours after the test. Fortunately, I have never had a bad test. Now that they are coming up with positives months later from frozen samples, I no longer want to be a trainer of record.

Hardly Hardship Duty

With Uncle Sam indicating he was about to call me into the service, I enlisted in the Navy in late 1942, got security clearance to distribute secret films from a New York lab, and was provided subsistence to bivouac in a cheap hotel near Times Square. It was the best duty I could draw. The lab did not operate nights or Sundays, and I put those hours to good use, buying and selling by night, and visiting Belmont or Jamaica Racetrack on my one day off. I even found a way to keep my name "alive" by writing a weekly column for *The Thoroughbred Record*, titled "Memos From Manhattan."

In Uncle Sam's silks.

I came out of the Navy in the fall of 1945 with a poor man's fortune because the Thoroughbred market had been rising constantly during the previous three years. I reopened my office. If 1946 was a good year for me (and it was), 1947 was even better. Two major clients came my way that year—John D. Hertz, on the recommendation of Bull Hancock, and Captain Harry F. Guggenheim, who employed me upon the suggestion of Joe Estes. "E" sent me customers from the first day I opened an office, and two other cherished clients that he guided to me were Crispin Oglebay and Dr. Eslie Asbury. Also in 1947, I bought my first farm, a 22-acre tract abutting Keeneland.

Figuring Out Quiz Song

It has long been my thought that more horses have been "whipped out of the money than in." I claimed the best horse I ever owned, Quiz Song, for $15,000 because I thought that whip abuse was causing her to sulk and that, by abandoning its use, I could improve her. It was at Hialeah in early 1952. I went to the stewards and asked for permission to remove the whip from her

Quiz Song, the author's pride and joy.

racing equipment. It was not granted, but Jack Campbell told me: "The rider must carry it, but he won't have to use it for the next few starts—we'll understand."

Quiz Song was not struck with the whip again while she was racing. By year's end, she had won three good allowance races and the Correction Handicap (beating Sickle's Image, champion handicap mare the following year), the only stakes I ever won in New York.

The Great Persuader

In 1958, I went on a mission of mercy to help my pal Jim Edwards conduct his first meeting at Waterford Park, a "leaky roof" West Virginia track he had bought the previous fall. "What do you need of me?" I asked when he insisted I come to his aid. Edwards replied: "Your savvy of horsemen and racing. In fact, your eyes, your ears, and your mouth, if I need any talking done on my behalf." It was a challenge.

The first day I was there, the sheriff arrived at Jim's apartment above the grandstand and demanded "a binding of their friendship—with cash." He noted that the previous owners always accommodated him with funds from the parking concessions. "If I don't?" parried Edwards. "Then the roads to the track will be kept torn up throughout the meet." Jim invited the officer into his bedroom, pressed the nose of a Colt .45 into his right ear, and said: "If I have occasion to meet you again over the roads, we'll be just like this—except I'll be pulling the trigger."

No roads were bothered.

One night at dinner, John Hanson, an agent for the Thoroughbred Racing Protective Bureau, "confided" to me that he was about to start searching tack rooms and automobiles for contraband. Historically, the "leaky roof" trainer is his own vet, and we had plenty of them there. A raid would have closed down the meet. On the next overnight came this announcement: "This is a Thoroughbred Racing Associations track. Starting immediately and continuing throughout the meet, raids should be expected by the TRPB."

I thought John pulled my leg on that one, but if he did, it was for a good purpose. Everyone suspected that Waterford trainers were illegally medicating, even Jim Edwards when he was chairman of the West Virginia Racing Commission. "Who me?" Jim said in mock surprise when I mentioned it to him. "Never heard a thing."

Jim, like most of us, could not get too much of a good thing. With no political payoffs, expenses down to the bare bones, attendance and mutuel play far exceeding expectations, it was only natural for Edwards to announce a "double daily" program for Friday, July 4, 1958, with some 16 races spread over the morning and afternoon. Jim had been smarting for a confrontation with the mutuel clerk's union—actually wanted it—and he knew July 4 was the day he would get it.

It was my job to go to the track kitchen each morning, stand on a table top in my stable clothes, and fire up the horsemen. "Are you gonna let them mutuel clerks break up your livelihood?" They shouted back: "Hell no!" "Do they put bread on your table?" "Hell no!" "Do they hold the water hose on the sore leg of your old mare?" "Hell no!"

On the Fourth of July, the clerks went out and the horsemen stepped in, amazed at the simplicity of selling and cashing tickets. At the end of the day, the mutuel ledger balanced, and there were no patron complaints. Jim paid them regular mutuel wages—and raised the purses.

Teaching Manners to a Rogue

In December of 1963, I purchased Pocket Ruler, a son of *Nasrullah, then age nine, from Elizabeth Arden because she feared he would injure a stud groom. She said, "Give me $100,000 for him and get him off my farm today." That was a bargain price and I jumped on it. At the time he had but 15 foals of racing age, and four of them were stakes winners. But he was vicious—he would paw, kick, or bite you, all three in the same setting if he had time.

We had to catch him in his stall with a long pole with a hook on it, then lead him with two men, one on each side. You could not get to him to punish him. But I found a way: On his back. Each morning we would get my polo tack on him and I would ride him as long as it took to tire him, spurring him and

Pocket Ruler under orders from Clark.

whipping him continuously. He soon learned that, if he would be kind, the grooms and I would treat him kindly.

I stood him at stud the seasons of 1964, 1965, and 1966, then sold a well-mannered Pocket Ruler to Jim Sabiston of Ontario, Canada. He turned out to be a lucrative investment for me after I altered his attitude.

Be Certain of Your Horse

The first lesson I learned in tradin' horses was to ascertain identity. In my teenage years, I bought a broodmare prospect, a fairly well-bred mare with a decent race record, for $500. I gave my check and trailered her off the farm of the seller, a reputable dealer who each fall bought large numbers of fillies off the racetrack. This was before lip tattoos were used for identification.

I received the filly's Certificate of Registration by mail a few days afterwards. Just to learn how to relate the markings of a Thoroughbred to the description on the certificate, I compared them and learned, much to my chagrin, that they did not agree. The dealer, informed of the discrepancy, came immediately, acknowledged his mistake, and apologized. Convinced he had not tried to flimflam me, I did not take the refund he offered me, but instead applied it toward another filly he offered in exchange.

In real estate, the three most important factors are: "Location, location, location." Similarly in tradin', the three major concerns are "Identity, identity, identity." The Jockey Club recommends to breeders that, when the Certificates of Registration are mailed to them, they check the certificates against the foal's or yearling's markings and make any corrections promptly. Some people fail to do this, and some come to regret that they did not.

By the time a horse is ready to make its first start and is presented for lip tattooing, thousands of dollars have already been spent. The horse cannot race without a tattoo number, and the technician will refuse to make the imprint if there is a discrepancy between the markings and those listed on the certificate. In a few weeks, these matters can generally be cleared up by the Jockey Club correcting the certificate—after considerable paperwork, cost of training, lost racing opportunity, and aggravation.

I have been doing consulting work since 1980 for Fireman's Fund Insurance Companies, which insures veterinarians against malpractice largely by assisting its attorneys in preparing a defense in litigation alleging negligence and by testifying at trial about the value of the horses involved. Most of the cases are settled.

Several years ago, Tom Brown, an adjuster in the Tampa office, phoned and asked: "Mr. Clark, do you do trotters and pacers?" "Nope," I replied, "but my brother Charlie is big in that game. He'll help me, and I'll give it a try. Send me what you've got." He noted that the complainant had not yet filed a suit and wanted to negotiate a settlement.

Shortly thereafter, photocopies of the filly's Certificate of Registration arrived in the mail, as did statements from two veterinarians located 200 miles apart, each reporting the filly's name, tattoo number, and their finding, upon examination, of paralysis of the left side of the larynx (wind-broken to you and me). It was their judgment that the offending vet had injected a substance into the laryngeal nerve.

I immediately checked for identification. The tattoo number the vets listed was the same, but it was different than the number assigned to her by the United States Trotting Association. The USTA assigns a tattoo number on the original Certificate of Registration. A quick call to the USTA confirmed that there had been no change in the assigned number for the filly in question, and that the number on the vet reports belonged to another horse. When I reported this to Brown and he relayed the information to the "aggrieved" owner, that ended it. The guy had broken the law by making a fraudulent claim. The vets had protected themselves by listing the tattoo number of the filly they examined.

Last year, I was called on to arbitrate a dispute between two friends, both of whom were also friends of mine. They agreed that my decision would be final, and they also agreed to split my fee 50-50 for the appraisal work in the matter. To protect their identities, I will refer to them as "Oaks" and "Doaks." Oaks is a breeder-owner and Doaks an owner-trainer. For several years, Doaks had bought one yearling privately from Oaks, and it was a deal that has worked out to their mutual satisfaction.

In the fall of 1988, Doaks went out to Oaks's farm to make his annual purchase and was given a computer-generated pedigree to review as each colt was led out for examination. The problem arose because there were two look-alikes, one priced for $10,000, and the other for $15,000. Doaks selected the cheaper one, wrote his check for $10,000, and Oaks delivered the colt to Doaks at the Kentucky Horse Center near Lexington.

Come spring, Doaks presented the colt for tattooing, and the crew turned him down because the horse did not have two cowlicks and white inside his left hind heel. Doaks immediately phoned Oaks, who checked the look-alike and reported back that he had delivered the $15,000 colt. Then the friendly debate began.

They came to my office, and each stated his case. Oaks offered to switch papers for $5,000. Doaks countered that he would trade the colts even. "No way," each said to the other. I pointed out that there was also "no way" either of them could get duplicate certificates from the Jockey Club, short of a court order, and that, as matters presently stood, each colt was worthless.

I asked them to return the next day for my decision, which was: They were to switch papers, and Doaks was to pay Oaks $2,500. They were both at fault, Oaks for delivering the wrong colt, and Doaks for not checking what he had received. I found no malice on the part of either.

They were both stunned at first, but the mood changed when we started chatting about other things in our business. They both left the office happy and are still good friends. Upon their departure, I telephoned Mike Meuser, a brilliant young lawyer in Harry Miller's firm in Lexington with good knowledge of our business, and asked him his opinion on how a judge would have ruled had this case ended up in court. He replied: "He would have rescinded the sale, Doaks would have gotten his $10,000 back, plus expenses incurred, and interest on his $10,000."

It Ran in the Family

The topic of horse identification reminded me of an amusing story. Warren Wright Sr. and his father, William M. Wright, shared a common trait. Neither could identify their horses. Another thing they had in common was the sense to seek out the best advice and follow it.

In 1920, when the elder Wright established Calumet Farm as a Standardbred nursery, he instructed his trainer and farm manager, Dick McMahon, to buy one—and only one—gray broodmare. When he would drive out to the broodmare field with guests, he would point to the gray mare, Zombrewer, and say: "There's probably my best mare. Dick, you can tell them about the rest." Zombrewer later was to become famous as the grandam of Greyhound, one of the greatest trotters of all time.

Warren took over Calumet upon his father's death in 1931 and converted it to Thoroughbreds. Recently I asked H. A. "Jimmy" Jones, for 20 years Calumet's trainer, if it were true that his boss could not identify his horses. Jimmy laughed and said: "Only one and that was Whirlaway. He was the only horse we ever had whose tail was so long it touched the ground."

The Stress of Shipping

I have always believed that you cannot start too early to familiarize a Thoroughbred with things that later will cause fear or stress. Two that I always work on are the starting gate and the van-trailer. Warren Wright concluded that the anxiety of shipping stressed a Thoroughbred so much that he bought a six-horse van. From the 1930s until his death, the Calumet youngsters were hauled around the farm from the time they were weaned until they went into the training stable as yearlings.

For years I have schooled young horses to load and unload themselves into and from a two-horse trailer. I did this by setting aside one paddock for two youngsters, and in it I had parked the trailer, tailgate down and the wheels securely blocked. For the first few days, they would be led into the rig, where their feed tubs, with grain, were in place. Thereafter, when they would see the groom walking toward the trailer with grain, they would be loaded and ready for dinner by the time it was poured into their tubs. The next procedure was to hitch the trailer to a truck, close the tailgate, and drive them around the paddock. Once they graduated, they would be replaced by two more horses for the same education.

Demystifying the Starting Gate

To break well, a horse must be relaxed with all four feet on the ground. A lot of horses are overtrained and overraced, but I have never seen one overschooled at the starting gate. I began gate schooling with the start of the breaking process. Not owning a starting gate, I construct four parallel partitions, 2½ feet apart, solidly boarded on both sides, 60 inches high. Each time the youngsters leave the stable for exercise, they enter my "gate" and stand several minutes. Upon their return, they do the same thing. The first few days they have to be led in, but after that they can be ridden in without urging.

The first time I take them to the starting gate—if the starter will work with me, and most have—I break them four or five times in a row, letting them go a sixteenth of a mile before being pulled up, then return them to the gate, where they stand until completely relaxed and ready for the next "go." With the preliminary training they have had in my improvised gate, and the calming periods between breaks in this "crash" course at a regular starting gate, their fears of the gate are dispelled—except for a few individuals that require more time and special handling. In nearly 50 years of training, I never had a horse of mine placed on a starter's list.

A Threat to the Industry

Perhaps my proudest honor in the business was being elected president of the Thoroughbred Breeders of Kentucky by acclamation in late 1965. Captain Harry F. Guggenheim, for whom I had previously worked as a consultant, admonished me at lunch at Aqueduct one day. "You better get back to Kentucky and inform those breeders they badly need a lobby in Washington," Guggenheim said. "The Tax Reform Act of 1969 is going to disallow the expense of raising and racing horses as well as performance horses." Captain Guggenheim had close ties with Washington, D. C.

Upon my return to Lexington, I started to put together a game plan on how best this near impossible task could be accomplished, and I arranged a meeting with Warner Jones Jr. and Leslie Combs II to discuss it. Though this was the most serious problem facing the industry, we had still others that badly needed confronting with a united front. Warner and Leslie were ready to put up a fight against this industry-killing change in the tax code. "You are our leader, tell us what to do," exclaimed Jones. "And," added Combs, "if the people you ask to come along and help don't, they won't breed at Spendthrift Farm."

I stated that first we would need a state breeders organization to get the others throughout the country to join us in setting up a national lobby. I suggested we reconstitute the Thoroughbred Breeders of Kentucky, which had ceased to function. It was agreed that everything had to be done in haste. A time and date were set for a meeting in the ballroom of a local hotel, and the notice I mailed out announcing it, over the signatures of Jones, Combs, Bull Hancock, John Gaines, and myself, stated its purpose was to discuss "urgent matters of a very serious nature to the Thoroughbred business."

I presided. The hall was packed. As if the proposed changes in the Tax Reform Act of 1969 were not enough to set those in attendance afire, I added a couple of other stingers. The blacksmiths, without reasonable cause, had recently increased their rates for shoeing and trimming, and the local van

Telling tales at Keeneland.

men had applied to the Kentucky Department of Transportation to be regulated. The latter meant that no longer could a farm operator transport any horses other than his own, "and that will virtually close down the breeding and racing industry in Kentucky, for they do not have one-fourth enough equipment to accommodate the necessary service."

A motion made, seconded, and passed, made this an official meeting of the Thoroughbred Breeders of Kentucky. Next, I breezed in as president for 1966. Most of my term was spent revitalizing the organization. The following year, with Warner as president, we were able to start work toward forming a national lobby. Hancock and Jones persuaded Albert Clay to come aboard. Clay, a quiet man who works in wondrous ways, knows his way around Washington. It was largely through his efforts years before that the tobacco lobby was established. Soon, Clay was in the horse business, the American Horse Council was formed, and the Tax Reform Act of 1969 did us no harm. Albert Clay remained very active in Horse Council affairs, helping to keep our business out of harm's way.

I cannot imagine what life would have been without horses and horse people. One is indeed blessed when his vocation is his avocation and the greatest joy in his life.

Chapter 2
Colonel Phillip T. Chinn

Colonel Phillip Thompson Chinn, the self-proclaimed "greatest deficit spender of all time" and one of my first mentors in the tradin' business, left this mortal sphere in February, 1962, at the age of 87. He was a happy soul, and he delighted those who were fortunate enough to become his acquaintances with stories of his life, most of them portraying himself as the goat. The scams and the shenanigans always overflowed with good humor.

Noting that he had always "traveled skeleton-rigged" as far as finances were concerned, he would add: "With some frequency I've gone bust during a depression, but just as often I've gone down in a boom." Spending more than he took in was a way of life for him. Buying brought him more joy than selling, but he could never balance his ledger because he did both on "terms." He was the ultimate "paper man," and there rarely was enough cash flow from his tradin' to pay the help.

Chinn once told me: "I like buying from rich people. They generally have well-bred horses and, more importantly, they're able to offer terms." Once when I was with Chinn at Dr. Eslie Asbury's farm looking at the physician breeder's entire crop of weanlings, he asked the good doctor: "What'll it take to move that chestnut colt to Old Hickory?" Old Hickory was the name of Chinn's farm.

While Dr. Asbury was meditating, P. T. added: "And to hell with the price. What are the terms?" Chinn's anchor in times of financial trouble was his friend from boyhood, Rodman Keenon, a very successful lawyer.

Colonel P. T. Chinn.

Chinn was forever borrowing from Ike to pay Mike. He laughingly referred to a debt he owed or one owed to him as an "open account." He and his longtime friend, W. T. "Fatty" Anderson, who had just as many ups and downs, frequently traded positions on the ledger. Back in 1926, when Fatty won the $65,000 Coffroth Handicap at Tijuana with *Carlaris, a horse he had purchased on the cuff from Chinn, the colonel telegraphed him: "Congratulations. Chinn can use $5,000. Phil." Accompanying the money order for $10,000 that came the same day was the message: "Anyone who needs five can use ten. W. T."

Max Hirsch, the Hall of Fame trainer, once told me: "If everyone paid Chinn what is owed him, and he paid off all he owed, he'd net out a millionaire." Instead, he died busted, but he took to the grave the best "eye" for a horse that I ever encountered.

Boosting a Buyer's Account

One day during one of our regular lunches at the Canary Cottage on the ground floor of the Hernando Building in Lexington, Chinn asked if I would assist in correcting a financial situation that afternoon. I said I would if it did not involve my bank account, which was then crowding zero. "Not at all," he replied. "We're going to build up another man's bank account so I can buy a horse that I don't think I can live without, from a man who insists on cash."

The man whose account needed boosting had bought a horse from Chinn, but his check had twice been returned to the colonel with a slip noting "NSF," insufficient funds to cover the check. Chinn then surmised that his customer was deliberately keeping his bank balance below the face value of the check to buy time and test the horse before accepting or rejecting him. Ingenious thinker that he was, Chinn contrived a plan to counter that.

For several days, the colonel had telephoned the bank on which the check for $2,500 was drawn. Each day, he would state the check was for $100 less than the amount he had reported the previous day. Just before lunch that day, the bank had told Chinn the check would work at his stated amount, $2,200. Needless to say, we did not have dessert. Chinn was in a hurry to execute his plan—and then buy another horse.

When we arrived in front of the bank at the nearby country town, the colonel gave me $300 in folding money and instructed me to write out a deposit slip, then make the deposit to the purchaser's account. I looked at him curiously. "Don't worry," he said. "Banks aren't stuffy when you put money in. They're only fastidious when you take money out."

The deposit completed, Chinn directed me to drive around the block, then stop again at the bank. This time, the colonel went in. "The check worked this time," he chuckled as he got back in the car. "I cashed it. Remind me to have Miss Elam bill him for that $300 deposit. Now drive me to Charlie Nuckols's place. My option on that colt I've been trying to buy from him runs out tonight."

The 'Must Pass' Student

Phil Chinn was the son of Colonel Jack Chinn, who had a well-deserved reputation as a brawler and a Bowie knife fighter. Chinn himself said his father "was a fair and pleasant man to deal with, but, to those who lied to him or double-crossed him, he'd inflict unmerciful, physical assault." Indeed, *The Thoroughbred Record* in its November 19, 1892, issue reported that the elder Chinn "attempted to stab a bookmaker named Downing for some previous misunderstanding. Downing's life was saved by the fact he expected Chinn's assault and wore a breast plate of steel under his shirt."

Colonel Jack could take it as well as dish it out. "Twice people he had walloped returned with pistols and shot him, thinking he was dead upon their departure," his son said. "But when hospital reports indicated he was going to survive, the two assailants sold their farms and moved out of state."

Colonel Jack Chinn.

Colonel Jack also was a strong defender of his son's reading preferences. The principal of Mercer County High School (in Central Kentucky) made the mistake of writing a letter to Colonel Jack that said: "Phillip is not going to graduate because he devotes more time in school reading *The Thoroughbred Record* than his textbooks." This prompted Colonel Jack to call on the principal the next day during recess. He knocked the principal down, then picked him up and put him down again five times before the entire student body. Thereafter, the teachers in Mercer County knew well that Phillip "must" pass each semester regardless of his monthly grades or final examinations. "I graduated," Chinn mused, "but was not my class's valedictorian."

Chinn Promotes the 'Bull from Boston'

Phil Chinn even attended college, but he was better known for his promotional skills than his scholarship. In his freshman year at Centre College, at nearby Danville, Kentucky, Phillip didn't take on a part-time job, as did most of the students. He opened up with an enterprise he called "Chinn Promotions," which was to bring special attractions to the campus.

He was doing very well, although he was frequently called on the carpet by the dean of men for "overselling the house" and for not providing refunds to those who purchased tickets in advance, arrived a bit late, and found themselves crowded out of even the standing-room-only sections.

A pretty good amateur prize fighter himself, P. T. convinced the college champ he could gain national recognition—and start a lucrative career—if he could knock out "The Bull from Boston, Ferocious Frank," the champ at Harvard University, in a "six rounder." The kid agreed.

Promotion started immediately. This time, Chinn called on the dean of men instead of waiting to be summoned. He promised that he would follow previous admonishments and not oversell the house, but it would be necessary for him to sell two types of admission tickets, one at student prices and the other at non-student prices. He allowed that it was going to be quite expensive to bring down the young man from Boston. Permission was granted.

Chinn then went to the printers and struck a deal. In exchange for their printing the tickets and about 200 posters, they were to receive a reasonable number of non-student tickets for themselves and their best customers. Shortly thereafter, the town of Danville was plastered with posters announcing the match.

Strangely, the student tickets were sold out within an hour, but plenty of non-student tickets were available at the higher price. There were some complaints and accusations about the absence of lower priced ones, but the "happening" was a sellout a week before the match.

There really was not any travel expense. "The Bull from Boston, Ferocious Frank" was, in reality, a big, burly farm kid from a small village in Mercer County who ran four miles every night after a hard day's work, then hit a punching bag for an hour. Prize fighting was that small village's favorite sport. The kid had knocked out not only all the local boys and men, but also all interlopers who challenged him.

At weighing-in ceremonies, attended by a throng a few hours before the match, the Centre College champ took one look at "Ferocious Frank," whose arms and muscles and hands were twice the size of his, and motioned Phil to one side and presented him a "light" problem—"I just got a bad case of diarrhea. Get somebody else," the champ told Chinn.

Believing he could persuade the farm chap "to go easy," Chinn instantly announced to the crowd: "My dear friend and school chum here unfortunately had something for lunch that has given him a gastrointestinal pain. He's willing to go on, but I don't think it's fair to let him in his condition. Therefore, I shall take his place." Wouldn't it be something if the freshman champ from Centre knocked out the senior champ from Harvard?

Promoter Phil thanked all for coming and, with a "see you all tonight," walked away with the farm lad, explaining to him: "Now you'll have to go easy with me. I've been working pretty hard on this big event and haven't had time to work out. Let's just spar around for a round or two, then you hit me a hard, glancing blow—and I do mean glancing—and I'll go down and be counted out. For this, I'm going to give you $40 instead of $20. "Ferocious Frank" agreed.

The fight is now under way in the first round, and "Ferocious Frank" is throwing bombs and barely missing the head of P. T. The crowd's rooting for their college freshman—"Knock him out, Phil; knock him out, Phil"—angered the Mercer County boy, and he started fighting in earnest. Now I'll let Colonel Phil finish his story.

"With two blows to my body—it felt like his fists went through me both times—I was in the corner. I see this right coming at my head. I didn't duck; I collapsed against the ring post. He grazed the top of my head but hit the ring post with full force and broke his hand. I pulled myself off the canvas, expressed my deepest regret to him and the loyal boxing fans, noting the fight was over.

"He and I dashed back to the dressing room, put on our robes, gathered up our clothes. I took him immediately to the hospital, not the nearest one in Danville, but the one the next town over in Harrodsburg, Mercer County."

The next day, Phil T. Chinn was notified to report to the dean of men.

A 'Good Thing' Is Not a 'Sure Thing'

Once in Mexico, P. T. had a "good thing" that needed backing in the books very badly, and he had run out of sponsors. Being at Juarez, he had heard that General Pancho Villa was encamped with his troops nearby. Ingenious man that he was, the colonel arranged a meeting and a satisfactory arrangement with Villa.

Just a few hours before the race, one of Villa's lieutenants arrived at the Chinn stable. "The general told me to tell you," he began in broken English, "the money is down, but the horse *must* win."

A quick-thinking man, Chinn replied: "Please offer the general my deepest regrets. This colt has unfortunately just developed colic, and I'm going to have to scratch him."

Pancho Villa to the Rescue

Master promoter Matt Winn and Pancho Villa.

However, Pancho Villa did help Chinn to overturn a ruling by presiding steward Charles F. Price. After a heavily bet horse owned and trained by Colonel Phil performed as planned and won in a flagrant form reversal at the old Juarez track, Judge Price sent word to Chinn that without a hearing, he was "down for the meeting."

That night, while delivering Pancho Villa his cut of the coup, Colonel Chinn told the Mexican general of his plight. The next afternoon a squad of Villa's soldiers stormed the stewards' stand, chanting: "Chinn go back up,

Chinn go back up." Discretion being the better part of valor, Judge Price immediately vacated his ruling.

Chinn's 'Sure Thing' on the Atlantic

Colonel Phil once recalled for me some of his gambling coups, both as a layer and a player. In the old days while racing at Havana, Cuba, and Juarez, Mexico, it was not unusual for him to have a slate in the betting ring, but he had a "sure thing" only one time, and that was not on a racetrack.

"It was on a luxury liner when I was coming back on a dry run I had made to France to try to sell some of James R. Keene's horses to the Rothschilds," Chinn recalled. "Well, the Germans had torpedoed and sunk the *Lusitania* the day before (on May 7, 1915). There were no lights used on the boat the rest of the trip and the passengers were panicky. One told me he sure wished he could get some more life insurance. I told him I'd accommodate him for $1,000 even money that we'd embark safely. Word got around, and in an hour or so I had faded about 20 people. When the captain, who was holding the stakes, gave me a fishy eye, I winked back to let him know he was "in." This was the best of "sure things." If the boat goes down, I lose anyway. If we arrive safely, I collect."

Chinn's Horses Come In 'C.O.D.'

The "house horse" has long been a beef of the Horsemen's Benevolent and Protective Association. The horsemen's organization has charged that horses owned by people with direct or indirect influence on track management get preferential treatment in writing races, in formulating race conditions, or in assigning weights for handicaps.

Colonel Chinn invented his own version of the "house horse." He sent his horses in "C.O.D." "I'd tell the tracks I had some nice horses but no shipping money. Many of them would let me ship in 'C.O.D,' pay my transportation charges, bed my stalls, and put in an ample amount of feed. Those bills would be deducted from the earnings of my horses. That way, I never had to worry about conditions in the book until after the track had gotten square with me," he said.

An Unerring Eye for a Horse

In 1940, when I was far enough along in my horse tradin' to need a downtown office, I rented one in the Hernando, whose tenants then included Colonel Chinn, W. Arnold Hanger, and the Kentucky Racing Commission. It was located on Main Street between Lexington's two best hotels, the Lafayette and the Phoenix, and adjacent to the railroad station. John E. Madden had maintained an office there until his passing in 1929. No horse trader's office could be better located.

Nearly every day, the colonel and I lunched together in the Canary Cottage, and in the afternoons I would drive him to his farm or other places where he had business. I thirsted for his knowledge and spent every minute possible with him.

When he was buying for resale—pinhooking—he could arrange "terms" if the sale price was below $1,000. Above that, if he could not cuff it, he would get a backer and refer to him as a "sponsor." G. Ray Bryson, president and general manager of the Bel Air track in Maryland and the owner of a sizable racing stable, did quite a number of sponsorships while I was around Colonel Chinn in the 1940s.

At Chinn's price, Bryson bought many off-bred horses that made excellent runners. He would purchase them as yearlings, then sell them for big prices off workouts as yearlings or two-year-olds. One that he told me about was Sarazen (whom he purchased for about $500), which he sold for $35,000 to Mrs. W. K. Vanderbilt III, who turned him over to Max Hirsch for training. Sarazen was Horse of the Year in 1924 and 1925, champion three-year-old male of 1924, and the handicap champion in 1925 and 1926. Max considered him and Assault to be "the best two I ever trained."

One summer afternoon in 1940 as Colonel Phil and I were motoring out the Paris Road, he interrupted his story and said: "Turn right up here at the Terry Brothers store. I think I have some business down the Huston-Antioch Pike." As soon as I had turned, he exclaimed: "Stop the car! Look at that colt over there behind that wire fence on the right—there's a runner if I ever saw one." The youngster was no nearer than 100 feet. Never getting out of the car, and after looking at him for less than 30 seconds, he instructed me: "Back the car up to the store and go in and ask George Terry how much he is going to charge Chinn for that colt."

"Don't you first want to know how the colt is bred?" I inquired. "No," he replied. "I want to buy him regardless of his breeding, but you can ask about it."

Upon my return, I reported: "Seven hundred dollars cash to you or anybody else. He's by Jack High and is the first foal of a mare that didn't race. She's by Terry and out of a mare by Great Britain, a horse I never heard of."

"Go back and tell George we'll be right back with the check," he said. Then, in a nearly inaudible murmur, he said: "I think, I hope, I have $700 in the bank."

The horse was With Regards.

The next spring, when the colt showed that he had unusual ability, Chinn sent him to his old friend, T. D. "Pinky" Grimes, "on consignment," which meant Pinky could buy the colt himself or sell him for Chinn. Pinky did the former and made no mistake. That year, the good-looking but obscurely bred colt won half of his six starts, and the following two years finished first or second in 14 major stakes, including victories in the Arkansas Derby Stakes in 1942, and the Paumonok and Aqueduct Handicaps in 1943.

The Day the Quarter Pole Moved

Although Chinn's escapades often were spiced with chicanery in its most humorous vein, I never knew him to cheat anyone in the 25 years I was closely associated with him in business and social life—and I was with him almost daily.

He loved to embellish lavishly on his pranks, but there was one that he would never discuss. He would not deny it; just would not talk about it. This was the most famous of his alleged capers: *The moving of the quarter pole.*

Eastern buyers would come down to the old Lexington Association track for Chinn's yearling trials. The yearlings would work a quarter-mile in sets of two or three, then be sold privately off breeding, conformation, soundness—and performance. One particular year, it is said, the Chinn yearlings were not so precocious, and it presented to him a "light problem" since he owed for most of the yearlings that needed very badly to be sold if their breeders were to be paid.

The "problem" was solved, but unfortunately, the solution was detected and later reported by an old trainer, John Rodegap, who always timed from a bench that aligned perfectly with the quarter pole and a large elm tree just outside the track. Rodegap could not believe his watch on the first set. He had trained there for years and had never timed a yearling in :22.

Looking at the quarter pole, thinking he had snapped his watch late, the old trainer in astonishment uttered to another: "God, in his infinite wisdom and mercy, has moved that there elm tree, or someone has moved the quarter pole." Rodegap, then in his 70s, timed the rest of the trials, then trudged across the infield to verify which of the markers had been moved.

He knew, but he just wanted to verify his findings. Sure enough, the pole had been moved during the night about 100 feet closer to the finish line. Fresh dirt at both points proved it to him.

The people from the East, as well as track management, left the grandstand for the Chinn stable for a final inspection of the yearlings who had had their trials, and thence downtown to the Phoenix Hotel for a typical "Kentucky buffet" consisting of old ham, fresh garden vegetables, and mint juleps.

It was not until Monday, after the Saturday trials, that Rodegap could report his findings. The Saturday buffet had been quite a success. All the yearlings were sold. The track superintendent had not shown up on Sunday morning. He, too, had enjoyed the party.

By Sunday morning, the quarter pole had been returned to its proper location. Rodegap said it had to have been moved back there during the night. He took witnesses with him to show them the fresh diggings at the "proper and fraudulent locations of the pole." One of them admonished trainer Rodegap that he was impugning the reputation of the son of the chairman of the Kentucky State Racing Commission, the fearsome Colonel Jack Chinn.

An anonymous letter reported the matter to the racing commission, and not only did Colonel Jack decline to disqualify himself from the proceedings, but he also appointed himself chairman of the subcommittee to investigate the matter. The panel did find fresh dirt at the two locations. But strangely, although the moving of the pole had been the "talk of the track," not a single soul there knew anything about it, not even Rodegap.

At the next meeting of the commission, Colonel Jack stated to his board: "My subcommittee has made a thorough investigation of the charges brought against my son by some scurrilous individual so cowardly he did not sign his name. There is not a scintilla of evidence; there are no witnesses to give testimony. I am delighted, for I would rather fall on my Bowie knife in the presence of you gentlemen than to think my son, Phillip Thompson, would commit a dishonest act. Case dismissed!"

A Friendly Wave Seals a Sale

Gus Ring, a leading Thoroughbred owner of the 1970s and 1980s, picked and purchased horses with a minimum of counsel. I represented him for 35 years, off and on—the interims being after he or I had fired the other. Gus parlayed a low-paying bricklaying job into millions.

Chinn knew how to help people make up their mind.

I never knew but one trader to put it on Ring, and that was, you guessed it, Colonel Phil. He intercepted Ring just after he detrained from Washington for the Keeneland July sale. With his disarming charm, the colonel escorted him to the Lafayette Hotel and then whisked him away to his farm to "look at a colt that's the spitting image of Sarazen, a good horse I had to sell because I was traveling skeleton-rigged, very much in the shorts."

Chinn knew he was tuning Gus in just right. Gus had never seen Sarazen. Gus told Chinn: "I'm almost persuaded. Drop me off at Keeneland. I want to look at a couple of yearlings. Meet me in the hotel lobby at noon and I'll give you my answer. It would be nice if I could see his pedigree."

They met on schedule. Gus told the champion horse seller of all time: "Give me about 20 minutes. I'm going up to my room, phone my office, wash up a bit, and read this pedigree."

"Can't do that," was Chinn's quick reply. "Your option expired at noon, and it's now ten after 12. I've got to honor the second option I've given to that Texan with the big Western hat sitting over there in the corner."

"Where?"

"Right over there," Colonel Phil said as he pointed and waved to the total stranger, who politely nodded and waved back.

"Okay, I'll take him," Gus replied, and he immediately wrote the check.

I was chauffeuring the colonel that day and witnessed it all. Putting the check in his pocket as Gus departed for the elevator, he turned to me: "Now there's another lesson for you, young man. You have to help people make up their minds."

"By the way, go over there and find out that gentleman's name, just so I can tell Gus if he asks. Tell him also I'm P. T. Chinn if he's interested in buying a horse."

The Back-Rent Diversion

You will recall how I netted my first major commission, $250 for selling a horse to Senator Johnson N. Camden. With check in hand, I raced from my office on Hernando's fourth floor, down the staircase to the third, and into the office of Colonel Chinn.

"Hmmmmm," said Chinn, looking at the check, "Chinn needs badly to sell a horse. I was to pay Mason-Hanger the rent on the farm I have leased on the first of the month. I am to discuss my ten-day delinquency today at lunch in the Canary Cottage with Horatio. I've called down to Fish Wheeler for a table for four at noon. Could you ease in there with that check about five minutes after noon? I'll invite you for lunch since it's my turn with Horatio, and I'll then give you a list of about 20 horses I've got for sale at prices that will move them. Just remember, if Horatio brings up the rent, you change the subject back to my 20 horses."

I told Colonel Chinn I would—and I did—because I needed listings badly. Horatio, gentleman that he was, never brought up the back rent at lunch, and in a few days I had sold a horse for Chinn that enabled him to pay the back farm rent—and a sales commission to yours truly.

The Good Ones Go Home

Colonel Phil, who knew all the tricks of the auction ring and used them, once told me: "If you know a man bids up his horses at auction, don't bid on them. Wait until the auction is over and buy the ones you like that he takes home. Be assured he won't back one that is bad."

The Blind and Gentle Mare

Back in my early days as a horse trader, I was able to buy a well-bred mare, guaranteed in foal, with a good production record, for a few hundred dollars. I could not wait for such a bargain buy, so I completed the transaction hastily over the phone, sight unseen. When the check cleared, she was delivered, totally blind.

Hearing my lament, Colonel Phil took her off my hands at my cost. "The best-looking foals I've ever raised have been from blind mares," he said. "They move about slowly, don't run their foals to death, and their foals are always able to nurse at their will. I now have five blind mares." The good colonel always kept a special field or paddock for blind mares.

Yes, Colonel Phil might have been something of a good-humored rascal. But, when it came to using his "eye" for good horses and to tradin', he had few equals.

Chapter 3
From Keene to Keeneland

Keeneland Race Course, Lexington's self-described monument to "racing as it was meant to be," is an institution with deep and rich traditions—even though the first race meeting occurred in October, 1936, less than 60 years ago. Following are some anecdotes about the people associated with the Keeneland property and the men who shaped that first, radically innovative racing season.

The Right Man for the Job

Back just before the turn of the century, James R. Keene had one of the most powerful racing stables in the country, and he decided he wanted to start breeding his own runners in Kentucky. The right man to run the operation, he knew, would be the key to its success.

Major Foxhall A. Daingerfield, his brother-in-law, became available through adversity. His home and law library at Culpepper, Virginia, which were uninsured, had been leveled by fire. Major Daingerfield, a very knowledgeable horseman in his own right, had been counseling Keene on racing matters for some time.

By 1904, operating with a free hand, Major Daingerfield had purchased Castleton Farm and adjoining tracts to increase the property to 1,072 acres. Also by then, he was breeding the highest percentage of top stakes horses raised at any farm in the world. That success rate was to continue until the

James R. Keene.

deaths of Keene and Daingerfield, which came a few days apart in January, 1913. Because of failing health, Keene, a couple of years before his death, sold the farm to David M. Look (Standardbreds), and he also dispersed eight stallions, 45 mares, and 36 yearlings.

During the entire period that Keene bred horses in Kentucky, he visited the farm but twice—a clear indication of his trust in Daingerfield's judgment and his satisfaction with the horses raised at the Kentucky farm. The following is only a part of the record:

• In a span of 14 years, 1898-1911, Daingerfield raised five Belmont Stakes winners at Castleton. In addition, Keene had raced the 1879 winner, Spendthrift.

• From 20 named foals in his only two crops, Keene's stallion Domino sired eight stakes winners, including a champion, Commando, and Cap and Bells, winner of the 1901 Epsom Oaks.

• In four small crops of just 25 foals, Commando sired nine stakes winners, including the undefeated Colin and Peter Pan, winner of the 1907 Belmont.

What were the breeding theories and environmental factors that enabled Major Daingerfield to produce such results? I have gathered bits of this information from his grandson, Keene Daingerfield, a successful trainer and the retired dean of American stewards, and from the late Colonel Phil T. Chinn, who once told me: "Major Daingerfield was the greatest breeder of all time. Keene left all decisions to him in the breeding and raising of his horses as well as the farm management."

The stallions were exercised five to ten miles daily under saddle. Often, they were ridden to town and back. Once when Delhi had not returned on schedule, Major Daingerfield rode out in search of him, only to find him tied outside Pat McCann's saloon at Third and Upper Streets in downtown

Lexington. The mares booked to a stallion were teased by that stallion. If the major deemed that they were incompatible, he would change bookings to attain that "chemistry."

Pastures and paddocks were rotated each year, and they were never used two years in succession. Because they were rotated and undergrazed, they always provided an abundance of fresh, nutritive grass. The horses were kept outdoors in all but extremely cold, rainy weather.

Major Daingerfield personally inspected every horse on Castleton every day. He is said to have had the most discerning eye for anything that needed attention. A tireless worker, the major still found time to write eloquently on racing and breeding. He was an unofficial adviser to *The Thoroughbred Record* on editorial matters and served several terms on the Kentucky State Racing Commission. On January 10, 1913, he rested.

An Epitaph for Domino

One of the finest epitaphs ever written to memorialize a racehorse was dashed off in minutes. In late July of 1897, when the great Domino died from what his veterinarian diagnosed as "meningitis," Major Daingerfield telegraphed the news to Keene. Almost immediately came this return wire from Keene: "Bury him on Major Thomas's farm, if he consents, and place a slab over him with this inscription: 'Here lies the fastest runner and as game and generous a horse as the American Turf has ever seen.' James R. Keene."

The headstone stands today with the horse's name and the epitaph still readable near Lexington on Huffman Mill Road, on land that was once owned by Domino's breeder, Major Barak G. Thomas.

The Raceland Disaster

The early 1920s began a new era for Kentucky racing. The sport had been going along in nice fashion at the "Three Ls," Lexington, Latonia, and Louisville. To fulfill the racing needs of Western Kentucky, Dade Park, named after the famous starter, A. B. Dade, had been constructed along the banks of the Ohio River. There, just north of Henderson and south of Evansville, Indiana, the Green River Jockey Club offered its first meet in November of 1922.

That meet went rather smoothly. The next one, however, was tainted by "past posting" at its worst. (Past posting involves confederates betting with a bookmaker on the winner after the race is run. Someone inside the track has to inform the bettors in this scam.) Without warning, track manager Bradley

Wilson immediately barred all telegraph operators from the track, including those for the media.

Governor Edwin P. Morrow (1919-'24) intervened, as did the racing commission, and only after the proper safeguards were instituted did Wilson allow the communications men back on the grounds. Thereafter, things went well.

Jack Keene.

At about this time, J. O. "Jack" Keene—the dreamer of all dreamers—conceived the idea that the people in Eastern Kentucky also needed a racetrack. He drove up there and did his own "feasibility study," finding a tract of land near the Ohio River northwest of Ashland, a location that Keene deemed to be perfect.

Upon his return, Jack Keene (no relation to James R. Keene) called a meeting of Lexington-area horsemen. The perfect name of the new plant, they all agreed, was the one that he suggested, "Raceland," a word play on the sport and the nearest city. The track, he assured them, would draw not only from Ashland but also from the reasonably nearby cities of Portsmouth in Ohio, and Huntington and Charleston in West Virginia. "There's a lot of coal and oil money over in that area," he was said to have assured them.

Jack Keene could talk. Nearly everyone present at the meeting invested, although only Keene had seen the property. Tom Cromwell laughingly told me years later: "Jack was so persuasive, he got financial backing from the most tight-fisted, skeptical group this community has ever known—Hal Price Headley, Charlie Berryman, Timmy Hay, Tony Wallace, and others, including me!"

I asked Cromwell: "You've left out Chinn, where was Colonel P. T.?"

"Oh," he replied, "he was meeting with the president of the Bank of Commerce. He said he was unduly detained by him over a minor matter, something about making some arrangements to take care of some promissory notes that had matured. Later in the day, he did drive out to Jack's farm and gave his note for a piece of the action."

Jack Keene was not at all fiscally minded; never cared much for financial planning, detailed budgets of costs, or cost overruns. He just honestly guessed the cost of building something—and missed by a country mile. The advance payments that he received and the commitments that were originally made toward Raceland turned out to be merely start-up money. But he kept on building at a snail's pace as he slowly attracted additional investors.

In later years, Jack Keene told me where he got the last chunk of money to finish Raceland. "I went to Charlie Shaffer. He knew real estate; had made millions in it in Chicago," he recalled. "Charlie had a few years before bought Milton Young's old farm—Hanover stood there—and had become very 'strong' for Kentucky. Renamed it Coldstream Stud. I told him my plight with 'piker' investors, and he wrote the check."

The track was soon operational, but just barely, and the first meet was underway. Colonel Chinn called on his friend, W. T. "Fatty" Anderson, to bring in *Carlaris, one of the top runners of the day. The scheduled appearance of *Carlaris on opening day was certain to attract national publicity—and it did, but not in the expected way. No one would enter against him. Chinn took care of that, however, by instructing racing secretary Tony Wallace: "Put my little gelding Grover B. in with him, make it a two-horse race. He won't get beat any worse than the best stakes horse in New York."

Wallace complained to the colonel that he had so few horses on the grounds and so few entries that he could not complete the opening day card without at least one more entry in the last race. "Put Eleanor C. in the last." "But," Wallace protested, "she's already in the first." "I know," replied P. T., "she'll run in both."

The opening-day patrons had no trouble finding parking. Eleanor C. surprised by winning the first race, and—to the shock of the few patrons in attendance—she won the last race as well. To complete the disaster, the claiming gelding Grover B. beat the great stakes horse *Carlaris by six lengths! Nothing went right that day for Raceland, or any other day until its early demise.

A Raid on the Japan Derby

Jack Keene was an early proponent of international racing, and not only the classic races of England and Ireland. An adventurer at heart, Keene had trained for the nobility in Russia for two years, 1902 and 1903, winning every major stakes in his tenure there. In one span of three months, he won 116 races for Michael Lazerev, the immensely wealthy husband of a cousin of Czar Nicholas. It was suggested that Keene was helping his horses chemically, but he told me years later: "The difference was in the shoeing." He was using lightweight American plates; the Russian trainers insisted on using the much heavier "keg shoes." To get rid of Keene, the Russian Jockey Club ruled that only Russian-born trainers henceforth would be allowed.

A year or so later, Keene was racing a couple of nice two-year-olds in San Francisco when a Japanese-American talked him into shipping for the Japan Derby. The entries were duly accepted, and Keene and the colts arrived after a long steamship journey across the Pacific Ocean—only to find that he had not checked quarantine regulations, which caused him to be stationed on a beach until one week before the race.

"That beach," he told me years later, "was the best track I ever trained over. When I took my colts to the track, they were fit, and they ran one-two in the Derby, to the astonishment of the Japanese. After the race, I was besieged by buyers, each making higher offers, each bidding again and again. I told the two highest bidders I'd accommodate them if they'd pay me the next day in U.S. dollars. They did, and I packed and returned once again to Kentucky."

This Crooked Horse Could Run

When I first started writing on Thoroughbred subjects back in my teens, I wanted to apprentice myself as a typist to some authority, in exchange for tutoring on racing and breeding. Luckily, I was able to strike an accord with Jack Keene, who was to become one of my best friends and boosters.

In the fall of 1936, we were filling out name applications for yearlings. He instructed me to name a Jean Valjean colt out of Betty Smith after a placing judge who he believed had erred in not putting Jean Valjean's number up in a tight finish. (There was no photo finish in those days.)

"I gave him a thorough tongue-lashing after the race, and I told him I was going to name the worst son of Jean Valjean for him. The colt is so crooked I was going to destroy him at birth, but I saved him for that name." Mr. Smith, the horse, raced eight seasons on those crooked legs, started 122 times, and won 23 races.

The Genesis of Keeneland

Jack Keene was a flamboyant earner and spender who managed to keep himself either very rich or heavily in debt throughout his life. He was either one or the other. By contrast, his brother, George Hamlet Keene—better known as "Ham"—was conservative, methodical, and painstaking.

Both were born at Keeneland, a tract of land that came down to them from forebears who had received it in the 1700s as a land grant. Upon Ham's death in 1927, his share of the property passed to Jack, who set out to build a racetrack, stone clubhouse, and stone stables where he and his friends could meet with their horses and conduct private race meets.

The Depression arrived in short order, but it did not deter Jack. After he had poured more than $400,000 into his dream project—and it still was less than one-fourth completed—he was broke again and heavily in debt. To bail himself out once more, he sold the 147 acres on which he had placed the improvements for $140,000 on August 29, 1935. The nonprofit group that purchased the property retained the name and, led by fiscally minded presidents (first Hal Price Headley, then Louis Lee Haggin II, James E. "Ted" Bassett, and William C. Greely), Keeneland has grown to 893 acres, with racing and sales facilities that could not be replaced for $200-million.

It Beats Walking Behind a Mule

Jack once told me how he finally got Ham into racing. "Ham didn't like the Thoroughbred business, perhaps because of my ups and downs in it. He was a good horseman, however. Late one very hot July afternoon, I rode over to where he was plowing between rows of corn. He was exhausted, his shirt wet with perspiration, and he was knocking beads of sweat from his forehead. 'How long are you going to be walking behind that mule?' I asked him. 'You can make big money training horses.' He didn't answer me, and went on.

"But the next time by me he stopped and told me: 'I'll start tomorrow. Training horses has got to be better than plowing with this damned mule.' We did a lot of good together until Joe Widener hired him away from me."

For Jack, Ham trained the stakes winners Jeanne Bowdre (a foundation producer and the dam of Grand Slam) and Alice Blue Gown. For Widener, he trained champion sprinter Osmand, and stakes winners *Kiev, Chance Shot, and Haste. While Ham was with Widener, Earl Sande was the stable's contract rider.

Ham died unexpectedly from heart disease at age 53. Although his career as a trainer was relatively short, at the time of his passing he was considered equal in ability to the top conditioners of the day, Sam Hildreth and Jimmy Rowe.

A Foal Between Courses

Back in the early 1930s, Fannie and John Hertz were at dinner at Jack's "pneumonia" cottage, Keene's abode until he had completed his residence, which is now a part of Keeneland's beautiful stone clubhouse. Buck Jackson, Keene's "all-around man," announced: "Dinner is served."

Hertz recalled: "Buck took off at a fast pace, not his usual style, and returned in a jiffy with the first course, three huge bowls of hot soup, so hot it was almost boiling.

"We'd dined there many times. Buck was a wonderful wine steward and waiter, and there was no finer cook of country foods than his wife Caroline. We knew something was up, Fannie and I giving each other the eye. It seemed an eternity before the soup cooled to the point we could devour it, and another eternity before Buck returned to collect the soup bowls and spoons and serve the next course.

"As Buck walked into the dining room, still adjusting his white serving jacket, he said softly to Jack: 'Jeanne Bowdre has just presented us with a nice, strong chestnut colt by Chance Play. Caroline now has the next course ready for me to serve.'

"Buck, knowing the foaling was imminent, had delivered Grand Slam between courses, and Caroline had steamed up the soup to give him time to do it." Grand Slam turned out to be a top two-year-old of 1935.

Tales of Buck Jackson

I knew Buck and Caroline Jackson well during the last 15 years of Keene's life, and I was with the master of Keeneland daily up until I joined the Navy in late 1941. He passed away in late May, 1943, and I felt honored that *The Thoroughbred Record* sought me out to write his obituary.

Buck came to Keene as a wee lad, and over the course of 50 years Keene taught him how to do everything there was to do around a horse farm and training stable. He did nearly all of the teasing, breeding, weaning, yearling breaking, hoof trimming, and shoeing. A good-natured soul, everything was fun or funny to Buck. He constantly told jokes on himself and Keene to get laughs from his listeners. The late Charlie Kenney told this one on Buck.

"I was teaching German at the University of Kentucky, and one day when I was commuting on the old interurban (a rail transit system) from Paris, Kentucky, the passenger beside me was reading a horse journal. I engaged him in conversation, told him I'd like to learn the horse business. He turned out to be Tom Cromwell, about whom I'd read a considerable amount, and he immediately said: 'I can get you on with Jack Keene. He is always ready to help a young man. I sent him my paper boy, Jimmy 'Goggles' McCoy, and he made a top jockey out of him!'

"My first day on the job, I was turned over to Buck Jackson, who led me to the barn. 'Now, Mistah Cholly, I'm going to muck the first stall. You watch, and you'll do the second one.' I followed the instructions and procedure, and when I had finished mine, Buck said: 'That's good. Now, Mistah Cholly, you have trodden the path that I just tridden.' " Charlie became one of the finest, best-informed farm managers in our business.

The Contributions of Hal Price Headley

If you asked me the one person in Thoroughbred racing and breeding who built more monuments for the industry without any personal gain over his lifetime, I would unhesitatingly say Hal Price Headley. He never wanted any credit, but he wanted the job done—now. I was honored to handle the dispersal of his broodmares back in 1953; greatest guy for whom I ever worked.

Price Headley did the work—and thinking and planning—of five men. Outwardly, he was rude, abrupt, brusque. Those were, I believe, mechanisms that he maintained so that he could keep up his fast pace without interruption. If you were invited into his privacy, you found a man of great charm, compassion, and literacy, and he was a delightful conversationalist.

I have never known another person with Headley's power to motivate people. With Major Louie Beard, it was Headley who fronted and guided those who got Keeneland started, and then he quietly retired from the forefront while calling the plays from behind the scenes.

It was Headley who put together the Breeders' Sales Company as a cooperative in 1944 to conduct sales at Keeneland. Those sales now are a part of the Keeneland operation and the best-known bloodstock sale in the world.

It was Headley who conceived the idea of selling selected Thoroughbred yearlings on an annual basis at Saratoga Springs, New York. A great race meet went on there each August, and the wealthy owners were present to duel with their dollars for horseflesh rather than for chips at the nearby gambling casinos. A veritable

Hal Price Headley.

who's who of society, stage, and government as well as foreign dignitaries were also there. But there were no yearling sales.

Treacy and Walker sold Thoroughbreds at auction in Kentucky in those days, but they told Headley they were not interested in setting up a Saratoga operation. Headley told me: "All you needed was an outfit that knew how to run a blooded-horse auction, so I got hold of Jim Tranter, owner of Fasig-Tipton Company, which sold only Standardbreds up to that time. He went for the deal."

Headley always gave A. B. Hancock Sr. immense credit for helping bring in support of other important breeders and owners for the Saratoga sale and the establishment of Keeneland as a racetrack and Thoroughbred sales center.

Tranter, so heartened by the sale of Thoroughbreds at Saratoga, opened up a Kentucky operation that put Treacy and Walker out of the Thoroughbred sales business. But after Tranter's death, Fasig-Tipton started foundering until it was purchased by Kenneth Gilpin, who brought in Humphrey Finney to guide its destiny. By then, however, Kentucky breeders had established themselves at Keeneland.

'Confidence in Tomorrow'

When he was at work, Hal Price Headley was all business. As I said, he had a reputation for being smart, but rude, abrupt, and unduly hurried in his personal encounters. But he revealed his other side—the side that I came to know—in his remarks at a testimonial dinner given in his honor by the Thoroughbred Club of America on October 18, 1941.

"I want to talk a few minutes about what association with the Thoroughbred has meant to me," Headley said. "Perhaps first of all, it gives one an outdoor life. It also gives one a confidence, a kind of hope that is possessed by few other men of my acquaintance who are not horsemen. No matter how poorly the entire stable may be doing, the horseman feels sure that in the next crop of yearlings there will probably be a Man o' War. No matter how bitter his disappointment is today, the horseman never loses confidence in tomorrow." Could a cold, callous person utter such inspiring remarks?

Duval Headley, the antithesis of his "Uncle Price" in personality and one who never ceased to bring joy and good humor to friends and strangers alike, knew and liked all sides of his mentor in the horse business. As Headley left Duvie one morning at Keeneland after "explaining" some things to him, Ralph Kercheval jokingly asked him: "Is Uncle Price mellowing with age?" To which Duvie ribbed back: "Yesiree, just like an old pistol."

Back in Two Hours at the Same Speed

Hal Price Headley was a no-nonsense guy—and always in a hurry. He saw to it by rigid supervision that everyone who worked for him achieved full productivity. The sight of Headley approaching on his saddle horse always put his employees into high gear. He had a set pattern of making his rounds and returning. Sometimes, he would trick them by not returning at the customary time.

If he had a horse running at Churchill Downs, he would ride through the farm to a distant corner, hitch the pony, and jump the fence, where he would be met in his car by Harold Fallon, his office manager. He would then return Harold to the office and take off for Louisville at a high rate of speed, then reverse the process and mount the pony when he got back.

Once when he was stopped for speeding while going through Shelbyville, approximately halfway between Lexington and Louisville, he told the arresting officer to write two tickets. "I'll be coming back through here in about two hours at the same rate of speed!"

An Insult at Suffolk

Hal Price Headley also was a man of great pride, and Suffolk Downs ran afoul of him in its overzealous efforts to attract War Admiral to the 1938 Massachusetts Handicap. The Triple Crown winner and Horse of the Year in 1937, War Admiral was still virtually invincible. To lure owner Samuel Riddle into starting him, the Suffolk Downs people practically had to let him dictate how much weight his champion would carry.

A luncheon was given in Riddle's honor before the race, and the dining area was decorated in his black-and-gold colors. A blanket trimmed in the stable colors was placed in the winner's circle awaiting War Admiral's anticipated triumph.

War Admiral was never a factor in the race. Price Headley's Menow, un-

Duval Headley.

der 107 pounds and ridden by Nick Wall, took the lead at the break and led throughout to win by eight lengths. Busy K. (107) was second, and War Minstrel (106) finished third, a nose ahead of War Admiral, under 130 pounds. The outcome extremely displeased the cantankerous, unsportsmanlike Riddle, who failed to congratulate Headley.

After the race, when invited to the track's club room for a victory celebration, Headley replied: "No thanks. You counted me out before the race; didn't invite me to the luncheon, didn't prepare a blanket in my colors, so I'm going back to the barn and celebrate with my stable help and my trainer, Duval Headley." And that he did.

In those days, you never counted Headley out in a handicap. The year before, he had shipped Preeminent from Keeneland to New York to take the Toboggan Handicap and win the biggest bet of his life.

Don't Underestimate Price Headley

Among my fondest memories of our game are the nightly get-togethers of horsemen at the old Lafayette Hotel in Lexington in the mid-1930s. At that time, it was by no means a foregone conclusion that Keeneland would be successful.

Carey Ward: "Keeneland will never make it . . . it's way out in the country with no public transportation . . . no free passes . . . no public address system . . . gets its water from Manchester spring, which it sure as hell will pump dry. (Keeneland did have to haul water one hot summer.)

Bill Caskey: "Don't underestimate Price Headley. He can flip a silver dollar into the air and have it come down gold."

A Vote of Confidence

When John Hay "Jock" Whitney passed away at age 77 on February 8, 1982, the media, with its restrictions on time and space, were able to highlight only select contributions that he made to his country and to racing. In fact, none of the obituaries covered two very important contributions that he made to racing at Keeneland.

When Headley and Major Beard had grave fears that they would not be able to raise the necessary funds for their dream track, they told Whitney of their concern. "Go ahead with your plans," he told them. "I'll provide what you can't raise." Years later, Price Headley told me: "Without Jock, there probably wouldn't be a Keeneland. He gave Louie and me the confidence and drive to make it work. We never had to go to him."

To the track's first meeting, in October of 1936, Whitney sent from New York a string of his horses, head trainer Jim Healy, and contract jockey Johnny Gilbert. His filly, Royal Raiment, won the first race ever contested at the track. By closing day of the first meet, he had purchased Miss Merriment, the fastest mare in the East, and had her there to give still more prestige to the meet for a purseless, betless, match race with Myrtlewood. The latter won by three lengths on October 24, 1936. Whitney was in attendance throughout the meet—again, giving of his time.

In 1940, when Fred Post was putting together a group to build the Aiken Mile training track, Whitney became a major investor, along with Mrs. F. Ambrose Clark, John Schiff, Pete Bostwick, and others. From the track's opening in 1941, Whitney wintered at Aiken the horses that were not sent to Hialeah.

An excellent horseman himself and a high-goal polo player in the 1930s, Jock had a great love for racing and breeding Thoroughbreds, and a knowledgeable and keen insight into it. I did not know Whitney well, but, in conversations I had with him on his visits to Aiken during the winters of the 1960s, I found him to be a friendly, kind, almost shy soul with a great concern for his fellow man.

Working Behind the Scenes

In the Thoroughbred lore of Central Kentucky, the name of Major Louie Beard is rarely mentioned, and for good reason. He was the most influential "behind-the-scenes man" I have ever known. He kept a low profile, never sought or encouraged notice, and placed the Thoroughbred industry ahead of all else. "Write about the owners," he once suggested to me. "They're the ones who pay the bills and make our wonderful sport what it is."

About the only time I recall that Major Beard acquiesced to recognition was when he

Major Louie Beard.

accepted the invitation to be the honored guest at the Thoroughbred Club of America's testimonial dinner in the fall of 1945. To my knowledge, he was only the second salaried individual (after Colonel Matt Winn) to be so honored by the TCA.

Major Beard ranked high among the graduates of the class of 1910 at West Point, where he captained the Army polo team that defeated the British in a famed international match. Harry Payne Whitney, a high-goal player himself, persuaded the major to resign from the Army in 1925 and take over the management of the racing and breeding interests of himself and his son, C. V. Two years later, he accepted the additional supervision of the Thoroughbreds of Mrs. Payne Whitney (Greentree Stud), her son John Hay Whitney (Llangollen Farm), and her daughter, Mrs. Charles Payson (Manhasset Stable). Many noted runners were bred and raced by the Whitneys during his tenure—Equipoise, Twenty Grand, and Top Flight, to name three.

Hal Price Headley once told me: "Don't give me too much credit for the success of Keeneland. Louie Beard has done just as much as I." When William T. Bishop wrote Headley's obituary in March of 1962, he noted that in the uncertain, early days of the track in the mid-1930s, "Major Beard raised the money; Price Headley spent it wisely."

Major Beard was a guiding light in the formation of the American Thoroughbred Breeders Association and, with the help of Arthur Hancock Sr., arranged the purchase by that group of *The Blood-Horse* from Tom Cromwell. He also engineered the largest, most prestigious private sale of a farm and its Thoroughbred holdings in the history of the sport to that time. That was the November, 1946 purchase—by a syndicate composed of Greentree Stud, King Ranch, and Ogden Phipps—of the recently deceased Edward R. Bradley's Idle Hour Farm and Thoroughbred holdings, a fully equipped and developed farm of 1,292 acres, two stallions (Bimelech and Blue Larkspur), 32 mares (*La Troienne among them), 19 yearlings, 20 weanlings, and 15 horses of racing age. The package price, $2,681,545, was the biggest "steal" since the Louisiana Purchase. The major took not one red cent for masterminding the deal, nor any for other transactions. Had the major been commercial-minded, he could have made millions in the business. His thinking was always: "What's best for the sport."

In the Depression year of 1932, George Wingfield of Reno, Nevada, had to disperse all of his Thoroughbred holdings because a dozen banks under his control were unable to collect loans made to distressed sheep farmers and cattlemen. The dispersal of 25 of his horses in November at Lexington threatened to put a crimp in the revenues that young Tom Carr Piatt received from boarding the Nevada Stock Farm horses.

Luckily, Tom had come up the year before with a "new man" who was to volunteer him aid—John Marsch, of Chicago. Marsch told him to buy the best from the dispersal, which he did. Piatt, however, overlooked Chicleight, whom Major Beard had bought for Greentree Farm for $2,000. Piatt explained his plight to the major, offering him a profit.

"You don't have to pay a profit. I'll transfer her over to Mr. Marsch at the same price," the Greentree manager said. "I know you need the board money you'll get on her." At Crestwood Farm, Chicleight would produce the best racemare ever owned by Marsch, Blue Delight, a winner of six major stakes.

In turn, Blue Delight would become a foundation mare for Calumet Farm. She produced five stakes winners, including champion Real Delight, Bubbley, and Princess Turia. Her daughters, granddaughters, and great-granddaughters have produced a multitude of Calumet stakes winners, among them Alydar, Forward Pass, and Our Mims. It is a toss-up whether Blue Delight or Two Bob contributed the most to Calumet's success.

Major Beard gave freely of his time and good counsel when asked, and he was the confidant of the giants within the industry. He had a gentle, kind, persuasive personality; he spoke softly yet authoritatively.

The proletariat of the business, offended because he had no time for their small talk and hobnobbing, gave him the undeserved reputation of being a snob, which he was not. I know. As a budding Turf scribe in my teens, knowing little about writing or my subject matter, he took great patience in answering my questions about the activities of the Whitney farms and racing stables.

In manner, Louie Beard was the antithesis of Price Headley, each other's closest friend. Headley: "Have I told you everything you want to know? Okay, I'm busy, I got to go." I once asked trainer Tom B. Young: "Why are Major Beard and Mr. Headley such close friends, yet dissimilar in manner?" Tom, always waiting for a chance to turn a funny line, replied: "They each have a challenge toward the other. Price is trying to make a horseman out of Louie, and Louie is trying to make a gentleman out of Price—and they're both failing!"

In the fall of 1935, tough, rough, old Sam Riddle, in appreciation of Louie Beard's unselfish contributions to the industry, gave the major a free breeding season (priceless!) to Man o' War. "I'll accept it," Beard said, "if you'll let me pass it on to my best friend, Price Headley, for his best mare." Riddle agreed. The result of the mating of Man o' War and Alcibiades was Salaminia, one of Headley's best runners and producers.

Headley later returned the favor by giving a gift—a yearling filly, later named White Cross (by Revoked and out of Salaminia), who placed in two major stakes and was the dam of the top filly and $235,525-earner Firm Policy—to his friend's only son, Clarkson, the year before Major Beard died at age 65 in 1954.

The Lore of the 'KA' Post

The large, beautifully molded cast-iron post at the entrance of Keeneland—with its distinctive "KA" monogram—predates the Keeneland Association, perhaps by more than a century. The post is believed to date back to 1826, when the old Kentucky Association track was built inside the city of Lexington—on Race Street, where else? The street is still there with the same name, but the barns, fences, and grandstand were razed in 1935 for what is now a housing development.

Price Headley and William T. Bishop (then superintendent for Keeneland and subsequently general manager at Oaklawn Park) went out to the old track to determine what salvage they could buy, or beg, for the new Keeneland track, which had the lowest construction budget of any track in the last 75 years.

Keeneland's entrance post.

The late Hobert Burton, the longtime Keeneland superintendent, recalled: "Just for the dismantling, we got all the framing material and stall doors for five barns. Only had to buy siding and roofing. Then there was that cast-iron post."

"Get that, too," said the quick-minded Headley, knowing exactly where he would place it. He had seen that post thousands of times since he was a young boy. "Don't care how many men it takes to get it loaded, but get it." Not until "Bish" and Hobert had loaded the post did they realize Headley's foresight. The "KA" henceforth was to be the Keeneland Association emblem. Today, that entrance post is one of the most valuable antiques in racing.

The Silence of Keeneland

There always have been and always will be those who think Keeneland should have a public address system, among them being the late Brownie Leach (director of public relations, 1936-1946) and his successor, one John H. Clark (1947-1954). But it is hard to argue against success.

At the time of Keeneland's early planning, the use of loudspeakers at most U.S. tracks was abused by constant, inane announcements—such as: "The next race will go off in 27 minutes . . . the horses are now on the track . . . it's 20 minutes before post time . . . it's 15 minutes before post time . . . it's ten minutes . . . it's five minutes . . . this is your last warning, you still have time to get your bets down"—not to mention other nuisance announcements and the same music played daily from worn-out records.

I shall never forget one day in 1939 at Thistledown Racetrack when the placing judges posted the wrong order of finish. While the crowd was protesting with Bronx cheers and every other vocal manifestation that came to their minds, announcer Eddie Miller immediately played the old song, "Three Blind Mice," over the sound system. Instantly, track manager King Lear raced up the steps from the ground level to the roof, took the record off the player, and broke it into many pieces. Lear also had a few choice words of his own for Eddie.

It was primarily the decision of Price Headley and Major Beard that the track should not have a public address system. That idea has survived for more than a half century, but some other ideas did not.

They Bought the Steam-Heated Track

Brownie Leach was the most believable tall-story teller of my time, but sometimes truth was stranger than fiction. The first Keeneland race meet was, as I have noted, to be run under the most unprecedented and bizarre circumstances ever in the history of organized racing in the United States. Not one out of a hundred horsemen I talked with then thought it would succeed.

Keeneland was located on 147 unfenced acres. Only the clubhouse, grandstand, and paddock were enclosed, and you could get into those areas without paying admission simply by hopping over a couple of low fences. It was "out in the country"—eight miles from Lexington, and not served by pubic bus or streetcar transportation.

Only the racing secretary, his staff, the starter, and his crew were paid for their work. The stewards, placing judges, patrol judges, and paddock judges were to be horsemen with no previous "official" experience and would serve

Brownie Leach.

without pay—not even a parking director. There would be no photo-finish camera, no movie patrol, no public address system. The stockholders were to be paid no dividends. Any profits were to go to charity.

Brownie Leach stated these facts in a speech before the Lexington Rotary Club. Although each and every one of them was true—and were to be successfully implemented—the Rotarians, good businessmen that they were, did not believe him. The most optimistic of them said that, at best, the track had only a slim chance of survival.

Then Brownie, in his best performance ever at deception, told them the tallest tale he could think of—the "steam-heated track"—and they bought it.

"MIT," he said, "the Massachusetts Institute of Technology, has just completed plans and specifications to drain all water and snow off the racing surface of the track and steam heat it dry in inclement weather so the track can be kept fast and safe 365 days a year. This, of course, will be quite expensive. We'll have to build the plant to generate the steam and we'll have to bury beneath the top surface miles and miles of drainage pipe and steam pipe. It will be a few years before Keeneland will be financially able to put this system in place, but it will pay for itself in ten years."

The Rotarians nodded their heads in agreement. As soon as the meeting adjourned, A. P. Bryan, a reporter for the Lexington *Leader* who was covering the speech, rushed Brownie and exclaimed: "You've just told your biggest lie."

"What," Leach asked, "about the steam-heated track?"

"No, about all those guys working for nothing," returned A. P., whose specialty was investigative reporting.

No Haven for Haltermen

At the inaugural Keeneland meet in the fall of 1936, Price Headley let it be known indirectly that Keeneland was to be no haven for haltermen, no place for them to enlarge their stables. Nor was the track a place for horsemen to run their claimers below their true competitive level. Offenders would not be welcomed back in the future.

H. H. "Pete" Battle would have none of that, or so he thought. One day during the opening meet, he walked into the racing secretary's office and demanded of assistant racing secretary Sidney Brown: "Gimme a claim blank." Sid laughed. "Pete, we not only don't have any, we ain't even got a claim box!" The inaugural meet was a success, of course, and there were claim blanks and a claim box at the next meet, in the spring of 1937.

A Late-Blossoming Relationship

Hal Price Headley had a greater impact on my life than anyone else in the Thoroughbred business. My fondness for him was, shall we say, relatively late blooming. From the start of my Turf writing career in my mid-teens until a dozen years later, when I was established as a horse trader and consultant, I was never able to engage Headley in conversation. When I endeavored to do so, he would dismiss me in a gruff manner.

I admired him professionally, but my personal feelings for him were quite the opposite. He was not only the "horseman's horseman," but he was also their leader. They did what he asked them to do because they knew it was right—not because they liked him. He spared no one's feelings while rushing full speed ahead to complete Keeneland in one year's time for its inaugural meet. It was not unusual for him to ask the board of directors to approve plans for a barn or building that had already been completed.

In 1940, with the track a success, Headley turned over the day-to-day management to his son-in-law, Louis Lee Haggin II, a well-liked, capable administrator who guided the track to still greater recognition—at considerable sacrifice of his time. ("But Pappy keeps looking over my shoulder," he once joked to me.)

By 1947, I finally got Headley's attention. I was moving up in the business and needed a small farm. I bought approximately 21 acres, fronting Versailles Road and running alongside the eastern perimeter of Keeneland, for $25,000 from an heir of Jack Keene. It was the best land buy I ever made. There was no way for me to lose. One day, Keeneland would have to pay me dearly for it if the track wished to expand, and meanwhile, because of my "nuisance" value, I could build a barn and paddocks and train horses there as though the farm were a part of Keeneland.

The ink had hardly dried on the sales contract before the phone rang in my downtown office. "Johnny," said a very disturbed Headley, "get out here to my farm right away. I've got something to talk to you about that is very important!" I replied: "I'm on my way." I was overjoyed. After 12 years, Headley was going to have his first conversation with me—and on my terms.

I will not bother with the details, but this is the deal we made: Keeneland would pay me $12,500 for four acres near the track's entrance, rent me the stone cottage (now the security office) for an office for ten years at $1 a year, furnish me water, allow me to bring horses over from my remaining acreage to use Keeneland's training facilities, and I would give Keeneland first refusal to buy the rest of the land at any price I was ever willing to accept from another party. As I departed, Headley congratulated me on being a "good businessman," and noted he would be calling on me in the future to handle some "matters." (In 1962, Keeneland bought 16 more acres for $160,000.)

One month later, before I had moved my office to the stone cottage, Louis Haggin retained me to handle public relations for the track "for a couple of years." The "couple of years" actually lasted seven.

Price Headley became my biggest booster. He gave me all the time I requested to answer questions that improved my knowledge of the business. More importantly, he gave me confidence in myself because he believed in me.

In July, 1953, when I was nearing age 34, Headley said to me: "Johnny, I'm going on 65, and I want to start getting out of the business. I want you to handle this for me, handle every detail. Think about it and get back to me. I don't want anybody to know about it until we agree on a plan."

I was startled, not only because he had such respect for my judgment and trust in me, but also because he was a man I thought would die with "his boots on" in a game he loved. Rethinking, I realized it was typical Headley. Everything planned.

At our next meeting, which took place the following week, I proposed the following: 1) Sell his half interest in *Rico Monte; 2) syndicate Revoked to stand at his farm; 3) sell his 37 mares the first Monday of the Keeneland November sales; 4) sell the older racing horses privately or at a paddock sale at Belmont; and 5) keep the foals of 1952 and '53 and dispose of them at a later date.

"What is this going to cost me?" he asked. "I mean, for your services."

"Nothing on the sale of *Rico Monte, I can sell your half interest to Lou Doherty over the phone. One share in Revoked, and I'm sure he'll syndicate quickly. On the mares, $10,000 if you think they sell well. Otherwise, $5,000."

"What do I have to do?" he inquired.

"Just sign the papers I put in front of you and come to your sale."

"You got a deal," he said, and we shook hands on it. Nothing was in writing.

Headley's interest in *Rico Monte was sold the next day to Doherty. I syndicated Revoked in a week's time, and the mares sold well. After the auction, Headley walked to where I was standing, squeezed me with a two-arm hug, and said, "Come by the office tomorrow and pick up your check for $10,000."

The Contributions of 'Bish'

No one in racing was more respected or better liked than William T. Bishop, who served as the general manager of Keeneland. "Bish," or "W. T.," or "Willy T.," as he was variously known, came to Lexington in the 1930s from a small town in Western Kentucky at the urging of an older friend from that neck of the woods, Joe A. Estes, who later was to be acknowledged as one of the true geniuses of our business.

Joe at the time was associate editor of *The Blood-Horse*, and he lived on the second story of the building that housed the magazine's offices with a young college professor by the name of Joe E. Palmer, who was later to become Turf columnist for the New York *Herald Tribune*. Bish received free lodging from them in return for housekeeping.

While he was attending the University of Kentucky, from which he graduated with high honors, Bish had to work numerous outside jobs to provide funds for his subsistence and school expenses. But housekeeping was not his strong suit. About once a month, he would receive messages written by a finger on dusty mirrors that said such things as: "Get on the ball. Clean up this joint!"

Estes, who had been in on the planning of Keeneland, recommended to Price Headley and Major Beard that they make W. T. their

William T. Bishop.

right-hand man. "What'll I be doing now that I have the job?" Bishop asked Estes, who replied: "Knowing Price Headley, I'd say about a hundred different things—from pushing a wheelbarrow to doing the books, payroll, and accounting. You will learn a lot about how to build and run a racetrack." He did.

Keeneland came a long way in a hurry. In the mid-1970s, after the track had attained national prestige of the highest order, Bish moved on to Oaklawn Park. There, he and Charles Cella succeeded for many years with what was once a sleepy Midwestern track in a sparsely populated area.

An extremely sensitive, tireless worker in civic and charitable endeavors while in Lexington, Bish received nearly every award and honor bestowed on citizens for contributions to the betterment of the community. It was in this work that he became a close friend of another person cut from the same cloth, Judge Bart Peak.

In the 1960s, a kindly, quiet, likable hotwalker made Emerson Davis's tack room his living quarters at Keeneland and did menial tasks for him and other trainers. On occasions, when the hotwalker would become disturbed and needed to be hospitalized, Bish would have taken him to the institution. The hotwalker trusted Bish, and he always would go willingly for Bish, except one time.

W. T. raced into Lexington and asked Bart, then a county judge, to make out an order for the hotwalker's commitment to Eastern State Hospital and to have a police officer follow him to serve the papers and take the hotwalker to the hospital. As Judge Peak filled out the order, he listened to a quick report from Bish on the new Boy Scouts camp, a construction project that W. T. was supervising. This distracted Bart—and caused an amusing incident.

When the hotwalker was found walking along Versailles Road, the officer apprehended him and had barely started reading the commitment order when he suddenly stopped, looked at Bish in astonishment, then gasped, "Mr. Bishop, Judge Peak has committed *you* to the asylum!" The hotwalker stayed with the officer willingly, and Bish returned in 30 minutes with the commitment properly executed. A month or so later, Bish went to the hospital, picked up the hotwalker, and returned him to Keeneland.

It Must Be in the Genes

Historically, Kentucky has been blessed by the character, knowledge, and dedication of the chairpersons of its racing commission, but unfortunately so many of them have not had sufficient time to devote to the position that it really requires.

But that was not the case with Martha Broadbent, the first woman chairperson, who was appointed by the commonwealth's first woman governor, Martha Layne Collins. Markie Broadbent was at the commission office some part of every work day, got to all the tracks—including their stable areas—and was "GI" but reasonable. On one occasion, when one of Markie's horses was being groomed by a man not wearing his identification badge, she fined her trainer.

I was honored to be among a few horsemen invited to an informal reception tendered her by her fellow commissioners after the end of her term as chairperson in January, 1988. "She's worked hard, she's been firm but fair, and she's done a very good job," I remarked to her fellow commissioner, Kenny Platner. "Why wouldn't she?" he quickly returned. "She's by Louie Lee Haggin II out of a daughter of Hal Price Headley."

Chapter 4
Giants of the Bluegrass

Central Kentucky ascended to the pinnacle of the Thoroughbred industry not only because of the richness of its soil and the sweetness of its bluegrass. No, it became dominant within the industry because of the intellect, insight, and hard work of the horsemen who grew up in the Bluegrass or settled there. In the following pages, I will tell you about some of the great Kentucky horsemen I've come to know, or know about, in my years of tradin'.

The Master of Hamburg

In 1905, you could buy a pretty good yearling for $1,000. That was the average price John E. Madden got for the 55 yearlings he sold at public auction that year. He estimated it cost him $250 to breed and raise a yearling at that time, even computing in interest on the cost of the mare and allowing for barren years.

"Shed raising" of yearlings is not new. Madden raised all of his that way. From 1898, the year he bought Hamburg Place, until his death in 1929, he produced 182 stakes winners—19 in just one year, 1914. Madden bred four Kentucky Derby winners: Old Rosebud, 1914; Paul Jones, 1920; Zev, 1923; and Flying Ebony, 1925. His four winners tied him with 19th century breeder A. J. Alexander and is second only to Warren Wright, who bred five Derby winners at Calumet Farm. In partnership, Madden also bred Sir Barton, the first Triple Crown winner in 1919.

Madden bought, sold, bred, owned, and trained horses by the hundreds at all levels of the market, and he had an almost uncanny instinct for when to buy and when to sell. When the market was going up, he sold. When it was on a downward trend, he bought. In 1915, he registered 96 foals. In 1920, he sold 76 mares. Yet, in the next seven years, he led the breeders' list three times and was second in the other four. At auction, he never bid away his profit, and in private transactions he bought only at a figure he considered to be reasonably below the price he thought he would get on resale. Madden's maxim was: "It's better to sell and regret than keep and regret."

A Persuasive Salesman

Madden was perhaps the best horse salesman of all time. In the old days, long before Lexington had an airport, most Eastern horsemen commuted to the Bluegrass on the Chesapeake and Ohio's "luxury" George Washington. The train arrived at around eight in the morning in Lexington and departed for Washington around four in the afternoon.

Smoke Johnson, Colonel Phil T. Chinn's faithful manservant and chauffeur, knew all horsemen of note. One of his jobs was to observe who arrived each day and report their names to the colonel, who then would figure a way of encountering them within the next few hours so they would not leave town without a horse.

One morning, Smoke breathlessly reported to Colonel Phil: "I can't think of his name—he's the tall gray-haired man with that big diamond tie stickpin you sold a High Time colt to last year—just got off the train. I just said hello to him, but he told me to tell you he wasn't buying nothing. He had come to town to close out a sale of all of his horses to Mr. John E. Madden."

The colonel instructed Smoke to be present that afternoon when the passengers boarded the George Washington and to bid the gentleman goodbye. "He may get

John Madden.

back into the business, and I can accommodate him with a nice racehorse," Chinn said. Smoke's report to the colonel that night was dismaying—for Chinn, at least.

"Why, he was the happiest man I ever saw when he was leaving, came over and shook my hand, told me Mr. Madden had convinced him his horses were too good for him to sell. He should by all means keep them. He said Mr. Madden made him feel so good, he bought two mares and two yearlings from him," Smoke reported.

Another time, upon learning that Pierre Lorillard would be arriving the next morning on the George Washington, Madden arose early and had his chauffeur drive him 150 miles northeast to Ashland, Kentucky, where he boarded the train. When Lorillard arrived in the dining car, Madden invited him for breakfast. Between Ashland and Lexington, a deal was struck, subject to the tobacco tycoon's approving the horses upon his arrival in Lexington.

It Depends on the Intent

Madden was grazing a two-year-old colt at Saratoga on an August day in 1897. "Young man," asked an approaching stranger, "do you own that colt?" Never at a loss for words, Madden replied: "That depends on whether you want to buy him or attach him!" The stranger was the copper king Marcus Daly; the colt was the great Hamburg. A sale was made at $40,001, the highest price paid to that date for an American Thoroughbred.

Preston Madden's Mark

Preston Madden has never attempted to emulate his legendary grandfather John E. Madden. But, in a quiet, low-profile way, he has made his mark in racing. Never owning more than a dozen or so mares, he has personally bred 24 stakes winners, and in partnership many more. One of his foremost accomplishments has been the breeding of Alysheba, the world's all-time leading money winner with $6,679,242.

Perhaps Preston's greatest accomplishment before Alysheba was his purchase of T. V. Lark, a rather lightly bred four-year-old by *Indian Hemp out of a Heelfly mare. The rags-to-riches runner, raised in his breeder's back yard in Arcadia, California, won $902,194 from 15 stakes victories. The other foals out of his dam had earnings as follow: $12,375, zero, $24,740, $1,600, and zero. T. V. Lark was sold as a yearling for $10,000 to Chase R. McCoy, who sold him in September, 1961, to a syndicate headed by Madden.

"Presto" figured that T. V. Lark had "made" his own pedigree by beating Kelso on the dirt in the 1960 Arlington Classic Stakes—the gelding's only defeat that year—and on the grass in the 1961 Washington, D.C. International, a victory that sealed T. V. Lark's title as grass champion for that year. In both years, Kelso was voted Horse of the Year. Still, selling syndicate shares in T. V. Lark was difficult, and the buyers of them were primarily friends of Madden who respected his knowledge and knew him to be a straight shooter in his horse dealings.

Preston Madden with Bel Sheba, dam of Alysheba.

T. V. Lark became the leading sire of 1974 and had been second in two other years before his untimely death at age 18 in 1975. "Presto," like his grandfather before him, has had many partners through the years, but I have never known one to leave him before death or retirement from the business. Pretty much the same can be said about his employees. As we say about the uprights in our game: "His word is good."

Colonel E. R. Bradley Arrives

It was in 1933 at the age of 14 that I first met Colonel E. R. Bradley, and I was indeed awed to be in the presence of the only man who, at that time, had ever owned four Kentucky Derby winners. I was out hustling racing notes and was in the stable of Hunter Moody at the Lexington trotting track watching Burgoo King, winner of the Derby the previous year, being harnessed and hitched to a driving cart. Also in the stable at the time for training in harness was that year's Derby winner, Brokers Tip. Bradley was experimenting with preparing sore-legged horses for a racing comeback. His theory was that keeping weight off their backs would protect their ailing legs.

As a stately, erect, tall, gray-haired man walked into the stable, Moody remarked to me: "You'll have to excuse me. That's Colonel Bradley." Overhearing the remark as he continued walking toward us, Bradley said: "No, let the young man stay. What is your name, son?" "Johnny Clark, sir," I replied. "I

Colonel Edward Riley Bradley.

have a brother named John," said the colonel. "You come along with me and we'll watch Mr. Moody work Burgoo King." We did. I found Bradley to be a quiet, matter-of-fact sort of man. His comments on that occasion indicated to me he had a deep, warm concern not only for his horses, but also for his fellow man.

Born December 12, 1859, in Johnstown, Pennsylvania, Bradley saw little future for himself as a steel worker and at a relatively early age headed beyond the Continental Divide. There, as a gold prospector and miner, he accumulated enough capital to return east to Chicago, where he invested with fabulous success in real estate.

Because of the intense strain he placed upon himself, Bradley, at age 39, was advised by his doctor to get himself emotionally involved in some outdoor activity. When his first horse won first time out for him that year, 1898, at the Harlem track near Chicago, Bradley had found his hobby. Shortly thereafter, he bought a stakes colt and soon was naming all of his horses with words starting with the letter "B."

Soon, Bradley decided he liked racing so much he wanted to try his hand at breeding as well. He bought a 335-acre tract in 1906, five miles west of Lexington, and named it Idle Hour Farm. By the time of his death at age 86 in August of 1946, he had expanded the farm to 1,292 acres. His horse inventory included two stallions (Bimelech and Blue Larkspur), 41 broodmares (19 of them stakes winners or stakes producers), 16 yearlings, 19 weanlings, and 15 horses of racing age (ten of them current or future stakes winners).

In the early 1920s, Bradley bailed out Fair Grounds racetrack in New Orleans and established first-class winter racing there. In 1929, after Hialeah had gone under, he refinanced that track with the help of Joseph E. Widener and did not sell his stock in the Miami-area landmark until 1943, after it was firmly established as the capital of winter racing. His stock was purchased by

Joseph P. Kennedy, father of the late President John Kennedy, acting along with a number of other "Eastern interests."

Previously, in 1912, Bradley had inadvertently rewarded himself through a kind deed. William A. Prime, a Memphis cotton broker, sought and accepted the colonel's advice to buy the entire yearling crop of colts of James R. Keene, 16 horses, for $25,000. Two weeks later, when Prime lost a fortune in the cotton market, he telephoned Bradley and told him he did not like the deal, while concealing his financial reverses. "I will take them off your hands," Bradley replied, "although I have a sufficient number of yearlings now for my racing stable. I'm doing this because I never give advice I would not take myself."

The 16 yearlings were shortly thereafter offered at auction at a sales barn in downtown Lexington. The sale grossed $57,650, of which Bradley spent $32,400. In other words, Bradley netted his cost, $25,250, and got four colts. One of those four Bradley bought in (for $1,600) was to be named Black Toney, who would become the cornerstone of his breeding operation. Black Toney stood at Idle Hour after his racing career. At the same sale, Harry Payne Whitney purchased the following year's Futurity Stakes winner and later foundation sire, Pennant, for $1,700, with Bradley as the underbidder.

'I Am a Gambler'

After Bradley's death, Father D. J. Boland, a close friend, characterized him well: "Only those who knew him intimately are able to estimate him as a benefactor to humanity. His virtues were kindness to the poor, love of truth, and strict adherence to the principles of justice." Through his 40 years at Idle Hour, Bradley contributed from $25,000 to $50,000 annually to Kentucky charities.

Unable to shake down Bradley during the time that he owned Fair Grounds racetrack, the demagogue Huey Long hauled him before his Senate committee in Washington. Asked his business, the colonel answered straightforwardly and without any hint of shame: "I am a gambler."

Bradley had his own private training track at Idle Hour and his own private betting agent, Mosey Cosman. He was no piker when it came to backing one of his horses, but he never ran them "hot and cold." He was socially accepted in Palm Beach, Florida, where he owned the posh Beach Club casino, better known as "Bradley's." He allowed no professional gamblers, only the winter residents and their properly introduced guests who could afford to lose. His benevolence to the community there was also great.

An $83,000 Side Bet on the Derby

In 1925, William R. Coe was bragging a bit about his colt Pompey in front of a group of friends. He was immodestly proud that his youngster was to be acclaimed champion two-year-old of the year off his wins in the Hopeful Stakes and the Futurity. Colonel Bradley told Coe he had a pretty nice colt named Bubbling Over, and he would match him horse for horse, with the winner to take the other's prize runner, over any distance at any track.

Coe declined, not wanting to risk losing the horse for whom he had been waiting a lifetime. "Okay," Bradley replied, "I'll race you for $100,000 a side." Coe demurred again, stating: "We'll do that next year in the Kentucky Derby." When Derby time came around, the most money that Coe and his friends would fade Bradley was $83,000. Before the race, the high-rolling Bradley told his jockey, Albert Johnson: "If you win, you get 20% of the purse. If you are on the board and beat Pompey, you get 10% of the winning purse."

Albert put Bubbling Over on the lead—the "Bill Daly," as it was popularly known then—right at the start, led all the way, and won in a gallop by five lengths. Pompey finished fifth, beaten 12 lengths. It is said to be the biggest bet that Colonel Bradley ever won on a horse race. Bubbling Over, one of Bradley's all-time favorite horses, sired Burgoo King, one of Idle Hour's three other Derby winners.

Suspicions About Fair Play

Colonel Bradley bred horses at Idle Hour for 35 years before he accepted the blood of Fair Play. Although Samuel D. Riddle invited him to breed to Man o' War, he did not accept—even though the son of Fair Play was probably the greatest racehorse ever bred in this country. Always the gambler, Bradley said he had observed "too many sulkers, too many dishonest, high-strung runners" with Fair Play blood.

When War Admiral retired to stud, Riddle came to him again. "I'll breed a few mares each year to him and see how things go," Bradley told him. "War Admiral is out of a mare by Sweep; that may offset the objectionable traits handed down by Fair Play." Bradley told his farm manager, Olin Gentry, to select mares with good dispositions for War Admiral, and to double up on Sweep if possible.

The mares that Olin selected made War Admiral as a sire. In a span of five years before Bradley's death in 1946, the arrangement produced Busher (champion three-year-old, Horse of the Year, leading money-winning female upon her retirement from racing), Bee Mac (the top two-year-old filly of her year up until she was injured), Bric a Bac ($103,225), and Mr. Busher. At Bradley's death, Businesslike (by Blue Larkspur and in foal to War Admiral) was sold carrying Busanda, who later won the Suburban Handicap and was the dam of champion Buckpasser.

Bradley's Foal Insurance

Bradley may have been the first stallion owner to sell live foal insurance. Back in the 1930s, he charged only 10% of the stud fee for the insurance, payable with the signing of the contract. I once asked Olin Gentry, who managed Idle Hour for 24 years,

Olin Gentry.

how it worked. "Colonel Bradley knew odds and risks better than anyone," said Gentry, "and he knew that only about 70% of the mares bred produced live foals. He was a generous man and always gave the other fellow the best of it in any deal. The stud fees he set for his stallions were always more than reasonable."

For the breeding season of 1933, he stood Black Toney for $2,000, Blue Larkspur and Black Servant for $750, *North Star III and Bubbling Over for $500. "Some of the fellows who didn't insure and failed to get a live foal squawked," Gentry recalled, "but most of them paid because they wanted to continue to breed to our stallions."

Bradley's 'Sunning' Stalls

The colonel also believed in experimenting for the betterment of his horses. Few of the experiments proved out, but, up to his last years, he continued trying new ideas. At Idle Hour, he built "sunning" stalls for his horses in training. On days of favorable weather, they were placed in the stalls during daylight hours. He also tried glasses for horses he thought had poor vision.

Source of Phipps's Success

Ogden Phipps and his highly successful breeding operation owed a great debt to Colonel Bradley. Five of Phipps's eight champions trace in direct female line to Bradley bloodstock, which he purchased from Bradley's estate in November of 1946.

Major Louie A. Beard, who could orchestrate the doings of the rich and famous in racing better than anyone in my lifetime, put together a group to buy all of Bradley's Idle Hour Farm horses after his death in August of that year. The total package cost was $2,681,545. It was probably the best deal since Samuel D. Riddle had taken Man o' War from the Saratoga sales ring in 1918 for $5,000.

Beard's group of buyers were Phipps, King Ranch (Robert J. Kleberg), and Greentree Stud (John Hay Whitney and his sister, Joan Payson). Each of the three entities selected what they wanted, and then they sold off the balance to Charles S. Howard (racehorses) and Edward S. Moore (broodmares, yearlings, and weanlings). The stallions, Bimelech and Blue Larkspur, were transferred to Greentree Stud and stood as the property of the three original investors.

No one made out as well as Phipps. Champions Easy Goer and Relaxing trace to Big Hurry; Buckpasser to Businesslike; Numbered Account to Baby League; and Queen of the Stage to Flitabout (an unnamed yearling filly at the time of the purchase). In addition, 1989 two-year-old champion Rhythm—bred and owned by Phipps's son, Ogden Mills "Dinny" Phipps—also traces directly to Baby League.

The Best Was Bimelech

Although Colonel Bradley won the Derby four times, his best horse, Bimelech, finished second in the Churchill Downs classic. Olin Gentry affirmed that Bradley had often said Bimelech was his best, "but he was so much a gentleman he'd never once criticize Bill Hurley for the way he brought Bimelech into the Derby." Olin remembered it with a good bit of regret.

Bimelech, the champion colt at two in 1939, was so impressive in his final start that year, a victory in the Pimlico Futurity, that Bradley offered to match the colt immediately against "any horse of any age at any distance for any amount of money," Gentry said. There were no challengers.

Instead of taking the great colt to warmer climes to prepare him for the

Derby, Hurley wintered him at Idle Hour and trained him there for his first start at three, the Blue Grass Stakes at Keeneland. On Thursday, April 25, 1940, he won easily, yet he put enough into his effort to get himself thoroughly fit for the big race nine days later. "Ben Jones told me: 'Now if Bill doesn't run him again and only works him lightly, Bimelech's a cinch in the Derby,'" Gentry said.

But Hurley had other ideas. He ran Bimelech the next Tuesday in the one-mile Derby Trial Stakes. Bimelech won, but he went into the Derby a tired, sore horse. At 40 cents to a dollar, he gave his all to finish second, beaten 1 1/2 lengths by the 35-to-1 shot Gallahadion, a colt who had only once before won a stakes and was never again to win another. The chart of the race carries notes indicating that Bimelech was not at his best: "(he) went wide throughout . . . bore out on the stretch turn."

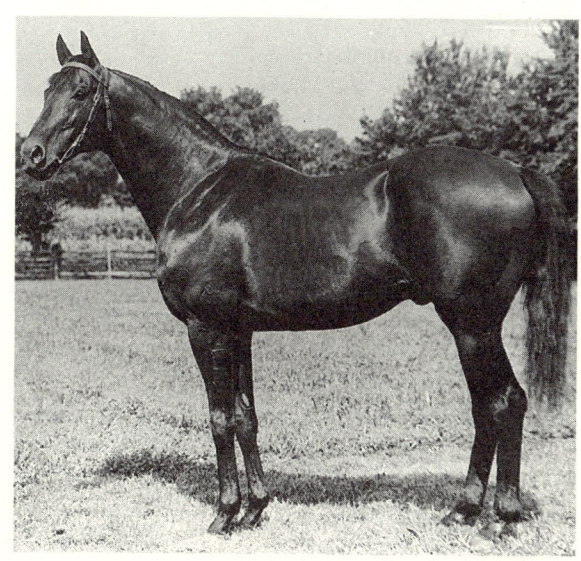

Bimelech.

With a little rest, Bimelech was a different horse two weeks later for a smashing victory in the Preakness, with Gallahadion third. He then won the Belmont, with his previous conqueror unplaced. It is indeed sad that the mishandling of Bimelech denied such a fine sportsman as Colonel Bradley his fifth Kentucky Derby winner and his first Triple Crown champion. But he did receive some solace when Bimelech was voted champion three-year-old colt of 1940.

There is no mental and physical uplift for a person in the Thoroughbred business quite like the knowledge that one has a good racehorse developing. Colonel Bradley seemed to be losing interest in his horses and life in general for several years prior to Bimelech. When the colt by his favorite sire, Black Toney, proved he was a good one at two, he instantly regained interest and maintained it fairly well up to his death in 1946.

The Roots of Claiborne

The year of 1875 was very significant for the American Thoroughbred. It marked the advent of Kentucky Derby and the birth of Arthur B. Hancock Sr. Hancock was born at his parents' Ellerslie Stud, near Charlottesville, Virginia, where he entered school at the age of four in a one-room brick building on the farm presided over by a strict tutor who instructed the Hancock children. With such a thorough educational foundation, it was no surprise he went to college at 15, graduating from the University of Chicago with a degree in engineering.

The lure of horses, however, was greater than engineering, and after college he joined his father, Captain Richard J. Hancock, as a junior partner in Ellerslie. By age 32, he had established such a national reputation as a first-class horseman that he was invited to judge the Thoroughbred classes at the 1907 Blue Grass Fair in Lexington. It was an honor previously accorded only to veteran horsemen. He accepted.

While in Lexington for the fair, Hancock met Miss Nancy Clay of Paris, Kentucky. They were married the following year at her parents' home. Three years later, they were to return to the Paris area permanently to establish Claiborne Farm on 1,300 acres that Mrs. Hancock had inherited upon the deaths of her parents, who had passed away within four days of each other.

A. B. Hancock Sr.

The Hancocks operated Ellerslie in conjunction with Claiborne until 1946, when the Virginia farm was sold and *Princequillo was moved to Kentucky after that breeding season, in which he sired Hill Prince.

Hancock developed Claiborne quickly and with the same zeal and skill that he accumulated top stallions and mares—and very rich, influential boarding clients who took blocks of shares in stallion syndications. First, and maybe foremost, among his boarding clients was William Woodward, for whom he raised three Kentucky Derby winners.

The first stallion that Hancock purchased was Celt for $20,000 in 1913, at the dispersal of the James R. Keene horses at Madison Square Garden. In 1921, Celt became the first Claiborne stallion to head the general sire list. Since then, no farm has come near the Hancock nursery's record for having sires at the top of the list.

Hancock laid a good foundation at Claiborne for his son and successor, A. B. "Bull" Hancock Jr., who was to guide it to its greatest heights. While the senior Hancock was near par excellence as a breeder, Bull was a genius. I knew them both. It was not until the early 1940s, when the old gent was in his late 60s and Bull in his early 30s, that the younger Hancock was allowed in on decision-making. Some of the stallions who stood at Claiborne during Bull's tenure were *Princequillo, *Nasrullah, and *Ambiorix (all to become leading sires), not to mention Double Jay and *Court Martial. Later he was to bring in Round Table, *Herbager, Sir Gaylord, Sir Ivor, Nijinsky II, and Bold Ruler. Those 11 are among the 40 leading sires of stakes winners in North America during the current century.

Bull Hancock.

When he got full control in 1949, Bull also started to cull the Claiborne-owned mares. Nearly every one was replaced by mares who had already proven themselves as producers or young mares with a racing record and reasonably good pedigree. "I won't buy a mare just because of her pedigree," he once told me, "or just her racing record. I want all, or a reasonable amount of both." He once bought such a mare from me.

Bull demanded a lot of himself. He read—and retained what he read—reliable publications on racing and breeding throughout the world. No one was better informed. Nor did anyone have a better eye for a horse. On sight, he could identify and recite the names and pedigrees of the some 500 mares, yearlings, and foals that inhabited Claiborne. During his stewardship at Claiborne, more than 40 champi-

William Woodward Sr.

ons were raised for the farm and its customers. Seven of them earned Horse of the Year honors.

Bull played with the same intensity that he worked. He got his nickname in prep school at Woodbury Forest by crashing into a second baseman. "What do you think you are," admonished the coach, "a bull in a china closet?" He was a gracious winner or loser in public, but in private he gave vent to defeat, often throwing away golf clubs or tearing up decks of cards. But his close friends, particularly Charlie Nuckols and Warner Jones, adored him and his tantrums.

Bull passed away in mid-September of 1972, and such genius in our business I never again expect to see. His son, Seth, took over the management of Claiborne, the fourth of a great line of horsemen.

Two Yearlings in the Ring

Did you ever hear of two yearlings being put into the sale ring at the same time, with the successful bidder taking his choice? Well, Arthur Hancock Sr. did it in July of 1944 at Keeneland. By coincidence, he wound up selling both. That year, Hancock could not decide which of two fillies he wanted to retain for breeding, so he let the sale make the decision for him. One was by Stimulus out of Risk, and thus a half sister to Sky Larking. The other was by *Sir Gallahad III out of Sun Gamonia.

From $15,000 on, there were only two bidders, Elizabeth Arden and Fred Hooper, and Miss Arden prevailed at $22,000. She selected the Stimulus filly. Hooper then walked over to Hancock and asked to have the other for the same price, noting she was the one he was bidding to buy. (At the time, Hooper had in his stable a *Sir Gallahad III colt he regarded highly—Hoop, Jr.—destined to win the 1945 Kentucky Derby for him. He had bought him at Keeneland for $10,200.)

Fair man that he was, Hancock granted Hooper's request. Later, when I asked Hancock why he had done so, he replied: "I felt obligated. In actuality, I was selling two fillies with only one underbidder, which is not the way I do business. I'll not do it again. I doubt if the fillies sold individually would have brought a total of $44,000."

The Stimulus yearling was Beaugay, champion two-year-old filly of 1945, winner of seven stakes and $148,070 before retiring at four. Fred Hooper's filly, named Gallonia, won only two races and $4,700 in 13 starts, racing two years. Neither Beaugay nor Gallonia did much as broodmares.

The 'Cantankerous' Stallion

In the mid-1950s, Dr. Gerald McElligott, the Irish veterinarian and director of the British Bloodstock Agency, lamented to me that he regretted he had not retained *Nasrullah— one of the most influential stallions of this century— for a longer time. As a racehorse, he said, *Nasrullah had the most "cantankerous" kind of disposition. "That's why the Aga Khan sold him to Bert Kerr and me for $50,000, after he'd been the second best of his crop at two and three. If he'd been a bit more cooperative, he would have been champion both years. It was a very cheap buy, considering his racing record, breeding, and conformation. Bert and I thought after we got him to the farm he'd settle down, but he didn't. If things didn't go his way, he just didn't go. You couldn't force him.

"Bert and I didn't sleep a wink at night until we got rid of him," he continued. "We priced *Nasrullah to Joe McGrath for $76,000, and he bought him immediately. We'd have taken a loss on him if we had to, but Joe gave us the asking price."

*Nasrullah had entered stud in 1944, as a four-year-old, at Barton Stud in Suffolk, England, before moving to McGrath's Brownstown Stud in Ireland

*Nasrullah at Claiborne Farm.

the following year. He was a success from the start. His progeny proved to be a bit high-strung but tractable. Such was the record of his initial crops that Bull bought him from McGrath for $340,000, again a very cheap price, in December, 1949, with the understanding that delivery would not take place until the horse had served his 1950 book, to which nominations already had been confirmed. Joining Claiborne Farm in the purchase of *Nasrullah were Harry Guggenheim, William Woodward, and John D. Hertz.

*Nasrullah died in 1959, but until Northern Dancer overtook him in the 1980s, he was the all-time leading sire of stakes winners in North America, with 99. His influence on world-class racing has been immeasurable. He is the all-time leading sire in percentage (23.4%) of stakes winners to foals sired (423). His sons (primarily Bold Ruler, Never Bend, Nashua, and Fleet Nasrullah) and grandsons (Bold Bidder, Cornish Prince, Bold Commander, Raja Baba, What a Pleasure, and Gummo, to name a few) established a preeminent sire line in the 1970s and 1980s.

In the eight years that *Nasrullah stood at Claiborne, Colonel Floyd Sager, the farm veterinarian, was never able to give the cantankerous stallion as much as a tetanus shot. One day when Sager reported "another problem" he was having with *Nasrullah, Bull replied with a bit of chagrin: "Colonel, I just guess we'll have to put up with him."

Bull Passes Up Kingmaker

It was nearing bedtime one Saturday night in August of 1957 at the Reading Room, a private club on the Saratoga track. Kingmaker, by *Princequillo out of Raise You, had been an impressive winner of the Whitney Stakes that afternoon. "Hey," a group hailed Bull as he walked in, "we've formed a syndicate, have it half sold out, to buy Kingmaker for stud. Do you want in? Will you stand him?"

"What kind of liquor are you guys drinking?" Hancock laughed. "Wouldn't I look funny standing a gelding at stud at Claiborne? You guys better turn in." Kingmaker's younger half brother did go to stud and sired horses that made racing history. His name was Raise a Native.

Either Weight or Money

A true rarity on the racetrack is a trainer who is happy with the weight assignment for his horse in a handicap. One young trainer was knocking handicaps to Bull Hancock, contending that races other than maiden or claiming should be run solely under allowance conditions. "Son," Bull replied in a fatherly way, "you're wrong. In a handicap, you either get some weight off or some money."

The Sheikh of Spendthrift

To recite Leslie Combs's contributions to the Thoroughbred industry—and what it has done for him—would require months of research and writing. Just take my word, he, Bull Hancock, and Hal Price Headley were the principals in making Central Kentucky the world capital of the industry, greatly enhancing the value of the region's horses and the Bluegrass's improved and unimproved land.

Leslie sold his insurance business in Huntington, West Virginia, in 1937, and bought the old Hugh Fontaine farm of 127 acres on Iron Works Road. He started out boarding horses, and, to make ends meet at the same time, managed Robert W. Mellwain's nearby Walmac Farm. By 1980, Spendthrift Farm had been expanded to 4,000 acres, with an average annual horse population of 500.

Leslie was born at Belair Farm, the ancestral home of the Combs family in Fayette County, on October 22, 1901. He attended tiny Centre College in the nearby town of Danville. He was on the school's "Prayin' Colonels" football team that upset Harvard University, at odds calculated to be something like 1,000-to-1, thanks largely to one of Centre's all-time great quarterbacks, Bo McMillan, and a super running back, Red Roberts.

The team got its nickname from the fact that the coach, Uncle Charlie Moran, had the team members pray before and after each game. When I would point out to Leslie that he has not prayed much before or since but has done a lot of preying on other horsemen's customers, he laughed: "Yes, that's right, that's right."

"I never could understand how I made the team in the first place," he recalled. "I couldn't kick, pass, or run." Knowing Leslie's power of persuasion, I could. He noted he went out for the team "to get extra clout" with the girls. On Thanksgiving before a big game, he accepted a girl friend's invitation to have dinner with her parents. "Knowing I wasn't going to play—hadn't played a second in three years—I stuffed myself so much I thought I was going to colic. In the locker room before the game, Uncle Charlie, who never missed anything, noticed my condition.

"The game was hardly under way when Uncle Charlie yelled out: 'Combs!' and I made like I didn't hear him. In anger, he walked down to where I was on the bench, grabbed me by the shoulder, and lifted me to my feet, shouting: 'You're in. Tell Bo to run that draw play for you.' I didn't run out on the field; the best I could do was a jog.

Leslie Combs II.

"McMillan hit me in the stomach so hard with the ball I thought it was going clear through me. I fumbled it as I collapsed to the ground, then up came the turkey, the oyster stew, the cranberry sauce, the pumpkin pie, and everything else I had eaten. Red Roberts recovered the ball and helped me to my feet. My playing time for the 'Prayin' Colonels' was over, although Uncle Charlie did let me scrimmage and dress for the games."

After college, Les took up business in Huntington, where he established the city's largest insurance firm, played polo, headed the West Virginia Racing Commission (two terms), and caught the hand of the most beautiful—and wealthy—woman in the state, Dorothy Enslow. Their son Brownell and daughter Juliette (who married developer David M. Trapp) were born in Huntington.

It's Preferable to Hindoo Farm

By 1937, Leslie no longer could resist the lure of the Bluegrass and the horse business. It was through the process of elimination that Spendthrift Farm got its name. Leslie and Dorothy had just taken possession of the old Fontaine farm when Dorothy suggested: "Leslie, your family has been in the Thoroughbred business for several generations here in Kentucky. Why don't we name the farm for its best horse?"

"Good idea," replied Leslie. "Guess that it would have to be for one of the horses of my great-grandfather, Daniel Swigert, who was the foremost breeder of his day—bred three Kentucky Derby winners in a space of six years before the turn of the century.

"Let me think," Combs continued, "there was Spendthrift, whom he bought as a yearling (from A. J. Alexander's Woodburn Stud, then later sold for a record price to James R. Keene), then turned out to be a great racehorse and sire. He was left at the post in the Belmont but came on and won it, anyway. He was also the paternal great-grandsire of Man o' War."

Dorothy was listening intently. "Then there was Hindoo, whom he bred. He ran 35 times, won 30, 18 in a row, including the Kentucky Derby. He sired Hanover and a lot of good . . ."

"Now, Leslie," interrupted his charming wife, "the farm's name won't be Hindoo!" And so it became Spendthrift.

Dorothy did a beautiful job in restoring the main residence and adding wings to it to create a most attractive and charming Colonial structure. The center section was built in 1804 by Major Hector P. Lewis, and logs from trees felled on the farm for its understructure are still in place.

Spendthrift House, until Dorothy's passing and Leslie's retirement, was the scene of many lavish luncheons, dinners, and dances, particularly the ones held during the time of the Kentucky Derby or the July yearling sales. Leslie always managed to have in attendance buyers of high-priced yearlings as well as those he believed ready to play the game on that level. Elizabeth Arden, Jack Knight, and Eugene Constantine were regulars, even house guests, and as long as Cadillac dealer Emil Denemark, brother-in-law of Al Capone, was buying big, he was there (attired in bulletproof vest and pistol in a shoulder holster). Such was the charm and salesmanship of Leslie that he could mix the most diverse group of people at one party and make them all comfortable.

Acquiring Nashua

For the longest time, Combs always seemed to be in the right place at the right time. Additionally, he always had one man who could write the "big check" to tie up a horse that he then could syndicate at share values considerably above cost. This is the Nashua story.

Awakened by a dog's barking in the middle of the night of October 30, 1955, the young wife of William Woodward Jr., owner of Nashua, grabbed her shotgun and blasted at close range a person she thought to be a prowler. Her 35-year-old husband, in the wrong place at the wrong time, died instantly.

A few weeks later, when a New York bank announced that it would sell Nashua by sealed bid in December, Combs paid no particular attention to the matter until he got a call from Chris J. Devine, a New York financier, who asked if Combs would syndicate Nashua and what the bid price should be.

"I'll syndicate him," Leslie replied, "but I want to wait until the night before to give you the exact bid. It'll be around a million."

Strangely, there was little talk around the industry about selling Nashua in this manner. No syndicators were interested because there was not a lot of time to get commitments from shareholders, and there were fears they would "talk" and ridiculously overbid or underbid, in either case making themselves look like "damn fools."

Lou Doherty, always a close friend of mine, confided to me that he was going to bid with the backing of independent financial institutions ("no horsemen"), but he did not state his figure. "There's only one guy who can screw me. That's Combs. He's slick," Lou said. Five sealed bids of $1-million or more were received. Maxwell Gluck offered $1-million, accompanied by his certified check for $100,000, a required 10% downpayment. Lou Doherty came in at $1,251,000. Chris Devine topped both at $1,251,200, a mere $200 over Doherty's bid. The Sheikh of Spendthrift had struck again.

Doherty was livid. "I outbid Gluck by 25%, Combs's man outbids me by .01598%. Somebody in one of the banks had to have talked. I will find out if it is the last thing I do before I die," he said. Lou died January 28, 1988, at the age of 76. He never found out "who talked."

William Woodward Jr. leading in Nashua and Eddie Arcaro.

He Has Money, Too

The big yearling buyer in the 1940s was Elizabeth Arden. Leslie picked the ones for her to purchase, and in return she would buy one from him. Les did the bidding. He once told me: "She never ever gave me a limit. She'd just say, 'Buy him, or buy her,' and that was it." The same year she purchased Beaugay, she also bought the next year's champion juvenile colt, Star Pilot, for $26,000. The next year, Elizabeth bought her Kentucky Derby winner, Jet Pilot, for $41,000.

She would do the bidding herself on Leslie's horses, and she got Myrtle Charm, the champion two-year-old filly of 1948, from him for $27,000. Another she bought from him was the "quickest-sold" yearling in auction-sale history, Look Out Jeep. The bidding lasted less than 30 seconds. Someone opened at $10,000, she nodded right back with $20,000, another person instantly jumped it to $30,000, and then she threw in the clincher, $40,000. I was sitting at ringside with Charlie Nuckols, and we looked at each other in amazement. "If that sonofabitch runs as fast as he sold," remarked Charlie, "he'll be a champion!" He did not, earning only $14,437 in four years of racing.

I never saw Elizabeth back off but one time. John Marsch had two very good talent scouts spotting yearlings for him, Roscoe Goose and Burley Parke. Many yearlings that they had selected for him were also on Leslie's list, and on those Marsch invariably finished second. Noticing Marsch bidding against Leslie on the last day of a Keeneland July sale, Elizabeth whispered to Combs: "Let Mr. Marsch have this one."

When the youngster was knocked down, Marsch shouted so all could hear: "I got money, too."

Brownell's Birthday Present

Juliette Trapp, like her father, is quick with a repartee. A day or so after his 70th birthday, Leslie showed me his new Cadillac. With a great deal of pride, he noted: "Brownell gave it to me as a birthday present." Then he continued: "The first place I drove it was over to Juliette's, and I said: 'See, honey, look what Brownell gave me. What are you gonna gimme?' She just laughed. 'I have a nice present for you, but it's not that expensive,' she said. Then she told me: 'Brownell ought to give you something like that for all the trouble he caused you in raising him.'"

In 1968, Leslie was the honored guest of the Thoroughbred Club of America's annual testimonial dinner in recognition of his outstanding contributions to Thoroughbred racing and breeding. But that was not his swan song. Combs, with his infectious grin, laugh, and good sense of humor, continued to be a popular figure at bloodstock sales, the races, and dinner parties until the final year of his life in 1990.

Chapter 5
Plain Ben and Jimmy

Thoroughbred racing has had several notable father-and-son teams of trainers. The Van Bergs, the Jolleys, the Veitches, the Lukases, and the Burches spring immediately to mind, and they are only a few of the family partnerships. But none of them had nearly the impact of Ben and Jimmy Jones.

They worked as a team, first with their Parnell, Missouri, homebreds (mostly by Seth) in the 1920s, with Herbert M. Woolf's Woolford Farm runners in the 1930s (1938 Kentucky Derby winner Lawrin and the champion two-year-old filly of the same year, Inscoelda), and then with the great Calumet Farm runners from the 1940s to 1964, when Jimmy retired. Ben had retired in early 1957.

B. A. "Plain Ben" Jones was voted into the National Museum of Racing's Hall of Fame in 1958, and his son, Horace A. "Jimmy" Jones, was inducted the following year. They were, of course, the first father and son to be so honored, and the proximity of their inductions provides the proper perspective on their places in racing history. Although Jimmy sometimes appeared to have been in his father's shadow, they were, in fact, two great trainers.

Their record in the Kentucky Derby is nothing short of phenomenal. Out of the 15 horses that they started in the Derby, only three of them finished off the board, and they were all fifth-place finishes. Some people would be happy to finish fifth in the Derby just one time. Ben was the trainer of record for a record six Derby winners, including the Triple Crown champions Whirlaway and Citation. Jimmy, in fact, trained Citation, but the colt ran in Ben's name at Churchill Downs so that the elder Jones could equal the record of four wins

Ben and Jimmy Jones at Keeneland.

set by H. J. "Derby Dick" Thompson when he was training Colonel E. R. Bradley's Idle Hour Farm powerhouse.

Ben told me half jokingly after Lawrin's Derby victory: "Now, I'm going after Dick Thompson's record of training four Derby winners." Thompson, who was given the "Derby Dick" nickname by Damon Runyon, had tightened the cinch on Behave Yourself (1921), Bubbling Over (1926), Burgoo King (1932), and Brokers Tip (1933).

Ten years later, Ben was to accomplish what he had half-joked about when Citation crossed the finish line 3 1/2 lengths ahead of Coaltown, who also was trained by the Jones boys. Ben's other three Derby winners were Pensive in 1944 (also prepared by Jimmy, in Maryland), Ponder in 1949, and Hill Gail in 1952.

Jimmy, who resumed training Citation after the 1948 Derby and saddled him for victories in both the Preakness and the Belmont Stakes, trained two more Derby winners after his father's retirement—Iron Liege in 1957 and Tim Tam in 1958. Jimmy also was the trainer of record when Citation became the first $1-million earner in racing history and when Bewitch set the record for highest earnings by a female runner.

No matter whose name was on the program, the Jones boys shared more than the bond of a father and son. They each respected the other professionally, and they shared the wealth. When Jimmy was in the Coast Guard during World War II, Ben sent him half of his trainer commissions. When Ben retired, Jimmy did the same for Ben until his father's death in June of 1961.

Jimmy retired from training in 1964, and for many years served as director of racing at Monmouth Park.

The Choice Was Relatively Easy

I once asked Ben, who still is regarded as one of the best horsemen of all time, why he chose to become a horse trainer. "My dad, Horace, raised cattle and horses and ran a small dairy at the family farm near Parnell, Missouri, a town of less than 500 population," he told me. "When I was just a little kid on his knee, he'd ask me: 'Now Ben, what do you want to do when you grow up?' and I would always say: 'Run the dairy or train the horses.' I loved Holstein cows and Thoroughbreds. I made my decision quickly when I got old enough to help out with the milking."

Ben Applies a 'Schooling'

In the 1930s, when Ben was hustling to make ends meet while racing his own horses at Oriental Park in Havana, Cuba, he incurred the wrath of Butsey Hernandez, an ex-boxer, by claiming a horse from him. Hernandez immediately announced that he would "school" Ben the next time he was near him. Knowing he would have no chance at fisticuffs if they met on even terms, Jones jumped Hernandez by surprise with a swift kick in the groin, got him on the ground, buried his teeth into his ear, threw punches to his body, and kicked him in the midsection with his knees until he was out of breath. Butsey did not ask for a return match.

Buying Out the Battery Man

No one ever seriously questioned the honesty or the horsemanship of the Jones boys. I once was told that, when Jimmy was a youngster, Ben was racing in Juarez, and they were stabled in the first barn inside the stable gate. One day, a suspicious-looking character walked under the shedrow, asked for "the trainer of these horses," and was directed to the tack room where Ben was studying the condition book. Jimmy, observing the stranger enter the room and leave a short bit thereafter, hastened to find out what "this guy was about."

"He had 12 batteries," Ben replied as he pointed to them on a trunk, "and I bought all of 'em." Jimmy was in a quandary. "I never knew you to use a battery on our horses," Jimmy said with a note of disappointment in his voice, "and if you plan to, I'd think you'd only need one, not 12."

"Ain't gonna use any of 'em," Ben replied as he calmly turned to the next page. "I just bought 'em all so I won't be running against any of 'em." B. A. as Jimmy referred to him, was always thinking ahead.

Protection from Pancho Villa

Ben also used his foresight against the forays of Pancho Villa onto the racetrack. One winter, after Ben had settled into Juarez, a fellow trainer noticed the legs of all of B. A.'s horses. "Ben," he said, "you must have a bunch of bad-legged horses. All of them have bandages or mud smeared over their legs." "Nope," replied Ben, "just protecting them from Pancho Villa. His men sometimes raid these grounds for fresh horses for his cavalry. They won't take one they suspect is unsound." The Mexican general preferred black horses, but he would horsenap a good-looking, sound one of any color.

Everybody Gets the Cough

Ben utilized his foresight and insight throughout his career. One winter at Hialeah in the 1950s, he was seen leading a sick colt, coughing and running at the nose, to the front of the stall of each Calumet youngster. All got nuzzled by the ailing two-year-old.

"What the hell are you doing, Ben," asked his old friend, John Partridge, "trying to get 'em all sick at one time?"

"Exactly," replied B. A. "I want 'em all to get this bug, get sick, get over it, and get their immunity so I won't have to deal with 'em one at a time the rest of this winter. It's gonna pass through the whole stable anyway."

Ben Picks Up 'Slow and Easy' and 'Pinky'

A racetrack hustler walked into Ben's stable early one misty morning in the 1930s at Tijuana and exclaimed: " 'Slow and Easy' wants you to get him out of jail. He's afraid those Mexicans are going to kill him. He was the only person around last night when that next barn over there burned down, and the Mexican police have charged him with setting it on fire. John and George Colburn won't have any need for him—their horses got burned up, too." Ben replied: "When I finish with the last set, I'll go into town right away and see what I can do."

Ben had become acquainted with most of the town's politicians by giving them tips on his horses, figuring one day he might need favors from them. When he and the chief of police arrived with an order for the groom's release at a site a few miles out of town, "Slow" had just completed digging a hole three feet wide, eight feet long, and four feet deep. "Why's he doing this?" Jones inquired of the police chief. He replied: "Our jails are overcrowded, so we make these bad criminals dig their own grave."

Ben had been "clocking" Slow and knew he was a good groom. On their way back to the track, Slow said: "Mr. Jones, I'm going to rub horses for you for the rest of my life, which would have ended in another five minutes. All you'll have to give me is enough money to buy food and clothes. I'll sleep at the barn."

At the same Caliente meeting, a young man walked into Jones's stable and asked for a job as an exercise rider. He looked not at all like the average exercise man—he was tall, lean, and appeared a bit awkward. Later, Jones was to observe that the man, an albino, had poor vision.

B. A. handed him a bridle and saddle, then pointed to a horse who was to go out in the next set, saying: "I'll try you out." He passed Jones's first test—his stirrups were low enough for his knees and legs to engage the saddle, and his hands were down. The trainer allowed no "three-point stands," by which riders balanced themselves on two stirrups and the bit.

On the track, the rider suited Jones even more, and Ben came out of Caliente with the best exercise man, "Pinky" Brown, and the best groom, "Slow and Easy" Martin, that he and son Jimmy were ever to have. Ben and Jimmy treated them as though they were family and encouraged them to invest their stakes in savings accounts as a "set aside" for sickness and their later days when they no longer were physically able to work.

Slow rubbed champions Bewitch and Coaltown, and many other good ones. Pinky galloped all the "goofballs"—including Whirlaway and Hill Gail—as well as the most important runners in the stable.

A Late-Blossoming Opportunity

Despite his abilities, Ben Jones could not be fairly described as an overnight success. He was 50 years old when he got his first big chance, and 57 when he got an even better opportunity. When the dark days of the Depression arrived, Jones lost his meal ticket—the stallion Seth died in a paddock accident—and "I was just about busted," he later told me.

"I got a call from Herbert M. Woolf, a Kansas City, Missouri, merchant who was getting into the game and who had just fired his first trainer, Danny Stewart. That was in 1932. Woolf, I'd heard, was a tough man to get along with, but I took the job for a small salary and a percentage of the winnings. At least, I wouldn't be paying bills."

In Jones's first years with Woolf, who raced under the name of his Woolford Farm, Jones won stakes with Lady Broadcast and Lucille K. in 1932, Risky Miss and Trinchera in 1933, and Navanod in 1934. (The last three raced

Herbert M. Woolf.

under the name of Woolf's friend, Tom Worden, but Woolf paid the bills.) Jones was off to a good start.

Jimmy had remained behind at the Jones Stock Farm in Parnell to get rid of the horses there "at any price," the younger Jones recalled. " That was no easy job. When I got down to the last eight mares, I packaged them and sold them to a man who never sent the check. I called him and said he could have them for nothing if he'd haul them off the place, and he agreed. But he didn't do that. So I paid for it, shipped them to him, then hurried to join B. A."

He Wanted to Know When He Won

In the late 1920s, Woolf had one of the nation's top stables of American Saddlebreds. I first met him then, but I got to know him in the 1940s and 1950s while doing consulting work for him. In 1941, I asked him why he got out of the show horse game and into Thoroughbreds. "It certainly was a smart move; in a short time you've come up with two champions, Lawrin and Unerring," I told him.

"I wanted to know when I won," he began. "I had a great stable of show horses—you know, you were riding in kid horsemanship classes at the time—and my very best one was Roxie Highland, undefeated. We're showing in Chicago, and a man from your town, Bob Moreland, has Dark Rex in the same class with Roxie. Much to my surprise—and the crowd indicated their indignation by booing—Dark Rex was tied for first with her. She got the red ribbon.

"I confronted Bob immediately and accused him of getting to the judges. He admitted it. 'Herb,' he said, 'you had the best horse, but I had the judges,' and that very moment I started selling."

Perhaps It Was Gambler's Luck

Ben was not at all impressed with the quality of bloodstock that Woolf had begun assembling in 1929 to breed Thoroughbreds. Nor was I or anybody else to my knowledge. But Woolf was a risk-taker and a high-stakes gambler. Despite my opinion and those of anybody else, his gambles certainly paid off for a while.

As Woolf sold his saddle horses, he began buying Thoroughbred breeding stock. Rush McCoy, in November of 1929, bought the eight-year-old mare Margaret Lawrence for him at the Lexington Sales Paddocks for $2,000. In 1932, he sent Rush back to the same sales to buy a stallion. He got Insco for $500. In three successive years, 1935-'37, the mating of Insco and Margaret Lawrence were to produce Lawrin, Unerring, and 1940 Kentucky Oaks winner Inscolassie for Woolf.

Insco had some credentials for success at stud, and his depressed sale price can be attributed to the Depression. Bred by Admiral Cary Grayson, Insco was by *Sir Gallahad III and out of *Starflight (a sister to 1916 Middle Park stakes winner *North Star III). He was the seventh-highest-priced yearling of the 1929 Saratoga sales, going for $22,000 to Griffin R. Watkins, president of the International Shoe Co., whence came his name.

At two, Insco showed great potential. He won 4-of-7 starts, including the Post and Paddock Stakes and an allowance race at Arlington Park, lowering the track standard for 5 1/2 furlongs to 1:05 in the latter. An injury shortly thereafter compromised his racing career. Though raced at three—he was sixth in Twenty Grand's 1931 Kentucky Derby—he was so impaired that he was unable to reproduce his early form.

For Woolf, buying Insco was tantamount to "catching lightning in a bottle." The old saying, "A good sire is half a stud, a bad one all of it," was hardly appropriate in the case of Insco. He definitely was all of it at Woolford Farm. Bred to ordinary mares, he sired 13 stakes winners (11%) from 116 foals, including the two champions out of Margaret Lawrence.

In the light of Ben's later record as a trainer, Ben Jones either made Insco or Insco made Ben Jones. But I would give most of the credit to the trainer.

Calumet Farm foundation sire Bull Lea.

A decade later, he took the offspring of another unsung stallion prospect, Bull Lea, who stood at the time for $250 or $500, and by training his progeny elevated him to the champion sire of his day. Leslie Combs once told me that he would stand any sire at Spendthrift Farm, regardless of his credentials, if he knew Ben Jones was going to train most of his offspring.

The Right Trainer for Lawrin

Ben, a nonconformist, bucked tradition by getting Lawrin ready for the 1938 Derby by racing him over the winter at Hialeah. No other winner of the classic had raced in the winter except for Black Gold, winner of the 1924 Louisiana Derby. "Had we not taken him there," Jimmy said, "we would not have won the Derby. We shipped a dead-fit horse into Churchill after he won the Flamingo and Hialeah Stakes. But, in his last workout in Florida, he had sustained a separation of the outer wall of his left forefoot.

Kentucky Derby winner Lawrin with Ben Jones.

"We put a bar shoe on it and trained him lightly," Jimmy continued, "keeping our fingers crossed and hoping we could hold his condition. After the Derby Trial Stakes, in which he was second to The Chief on Tuesday, we replaced the bar shoe with a wide-web, conventional plate, and on the following Saturday he won our first Kentucky Derby—and also Eddie Arcaro's first."

But my old friend Tom Shehan recalled that Lawrin was beginning to shorten stride as he bore out in deep stretch. Meanwhile, Dauber was closing on him. "Arcaro got Lawrin three lengths on the lead in the stretch, but as he started to tire, a drunk stood up on a chair in front of Ben, impairing Ben's view of the race. Ben immediately took his binoculars and brought them down full force, downing the man but also drowning Ben's suit with the man's huge paper cup of beer. As he reached down to pick up the drunk and finish him off, Jimmy pulled Ben away, shouting: 'B. A., B. A., he held on by a length. We won the Kentucky Derby.' The two Joneses were then off to the winner's circle."

Time to Make a Move

When Insco died prematurely in 1939, Ben once told me, he knew it was time to look for another position. "When Insco died, I knew I was going to have to go elsewhere if I was to get quality horses to train. That's why I accepted Warren Wright's offer to come on as the Calumet trainer in the fall of 1939. My decision was correct."

Over the next two decades, Calumet Farm was to be the country's leading owner 11 times and would win the Kentucky Derby seven times.

Herb Woolf lost more than his trainer to Calumet. At a 1941 luncheon with Woolf in Kansas City, he listed with me the champion mare Unerring for $8,000. Upon my return to Lexington, I sold 1939's champion three-year-old filly sight unseen to Warren Wright. For Calumet, she produced only three foals, two of whom were Faultless (the 1947 Preakness Stakes winner) and Tige O'Myheart (dam of two-time champion filly Idun).

Warren Wright Sr.

The Record at Calumet

Warren Wright had been offering Ben the head trainer position since he had stood "the Turf world on its ear" with Kansas-bred Lawrin. When it was pointed out to him that Wright was hard to please—he had had three trainers in the eight years he had been in racing—Jones replied: "He can fire me, too, if I don't produce." But produce he did.

In 1940, Ben's first full year as Calumet's trainer, the stable was the nation's third-leading owner. In the next 16 years, up to his retirement, the Lexington farm led the list nine times, and was second in four other years. When Jimmy took over in 1957, Calumet led the list that year and the next, and again in 1961.

Jimmy Jones leading in Citation after the 1948 Belmont Stakes.

It was the first stable ever to earn $1-million in a year (1947). In 1948, when its winnings were $1,269,710, the second-leading stable earned only $490,832. In 1952, with earnings of $1,283,197, the next closest had $600,505. In three different years, Calumet had ten or more stakes winners from strings that averaged around 40 horses.

In five of the nine years from 1941 through 1949, a Calumet runner was voted Horse of the Year. Whirlaway was the first horse to earn $500,000; Armed, the first gelding to reach $800,000; Bewitch, the first filly to earn $460,000; and Citation, the first horse to go over $1-million. Oddly, Citation and Bewitch set their earnings records by running one-two in the 1951 Hollywood Gold Cup.

Warren Wright died on December 28, 1950, and unfortunately did not get to see the foundation of bloodstock he had assembled at Calumet carry it on for 11 more glorious years. Five times during that span, the stable headed the earnings list. Ben did live to witness the accomplishments.

Whirlaway Jumps Into the Derby

Pinky Brown was Ben's exercise man of choice for his Derby horses, particularly for Whirlaway and Hill Gail. (Freeman McMillen galloped Citation.) They were run-out horses, and only Pinky had the strength and balance to keep them on a straight course. But Pinky's poor vision once nearly caused Ben's already ailing heart to go into cardiac arrest.

Early one morning in Derby week in 1941, as dawn was breaking over Churchill Downs, Ben instructed Pinky to gallop Whirlaway a mile and quarter at a two-minute clip—"and don't let him get out with you." Pinky took Whirlaway right to the rail and let him gallop in a manner that appeared he was challenging "Whirly" to try to get out, a bad habit that had cost him several important races. Returning to Jones with the long-tailed colt, he remarked: "He didn't try to get out at all, but he was bobbing up and down and going choppy all the way. Something's wrong with him."

"He should have," Ben replied. "You just got through jumping every 'dog' on the racetrack, but I think I've just learned something. The dogs distracted him." On Saturday, Whirlaway ran in a one-eyed blinker, his right eye covered, and the rest was history. Whirlaway won by eight lengths, and Ben had his second Derby victory—and the first for Calumet and Warren Wright.

Trying to 'Make' Whirlaway

I once asked Jimmy how Warren Wright was to train for. "Tops," he replied, "because he was a good businessman and a realist. He looked at his horses objectively—except Whirlaway. He really didn't expect Bull Lea to be much of a sire. Stood him for $500 and bred him to what he thought were his worst mares. In fact, he sold the dam of Twilight Tear, Lady Lark, in foal to Sun Teddy, for $4,000 when Twilight Tear was a weanling and offered to sell Armful, the dam of Armed. Armed was to become the second-best horse (to Citation) we ever had, and Twilight Tear the best mare. They were in Bull Lea's first crop. Also, there were two other outstanding fillies, Durazna and Harriet Sue.

"By the end of 1947, the year we got the first Whirlaways, we had led the earnings list four out of the last five years, with Bull Lea putting us there with horses like Citation, Armed, Twilight Tear, Faultless, and Bewitch. B. A. went to Mr. Wright and said the Whirlaways are 'no account—their first race is their best, then they fall apart. Give Bull Lea the best mares.'

B. A. with Triple Crown winner Whirlaway.

"Mr. Wright said: 'No, I'm going to make Whirlaway a sire,' and B. A. replied: 'Well, give Bull Lea some good mares so we can afford the expense of the Whirlaways.' " Wright made few mistakes, and those he made he quickly corrected. Whirlaway was an exception. He bred to him three more years before leasing him to Marcel Boussac to stand in France, where he died in April of 1953, leaving no issue of note.

Armed and Coaltown

"Why did you cut Armed?" I asked Jimmy. "Couldn't train him," he replied. "He was studdish, he'd kick you, bite you—he was common! One day he kicked the hay out of the fork when his groom was entering his stall to feed

Horse of the Year Armed.

him. That was it. We sent him back to the farm, gelded him, and turned him out for a year. Then, when we put him back in training, he developed a little ankle trouble, and we had to give him more time. Didn't get him sound and rolling until he was four. But what a dead game racehorse he was." Armed was the champion handicap horse in 1946 and 1947 and Horse of the Year in 1946.

"And about Coaltown, you did race him as a two-year-old?" I asked Jimmy. "Coaltown always had some kind of respiratory problem," he replied. "We couldn't figure it out. One morning at Arlington as a two-year-old, just galloping, he fell, and he hemorrhaged about a quart of blood. Sent him home and turned him out until late fall, then got him ready for Hialeah. He still had that little respiratory problem. Without it, however, he still wasn't ever going to beat Citation."

Which One Was the Best?

During its glory years, it was not unusual for Calumet to finish first and second in major stakes races. On more than one occasion, the stable finished one-two-three in major events, and the one I remember best is the 1947 Washington Park Futurity: Bewitch (Doug Dodson up), Citation (Steve Brooks), and Free America (John Westrope). It was Citation's only loss at two.

Years later, I asked Doug Dodson if Bewitch was really the best that day.

"I don't think so," he replied. "Nearing the finish, Steve was right on the heels of Bewitch when she started tiring under me. 'Go with her, I can't hold this big sucker,' he yelled to me, but I couldn't. Bewitch was out of gas. I looked over my right shoulder at the finish, and Westrope had Free America bent double.

"Before the race, Ben Jones told us jocks: 'This race is between our three horses. We're going to finish one-two-three, and you riders are going to split the stakes evenly. Forget about the seven other starters. Just finish in the order you come up, but don't race each other.' He had the race figured right."

Bewitch winning the Washington Futurity over Citation and Free America.

Last to the Paddock

Ben Jones's record in the Derby can be attributed in part to the condition of his horses as they went onto the track for the race. Generally, they did not "wash out" in the wild, raucous paddock before the Derby. He accomplished this by simply being late to the paddock with his horse, entering it just in time to fasten the saddle and throw up the jock. Reacting to the pandemonium, the other starters were generally lathered up and were losing precious energy because of the excitement. Tension mounted on the jocks, too, as they wondered when Ben and his horse would arrive.

I once asked Ben whether the stewards had ever admonished or fined him. "They've told me not to do it anymore, but what is a $100 fine when you are trying to win the Derby? What is more important is that no Derby field has ever been late leaving the paddock because of me," he said.

Hill Gail Goes the Right Way

In 1952, the other Derby trainers took things into their own hands and told management that they would not start leading their horses over from the backstretch until Hill Gail left with them. The stewards called in Ben, told him of the threat, and asked him not to "provoke the other trainers into carrying it out, thereby causing a delay and inconveniencing the more than 100,000 spectators and the millions who watch on TV."

Jones agreed. "Hill Gail will be one of the first to enter on the track, if all the others are there to enter with him, for the walk from the backside to the paddock," he said. His statement was very carefully—and artfully—worded. Hill Gail was led by Harry Smith on a lead pony, and they were closely followed by Pinky Brown and Ben, who carried a canvas travel bag.

When Jones looked back and confirmed that all the entrants were being led clockwise around the track's clubhouse turn to the paddock, he yelled, "Now!" to Harry, who then led Hill Gail to the middle of the track and stopped. Ben pulled a saddle and saddle pad from the bag, buckled it on Hill Gail, threw up Pinky, and instructed them: "Now walk slowly the right way (counterclockwise) on the track, and I'll meet you at the paddock entrance." The other trainers were dumbfounded and furious. Ben had done it again.

Knowing the day would come when he would have to deal with the other trainers, Ben had timed that counterclockwise walk many times from that exact point during morning training. Hill Gail was in the paddock only long enough to be changed to Arcaro's tack and leave it when the paddock judge ordered the riders up.

Hill Gail clocked Hannibal for more than a half mile and then took command, opening five lengths at the head of the lane. Arcaro held him together through the stretch to win by two lengths over Sub Fleet. It would be the final Derby victory for two great ones, Ben Jones and Eddie Arcaro.

The 130 Pound Club

I once asked Jimmy Jones to tell me about the "130 Pound Club," and the Hall of Fame trainer complied. "Jack Campbell started that up in New York. Said B. A. was president and I was vice president, and made a big to-do about it, like we always wanted an edge. Armed was nominated for the 1946 Suburban Handicap, and Mr. Campbell phoned me down in Maryland and asked if we were going to run. I told him not with more than 130, and asked what he had in mind for the spread of weights. He said 132 down to 112. I suggested he take two pounds off each horse and the handicap would be relatively the same. He agreed. Armed won with 130. Reply Paid was second with 110. What was unfair about this?"

Champion sprinter and handicap horse Coaltown.

Campbell put 138 on Coaltown for the 1949 Suburban Handicap, a 40-pound spread in the weights to the lowest assignment of 98. So Ben called Ty Shea at Narragansett Park, who agreed to 130, and Coaltown was shipped to the Rhode Island track to win the Roger Williams Handicap in an easy gallop. "Now does that make sense?" Jimmy asked. "A horse that has to carry only 98 pounds to be competitive doesn't belong in the race. Obviously, we skipped it."

Chapter 6
Rascals and Writers, Hardboots and Hangouts

For many years, the term "hardboot" was used nationally to denote a Kentucky horseman. It originated, to the best of my research, before the turn of the century at the Sheepshead Bay, New York, yearling auctions. A groom from the Bluegrass could be identified by his rawhide boots, which were very hard when they dried out after being wet.

With the term went the reputation of being close with a buck. Colonel Phil Chinn once told me: "Never in history have two hardboots so much as torn a lunch or dinner check grabbing it. Generally, when a waiter approaches with it, each turns his head away in utter abandon."

The late Dr. Eslie Asbury, renowned writer and lecturer, once defined a hardboot as a horse seller who skillfully extols the good points of his horse's conformation and pedigree but adroitly neglects to reveal the faults. He is not lying, but he is not telling the whole truth, either. That is where *caveat emptor* comes into play. For me, it seems that the typical hardboot strives constantly to get more for his dollar than he is entitled to. He is described as being "a little tight with a buck," an "el cheapo," or a cheapskate.

There is an amusing story that I heard one night back in the 1930s at the "Horsemen's Corner" of Lexington's Lafayette Hotel, where trainers, owners, and breeders gathered nightly to swap the news of the business and, if there was not any news, rumors would do.

A tobacco farmer, new to the horse business, had stopped at the first stable inside the old Kentucky Association track looking for a "dollar a day" trainer for the yearling colt hitched to the rear of his horse-drawn buggy. In answer to questions at the first stable, he replied: "One friend 'gived' me the mare and another one 'gived' me a free season, so I raised myself this fine colt.... What, you supposed to trim his feet? Well, he ain't had that done to him.... Wormed? Well, he ain't never had that, neither."

The farmer was nearly to the last barn before he found a trainer in those desperate Depression days who would go for his deal. As an afterthought, the farmer added: "And save the manure. I'll come with my buckboard on Saturdays and haul it back to the farm." The trainer replied: "At a dollar a day, there ain't gonna be none."

A Genuine Hardboot

One of my favorite hardboot horsemen was E. Gay Drake, who frequently joined Colonel Phil T. Chinn and me for lunch on Saturdays at the Canary Cottage, where the fare was good and much cheaper than at the Lafayette or Phoenix Hotel. Colonel Chinn once told Gay: "When you get ahold of a dollar bill, you squeeze it longer than it took Washington to cross the Delaware." Additionally, he "enjoyed bad health," which Chinn and I thought was his excuse for his ordering a thrifty lunch.

E. Gay Drake.

Once, I recall that he said he was suffering from consumption, bronchitis, rheumatism, and a myriad of other disorders that would have kept him bedridden. "I'm only 46," he noted, "and I'm afraid I won't be with you boys much longer." Gay died 34 years later in 1974 at the age of 80.

To save on trucking, he bought a one-horse van. He hauled his own horses and charged others for the same service. The driver? E. Gay Drake, himself. The self-proclaimed little, "sick" man—he was thin and frail-looking and weighed less than 120 pounds—had no trouble lifting or lowering the heavy rear door of the van.

Gay also was a knowledgeable horseman. He could buy cheaper mares and pay lower stud fees and get better results than anyone I have ever known. And he would back up his faith in his judgment by putting one or two in training each year, which was not often done by commercial breeders in those days. He bred about 20 stakes winners from a small band of mares, and he kept the best one for himself, Swoon's Son.

If ever there was a well-managed horse, it was Swoon's Son, who was trained by Lex Wilson. In the late 1950s, he started 51 times, won 30 races, and earned $970,606, big money in those days, while racing almost exclusively in the Midwest. Gay never shipped him to New York or California. Round Table came to Chicago to take him on and was beaten by him.

When asked why he never shipped Swoon's Son for the big races away from Churchill Downs, Keeneland, Arlington Park, and Washington Park, Gay would act a bit displeased and reply: "I can't get Lex to ship." This was the same trainer who took Fred Alger's *Azucar to California to win the first Santa Anita Handicap in 1935 and rode in England's Grand National.

When Swoon's Son was running in Chicago, Gay would attend his Saturday races— and save a few bucks. He would take a second-class day coach on the train from Lexington to Cincinnati, then switch to a first-class sleeper coach on into Chicago and return in the same manner.

Swoon's Son got off to a good start at stud, siring three stakes winners in his first crop. Subsequently, he sired the New York Racing Association's filly triple crown winner, Chris Evert. He was always in demand, and his book could have been filled at a higher fee than Gay set for him. Though a bit miserly with himself, he never gouged anyone. Swoon's Son sired 22 stakes winners.

Gay saved himself some money in still another way—tree trimming. Once, well into his 70s, he noted a limb that needed to be removed from a tree in his front yard. He methodically carried his saw and ladder to the tree and did the job himself. About an hour later, while being x-rayed at the hospital, he insisted the ladder was resting on the trunk of the tree and not on the limb he had removed. He was not seriously injured, just badly bruised.

Drake was a quiet, soft-spoken man with a droll sense of humor, and he was well-liked in the Lexington community. In our many years of friendship, I never heard him criticize another person nor heard anyone knock him. His grandson, Jack G. Jones Jr., also an owner and breeder, is a successful Lexington lawyer who specializes in Thoroughbred-related matters.

'Fats' Came for the Money

Walter "Fats" Wilkerson came on the track first at Louisville's old Douglas Park— he could not get stalls at Churchill Downs—back in the Depression days of the early 1930s. Later, after he had trained a few winners, which he also owned, rubbed, and hot-walked, he was able to get into Churchill, Dade, Keeneland, and River Downs. He was not Ben Jones, but he did scrape out a living.

I will always have a soft spot in my heart for Fats. He sold me my first broodmare prospect, Joji T. My first racehorse was Cadence, who won 13 races—for other people, and not one for me. I was a real greeny. "Buy this old mare from me," he said. "I'm busted." I replied: "I ain't got no money." "You got this kind," Fats responded. "Gimme $400." I did, after researching her and learning she was a stakes winner bred by Hal Price Headley. (A. B. Hancock Sr. let me breed Joji T. to Fighting Fox for $250, and I sold her filly at Keeneland in 1946 for $10,300.)

I once asked Fats what prompted him to go on the racetrack. "Money," he said. "My mother ran a catering business in our home. Many of her customers were local horsemen and also racetrack men from out of town who came to Churchill. Those guys always seemed to drive new cars and have lots of spending money. And those were Depression days! I'd have been a damn fool not to go to the racetrack when my mother told me I was too old to be hanging around the house and kicked me out." (Fats's home was reputed to be the best bawdy house in all of Louisville.)

My favorite story about Fats—who was seldom addressed by his first name, Walter—concerns an incident that occurred in the paddock before the first race one day at Churchill Downs. Judge Charles Price, passing through on his way to the stewards' stand, observed Fats feeding a white substance to his horse. "Now, now, Walter," said the stern, old racing official, "are you getting yourself into trouble?"

"Not at all, Judge," Fats quickly responded. "It's just a sugar cube. Here, have one. I'll eat one myself." Tasting nothing foreign, Judge Price walked on. A few minutes later when jockey Earl Poole asked Fats how he wanted the horse ridden, Fats replied: "Put him right on the lead. The only two here that can catch you is me and the presiding judge."

I saw humor much like that story in everything Fats said or did, even in his physical build and the sloppy fit of his clothing. Fats was obese, as his nickname suggests. He walked fast but sort of waddled. His stomach protruded six inches out over his belt buckle, and his ill-fitting shirts were never buttoned in proper alignment. He was nearly always busted, but he never failed to pay his honest debts. His word was good. Fats had many pals on the racetrack, including me.

This 'Fats' Carried 'Swindle' in His Briefcase

William E. "Fats" Charles first came on the racing scene as a trainer in New England, as well as I can recall, and then migrated to New Jersey, where for some years he served as secretary of the state's Horsemen's Benevolent and Protective Association, a position he also held concurrently in Florida. His tenure in each position was promptly terminated with the results of the New Jersey division's raffle of a new Cadillac in the late 1940s.

W. E. explained to the division's executive committee that the raffle was a keen scheme to raise a few thousand dollars for its benevolence work, and he was told to "go on with it." He further secured his position by noting to them that, unlike other sweepstakes and raffles where employees or their relatives were precluded from participating, that prohibition should be waived in this case "since most of the tickets will be bought by you gentlemen and the members of our division." He made his point.

Well, the tickets are sold, and the time for the drawing arrives. Fats Charles reaches in, pulls out a ticket stub, and—faster than you can say "palmed"—nonchalantly observes: "Well, what do you know? That's my wife's number." Fats's lack of surprise was his indictment.

I once asked Fats—you could ask him anything without offending him—if he really put the fix on the drawing. He just laughed, without confirming or denying. "What's the difference anyway?" he replied. "She divorced me two years later, and the Caddy was in her name."

For health reasons, Fats dieted off about one-fourth of his weight without altering his clothes or buying a new wardrobe, and he did not exactly dress in the sartorial splendor that befitted his next means of

William E. Charles.

subsistence—selling racehorses and breeding stock. The sag of his clothes was accentuated by a sloppy gait. He walked on his heels as though he had a chronic case of ingrown toenails, and he always carried a frayed briefcase containing wrinkled copies of race records and pedigrees under one arm.

"What are you carrying in your satchel?" I once asked him. "Swindle, my boy, swindle," he replied.

Fats once put it on me as my agent in a sale. He said he had a "man" who wanted to buy a "tax mare" (at that time, a mare over 15 years could be depreciated in 12 months). I showed him the pedigree, a stakes producer with a good black-type family that cataloged well. She was in foal to Gun Shot, which gave him a good talking point because he was the sire of Gun Bow, who had just retired to stud with earnings of nearly $800,000 and had been syndicated for something like $1-million.

I told Fats he would have to complete his deal quickly, or else wait until I returned from Argentina (where I went on a commission to buy *Forli for Bob Hibbert, only to get nosed out by the Murty brothers and Bull Hancock). Fats hardly examined the mare physically, which reminded me of another hustler who cared nothing about the horse, only about how to move the merchandise. "Come back by way of Miami, phone me at this number, and I'll have the deal closed," he instructed.

Fats said payment would be "part check, part cash, with my 10% coming out of the cash." I said okay, thinking that would be the last I would hear of the deal. But, upon my return to Miami, he had indeed completed the deal. He had forged my name to a bill of sale for $25,000 (the amount of the check he presented to me) and handed me $1,000 in cash. I protested: "Hey, Charles, there's a grand missing!" To that, he replied: "I had to spend that on your behalf. I had to 'grease' the man's accountant to assure him he could write off the mare in 12 months." I am confident W. E. swung with my thousand. Obviously, that was my first and last deal with William E. Charles. Subsequently, we laughed, joked, and socialized with some frequency, but no business. The last time I saw him, he told me he was doing very well in the insulation business. "To avoid conflicts of interest, deals are going through me as a third party, and I get 10% of the rip off," he explained.

Barred from the Sales

The most loved—and hated—character ever in the Thoroughbred business around Lexington during my lifetime was John W. Stanley. He lasted only about a dozen years, and, upon his departure, there were only five horsemen who would pal with him—Gay Drake, Grant Dorland, Denzil Hollingsworth,

Phil Chinn, and myself. For some reason, we ignored his wicked ways and speech and enjoyed his humor immensely.

John freely admitted he operated on wife Hilda's money—and he was very generous with it. Hilda, it was said, discovered him in a car wash in Florida, bought him a wardrobe, and brought him to Kentucky in the early 1940s to go into the horse business. He knew nothing about it upon his arrival and less when he left, and during the interim he made many disturbing utterances and masterminded many dastardly deeds.

John got early recognition as a breeder. After Eddie Janss had bought Broomshot for $700, he gave Ed a hundred or so profit for her—and a good cursing for being so dumb to sell her. The second foal that J. W. bred from her was Double Jay, champion two-year-old colt of 1946 and later the sire of 45 stakes winners and the maternal grandsire of over 100 more, including John Henry.

John Stanley.

It was not long before John had fallen out with so many stallion managers that he could not book his mares anywhere, so he bought his own stud, Halcyon, who failed miserably for him. When the registrar of the Jockey Club informed him that his foal registration applications were improperly prepared, he telephoned back with a thoroughly profane description of every member of the Jockey Club and all of its employees. Those foals were nearly two-year-olds before I got the matter straightened out for him and all the youngsters registered.

Because he refused to withdraw or present horses he had cataloged for a Keeneland sale, he became the first—and last—consignor to be barred from selling there. Later, Fasig-Tipton barred him, too.

The turnover of employees at his Springside Farm was constant. When top grooms on most farms were receiving $50 a week, John advertised in the Lexington newspapers with an offer of $100 a week plus a $500 Christmas bonus. He was deluged with applicants, hired his quota—and earned the enmity of not only the farm operators who lost grooms, but also those who were informed by their employees that $50 a week was a subpar wage and that a Christmas bonus indeed was in order.

J. W. did not believe in electric traffic signals, stop signs, or speed limits. I was riding with him once en route to the races at Hialeah. I was terrified. When a traffic officer pulled him over and approached the driver's side of the car, John slapped his book of tickets and pen out of hand, shoved a $100 bill in his pocket, and shouted: "Bet this on No. 3 in the second race or give it to one of your women. I gotta get going." And go he did, leaving the traffic cop in total shock.

Looking for Loopholes

An old racetracker was in a Lexington nursing home with a terminal disease. Although he had broken nearly every cardinal rule of life—and racing—he had some endearing qualities because of the comical manner in which he had played out his scams. A visiting trainer stopped by the nursing home and was shocked to see the old racetracker reading the Bible. "Why are you reading that?" the trainer asked. The patient replied softly, but with a wink of the eye: "I'm looking for loopholes."

Willie Lee Nutter 'Manners' His Horses

Willie Lee Nutter was a most unusual person. He was a horse breeder and tobacco farmer, but he never dirtied his hands while pursuing those endeavors. He was always neatly dressed, wore the most expensively tailored—yet oddly designed—clothes. Any car less than a Cadillac was beneath his dignity.

To most people who knew him, he was Willie Lee or W. L. to his face and "Nut" behind his back. Willie Lee was a commercial breeder at his 100-acre horse farm near Georgetown, which is north of Lexington. The first and about the only good runner he bred was Can't Wait, a foal of 1935 who was still winning major stakes for Myron Selznick, the movie man, at the age of seven under the fine training of J. T. "Tommy" Taylor.

Nutter's horses were always fat and well groomed, but they were terrified of him. W. L. started "mannering" them almost from birth. If they did not obey his voice commands, they would be thoroughly lashed with a bullwhip. His son Bill, a sensitive soul, would cringe on those occasions.

"You like to ride," the old gent said to me on one occasion. "Come on out— you can ride Bill's horse—and I'll show you some 'broke' horses." I did. At their paddock, Willie Lee called to them, and they galloped through the open gate. They stopped instantly, side by side and stone still, in the barn in front of the tack room. There, we brushed and saddled them. Never before had I seen two such obedient horses.

When Willie Lee got his saddle horses going "his way," he would sell them off at fancy prices and start with new ones. He got little repeat business and a multitude of complaints. Without the whipping, the Nutter horses would not stay "broke."

Back in the 1940s, Mrs. Warren Wright, who had ridden extensively in her younger years, thought it would be fun to ride over the farm and watch from horseback as some of the Calumet horses trained. Dick McMahon, the farm manager, bought what he thought was Willie Lee's best for her to ride. The walking horse went very well for several days, but without W. L.'s refresher courses started falling into his old, unmannerly habits and became worse each day.

As was suspected, one day the Nutter "graduate" got the lady of Calumet off his back. Before she had extracted both feet from the stirrups, he dragged her for a short distance, leaving her with minor abrasions and contusions. McMahon, as tough an old Irishman as ever lived, immediately telephoned Willie Lee, unleashed upon him his unlimited command of profanity, and by nightfall had the unruly horse returned to Nutter and Calumet's purchase price back. Willie Lee did not recall any guarantee, but Dick convinced him he had made one.

People would drop by to see W. L.'s showing of a yearling he had up for auction. "This is a broke colt," he would tell them, "plenty of sense. Let me show you." With that, he would walk around the young-

Willie Lee Nutter.

ster and would use his cane to lightly strike the yearling on various parts of his body, including up between his hind legs. The colt never moved. Observers would walk away in bewilderment.

When World War II was in its early stages and the horse market was down, Willie Lee told Henry Knight that he wanted out of the horse business.

The same day, Knight gave him his asking price for all of them—Henry was a "package" man—and got a bill of sale from Nutter. Knight jumped on the phone and sold all of them, sight unseen, in two days. But, when vans from out of state arrived and picked up the horses, W. L. reasoned that he had been "had," the victim of his own trap—and his own asking price.

He phoned Knight and said the deal would have to be "renegotiated for more money," or else the certificates of registration would not be delivered. Henry took it calmly, but he told W. L. that his attorney would be in touch with him shortly. With one letter, the attorney explained the damages he expected to obtain for Knight in view of the fact that the check had cleared and Henry had a bill of sale. Willie Lee raced to the lawyer's office and surrendered the registration papers.

After the sale, Willie Lee told me: "I'm going to wait until the market comes down, then I'll get back in." It never did, and he never did. He died about ten years later, the market still on an upswing. Willie Lee had a good but slightly dull sense of humor and was rather well liked in Lexington— except by those who knew he would welsh on a deal and that he was cruel to horses.

'Chew Tobacco Charlie'

In the Depression days of the early 1930s, Charles R. Valentine was variously known as "Chew Tobacco Charlie," "One Horse Charlie," and "Big Valley," and he objected not the least to being addressed by any of them. There were other Valentines in the business, and he considered his nicknames to be a distinction.

The "Chew Tobacco Charlie" nickname came naturally. He constantly chewed an uncontrollable amount of the stuff, and a steady stream of tobacco juice drained from both sides of his mouth. You had to converse with "Chew Tobacco" at some distance, or you most assuredly would get sprayed. When he changed loads, he would stuff at least a quarter of a bag of Mail Pouch into his mouth, and then you would have to wait a minute or two until he got it worked up before resuming the conversation. If you were to follow "Big Valley" to the pay telephone in the Keeneland kitchen, it was highly advisable to take along a paper napkin to clean the mouthpiece.

Big Valley was the biggest bluffer and the most chicken-hearted character I have ever encountered in my many years in this game. He died a "maiden," never winning a "heat."

Valley's headquarters was Keeneland for the last 20 years of his life, and before that he was based at the Lexington trotting track, where he trained with a lead pony or by driving a cart. I never knew him to race farther away than 150 miles from his home base, probably because of his fear of becoming estranged from the man who footed the bills, Dr. J. R. McGinnis, a Lexington physician. For what they cost, they were good runners, earned back the initial investment, then were resold or claimed for a fine profit. This was repeated several times, each time with the same success.

Doc McGinnis once told me: "I well know Valley and I will never get a good horse, and if we should, he'll not know how to train it. But I love his optimism and immensely enjoy his reports on our one or two horses. He diverts my mind from serious, unpleasant matters. If you take out of your game guys like me who get kicks from such a person, you'll not have horse racing." I had to agree. It is true.

Valley was best at breaking and training young horses up to where they could perform a good workout, or rehabilitating crippled or sour dispositioned horses back into racing condition. But as a manager and trainer of racing horses, he was a total failure.

If you knew him well and he liked you, you could ask him any question without fear of offending him. I once asked him how he had come to the racetrack, and this is what he told me:

"My parents worked for the Barnum circus. I was about seven when it came to town and set up in the centerfield of the trotting track over here by Angliana Avenue. I wasn't around when the circus pulled out, and they left me here stranded—stranded, and hungry, too. A family over there on Curry Avenue took me in and had the police contact my parents at the next town. They said they didn't have a son. I guess I had been causing them a lot of trouble. So I moved over here to the trotting track and been here ever since."

Valley's future in the horse business was limited from the start. He had strong likes and dislikes and did not get along with fellow workers. He had to go it alone if he were to make it at all. He had no education—could barely read or write—and was completely free of social graces. He said what he had on his mind, always in loud tones, without any thought or concern about how it would be accepted. Thus, Big Valley was always limited to the number of horses he could personally handle: three, at most.

For quite a number of years, Valley's insults stuck. Valley was a big, physically fit looking Irishman, better than six feet tall, and approximately 180 pounds. If he could get in his bluff and make it stick, he would preen in a swashbuckling manner. But on the racetrack, most bluffs are called. The racetrackers lost their awe of him one morning when a 105-pound exercise boy stood on his tiptoes and decked him. Valley had a glass jaw and a chicken heart.

Once when Herb Stevens took exception to a remark made by Valentine in the Keeneland kitchen, Valley yelled so all could hear: "Meet me outside the front door. I'm going to close your mouth for good. I'll be there in a minute." Herb waited 15 minutes. No Valentine. When Howard Rouse was leaving the kitchen for his car, he laughed to Herb: "Don't wait any longer. Valley didn't even finish his coffee. He left immediately by the back door."

Valley was particularly good in mannering horses with vices—the kickers, the biters—although his discipline was sometimes abusive. Once, a big, burly owner caught Valley kicking his horse in the belly and bellowed: "Okay, Valley, come on out of that stall and get yours!"

"Now don't hit me," Valley begged. "You know I ain't just right . . . in fact, you ain't either, or you wouldn't be paying bills on this big, no account bum."

At a meet at the old Latonia racetrack in the summer of 1939, Smith Baker claimed from Valley a two-year-old Islam filly, Charlotte Dear, who had been winning. "Tell Smith," Valley told his groom, "I want to see him. I'm going to knock his head off." He noted he would be in his secretary's office.

Although much older and much smaller than Valentine, Baker was not one to be threatened. Knowing that Smith would answer the challenge, jockeys, agents, and trainers rushed there to observe the confrontation. Because of the big differences in the size and age of the two men, they thought this would be the first time Big Valley would do battle.

But they were wrong. Upon his arrival, Smith shouted: "Valley, I understand you want to see me." Trembling, Valley quickly replied: "That's right. I want to congratulate you on making a good claim. That filly will do well for you." Baker gave Valentine a dirty look, said nothing, and then turned and walked away. Valley quickly exited through another door. The next morning, Valentine found a chicken in the stall that had been vacated by Charlotte Dear.

For Chew Tobacco Charlie, age was no barrier to his cowardice. Once when an elderly owner came to his stable and said he was turning his horse over to another trainer, Valley flew into a rage, concluding his profane outburst with: "If you weren't so old, I'd grab you by the neck and throw you over into that manure pit."

"Don't let my age stop you," the oldster said as he started walking toward Valley. "Stop, stop," cried Valentine. "Don't hit me." Despite all of his bluster and goofiness, Charles R. Valentine was a good horseman, considering the class of horses that came his way. Few horses had a better caretaker.

Sparing with the Truth

Valley and I were pals from the very start, but once I got into a position (at age 15) where I could get his name in the newspaper, he had some "news" for me to print with undue frequency: a fast workout; the purchase of a horse as principal or agent; an offer he had made or turned down. No other person was looking me up to give me such reports. Modesty was not one of his virtues. He would say anything to get his name in the newspaper and gain some free advertising.

Colonel Chinn, the foremost wheeler-dealer of the day, put me hip to Big Valley. "Better check out what Big Valley tells you," he advised. "I'm not saying he is a pathological liar; he just uses the truth sparingly."

Chinn and Valentine were two different types of traders. Valley was strictly cash. If he sold a horse for $1,500, he would reinvest the whole sum in another. He never set aside any profit. He would roll over and roll over until he got stuck with a bum, then it was tap city. Then he would have to get a new partner to start again.

Paging 'Chew Tobacco'

Back in the 1940s, Chew Tobacco Charlie came up with a ploy to inform horsemen visiting Lexington for the race meets or sales at Keeneland that he was very much around. The city had only two major hotels, the Phoenix and the Lafayette, which were located a block apart.

At times when the lobbies and dining rooms would be filled with horsemen, Valley would call from one hotel to the other and have himself paged. Shortly thereafter, he would walk into the other lobby to receive messages from various persons that he had just been paged. Thanking them, he would proceed to the bell captain and go through the motions of writing down phone numbers. After that, he would go to the nearest pay phone and have himself paged at the other hotel. "Made a lot of contacts advertising myself that way," he later confided to me, "but when the bell captains found out my game, they shut me down."

Impressive Reading

Anybody who came to the Lexington area in quest of a cheap-to-moderate racehorse from the late 1930s through the early 1970s was not half trying if they did not encounter Chew Tobacco Charlie. If you were buying, Chew Tobacco Charlie would find you.

The front of his business card noted that he was an owner, trainer, dealer, and sales agent of Thoroughbred horses, and on the back of the card were names of many fine horses with which he had been associated in those pursuits. I once observed that he had had nothing to do with a number of those horses. "I know, I know," he replied, "but they are impressive reading."

Valley's Big Chance

Back in the 1930s, Calumet's Dick McMahon observed the good care that Valentine gave his horses and decided to give him a chance as a trainer. But first he had to clean Charlie up, get him fitted with false teeth, buy him some nice clothes, and a new automobile. Salary: $1,000 a month, pretty good for those days. Tobacco chewing was restricted. Valentine had to go Calumet style—first class.

Off to Hialeah with Valentine went a nice group of young horses—and Calumet's contract rider, young Eddie Arcaro. No young trainer ever had a better shot. He had hardly settled in before everything went awry. This is how Big Valley told it to me: "Dick tried to make a big man out of me too quick. It went to my head. I started chasing the girls and boozing at the bars. Arcaro got hurt on a motorcycle and couldn't ride. I wrecked the car. The horses that didn't get sick couldn't run worth a damn. I wasn't supposed to run Hug Again for a claiming price, but I did anyway, and Frank Kearns claimed her for $3,500. I got fired before the meet was halfway over. I blew my chance for glory!" Calumet bought Hug Again back from Kearns, and she became one of the farm's best broodmares, the dam of Sun Again and Fervent. Kearns was later hired as its trainer.

Valley's New Teeth

Once, I noticed Valley wearing some rather ill-fitting false teeth that rattled like castanets when he talked. About a week later, I observed a change in his dentures. "Isn't it a bit expensive to keep getting them changed?" I asked him. "Nope, the guy who owns an interest in this horse provides them for me," he replied. "In due time he tells me he'll get me a set that fits perfectly."

"Is your partner in this horse a dentist?" I inquired.

"No," he said nonchalantly, "he's an undertaker."

Discounting the Competition

Valley could be very humorous, although I doubt he intended to crack a funny line at the time. When I opened my office on Main Street in the Hernando in 1940, Colonel Chinn put the needle to Valley: "We've got competition now. Johnny Clark has announced himself as a bloodstock agent. That makes four of us in Lexington." Valley quickly replied: "Johnny's still wet behind the ears, old man Tom Cromwell don't have a year to live. And, colonel, you don't look like you're feeling well."

The Skills of Joe Palmer

Joe Palmer, it seems, is the most quoted Turf writer of my generation. He was every Turf writer's Turf writer. No writer ever had a greater knowledge of our business, nor more literary skill. People who did not know or care about horses would read him. The writings he left behind before his untimely death in the fall of 1952 are laden with an ingredient so lacking both before and after his time—humor.

Joe's command of the language was so complete that he wrote at a speed of 40 words per minute or faster, with no "typos," and he never struck out and reworded a phrase or changed a word before sending it to his office at the New York *Herald Tribune*. I cannot recall his exact wording, but in essence his philosophy ran like this: "I'm tired of reading of someone's 'love' for horses. Only a horse can love a horse. I like horses, but more than that, I like people who like them."

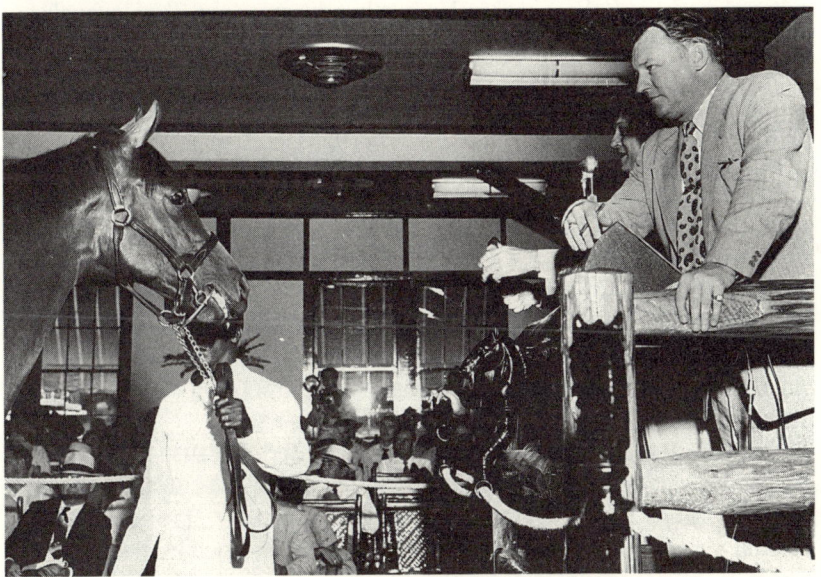

Joe Palmer announcing at Keeneland.

The Best Crash Course

When Joe Thomas arrived in Lexington to work for me in January of 1950, after a frigid ride from California in a horse rail car, one of his first assignments was to be at the Keeneland kitchen each morning. "There," I told him, "you'll get the best crash course in the country on nearly every facet of the horse business. There are oracles on every subject. You'll not only gain a lot of knowledge, but you'll hear a lot of stories about characters who have made our game more colorful."

In a few short weeks, Joe was writing the Turf column—one of the best who ever did it—for the Lexington *Herald,* and basing most of his columns on material he gathered at the Keeneland kitchen. Three years later, Joe was off to Windfields Farm, where he helped to build E. P. Taylor's operation into a world-class producer of racing and breeding stock.

The Charm of Uncertainty

"The charm of woman lies largely in our inability to understand her. The charm of the racehorse, and of racing, is their element of uncertainty—without which there could be no racing, and hence no racehorses." That was written by Walter S. Vosburgh, a leading handicapper and Turf journalist of the early decades of this century.

Brownie's Party for Ballot

Brownie Leach, Keeneland's first publicity director, was a champion prankster and liar as well as an excellent Turf writer and publicist. One of his more memorable events was a party at Keeneland commemorating the 33rd birthday of the great racehorse Ballot.

Raymond Gentry, Olin's brother, owned Ballot and was using him to promote a feed supplement he was selling by the name of Enza-Vita. If the old stud was not thriving as a direct result of the product, it certainly was not hurting him. He was in pretty good shape for his age.

Brownie and Raymond arranged the party, and, because it was a "freebie," it drew a record crowd of Lexington horsemen. Keeneland's publicity director dictated that Raymond must have the party "properly catered, meaning plenty of old ham, corn pudding, beaten biscuits, bourbon, and cigars." Gentry more than complied.

Just before noon, Ballot was led out onto the lawn in front of the Keeneland grandstand, and the throng applauded his condition and praised both Gentry and his product. Had Ballot been presented after the party, there would have been few in attendance.

Joe Estes set the tone for the party in the grandstand dining room. A hilarious master of ceremonies, he stated: "Now boys, there's plenty of bourbon here for us to drink. We'll go down before we run out. Now, I have a watch here before me, and at five-minute intervals we're going to toast Ballot for each of his years. I'll go first. "Here's to Ballot, as a yearling, bred by James R. Keene, foaled in 1904 at Castleton, one of the most honest and faithful and generous horses to ever set foot on the American Turf scene." Gulp!

I was then still in my teens, had not yet taken to bourbon, and I still recall watching and knowing more about the goings-on than most of those who were present. As best I recall, Ballot was only 17 years old when the party broke up. I was the last to leave, and when I got to the parking lot I counted fully 30 cars still parked there. Based on the number of people who had to be driven or carried home, the party was obviously a success.

Jack Griffin, a Louisville *Courier-Journal* writer and not much of a drinker, was gazing at all the cars when I walked out. "That's Brownie's car," he observed, "and he left on 14. I'll check on him, I live nearby. I'll phone you."

In a half hour, I had the report. "I rang his doorbell and Melinda, the maid, answered, and I asked if Mr. Leach was in. 'Mr. Griffin, I don't know if he's in, but he is here!' Never worry about Brownie, Johnny, he always makes it home—somehow!"

Joe Estes.

Brownie and the Blind Man

Shortly after moving from Keeneland to Churchill Downs, Brownie pulled another of his famous pranks. On a day when he knew Hal Price Headley would be in his Churchill box to watch one of his horses, he borrowed the adjoining box from a friend. Disguised as a blind man with dark glasses and a white cane, he was led to the box. Throughout the running of the race, he disturbed the Keeneland president's concentration by repeatedly appealing in a pathetic manner: "Sir, can you tell me who's in front?" Headley left in a huff after the race and told Frank Atkins, who was in charge of the boxes: "Get that man out of that box and don't let him in there again."

This Cucumber Kicked

One of my earliest teachers and sponsors as a Turf scribe was Clem McCarthy, who did much to popularize prizefighting and racing as a radio sportscaster for NBC. With a rapid-fire patter and a few breathless descriptions of things that were not happening, he kept interest alive throughout every contest.

While I was still in high school, on the recommendation of Phil Chinn, Clem hired me for what was then to me a lavish retainer to provide notes for his syndicated racing column. These funds largely enabled me to complete my high school and college educations. The association also bonded our friendship.

Clem McCarthy.

I guess a bit of Clem rubbed off on me if I take a few liberties in writing of people and events. Clem's funniest exaggeration was this: "I'm now here in the winner's circle with this great champion who's just won the richest race ever run, the Santa Anita Handicap. I'm going to walk around him and describe him. He's a big gleaming chestnut, about 16 hands high, and he's calm as a cucumber, not at all excited as you'd expect after running such a big race . . . "

Immediately, there was the sound of a thud, a silence, and then an unfamiliar voice came on. "The horse has kicked Mr. McCarthy to the ground, but he's getting up, and I don't think he's hurt." Clem was back at the mike instantly, but he never noted that he had misrepresented the horse's temperament.

Living Like a Millionaire

Bill Corum, noted columnist for the Hearst papers and successor to Matt Winn as president of Churchill Downs, managed to keep himself busted most of his life by high living and playing horses. "I never want to be a millionaire," he once told me, "just want to live like one."

They Were 1 and 1A

Not one of the obituaries of Red Smith noted his close friendship with Frank Graham. (Joe Palmer was acknowledged, and rightly so.) Outside of when I saw them in New York or at Churchill Downs, I swapped stories with them at Hialeah in the 1950s and at Aiken, South Carolina, during the 1960s. Each winter, they traveled together and bunked with each other in their tours through the baseball camps en route to Hialeah. Upon their return north, they would stop off for a day in Aiken. They were such good companions that they were nicknamed "1 and 1A."

Of all the sports they covered, racing was their favorite. Red loved racing and its participants. "There are more rags to riches to rags stories on the backstretch than in any other sport," he said. Each loved the backstretch yarns I would spin, whether they were fabricated or not. Everett Clay, the Hialeah public relations director, first put them on me, noting that I had "more stories than a hound dog has fleas." Upon meeting them each year, they would remind me of

Red Smith.

Ev's remark, then cajole: "Come on and give. . . ." Frank, indeed, was unique. He wrote with speed and excellence; neat copy without corrections or strikeovers. He never informed me about this, but I was reliably told he had a great disdain for the books published for children and therefore wrote all the books to be read by Frank Jr. in his early years.

I have fond memories of "1 and 1A," and others of that great era of sportswriters, the days of Grantland Rice, Henry McLemore, Dan Parker, Joe Williams, Bob Considine, Bill Corum, and Shirley Povich.

The Offending Headline

Oldtimers around Kentucky and Midwest tracks remember Phil McCann, but I doubt if any recall why or how he became a Turf writer. After high school, he broke into journalism on the Lexington *Herald* and soon worked himself up to assistant city editor. Over a story relating how an aged veteran at a Memorial Day service had become overly emotional, collapsed, and died of a heart attack immediately after the playing of "Taps," Phil wrote this headline: "Bugle Blows, Veteran Goes." The next morning, Editor Tom Underwood penned this memo to the managing editor: "Get McCann off the desk. Put him where he's harmless. In sports. Let him write racing."

A Favorite Meeting Place

Among my fondest memories of our game are the nightly get-togethers of horsemen in an alcove of the old Lafayette Hotel in the mid-1930s. If all the seats were taken and a person was observed standing, an obliging bellhop brought a folding chair. This became known as the "Horsemen's Corner," where a heap of good information, and some bad, could be obtained.

Uncle Johnny Furlong's

Gone from the inner city of Lexington now is the storefront restaurant of "Uncle Johnny" Furlong that I knew so well in the mid-1930s and into the 1940s. Furlong's was a nationally known eating place among horsemen despite its crude accommodations, the questionable manner in which food was prepared, and the place's lack of cleanliness. Few visiting horsemen ever left town without at least one meal there.

These included Mose and Jake Lowenstein, Humphrey Finney, Roscoe Goose, John Flanagan, Alec Gordon, Harry Trotsek, Frank Podesta, Cooper Phelps, Dr. Henry Harthill and his young son Alex, Doug Davis, Max Hirsch, and Jack Hodgins, not to mention racetrack hustlers "Umbrella" Herb or "Yum Yum" Dominic, when they could manage to get someone to pick up the check.

The eatery was owned and operated by "Uncle Johnny" and manned only by himself and an elderly black man, "Henry Boy," whom Johnny had raised from childhood. Henry had a propensity for overcooking and for highly seasoned food.

There was no menu; the fare and prices were listed on a signboard. Neither the bill of fare nor the prices changed in the 15 years I knew

Furlong's. Offered in generous portions—a total meal was $2 or less—were bean soup (cooked with ham hocks), chili, hot dogs, hamburgers, boiled or mashed potatoes, corn pudding or corn on the cob, vegetables in season, steaks, pork chops (no lamb), corned beef and cabbage, coffee (on the strong side), and pie.

The place was small, accommodating only about 16 at one time, and never was a check presented. Uncle Johnny had a computer-like mind and was very observant. When a customer would come to the old gent at the cash register near the front door, he would be asked what he had ordered. If he left out any items, Uncle Johnny would remind him—"Plus a bowl of soup and a piece of pie, that'll be 35 cents more."

Henry Boy showed no emotion, but he did resent complaints. I was there on one occasion when a guest suggested that his bowl of chili was cold and insufficiently seasoned. "I *shall* make it hot for you, both ways, sir. It *shall* be hot," Henry replied. After Henry had added a heaping tablespoon of red chili powder to it and placed the bowl in the oven to bring its contents to a boil, the customer stirred his chili for 15 minutes to cool it, then drank three glasses of ice water and ate four handfuls of crackers before he downed it.

In listing Uncle Johnny's bill of fare, I neglected to mention chitterlings (small pieces of swine intestines served fried or boiled), rarely served elsewhere, but you would never get them unless you ordered them by their colloquial name, "chitlins." Another I overlooked was lamb fries, which were lamb testicles breaded, fried, and served in a cream sauce.

The Same Gunman Returned a Second Time

In addition to the Lafayette's "Horsemen's Corner," anybody who came to Lexington in the late 1930s and early '40s and wanted to learn what was going on in the Thoroughbred business in Central Kentucky had to spend some time at Keith's Bar & Grill, a half-block west of the Lafayette. Horsemen big and small gathered at those two places in their off hours to recollect, tell stories, gossip, and pass on the "news." Only there could you find out which stallions were not stopping their mares, the farms with virus abortion, trainers about to be fired or hired, and other matters of a sensitive nature.

Joseph P. Keith, never at the cafe during lunch hour, had more than the restaurant going for him. On the second floor of a nearby building, he had a handbook, where patronage was rather heavy at noon. "Running both these joints is driving me crazy," he once confided to me. "I was catching the clerks holding the bets themselves, so I took in a partner, and what did he do?

"One day when I returned after having to be away for a half-hour, he stood behind the counter faking a tremble and pointing to the cash drawer, which was open and empty, and told me 'some big guy wearing a white cowboy hat' had knocked us off after sticking a gun in his face. I had to go to the safety deposit box at the bank to get operating money for the rest of the day, but I made up my mind I'd get even.

"The following Saturday afternoon, when nobody had picked a winner and the cash drawer was full, he stepped out for a few minutes. We weren't busy, nobody was coming in to cash. When he returned, I pointed to the open, empty cash drawer and said: 'That same big guy wearing the white cowboy hat came back.' Then I told him we were bad luck for each other and the partnership was finished."

During nights spent at his bar, Joe would regale us with stories of his training, owning, racing, and booking—all simultaneously—at tracks in the West, Canada, Mexico, and Cuba. Buddy Morrissey, an old racetracker himself, tended bar near the front door of the store. He seemed to know everybody in the horse business—local and out of town. When horse people would walk in, he would greet them by name, and nod to the hostess that they were to be seated immediately, whether there was a waiting list or not. Joe answered any complaints about this priority system by saying: "This joint is for horse people first and the general public last."

Joe gave away so much booze and food that Keith's Bar & Grill was not a moneymaker. When the federal government closed down the wire service and the handbooks, Joe sold the restaurant to Ralph Campbell (who later built the Campbell House) and opened a small sandwich shop nearby. It failed, and he died penniless a few years later. But he enjoyed life while he was here.

The Blind Man Took Off

A caller from Louisville once asked if I remembered Junior Garr, who ran a bar and grill across the street from Churchill Downs at Fourth Street and Central Avenue. I did; Dr. Alex Harthill and I ate there often, and I had met Junior when he owned a nice stakes filly by Wine List.

I asked the caller: "Is that elderly blind man with the cane and the tin cup still standing in front of Junior's before the races each day? He wore a sign saying 'Help the blind,' and he'd tap his cane to get attention."

"Hell, no," the caller responded. "He was a complete phony and could see better than most stewards, which doesn't necessarily mean he had good eyesight. One day when he misjudged the time and noted he might miss the daily double, he stuffed the tin cup, the glasses, and the sign in his pocket and ran like Jesse Owens down Central Avenue to the track. He blew his cover. He may be hustling some other corner near the track now."

Chapter 7
Legends of the Sport

In 1921, Man o' War was bred to his first mare. The previous fall, he had been retired from racing as the "Horse of the Century." Although the century was then very young, his legend is still very much intact. Other than Secretariat, no other horse in the history of American racing so captured the public's imagination. Man o' War's acclaim extended from his racing days in 1919 and 1920 beyond his death at age 30 on November 30, 1947. He has been to Thoroughbred racing what Babe Ruth was to baseball, Jack Dempsey to boxing, and Red Grange to football. In the following pages, I will tell you some more about Man o' War and some of the other legends of the Thoroughbred sport.

Man o' War's Birthplace

To be certain that he would not bring down the wrath of the industry and the general public by inadvertently removing a historic building, Catesby Clay requested in the late 1980s that I meet him at the farm where Man o' War was foaled, three miles north of Lexington on Georgetown Road. Catesby had bought (for one of his companies) 250 of the original 400 acres that constituted August Belmont's Nursery Stud.

"There's only one barn up, a brick shed-type with seven or eight stalls," he noted, "and, if Man o' War was foaled in it, I'm certainly not going to tear it down." I assured him that was not the barn but agreed to meet with him anyway.

Back in the late 1930s, I had asked Frances and Al Kane, as well as their brother Kenneth, where Man o' War had been born on March 29, 1917. All three were born and raised on the farm and were living there at the time of the horse's birth. I was told by each of them that it was the first stall on the left

Man o' War with groom John Buckner.

in the large wooden barn closest to Georgetown Road. Through the ensuing years and into the 1950s, I had observed the old barn deteriorate, leaning more and more, and finally falling from its own weight.

"This brick structure," I told Catesby, "was the stallion barn, and the wooden structure over there (about 200 feet away) was the breeding shed. A few days later, after both the buildings had been leveled, a Lexington newspaper columnist lamented that the brick barn in which Man o' War was foaled had been destroyed. The next day or so, the writer corrected himself when Dr. Charles E. Hagyard informed him the brick structure was the stallion barn, but he misquoted Charlie by saying that Man o' War stood at stud in it. Man o' War never returned to Nursery Stud after he was shipped away from there as a yearling to the Saratoga sales.

In fact, the Belmonts never owned Nursery Stud. The first August Belmont leased the property from Walsh Sutton and moved his breeding operations there from Babylon, Long Island, New York, in November of 1885. Upon his death in 1890, Major August Belmont II took over from his father and operated it.

Ed Kane came from Babylon with the first August Belmont and remained on as manager for Major Belmont until his passing in May of 1917, two months after he had supervised the foaling of Man o' War. His wife Elizabeth succeeded him as manager, and sons Al and Ken worked with the horses. Al, in later years, recalled for me many humorous experiences at Nursery Stud.

"Major and Mrs. Belmont were great patrons of the theater," he once reminisced, "and I shall never forget the time one summer they brought down from New York some actors and actresses to see the horses. He gave each of them a catalog of the horses, and he'd identify each by name as I'd lead them out. When I led out Fair Play, he had his back to them and proudly announced: 'This is Fair Play, the sire of Man o' War.' At that very instant, the old horse vigorously exposed himself. A young actress in the back, her face down reading the catalog, remarked: 'Why, Major Belmont, this horse has a marvelous pedigree.' Think-

August Belmont I.

August Belmont II.

ing her meaning to be a bit risque, he replied: 'Yes, and I'd love to have one just like it.'"

A Chance Purchase

Samuel D. Riddle, primarily a steeplechase devotee, bought Man o' War as a 'chasing prospect at the 1918 Saratoga auction, paying $5,000 for the yearling. Riddle became interested in him through a strange happenstance, which he related to me in later years.

"Major August Belmont," he said, "had accepted a special appointment with the Army—the U.S. was then in World War I—and had announced he was selling all of the yearlings of Nursery Stud. I sent my trainer, Louis Feustel, to Kentucky to look them over in their paddocks. But when he took me to see them at Saratoga, Feustel noted there was one not shown to him in Kentucky. Mrs. Elizabeth Kane, the farm manager, told us Major Belmont planned to keep that one but had changed his mind and included him. He was already named Man o' War." Riddle then decided that, if the colt was Belmont's pick, it was his pick as well. The fact that the colt had already been named had nothing to do with the decision.

Bad Start, Bad Ride

The racing record of Man o' War is well known; he was beaten only once in 21 career starts. Upset, in receipt of 15 pounds, defeated Man o' War by a

Upset handing Man o' War his only defeat, in the 1919 Sanford Stakes.

half-length in the 1919 Sanford Stakes at Saratoga Race Course. He probably should not have lost the Sanford, either. A bad start and a bad ride brought the great horse's only defeat. Man o' War was all but left at the post, and jockey Johnny Loftus rushed him into a pocket at very close quarters. Those two errors cost Man o' War much more than Upset's margin of victory.

In researching his career, I came upon some interesting facts that I had previously overlooked. Man o' War was odds-on favorite in every one of his starts, from 9-to-10 (in Saratoga's United States Hotel Stakes, immediately before his Sanford loss) down to 1-to-100 on three occasions. His average victory margin was 9.42 lengths. He carried 130 pounds or more in nine of his victories, including 135 in one and 138 in another. He set five new American time records in New York from one mile to 1 5/8 miles. He broke numerous other track and stakes records, and is reported to have been able to break more had he been urged.

Man o' War drinking from $5,000 gold cup after his last career start, with Feustel, left, and Riddle.

Early on, "Big Red" ran out of competition. Eight tried him in his first start at three, in the Preakness Stakes, but in the next ten starts that completed his racing career, he met only one opponent on six occasions, two in three races, and three in another. In short, a total of only 15 opposed him in his last ten starts.

Riddle was severely criticized for not racing Man o' War at four. It was unjustified. "Big Red" simply had no competition. About the best was Exterminator, then six. To entice any competition, Man o' War would have had to concede so much weight that the handicaps would have been meaningless. Even then, there were no guarantees that there would have been races for him.

To lure older horses to run against Man o' War, Kenilworth Park, at Windsor, Ontario, Canada, put on an "extravaganza" of "$75,000 in American currency," plus a $5,000 gold cup. Only two—Man o' War and Sir Barton—went to the start after Wickford had been scratched. Sir Barton was coming off a win in the Merchants' and Citizens' Handicap at Saratoga, in which he carried 133 and set a new world record for 1 3/16 miles.

Sir Barton, champion three-year-old and Triple Crown winner the previous year and a top handicapper in 1920, had to concede six pounds to "Big Red" because of the age difference, 126 to 120. At odds of 1-to-20, the Riddle colt galloped to an easy lead, winning "in hand" by seven lengths while lowering the track's record for 1 1/4 miles by six seconds, to 2:03. It was the final race of his illustrious career.

Can't Pick the Owners

Man o' War had three managers at stud, Miss Elizabeth Daingerfield from 1921 until 1930, Harrie B. Scott from then until 1944, and Paddy O'Neill, Riddle's chauffeur, from 1944 until the horse's death in 1947. Riddle had absolutely no knowledge of Thoroughbred conformation, racing performance, or pedigree. He interfered so unreasonably that both Miss Daingerfield and Scott flat quit. Riddle once told me: "It's senseless for me to buy good mares; $500 is enough to pay for one. Man o' War is the whole pedigree. He's so great, so dominant."

From 379 named foals, Man o' War did sire 64 stakes winners, most of which were bred by people other than Riddle. The horse, in fact, sired almost as many losers and non-starters as he did winners. Riddle did breed some good ones—War Admiral, War Relic, and Crusader—but his only recognized champion was War Admiral. Only one year (1926) did Man o' War head the sire list. It is unfortunate that horses cannot pick their owners.

An Owner Without Class

If ever there was an instance when the class of the owner did not match that of his horse, it was Sam Riddle. Riddle always told me that he would have paid more than $5,000 for Man o' War. I have been told by more reliable authorities that Feustel had to beg the owner to make the final bid.

He behaved in a graceless manner toward Major Belmont after the war. Belmont did not get to see Man o' War in any of his races, but he immensely enjoyed reading of them. While overseas, he bought a mare he felt would be an ideal mate for the great horse. But, when Belmont and the mare returned to the States after the war, Riddle refused to let him breed that mare or any other to Man o' War.

Riddle's second and last great horse was Man o' War's son War Admiral, the 1937 Triple Crown winner and Horse of the Year. This fine horse also enabled the crabby old man to speak and behave intolerably. Bryan Field told me this story. When it became apparent that War Admiral would breeze to a Triple Crown victory in the Belmont Stakes, Field made advance arrangements with Riddle for an interview over a nationwide CBS radio hookup immediately after the race. After Field introduced Riddle and congratulated him, Bryan asked the owner-breeder to define "class in a racehorse." Riddle responded with a horrible racial slur.

Samuel D. Riddle.

Field immediately interrupted him, thanked him, and walked away with his microphone. Field said the old man lighted the switchboard of every CBS affiliate in the country with protests, and he was told by the radio network never again to allow Riddle near his microphone.

In the fall of that year, Riddle was the honored guest of the Thoroughbred Club of America at its annual testimonial dinner. In his acceptance speech, Riddle poured more vitriol, this time directed at handicappers. Among his acid remarks was: "All any of them know about a horse is that one end bites and the other kicks."

The next year, the old man again showed his "class." He refused to let War Admiral run in a match with Charlie Howard's Seabiscuit unless all his conditions were met. The regular starter at Pimlico could not officiate; Riddle would bring in his own from New York. The start would be from a walk up, not out of the gate. But justice was served. Seabiscuit took the lead at the break, led every step of the way, won by four lengths, and was voted Horse of the Year off this performance.

A Tactless Rejection

Texas oilman W. T. Waggoner offered Riddle $1-million for Man o' War upon the colt's retirement. Riddle replied with characteristic tactlessness. "Not interested. Many people have a million dollars. Only I own Man o' War."

The Career of 'Old Bones'

John Hervey, the foremost Turf historian in the first half of this century, described Exterminator in the 1937 edition of *Racing In America* as "one of the most extraordinary Thoroughbreds that has ever appeared and one whose like, very possibly, we shall not see again." Nowadays, Exterminator seems all but forgotten. I never read or hear his name mentioned among the great horses of the century, perhaps because there are too few students of the rich history of racing. Let me recall what I read and heard about him back in my youth.

In the spring of 1918, Willis Sharpe Kilmer, who had accumulated 120 horses by his third year in the sport, needed a work companion for *Sun Briar, champion two-year-old colt of the previous year and then the winter-book favorite to win the Kentucky Derby. Henry McDaniel, his trainer, came to Kentucky and bought Exterminator from J. Cal Milam for $15,000. The gelding, winner of two minor races in four starts at two, was working sensationally for Milam over the old Kentucky Association track in Lexington.

Exterminator turned out to be better than a workmate for *Sun Briar— the gelding overextended him to the point that he broke him down. Kilmer had already made elaborate plans for a large party of his friends after *Sun

Exterminator after winning the 1918 Kentucky Derby.

Briar's victory in the Derby. After learning that Exterminator was also nominated to the Derby and not wanting to disappoint his friends, he instructed McDaniel to start Exterminator.

The tall (16.3 hands), skinny, three-year-old gelding was lightly regarded not only by his owner and trainer but also by the betting public. But he collared front-running Escoba inside the eighth pole and finally disposed of him in deep stretch for a one-length victory. He paid $61.20 to win as the longest shot in the field of eight. Because the Derby was his first start at three, he went into the race with earnings of $1,350. The Derby win increased them by $14,700.

When Kilmer was being interviewed after Exterminator's win, a reporter asked: "I understand you own 120 racehorses. You must be very wealthy. How did you make your money?"

"Swamp Root," he replied. "It's a medicine patented by my father."

"What's it good for?" continued the sportswriter.

"At least $2-million a year," Kilmer retorted gleefully.

I once asked Milam, who was very helpful to me in my early days as a Turf journalist, why he had nominated Exterminator for the Derby off two minor wins at two, one at Latonia and the other at Windsor, which was just across the Canadian border from Detroit. "Learned that from John E. Madden, smartest horseman I've ever known," he replied. "I went to work for him when I came to Kentucky as a kid from Alabama. Having a colt eligible for the Derby helps sell him. Henry McDaniel wasn't going to buy Exterminator until I told him I thought so much of him I had put him in the Derby. It works.

"I really outsmarted myself when I sold him for $15,000," he continued, "thought I was getting the best of it. Henry was in a bind, and that was a lot of money in those days for a colt who hadn't shown more in his races. He got

Willis Sharpe Kilmer with his world's leading money winner, Sun Beau.

sick on me at Kenilworth (Canada) in July, was green and growing, so I put him away for the year. Never got to run him beyond three-quarters." Then, after a slight pause, he winked an eye at me and said: "I lied a little to Henry when I told him I thought he had the makings of a Derby horse. You'll learn some day that horse traders don't always mean what they say."

This was the beginning of Exterminator's rise to fame—fame that he continually enhanced until he was retired at the age of nine with a record of 100 starts, 50 wins, 17 seconds, 17 thirds, and earnings of $252,996, a record for geldings. Although he was unplaced 16 times, in eight of those races he finished fourth and received a part of the purse.

Exterminator was probably the most traveled Thoroughbred in racing history before the advent of air transportation. He went by rail, racing at 19 tracks throughout the United States, Mexico, and Canada. It was said that, when loaded on a freight car, he would immediately lie down and would get up only to eat, drink, or loosen up his legs and body. He always arrived fresh at his destination.

"Old Bones," as he came to be known, compiled this great record despite—not because of—owner Kilmer and the handicappers. Kilmer ordered the gallant old warrior to be raced many times when his trainers—yes, nine of them—advised to the contrary. And the handicappers piled on the weight. He won 20 of the 35 races in which he carried weights ranging from 130 to 138 pounds.

Exterminator's best year was 1922, when he was age seven and won ten of his 17 starts and earned $71,075. In the process, he attained a title equivalent to Horse of the Year. In his final start of the season, the Pimlico Cup, which he had won the previous year, he suffered his most humiliating defeat, beaten 31 lengths. It was then, in respect for his glorious career and age, that Kilmer should have retired him.

But Kilmer continued on with him. The next year, 1923, the crippled old warrior, well beyond his better racing days, made three starts within 13 days in April, then gave way again, but he was game to the core in those three. He was third, beaten 1 3/4 lengths in the first, then won Havre de Grace's Philadelphia Handicap, and in the last he finished second, beaten a nose.

Amazingly, Exterminator held up for six months in 1924 at age nine, winning three of his seven races, even though his third and fourth starts were only two days apart in April. In late June he was retired—permanently! Rarely in racing history has such a great horse endured such heartless and cruel abuse. How much greater would his record have been had he been owned by a kinder man? I think John Hervey's evaluation of Exterminator as an "extraordinary Thoroughbred" was an understatement.

The only nice things Kilmer did for Exterminator were to give him a peaceful retirement in his own paddock, the company of a Shetland pony companion nicknamed Peanuts, and a proper burial when he died at the age of 30 in Binghamton, New York.

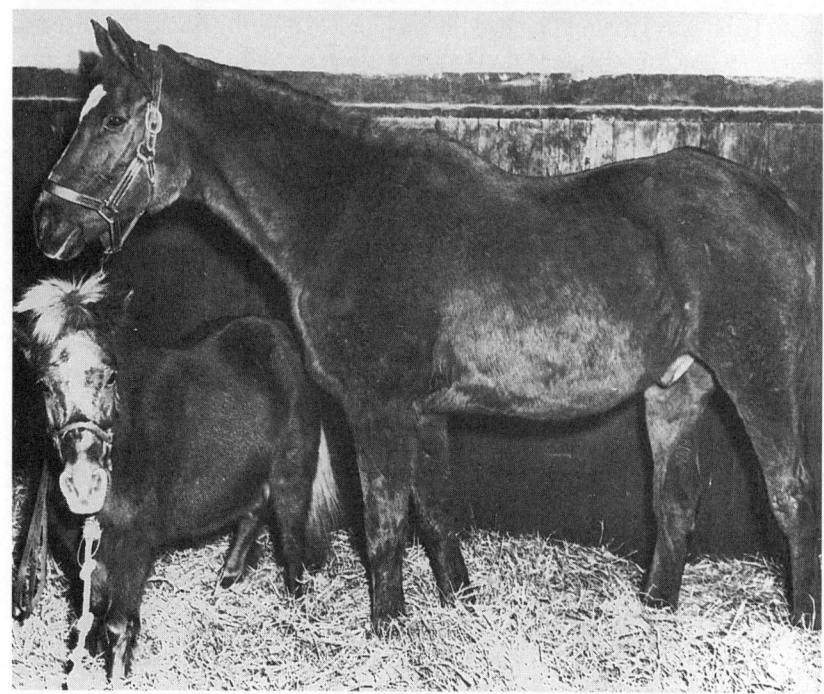

Exterminator, late in his retirement, with his companion Peanuts.

The Filly From the Tobacco Barn

Jack Keene bred and raced a lot of good fillies, but the best filly he ever bred was the one he least expected to get to the races—Nellie Morse.

In the fall of 1920 the master of Keeneland Stud culled out the 18-year-old mare La Venganza, whose foals in prior years had not been much, to a Woodford County tobacco farmer with the understanding that he could keep the old mare if he would deliver back to Keene at weaning time the foal by Luke McLuke that she then was carrying.

The next spring, La Venganza produced a bay filly. Time and again, the farmer asked Keene to visit the farm and inspect the foal. Keene finally acquiesced when the youngster was about three weeks old. "She was a beautiful filly," Keene recalled, "but the farm was the most unsafe I'd ever seen for raising a young foal—barbed-wire fencing, parts of cutting harrows and other farm machinery all over the place."

Nellie Morse, winner of the 1924 Preakness Stakes.

Keene instructed the farmer to place the mare and foal in a nearby tobacco barn, feed them properly, "but don't let that foal out of there until you get ready to house your crop, at which time you bring the foal directly to me."

Thinking that a filly raised in this manner would be too delicate for racing, Keene offered her at Saratoga's yearling auction the following August. Believing that he was doing them a favor, he steered all friends off of her. Alec Gordon, who did not check with him, got her on a $2,000 bid for H. C. "Bud" Fisher, creator of the "Mutt and Jeff" comic strip, who named her for his mother, Nellie Morse.

Keene was wrong about his hothouse filly; she was absolutely hickory. Gordon, a butcher trainer if ever there was one, started her 22 times as a two-year-old. She won the Fashion Stakes at Belmont and placed in four other stakes in New York.

The following season, Gordon asked even more of Nellie Morse—with unfortunate results. Second in the Kentucky Oaks, the trainer took her to Pimlico Race Course and started her three times in nine days. She won all of them—an allowance race, the Pimlico Oaks, and the Preakness Stakes. She was the fourth and last filly to win the Preakness, and the victory earned her the year's three-year-old filly championship.

As predicted by good trainers of the day, Alec finally "cooked" Nellie Morse. After the Preakness, she never again won a race. In the fall of 1931, Bud Fisher dispersed all of his Thoroughbreds at auction. Warren Wright, entering the business that year, bought Nellie Morse, in foal to American Flag, for $6,100. The resulting foal was Nellie Flag, champion two-year-old filly of 1934 and post-time favorite of the next year's Kentucky Derby. (She finished fourth to Triple Crown victor Omaha.) She was the first stakes winner foaled at Calumet, and she became a foundation mare of the great Calumet dynasty that was to come.

The Late-Blossoming Seabiscuit

About the toughest good horse of modern times was Seabiscuit. He raced 58 times at two and three before he really got "good." He was very good at four, when he won ten stakes from coast to coast, and better still at five, in 1938, when he was voted Horse of the Year. After standing at stud at six, Seabiscuit came back to win the prestigious Santa Anita Handicap at seven, then was returned to stud with a record of 33 victories from 89 starts and total earnings of $437,730.

It was the summer of 1946 when I became well-acquainted with "Silent Tom" Smith, one of my heroes since I first started to try to get a foothold in our business in the mid-1930s. He was at Keeneland training Jet Pilot and several other Elizabeth Arden horses. Tom had been a close friend of Phil

Seabiscuit trounced War Admiral in a match race at Pimlico in 1938.

Chinn, and the three of us would have dinner two or three times each week. Smith was not at all the silent type among friends he trusted, especially after a couple of mint juleps and a dinner of old Kentucky ham and fried chicken.

His first experience with horses came as a ranch hand, then as a rodeo rider, and later as a performer and horseshoer in C. B. "Cowboy" Irwin's Wild West shows. When Irwin began training Thoroughbreds, Tom became his assistant and blacksmith. In 1923 and 1930, Irwin was America's leading trainer by races won. After Irwin's death in 1935, Tom became the trainer for Charles S. Howard.

"Tom was especially good with mean, roguish, sulky horses," Chinn said. "They feared him more than any other man. He did use rather strong measures to get their attention. Horses that refused to break were no problem to him." Those were the days of "anything goes." A battery, or "joint," or "short stick," or "an Edison," as they were variously referred to, was standard equipment in a stable for morning training. "Nearly all the trainers had them; Tom just knew better how to use one," Chinn related. They were not allowed in races, but some jockeys took their chances and gave their mounts an electrifying ride.

For Howard's account in August of 1936, Tom had bought the sulky claimer Seabiscuit—twice unclaimed for $2,500—from the Wheatley Stable for $7,500. He had been trained by one of the greatest, "Sunny Jim" Fitzsimmons. Tom transformed Seabiscuit almost overnight, and rumors spread nationwide that he had done so with the assistance of a joint. In all likelihood, he had.

En route to meet Tom for dinner one evening, I suggested that Chinn work the conversation around to where he could ask Tom if he had "put run on Seabiscuit's mind" by using a "short stick" in morning workouts. "Johnny," he replied, "you don't ask another trainer such questions. The horse obviously had been cheating and Tom 'shook him up' with a battery." I pointed out to the colonel that "Mr. Fitz" had run Seabiscuit 35 times as a two-year-old and did not win a race with him until his 18th start.

When Tom "changed Seabiscuit's mind," he became an honest and tenacious competitor, as game as a fighting cock. He could do it all against the best horses of his day, go to the front, come from behind, and carry high weight. In his first two attempts to take the Santa Anita Handicap, the race his owner coveted most, he was second, beaten only a nose in each—the first time by the top-class Rosemont in 1937, and the second time by Stagehand, to whom he was conceding 30 pounds.

One evening, Tom recalled for us the match race between Seabiscuit and War Admiral in October of 1938 at Pimlico. As plans for it were being made, the general consensus of horsemen (me included) was that it would be a mismatch in favor of War Admiral. After all, 1937's Horse of the Year had nearly wrapped up champion handicap horse and Horse of the Year honors for 1938 before the Pimlico match. I do not recall a single Kentucky horseman who thought Seabiscuit had a chance. But they also had not factored in Silent Tom Smith.

"Mr. Howard left it up to me to work out the details," Tom said, "and almost daily old man Riddle wanted to change something. First, I was asked if I'd allow Mr. Riddle to bring in a starter from New York. They said he didn't like the Pimlico starter. And I said, 'Get anybody, it's okay by me.' Next day they came to me and said Riddle didn't want to break from the starting gate. He wanted the two horses to be walking and break from the sound of a bell. And I replied: 'That'll be all right, too.' Then I was told the old cuss wanted War Admiral to have the inside post position, and I agreed to that. The only things he didn't ask to be changed were the weight (each 120) and the distance (1 3/16 miles)."

War Admiral was a front runner and Seabiscuit a stretch runner, and Smith knew well that the horse who controls the pace has a big advantage in a match race. "I had to make some adjustments," Tom said, "so I took Seabiscuit to the track before dawn each morning and broke him off from a bell and let him go an eighth of a mile. Then I'd do it another time. He took to it good, got to leaving there like a Quarter horse." He had "the Biscuit" ready to be on the lead, and he had the jockey—Georgie Woolf—who could execute the plan.

"The only instructions I gave George were to warm him up good at a fast gallop, get to the front if you can, control the pace if possible, and if you are going to die, die in front," Smith continued. "He executed them perfectly." War Admiral, a high-strung colt, was walked to the starting point. By the time he arrived there under his regular rider, Charlie Kurtsinger, Woolf had Seabiscuit on his toes. Both horses got away on even terms, but, by the first turn, Woolf had a sufficient lead to move over to the rail.

Responding to Kurtsinger's whip, War Admiral reached even terms with Seabiscuit turning into the backstretch, and from there they raced as though they were locked together until the homestretch, when War Admiral weakened and Seabiscuit won by four lengths.

That victory clinched Horse of the Year honors for Seabiscuit in 1938. Not until two years later, however, were Howard, Smith, and Seabiscuit to have their finest hour on the racetrack.

In 1939, misfortune struck at Santa Anita Park. Seabiscuit came up horribly lame in his first start, a prep for the Santa Anita Handicap. With his racing career apparently over, he was sent to Howard's farm in Mendocino County, California. *Kayak II, the young Argentine horse whom Horatio Luro had purchased for Howard the year before, won that year's Big 'Cap and went on to become the year's champion handicap horse.

After the breeding season, Seabiscuit's injured leg appeared to be fully recovered, and Howard started using the gallant old warrior as his riding mount on the ranch. On a visit to the ranch, Silent Tom was startled by the amazing recovery and exclaimed: "Keep ridin' him and send him back to me in the fall. Let's give him one more chance."

Back at Santa Anita, the seven-year-old favorite of California's racing fans was brought along slowly, leaving him a trifle short for his first two races in 1940. In his third race, he was back at the top of his game and won the San Antonio Handicap while equaling the track record for 1 1/16 miles. He then won the Santa Anita Handicap in track-record time of 2:01 1/5, upping his bankroll to $437,730 and breaking Sun Beau's earnings record, which was set in 1931.

Mission finally accomplished, Seabiscuit was immediately and permanently retired from racing to the Howard ranch. Upon his arrival there, he was greeted by ten foals he had sired the previous year. On "Seabiscuit Day"

In his last career start, Seabiscuit won the Santa Anita Handicap.

in 1941 at Santa Anita, more than 35,000 fans turned out for the unveiling of Tex Wheeler's bronze statue of him, which still stands there today in the paddock area. Seabiscuit died in May of 1947, a week or so after his old trainer, Tom Smith, had saddled Jet Pilot for his Kentucky Derby victory.

Alsab the Underrated

Alsab was one of the most underrated horses of all time, perhaps because he raced during the era of Count Fleet and Whirlaway, and perhaps because he was an off-bred $700 yearling who raced for Al Sabath, a Chicago lawyer who was generally disliked within the industry. (Alsab ran in his wife's name.) No one had a higher respect for Alsab than Jimmy Jones, whose father Ben shared the same feelings.

They never forgot the day in 1942 when Alsab beat their Whirlaway in a match race at Narragansett. Whirlaway had been Horse of the Year in 1941, and had the title nailed down again in 1942. Whirlaway's forte was a scintillating come-from-behind stretch run, his fastest quarter in any race, and he used it repeatedly to demolish his tiring opposition. George Woolf rode him in that match, and the game plan did not work. Carroll Bierman, on Alsab, set a false pace on the lead, going a quarter in :25 2/5, the half in :50 2/5, and six furlongs in 1:14. The two horses hooked up in the stretch, and raced head-to-

Alsab nosed out Whirlaway in a match race at Narragansett.

head to the wire, with Alsab winning by a nose. They sizzled the last three-sixteenths in :17 4/5.

When Alsab went to stud, after winning 25 races and $350,015 in 51 starts, Sabath bought or leased a small farm near Lexington and stood the horse. Under the management of a popular, competent person, the horse would have attracted good mares at a reasonable stud fee. Instead, he stood for a substandard stud fee for a horse with his racing record and was "overbooked" to mostly inferior mares. His destiny at stud was obvious at the outset.

About that time, I had just been retained by Captain Harry Guggenheim to advise on the matings of his mares, an arrangement that was to continue for 17 years. When I recommended breeding Fighting Lady to Alsab, he stated he would prefer another stallion, saying: "I don't like Al Sabath." I replied jokingly: "We're breeding to his horse, not him," and he instructed me: "Go ahead. I don't deal in personalities." The resulting foal was Armageddon (nine wins, including the Champagne Stakes and Withers Stakes, and $191,700 earnings), one of the first good horses in Cain Hoy Stable's ascent to a title as America's leading owner in 1959.

I knew Al Sabath casually. I never liked or disliked him, but I had little respect for him because he forced Sarge Swenke to run Alsab when he should not have run, and because he bred Alsab to bad mares just to collect a stud fee. Mitigating circumstances, perhaps, caused me not to dislike him. I felt sorry for him because he was never allowed to see Alsab's races. He had a heart condition that caused his doctors to forbid him from watching the races. He stayed behind the grandstand or clubhouse during the running of each of those races.

Al Sabath with his namesake Alsab, and trainer Sarge Swenke, right.

An Edge in the Cutting

It seems that there was less gelding of young horses in the 1980s than in the previous 20 years. No hard facts to prove it; I just see a smaller percentage of two-year-old geldings when I read a racing program. Perhaps it was because horses cost more and owners were hoping that they would have residual value at stud. Nine times out of ten, they were wrong. And, it has been my observation that if you wait until an entire colt's disposition forces you to cut him, you have waited too long. It seldom improves.

Max Hirsch was adamant about gelding. "If my owners would let me," he told me many years ago, "I'd cut every colt as a yearling. Only 5% of the horses that go to stud make good, anyway. Geldings train and race better."

Back in 1957, Max and I met Arnold Hanger at his farm to look at a couple of yearling colts—a splendid-looking one by *Turn-to out of the top stakes-winning mare Harmonica, and another with entirely acceptable conformation by *Ambiorix out of Hadassah. Arnold had agreed to give each of us half interest in one of the yearlings for half of its earnings and sales price. We were to pay all of the bills. Max was to have first pick, and he selected the very valuable one, the *Turn-to, "providing you'll get the vet out here right away and cut him." I got the *Ambiorix, and left the decision on gelding him up to Arnold. He was not gelded.

Max proved to me, once again, that you could believe anything he said. The *Turn-to was immediately gelded and, named Waltz, won the 1959 Dwyer Handicap and Jersey Stakes. The following year, he placed in the Suburban and Brooklyn Handicaps before breaking a leg. In all, he earned $231,657. My colt, Clang, won seven races and had eight seconds in 26 starts, placing in two minor stakes and earning $26,905.

E. P. Taylor's Epochal Decision

Had E. P. Taylor gotten his price for Northern Dancer when he offered him for sale as a yearling, I doubt that the sire of no fewer than 144 stakes winners and 23 champions would ever have gone to stud. He would have been a gelding, and perhaps another Kelso or Forego.

But this story of fortunate decisions begins with Natalma, a filly by Native Dancer who crossed the finish line first in Saratoga's Spinaway Stakes, only to be disqualified to third. The next year, while being prepared for the Kentucky Oaks, she fractured her knee and was returned to Windfields Farm in Canada, where a decision was to be made on whether to breed her or to perform surgery on the knee in an attempt to return her to racing.

Taylor had not had much luck with knee surgery and decided to breed Natalma to Nearctic, then in his first year at stud. If she did not get in foal with one service—it was then late June—he still could have considered the operation, but he never had to make that judgment.

On May 27, 1961, Northern Dancer was foaled. He was a small colt, and he would stand slightly less than 15.2 hands at maturity. As a yearling, he was a thick, strong, well-muscled youngster, but no one wanted the colt when Taylor offered him for $25,000 at Windfields's annual private yearling sale. Taylor sold 15, but got "stuck" with the little bay that buyers said was "just too small."

Breaking him as a yearling was a problem. He threw his rider and ran loose with some frequency, but luckily he never injured himself. When sent to the track for training as a two-year-old, he was still about "half-broke" and he developed the disagreeable habit of biting. Throughout this period, Taylor was advised by the colt's handlers to geld the little toughy. And each

E. P. Taylor and Northern Dancer, with Bill Hartack up, after the 1964 Kentucky Derby, with trainer Horatio Luro, left.

time, his answer was: "No. Keep working with him. It's not that I'm thinking of him for stud. It's the fact that my experience has been that, once a colt starts acting ugly, his manners aren't improved by castration."

Northern Dancer finally calmed down enough to start racing, winning his first start in a breeze. The rest of his racing record is now history (18 starts, 14 wins, two seconds, two thirds, $580,647 earnings). His best race was the 1964 Kentucky Derby, when not yet a three-year-old by the calendar. He set a new track record of 2:00, a mark that stood nine years until Secretariat's 1:59 2/5.

Northern Dancer was another horse bred and trained by chance rather than design. Natalma produced four other foals by Nearctic, but not one of them won a stakes, and their earnings totaled $44,190. If Natalma had gone to the operating room instead of the breeding shed, there would have been no Northern Dancer. If Taylor had accepted the advice to castrate, world-class racing would have lost one of its most influential sires.

Untrainable as a Whole Horse

Dr. John Lee gelded five-time Horse of the Year Kelso when he was training him as a two-year-old. That has been well known for years. Carl Hanford, who took over Kelso's training at three, told me at Aiken, South Carolina, one winter that he never would have been able to train him as an entire horse: "Watch him, he's coming on the track right now, and he throws these numbers at you as a gelding."

We were leaning on the outside rail and, as exercise rider Dickie Jenkins moved him out of a trot, "Kelly" propped and buck-jumped for a quarter-mile before leveling off into a smooth gallop.

A Terror in His Stall

It took me more than a decade to find out who cut John Henry, the two-time Horse of the Year. While he was in my office one day, I asked Dr. Alex Harthill in jest: "Is it true you gelded John Henry?" "Yes," he replied defensively, "and he needed it worse than any horse I've ever seen. He was a holy terror in his stall—would eat you alive, walk around his stall on his hind legs like a dog, and hang his front legs over his stall screen. Do every common thing he could to threaten you or hurt you. You'd never have heard of him if he hadn't been gelded."

I do not think there is any doubt that John Henry was the greatest explater of all time. He ran for a tag five times in the first half of his three-year-old career in 1978, but not a single claim was dropped for him. He was ignored despite the fact that, in 11 starts at two, he had three wins, two seconds, two thirds, and earnings of $49,380, most of which he attained in winning the Lafayette Futurity at Evangeline Downs in Louisiana.

Like the legendary figure for whom he was named, John Henry had had his trials and tribulations. In July of his two-year-old season, he stumbled over a fallen horse at Jefferson Downs and fell in such a manner that onlookers thought he had broken every bone in his body. But John picked himself up immediately, came back a week later, and won.

Ole John's first claiming race was on February 15, 1978, at Fair Grounds. For a tag of $25,000 he finished next to last. He came back at the same track a week later to wind up next to last for $20,000. Then, a month later, he finished third for a $25,000 tag at the New Orleans track.

Harold "Bubba" Snowden Jr., who had bought him for $2,200 as a two-year-old in the Keeneland January sale and had resold him, purchased John Henry after the Fair Grounds meeting, freshened him, and then sold him to New York bicycle importer Sam Rubin for $25,000.

John Henry defeated The Bart in the inaugural Arlington Million.

In John Henry's first start for Dorothy and Sam Rubin, on May 21 at Aqueduct for a claiming price of $25,000, he won a six-furlong sprint by 2 1/2 lengths. Joe Trovato, as astute as any halterman, took the wrong horse out of the race, Royal Bengal, who finished sixth in the nine-horse field. In his next start, on June 1, John moved onto the grass, the surface over which he performed best, and won by 14 lengths for a claiming price of $35,000. Never again would he be exposed to the claims box.

In his illustrious career, he won the Arlington Million Stakes (G1) twice, and Arlington International Racecourse immortalized his 1981 victory over The Bart in the inaugural running in bronze, which is titled "Against All Odds." It is a fitting tribute to one of the legends of the game.

Chapter 8
Breeding, Buying, and Selling

I was fortunate to come into the tradin' business just as it was emerging from the depths of the Great Depression. From those dark days, the bloodstock business launched a bull market that lasted for more than four decades.

But, in the dreary, early Depression years from 1930 to 1933, averages for the breeding stock sales at the old Lexington Sales Paddock, conducted by Fasig-Tipton Company, were $573.41, $331.53, $194.56, and $275.83, respectively. And there were quite a number of good ones offered in those sales.

Hal Price Headley bought *Pharamond II (later sire of 35 stakes winners) for $7,500. For $400, he also got Summit (in foal to *Sickle and already the dam of Uppermost and later of Apogee). Herb Woolf got Insco (later sire of Kentucky Derby winner Lawrin and champion Unerring) for $500. Chicleight (in foal to *Epinard and later the dam of Blue Delight) went to Thomas Carr Piatt for $2,000. More bargains came out of these sales than any in history.

Tough Times, Even for Claiborne

Farm manager Dan Midkiff recalled the hard times of the 1930s. "Grooms were making $15-to-$20 a week—and showing up for work every day," he reminisced. "You could feed a horse for 50 cents or $1 a day, depending on if you bought in volume. Nobody had any money. Why, in 1938 I bought three of the best broodmares from Arthur Hancock Sr., including La France, already the dam of Jacola and Johnstown, for Louis B. Mayer for $30,000. Mr. Hancock said to me: 'Now, Dan, don't let this deal fall through, please. I need the money.' That's how tough times were."

A Well-Informed Prediction

It was back in early 1940. Present at this get-together (besides myself) were Joe Estes, Abram Hewitt, Dr. Eslie Asbury, and Ivor Balding, four of the most knowledgeable people on Thoroughbred racing and breeding it has been my privilege to have as friends—and teachers. There was an abundance of good horse talk.

I asked the learned group what the chances were of North America ever becoming dominant in the production of horses for international racing, and there was solid agreement that the odds were excellent. The question was posed because the war in Europe had enabled American breeders for the first time to buy some of the best stallions or sire prospects, not to mention mares, in France, England, and Ireland.

"We've already drained them of some of their best blood, and as long as the war goes on—and even after the war, with its ravages—we'll continue to be able to buy their best," one remarked, and the others nodded. (Already imported were *Blenheim II and *Alibhai, and later to come were *Mahmoud, *Nasrullah, *Royal Charger, *Khaled, and *Heliopolis.)

"We're not bringing over their plodding blood, nor will we in the future," one observed, "a mistake we've made in the past. Breed a plodder to a sprinter and you'll get a horse that can't sprint, get up at a middle distance, or stay. What we're getting now and will be able to get in the future is good middle-distance blood."

Abram S. Hewitt.

It was recalled that the best imported stallion in recent years had been *Sir Gallahad III, whom Arthur Hancock brought over in 1925. He could sprint or stay. In fact, he beat *Epinard at a mile. He was the fastest horse of his day and generally led throughout his races. To get him, Hancock had to pay a record price for a French stallion, and he was lucky to get him at any price. His record as a sire of runners as well as broodmares had been amazing.

It was further pointed out by my seniors that in North America we have other advantages over the European countries: 1) A more thorough test of our horses: "There are more tracks running, more races, more starters—by four or five times." 2) The manner in which our longer races are run: "They're hotly contested from start to finish, not just the last half-mile, as in Europe." 3) A larger percentage of our top stakes horses race beyond age three: "Most of the top ones in Europe retire at three because there are not many big-money races for them after that. In this country, there are many large purses for older horses."

It was the consensus that, with the influx of the best European blood and our more testing regimen of racing, our Thoroughbreds would become the best on an international scale in less than 40 years. How right they were.

Speed and More Speed

When I first came into Thoroughbred racing, speed was accented. There was an axiom that the most important attributes of a racehorse were twofold. The first was speed, and the second was more speed. Yearlings were "tried" at top speed for an eighth or a quarter of a mile. In January, there were five races a week at a quarter-mile for two-year-olds at Fair Grounds, and at three furlongs at Hialeah and Santa Anita Park. These trials and races fortunately have been abandoned—although Keeneland has sprints for two-year-olds in April.

There are those who believe that the stamina present in today's American Thoroughbred came from the imported French and British stallions. That is only partially true. The plodders failed miserably. Those who could both sprint and stay, as *Sir Gallahad III did, fared well. Many of the sprinters or sires of sprinters we imported did us well—*Pharamond II, *Bull Dog, and *Court Martial, to name three. But our own tough American strains gave us most of our stamina.

The Story of the American Stud Book

The first American Stud Book was published by its compiler, Patrick Edgar, in 1833. Because of its inaccuracies and omissions, it drew widespread criticism. The omissions were in part oversights, such as not including the great Sir Archy, but Edgar deliberately left out horses owned or bred by people he disliked.

The criticism killed Edgar's sales. He wound up keeping most of the 1,200 copies printed, losing heavily on publication costs. He vowed publicly that he would not start work on Volume II until the first was sold out, but his threat was not taken seriously.

Although records were kept in a somewhat disorganized manner by various individuals and publications in the ensuing years, it was not until 1868 that another American Stud Book was published, this one by Colonel Sanders D. Bruce. It was the product of his work-hobby of 28 years, but sales barely exceeded his publication costs.

Bruce notified the breeding industry that there would be a charge henceforth for registering horses in his next edition, Volume II. The response was

Sanders D. Bruce.

Robert Aitcheson Alexander.

mixed, but the majority of breeders agreed to pay $1 per horse. (It cost $160 in 1991.) In addition, Robert A. Alexander, master of Woodburn Stud, pledged financial assistance. Recalcitrant breeders fell in line. Volume II was dedicated to Alexander.

Volume II, published in 1873 was, like Volume I, accepted as authentic and reliable. For some time, Bruce and the Jockey Club cooperated on registering horses under Jockey Club supervision and including them in the American Stud Book. But, in 1896, they were at loggerheads over registration procedures. The Breeders and Owners Association in Kentucky interceded to bring the two parties together in a satisfactory settlement of their differences. When they were unable to do so, the association, acting on behalf of the Jockey Club, bought out the American Stud Book for $35,000 on April 29, 1896.

The American Stud Book certainly has stood the test of time. Even the Jersey Act, through which the English Jockey Club barred from registry in its General Stud Book "any horse that cannot be traced without flaw to it for eight generations." This went on for 35 years, 1915 through 1949, and was, in essence, a commercial embargo against American bloodstock. It prevented English and Irish breeders from buying our good American Thoroughbreds. Our breeders, nevertheless, bought theirs. The Jersey Act ban was rescinded on June 16, 1949. The ban would not have been dropped then, I was told by reliable sources, except for the intercession of Winston Churchill, himself a member of the English Jockey Club and the son of American-born Jenny Jerome.

George Swinebroad's Style

The late George Swinebroad rendered an inestimable service to the auctioning of Thoroughbreds. A former tobacco auctioneer, he developed the fast-paced sell—if you did not bid quickly, you did not get the horse. Other

George Swinebroad.

auctioneers have followed his style. With so many horses going to auction nowadays, without the "swingtime" pace, the sales would never finish. George knew horses (he started most of the bidding himself), and he knew people and just how far he could or could not go in cajoling them. He always got the top dollar. But once he did not—or maybe he did.

Some years ago, an ordinary sort was led into the ring, one that George was afraid to start himself, "Who'll start 'im at fi' thousen, who'll giv' fi' thousen," he chanted. An old timer in the back of the pavilion put up his hand, and there were no raises. "You got him, old pod'ner, on one bid. Congratulations." The bidder protested he bid only four.

"Now, old pod'ner, you put up your right hand with your thumb and four fingers clearly showing," George argued. "I did," responded the bidder, as he stood up and opened his palm for all to see. "But I ain't got no thumb on my right hand. I bid four thousand." Recovering quickly, George closed the matter by saying: "My eyesight must be failing. Okay, you git 'im for four thousen!"

Don't Call Him Little

Clifford Mooers suffered a fatal heart attack on November 13, 1956, at LaGuardia Field as he was boarding a plane to take him to Providence, Rhode Island, where his Traffic Judge was to have run in the next day's Narragansett Special. Clifford died in action; he was an action man.

Born in the state of Washington, he prospected for gold in Alaska ("Nearly froze to death in a goddam sleeping bag," he once said). And he "wildcatted" for oil in Texas. He did not strike gold, but he hit oil. He was a risk taker. Busted or rich, he always had a horse or two. Here is what he told Alex Harthill about winning his first big bet:

"Had this little gray mare at an abandoned racetrack in Texas. Rubbed her and galloped her myself. She could outrun horses that were shipping across the border to Juarez and winning. It was cold, and I got a real sore throat from the draft through the broken windows in the pickup truck pulling the trailer. Went to see this Mexican doctor, who told me both tonsils had to be removed. I was holding only about a hundred, and he told me it would be $60. He took out one for $30, which was all I could afford if I was going to bet. The next day after she won, I had about $500 in my kick, and I went back and had the other cut out." Clifford was self-educated and an avid reader. Somewhere along the line in his up-and-down days, he studied law through a correspondence course and passed the Texas bar exam.

He was short in stature, about 15.3 hands (five-foot-three), and sensitive about it. When conversing with a taller person, he would stand back a pace or

Clifford Mooers.

two so his looking up would not be so noticeable. He took great umbrage against anyone who would mention his height even obliquely. Otherwise, he was a very charming fellow with a humorous story, in most of which he portrayed himself as the goat.

Clifford came to Kentucky, oil rich in the mid-1940s with a large stable of American Saddlebred horses and bought the old Robert Sterling Clark farm on Muir Station Road. Immediately, he saw the Thoroughbreds were more fun and in 1947 dispersed his saddle horses at auction at the farm, which he had renamed Walnut Springs. He got $212,600. George Swinebroad, all six-foot-four of him, cried at the sale. Mooers was the first one to thank him and shake his hand. When George replied: "Well, Little Clifford, I too think it was a good sale," the big, burly auctioneer got the tongue-lashing of his life.

He's Not a Basket of Tobacco

George later told me that the Mooers incident was one of only two times that he had been so embarrassed. At Saratoga, Isabel Dodge Sloane, who apparently had had one too many cocktails, had pulled herself up out of the chair, stood half-unbalanced, and instructed him: "Now, Mr. Swinebroad, don't you be chanting and sing-songing on this next colt like he's a basket of tobacco. I'm going to be bidding on him." George, who could be temperamental, was so devastated that he started to leave the stand. Humphrey Finney, who was announcing, talked him out of it.

He'll Need a Lot of Stalls

In the 1940s, one of George's bid spotters was Max Self. One afternoon while I was sitting with Alec Gordon, Max had a particularly hot section of bidders. In the space of a couple of hours, George cried out "Max!" after knocking down about 40 yearlings to his section. "Tell me, Johnny," Alec asked as he scratched his head in perplexity, "where the hell is that Max gonna get all the stalls for the yearlings he's bought?"

He Couldn't Take a Hint

When W. H. Bishop retired from racing, he called on his friend, leading trainer Jack Van Berg, to auction off his racehorses and tack. Next to George Swinebroad, Jack is the best auctioneer I have ever heard. I happened to be there that morning at Arlington Park and was standing next to a prominent trainer. Jack looked directly into the trainer's eyes several times: "You better buy this tack . . . I can't give you better advice . . . Outfit yourself, you're goin' to be needing it." The suggestion went unheeded. After the sale, I asked Jack why he made those remarks only to the one person.

"Trying to help him," Jack replied. "He's gonna have to open a public stable. He's getting fired from that private job he has the first of the month. His man tried to give it to me, but I got too many horses. I know the man who is getting it. The dummy hasn't been told yet he's getting sacked. Private jobs are hard to find, so a guy has to start back up with a public stable."

Jack Van Berg.

Time to Look Like a Million

Back in the 1930s, Tom B. Young, one of my early mentors in the business, told me this story about his father, Colonel Milton T. Young, one of the leading breeders around the turn of the century. "My father was making money 'hand over fist,' but he had a hang-up about buying clothes," Tom told me. "He'd wear what he had until the clothes were virtually threadbare. One day, he drove back from downtown Lexington in his horse-drawn buckboard loaded down with boxes and bundles of new clothing. My mother exclaimed:

'Milt, have you lost your mind?' 'No,' he replied, 'I have to dress like a millionaire—we're broke.'"

Back in 1907, Colonel Young reported to "Registrar Rowe of the Jockey Club" that, of the 392 mares he had bred in 1906, he had received 178 live foals. By my calculations, that is 45.4%. It is amazing how veterinary science and good horse husbandry have improved over the years.

'Up a Grand Ethel'

In the late 1930s, Ethel V. Mars ruled the roost as the biggest and most flamboyant buyer of yearlings. While the auctioneers graciously accepted raises of $100, she would often bounce back with a $1,000 raise for one she really wanted. This got her the nickname of "Up a Grand Ethel." While some consignors were pleased with this tactic, others felt she was frightening off other bidders on their horses.

Frank Mars, her husband, had died at an early age in April of 1934 after purchasing 20 yearlings "at a price said to be in six figures" from Arthur B. Hancock Sr. the previous year. As the lone stockholder in Mars Candy Company, Ethel had the wealth to buy the best that came on the market for her Milky Way Farm Stables. She also had an excellent trainer with a good eye for a horse—Bob McGarvey.

Ethel Mars.

From a percentage standpoint, I do not believe anyone ever acquired as many top stakes winners from the yearling sales as Ethel. She defied the axiom that "you can't buy your way into racing," and she did it in a hurry. With auction yearlings that she bought in the first two years, 1934 and 1935, her Milky Way Farm became the nation's leading money earner in 1936. Nine of those purchases became first-rate juvenile stakes winners. For $3,000 in 1934, she got Forever Yours, who went on to be the 1935 champion two-year-old filly.

In 1936, she bought five more yearlings who became two-year-old stakes winners, and, in 1938, she got the one she had been waiting for—Gallahadion, a $5,000 purchase who upset Bimelech, Roman, Mioland, and other good ones in the 1940 Kentucky Derby. In his next start, the Preakness Stakes, Gallahadion was third to Bimelech and Mioland.

Not a volume buyer, Ethel bought a total of 22 stakes winners in the seven years she was an active buyer, from 1934 through 1940. Even more astound-

Gallahadion, winner of the 1940 Kentucky Derby.

ing was the fact that 18 of those horses won their first stakes at two. One who did not, Mars Shield, obliged by taking the Kentucky Oaks at three. Gallahadion was one of the others who failed to win an added-money event as a juvenile.

McGarvey trained the Milky Way horses through 1938. Roy Waldron succeeded him and remained her trainer until she retired from racing in 1943. Ethel V. Mars passed away on December 25, 1945, in La Jolla, California, but she did, indeed, leave her mark on racing. The best of her horses, I believe, was the ill-fated Sky Larking. Besides Forever Yours, other outstanding ones were Reaping Reward, Tiger, and Case Ace.

Reaping Reward won the United States Hotel Stakes at Saratoga and the Kentucky Jockey Club Stakes at Churchill Downs at age two. The following year, in 1937, he won the Latonia Derby and was third to War Admiral and Pompoon in a 20-horse Kentucky Derby field. Standing in the shadow of the great sire *Bull Dog at Coldstream Stud, Reaping Reward sired 18 stakes winners, including two-time champion sprinter Sheilas Reward.

Tiger won the Arlington Futurity and the Washington Park Futurity as well as the Arkansas Derby. With little opportunity at stud, he got 12 stakes winners, one of whom was Siama, dam of Bald Eagle. Case Ace took the Arlington Futurity and Illinois Derby. He sired juvenile champion Pavot and the dams of champions One Count and Raise a Native.

One of the greatest shocks and disappointments of my young career as a Turf writer came in September of 1937 when I read that Sky Larking had broken a leg at Belmont Park and was humanely destroyed. He was one of my heroes. I was quite impressed by the manner in which he took the Bashford Manor Stakes at Churchill Downs in the spring, and McGarvey had told me after the race: "He's not only the best I've ever trained, but the best I've ever seen."

Sky Larking had gone into the Champagne Stakes at Belmont Park with only one loss in six starts, and he was coming off back-to-back victories in the Albany Handicap and Hopeful Stakes at Saratoga. The even-money favorite over Menow and Bull Lea, Sky Larking was running easily, well within himself, when he stumbled and fell, sustaining a compound fracture of his right foreleg. Fortunately, jockey Alf Robertson was uninjured.

McGarvey hastened to the scene and, seeing the seriousness of the injury, instructed the track vet to destroy the colt. With tears in his eyes, he turned and walked away. Alf, also in tears, told a reporter: "He was running easily when it happened. I felt sure he was going to win by as much as I pleased and go on to become one of the best horses of all time. I know for sure he's the best I've ever ridden."

Henry Knight and the Package Deal

One of the fastest action men I have ever known was Henry Hudson Knight, who specialized in "package" deals. Like John E. Madden, Knight dealt in both Standardbreds and Thoroughbreds, but any similarity between the two men ended right there. Madden knew how to—and did—raise good horses. Knight did not. He "hot-housed" them to keep them fat and slick for either public or private sale. Although he did breed 30 stakes winners, few of them lasted long enough on the racetrack to live up to their pedigrees.

On the same land where his uncle, Dixie Knight, had raised probably the toughest class horse of all time, Exterminator (100 starts, age two through nine, 50 wins at weights up to 138 pounds), Henry is regarded to have raised the highest percentage of non-starters of any major breeder. His yearling fields and paddocks seldom showed paths along the fence lines, a telltale sign that his youngsters spent most of their time in stalls. Knight was a master buyer, and, if possible, a better seller. He knew how to "handle" people. He had quite a turnover in clients and very little repeat business.

Henry H. Knight.

Henry started "collecting" horses a few years after Dixie's tragic, unsolved murder in his sleep in 1932. He built it into a showplace and named it Almahurst, after his wife Alma. It was to be the only farm he still owned at the time of his death in 1959 at age 69.

His first large deal was in 1944, when he bought all the horses owned by Valdina Farm, 149 of them, for $250,000 and within three days resold all of them with the exceptions of the stallions Teddy's Comet and Valdina Orphan, whom he retained and improperly used; they were miserable failures. In July of 1944, Knight bought all but a few of the horses of Milky Way Farm, including the fine stakes mare Forever Yours.

In 1947, he bought the northern section of Coldstream Farm and operated it until 1951, when he sold it to Helen and Howard Reineman. In 1950, Knight sold all of his Standardbreds to Castleton for $500,000, then promptly restocked Almahurst with the same breed on a smaller basis. In 1951, he bought for $1-million nearly all of William G. Helis's horses, 184 of them, including the stallions Cosmic Bomb, *Olympic Zenith, and Rippey, reselling nearly all but the stallions, none of whom made it with the possible exception of Cosmic Bomb.

Also in 1951, Knight made his biggest deal. He bought all of the southern section of Coldstream Stud and all the farm's horses for $2-million. About this time, tiring of his huge dealings in land and horses and burdened with health problems, Henry started to lay plans for one giant liquidation. He retained most of the Coldstream bloodstock, including the successful 15-year-old sire, *Heliopolis. Under a tent at the farm on the rainy night of November 3, 1955, he had perhaps the most successful dispersal sale up to that time, selling 68 mares and 55 weanlings. The yearlings had been sold at Saratoga in August. In December of 1958, he sold the farm to the Commonwealth of Kentucky for experimental agricultural work for $1,123,500.

From that sale came one mare whose descendants were to make great achievements in racing and in the stud—Almahmoud. Knight had bought her as a weanling from her breeder, C. V. Whitney, resold her as a yearling to Bill Helis at Saratoga for $15,000, and repurchased her in the 184-horse Helis deal.

Danny Van Clief and his cousin, Betty Augustus (later Mrs. John Knight), bought Almahmoud, in foal to Citation, for $57,000. The first foal from her, after the Citation foal, was a Native Dancer filly they sold for $35,000 at Saratoga to E. P. Taylor. That was Natalma, dam of Northern Dancer. Previously, Knight had bred and sold Almahmoud's foal Cosmah. Gene Mori bought Cosmah at Saratoga in 1954 for $7,000 on the advice of Olin Gentry, and she became a top stakes winner and a Broodmare of the Year.

As a kid in the early '30s, I idolized Henry Knight. After all, he had bred and sold the great Standardbred, Greyhound. I was then working with and writing about Standardbreds—won my first race as a driver at age 14. Toward the end of that decade, I switched to Thoroughbreds, because there was neither money nor a future with the trotters and pacers. When Henry switched to the Thoroughbreds, I was one of the first people he consulted. But he learned quickly and, in a short time, did not need any advice.

My functions were mostly on the buying side—telling him the value of the horses he anticipated buying. I did not want to be in on the selling. I did not like his *modus operandi* in this department. It was generally difficult to detect the underbidders on the yearlings he sold at public auction. He had the clout to designate the auctioneer of his yearlings on "Knight's Nite" each year at Saratoga, and oddly that man turned up with a new Cadillac late each August or early September.

I shall never forget a conversation I had one July with my dear friend, Phil Chinn. "I'll see you up at Saratoga," he told me. "I'll be up there to protect Sam Riddle from Henry Knight. He tells me that Henry runs up his horses and that I, being a past master of it, will know better than anyone if any by-bidding is going on. If he is bidding on any of Henry's yearlings and is being run up, I'm to wipe my brow with my handkerchief to signal him to stop. I'll know which ones Sam likes, what he plans to pay—and, of course, I'll strike a deal with Henry before the sale. I'll come away from Saratoga with some money, and be able to take care of some of these accounts rendered I'm receiving each month."

After that "Knight's Nite," I asked the colonel how he had made out. "Good," he replied, "Sam got the three he wanted at his price, and I didn't have to wipe my brow a single time. I made some dough-re-me."

When John Marsch tired of breeding but continued racing, he sold out his breeding stock to Knight. In the package were three excellent Blue Larkspur mares—Blue Delight, Morning Lark, and Irvana. The logical buyer for them was Warren Wright, whose Bull Lea had already firmly established a "nick" with Blue Larkspur mares—siring Twilight Tear, one of the few fillies elected Horse of the Year, and champion Durazna.

Olin Gentry inspected Blue Delight and Morning Lark for Wright and recommended their purchase. Why Irvana was overlooked I have never known. Blue Delight became one of the four foundation mares at Calumet, dam of champion Real Delight, stakes winner Princess Turia (dam of Derby winner Forward Pass), and ancestress of many top runners.

'No Strings'

Knight generally got above market value on private sales. If he was not going to get his "excess," though, he would place a condition on the sale price based on the horse's performance. For a stakes win, for instance, he would receive an additional payment.

A year or so after he had bought all of Marsch's breeding stock, Marsch came back to Henry to buy the 1947 yearling filly by Occupation out of Irvana. "Now, Henry," said the old gent from Chicago, "there'll be no strings on this deal like the last one we had." That is how No Strings got her name, and she won for Marsch the Modesty Stakes and was second in the Princess Doreen Stakes. Later, she was to produce two very good horses, Nail ($250,230) and Globemaster ($355,423).

A Bad Cull

John Fellows, the noted French trainer, once lamented the health and financial adversities of Marcel Boussac, the renowned French breeder who died in 1980. "I used to work for him, sort of kept tabs on all his racing and breeding stock, and each Sunday morning he'd have me in for breakfast to report my observations," Fellows began. "On this particular Sunday, I reported that a new man in the business wanted to buy any one of his broodmares if he would select one and put a reasonable price on her. You know, Mr. Boussac had a multitude of mares, and I'd made a list of the ten I thought most unworthy of being in his stud.

"After looking over the list, he said: 'Young man, I'm not going to sell any; if you cull a mare you haven't tried thoroughly, she'll invariably come back to haunt you.' Then he told me of his greatest mistake in culling." In 1931, he culled out a young mare of ordinary conformation and modest racing ability and sold her for 1,250 guineas to go overseas to American breeder Colonel E. R. Bradley. "John," Boussac told Fellows with emphasis, "her name was *La Troienne."

He Did Ship Well

The death of Liz Whitney Tippett in 1988 took from our game a person whose life richly contributed to the wonderful lore of racing. I remember in particular one beautiful evening in August of 1956 at Saratoga. Liz arrived at the Fasig-Tipton sales grounds in high heels, beautiful gown, and abundant jewelry. In those days, it was not unusual for persons to come so dressed directly from a high-fashion dinner. She was there to buy the yearling whose conformation and pedigree was the best she had ever beheld, a gray colt by Hyperion out of Deodora being offered by Taylor Hardin.

Liz Whitney Tippett.

Liz had let the world know she was buying the colt, hoping to scare off other bidders. She even had her own van brought up from Virginia to haul him home. Liz started the bidding on the colt and fired back a higher bid instantly at every challenge, getting him for the then-record yearling auction price of $87,000.

As the colt was being led from the sales ring, much to the consternation of onlookers she grabbed the shank from his groom and—evening gown, high heels, and all—led and loaded the colt into her van, instructing the driver and her chauffeur to proceed to the edge of town, adding: "When I pay this much money for a colt, you can bet your life I'm going to see that he ships right." About 15 minutes later, Liz was back at the sale in her ringside seat.

*Rise 'n Shine was a good shipper, all right, but a poor runner. Liz raced him six years, and in 41 starts he won only four races. She stood him at stud at her place in Ireland, then sent him to France at age 14. I last saw *Rise 'n Shine in July of 1979, when I went to the Texas ranch of singer Ray Price to appraise a group of horses he was donating to Texas A&M University. They were to be vanned to the college the next day. Ray phoned me the following evening to assure me that *Rise 'n Shine "shipped just fine." *Rise 'n Shine was indeed a good shipper, but that was the only thing he did well.

A Close Call with Banquet Bell

Banquet Bell was the dam of two champions—Chateaugay, the top three-year-old of 1963, and Primonetta, the leading handicap female in the preceding year. But John Galbreath once came perilously close to losing this mare, the best broodmare he ever owned.

Olin Gentry selected Banquet Bell out of the 1952 Keeneland summer sale from the consignment of Ira Drymon and bought her as agent for Galbreath for $9,000. The daughter of Polynesian out of Dinner Horn showed a lot of speed and won the Gulfstream Turf Club Stakes at two for the Darby Dan Farm owner.

On September 4, 1954, Joe Metz raced into my office early one morning and asked me to look up the pedigree of Banquet Bell. "She's in the first race today at Atlantic City to be claimed for $4,000," he noted hurriedly, "and if she's got any breeding, I'm gonna

John Galbreath.

get her claimed for me. I know she won a stakes last year." He liked what he saw on the catalog page that I produced for him and was still more impressed that Olin Gentry had bought her for $9,000. "Olin Gentry wouldn't have bought her if she was bad looking. I'm gonna take her. See you," Joe said as he rushed out the door.

That night, a very upset Joe Metz phoned. He used his entire vocabulary of profanity to describe Western Union, which apparently had dawdled with the wire transfer of the funds for the claim to a friend who had agreed to halter the filly for Joe. By the grace of the delayed transfer, John Galbreath was able to retain Banquet Bell for a broodmare.

The Traveling Stallion

The stallion manager's name must be omitted, lest other mare owners request the same favor in the future. He had kept his crew at the breeding shed for a mare who was two hours overdue. Finally, came a phone call: "I can't get this mare loaded on the van. We've tried to coax her in with oats, tranquilized her, whipped her. She just won't load."

"Stay right there with her," replied the stallion manager, "I'll load the horse on my van and we'll breed at your farm. That's a good mare, and she'll help make my stallion." Within an hour the "mobile" breeding operation, stallion and crew, had completed the service and was back at home base.

Faith in Traffic Judge

Clifford Mooers, whom I mentioned earlier, did surprisingly well in the fewer than 12 years that he was in the Thoroughbred business. Early on, he won the Santa Anita Derby with homebred Old Rockport. He made Cyclotron, a cripple castoff he bought from Calumet (in the Ben Jones days!), into a top stakes horse who was still winning stakes at age eight.

The best two horses that Clifford bred were the half brothers Hasty Road (by Roman) and Traffic Judge (by *Alibhai), out of the good stakes winner Traffic Court. He sold Hasty Road at the 1952 Keeneland July select sales to Allie Reuben for $23,100, a pretty good price when you consider that the sale's average was $7,438. He was quite proud and bragged a bit about it.

But, when Dr. Art Davidson turned down Traffic Judge for the 1953 sale because of a calf knee, Mooers was slanderously outspoken about Art's knowledge of conformation. "Look," I said after he asked me to come to the farm and see the *Alibhai colt, "I've never known Art to be wrong. He looks at all the yearlings I'm going to bid on with other people's money. He can evaluate a fault better than anyone I know. He's okayed crooked horses for me that stood hard training and racing. The odds are against this colt."

"Odds my ass," screamed Clifford. "I'd bet on myself against Joe Louis if the odds were right. I'll race him myself and prove I'm right." And that he did. Traffic Judge was still winning stakes at age five. A year after Clifford's death, he won the Suburban and Metropolitan Handicaps for Lou Doherty.

The Overbred Stallion

Certain stallions in Kentucky now are serving from 75 to 100 mares each season. (Samuel D. Riddle limited Man o' War to 25, Hirsch D. Jacobs restricted Hail to Reason to 31.) It is to those greedy stallion managers I have dedicated one of my meter murders:

The Commercial Stud

Best of foal getters in the world,
He's booked to sixty mares,
I ought to breed him to twenty more,
He's virile, has no cares.
But that was early in the year,
He'd prance into his court,
And now that four full months have passed,
He doesn't even snort.
What he could do in seconds' run,
It now takes him an hour,
For even youngish, maiden mares,
He now has no desire.
The van men now are bringing lunch,
No longer do they look.
What's happened to my virile stud,
Guess forty is his book.

He's Not Welcome for Lunch

No one ever helped more people get started in our business than Charlie Kenney. He was always on the go, and his favorite mode of communication was the phone, but he always found time to help people, even strangers. His charming wife Buddy seldom knew how many people to expect for lunch.

Shortly after John Hertz died, Charlie agreed to stay on as manager of Stoner Creek Stud for its new owners, Norman Woolworth and David Johnstone, Standardbred breeders. "I may be a bit late for lunch today,"

Charlie told Buddy one morning. "I'm expecting Henry T. Adios. Don't know exactly what time he'll arrive."

"Charlie," she replied, "if you bring one more person to lunch this week, I'm walking out of this house." Henry T. Adios then was the leading money-winning pacer of all time and was arriving that day to take up stud duties at Stoner Creek.

Good Old 'Out of Bed'

The night before a yearling sale, a Lexington horseman invited a group of out-of-town horse pals down to his camp on Herrington Lake for a barbecue-and-drink bash. At the last minute, he invited an added starter, a friend who knew nothing of our business.

The stranger, bored with the unending horse talk in which he could not participate, entertained himself with a liberal amount of 100 proof bourbon and highly seasoned ribs. In a short time, he had to be assisted to bed.

In early morning, his "coils" hot and in need of ice water, he stumbled out of bed to feel his way to the kitchen. Trudging unsteadily, he stumbled and overturned a small table with many dirty glasses and dishes, causing a most disconcerting racket.

"Who the hell is that?" shouted one of the party. Replied the stranger: "Out of Bed, by Crack o' Dawn!"

Crimson Satan Was His Joy

The obituary of Peter W. Salmen in 1981 noted that one of his greatest joys was Crimson Satan and the horse's success in both racing and breeding. Salmen bred the horse and, upon his retirement, Crimson Satan remained his sole property. At one time, however, he felt differently about selling him.

Salmen was not at Keeneland when Crimson Satan was offered as a yearling in the July sale. His son Pete was, but he did not follow his father's orders to let the colt sell, regardless of the final bid. He took him back with his last bid of $13,700, and "caught hell" repeatedly for the disobedience. The criticism stopped the next spring, however, when Crimson Satan showed signs of being an exceptional runner. Crimson Satan was champion two-year-old colt of 1961, and, before retiring from racing, had earned $796,077. At stud, he sired 33 stakes winners and the dams of 66 others.

An Eye for the Classics

During the 1970s, bloodstock agent George Blackwell chalked up a notable record. In the space of seven years, he bought three Derby winners for his overseas customers. In 1972, he bought Prix du Jockey Club (French Derby) (Fr-G1) winner Caracolero (Graustark—Betty Loraine) for $75,000. Two years later, he picked out for $40,000 Irish Sweeps Derby (Ire-G1) winner Malacate (Lucky Debonair—Eyeshadow). These two were followed by his purchase for $24,000 in 1978 of Epsom Derby (Eng-G1) Henbit (*Hawaii—Chateaucreek).

In addition, he "stole" Ramirez (T. V. Lark—Dance Fan), who defeated Arc winners Allez France and Ivanjica in the Prix d'Ispahan (Fr-G1), for $20,000.

George Blackwell.

At the 1978 September sales, George "overlooked" a filly (Bold and Brave—Pidi) who went for only $12,000. When she came up for auction as an unraced two-year-old in California, he was there to land her for $70,000, but he invested well for his Texas client, Corbin Robertson. Bold 'n Determined earned $556,243.

I first met George in 1948 in London at the offices of the British Bloodstock Agency, where he was playing "third or fourth fiddle" in the chain of command, a post he left in 1956 to go on his own. I found him to be a quiet, modest, affable, humorous man. No one has a better memory of horses or people. He works slowly, but steadily, methodically, and tirelessly.

Like many top horsemen, he concentrated on the individual. For his clients with somewhat restricted budgets, "I sacrifice a bit on pedigree and try to buy very sound, good-looking horses. A horse that does not suit me on looks I pass up, regardless of how well bred he might be," he said. I asked George if there was a single "do" or "don't" about his buying. "Yes, indeed, I can be emphatic about this," he replied. "I have a very big 'don't' about buying from a consignor who does not raise runners. I don't even look at his horses."

John Finney.

From Right to Left

John Finney once told me how he reads a pedigree chart for his own pleasure when trying to predict the future of a racehorse, broodmare, or sire. "I first look at the eight horses in the fourth generation. If more than half of them failed, I eliminate the horse there. Otherwise, I continue to the four horses in the third generation, and the two in the second, following the same procedure."

A Nocturnal Pattern

Why do mares almost invariably foal at night or early in the morning? It is terribly inconvenient, especially to the overworked vet during the breeding season when he or she has to be called out of bed for a problem delivery.

Orville Huff, who served as John Gaines's head foaling man and attended more than a thousand births, said: "No one knows precisely. We assume it's because of the quietude of those hours." In 1980, Gainesway had 72 night foalings and only four during the day.

A Novel Way of 'Starting' Horses

Flag Is Up Farm lies in the flats of the Santa Ynez Valley, just west of Solvang in Central California, and about ten air miles north of former President Ronald and Nancy Reagan's ranch in Santa Barbara County. It is there that Monty and Pat Roberts, two lifelong horse people, both breed and train Thoroughbreds.

Monty does not "break" horses to the saddle, and he never uses the word. Roberts describes the process as "starting" the horses. "The two most traumatic things in a horse's life are the weaning and starting process," Roberts said.

Monty does in 30 minutes what normally takes two weeks by conventional methods. If ever there was a horse psychologist, it is Monty Roberts. I saw it with my own eyes in a high-walled, round pen that is 50 feet in diameter.

The yearling is brought into that area and turned loose. Roberts "clucks" or "chirps" to the yearling and the young horse canters around and around until it starts to relax. When the yearling relaxes, Roberts walks up to the young horse and gently pets it, then shoos it away. He calls this "joining up," and "advance and retreat." After this is accomplished, a bridle and a stock saddle are placed on the yearling, and it is cantered around the ring. Later, a rider mounts the yearling and guides it on a light rein in both directions, first at a walk, then a trot, and finally a slow canter.

"We never force a horse to do anything. We try to show a horse what we want to do and let him learn on his own," Roberts said. "You can't force horses—or people—and accomplish much."

Monty Roberts.

The filly I saw in the first day of her "starting" bucked the first three times around the ring. Her rider, Sean McCarthy, an excellent horseman, just held onto the saddle, never touching the filly's mouth with the reins, and then she settled down to a walk, after which she was guided clockwise and counterclockwise at a walk, trot, and canter. "Keeping a horse's mouth tender and sensitive to the bit is all-important," McCarthy said.

At Flag Is Up, a Thoroughbred has two sides. "Funny thing, the Thoroughbred is the only athlete whose right side is not developed in training," said the Robertses' assistant, Crawford Hall. "Now, when the filly goes to the track, like all others, she'll be trotted and cantered clockwise one day and counterclockwise the next."

I asked Hall: "How much jogging or trotting do you do?"

"Quite a bit," he answered. "Strangely, the worst, the slowest trotter we ever had was Alleged. We let them trot on a loose rein and go as fast as they want to. That year, we had a What a Pleasure colt in his set that went to the track and he'd open up an eighth of a mile on Alleged. But Alleged kept on developing physically and mentally and was a darn nice horse when Pat and Monty took him to the two-year-old sales at Hollywood Park."

Alleged spotlighted the Robertses' talent for spotting underdeveloped and undervalued yearlings who would blossom from age one to two. The Robertses had bid up to $34,000 on him in the yearling sales (the Hoist the Flag colts had averaged $91,000), but June McKnight took him back home for $35,000. The Robertses offered her $40,000 and got him. Robert Sangster had turned down Alleged as a yearling, but he and his group paid $175,000 for him at two. He was the first horse since *Ribot to win the Prix de l'Arc de Triomphe (Fr-G1) twice. Upon retirement from racing, Alleged was syndicated for $16-million.

The Second Coming of Phil Chinn

The evening before the start of the 1989 select yearling sales at Keeneland, Tom Gentry threw another of his $100,000 parties, which were annual affairs until a couple of years ago, when the banks started calling for payments on his huge borrowings and he filed for bankruptcy. At these extravaganzas, the featured entertainers have been the likes of Bob Hope, Burt Bacharach, and Paul Anka, who did not exactly perform for free. The ticket for Wayne Newton, to my understanding, was $50,000.

"How," a friend asked me, "could the banks and the court allow Tommy to give this party?" I replied: "That's easy. Tommy cultivated a friendship with his high-bidding customers by entertaining them and getting the big income that established his huge line of credit with the banks. Continuing these parties could help him make the dough to pay them back."

I have known Gentry since he learned how to research pedigrees and racing records working in my office while attending the University of Kentucky. "Don't worry about Tom," I continued, "he's a survivor." And, with his flamboyance, he is the second coming of Colonel Phil T. Chinn. Tom, I am sure, will go down as the most innovative merchandiser of Thoroughbreds in my lifetime. His lavish parties, giveaways (catalog covers, measuring sticks, pens, unique gifts of all kinds), and advertisements have spread his name throughout the horse world—even more so than from the goodly number of stakes winners he has bred.

Who but Tommy Gentry, I ask, could have interested former President Jimmy Carter in becoming a partner in a Thoroughbred, becoming the first President since Andrew Jackson to own a part of a racehorse?

Gentry Advertises a Claimer

Tom's most amusing promotion came out in California in 1982 when he had a horse he could not get sold or claimed. The day he was in for a price equal to his worth, Gentry took a full-page ad in the western edition of the *Daily Racing Form* offering the successful trainer a $5,000 commission, plus travel, food, and lodging for a weekend in Las Vegas. That got attention. Seven claims were entered for the horse, and the critter did not disgrace him. He finished second.

Brerry Preps for Football

Brereton C. Jones came to Kentucky from West Virginia on a visit in 1971. While here he made two important decisions. One was to marry Libby Lloyd; the other was to get into the Thoroughbred business. In due time, both things happened—and with big success. Late in the 1980s, he became Kentucky's lieutenant governor.

Most of this story was dug out of his adoring father, Bartow. When Brerry was a youngster, Bartow asked him what he wanted to do about his schooling. "I want to get a good education and, while I'm doing it, I want to play football in high school and college."

"Okay," replied Bartow, "but if you're going to play ball you've got to start getting yourself strong—it's a rough, tough game." Among other exercises he prescribed was rope climbing. He set up in the back yard of their home two telephone poles 20 feet high, the tops of which were connected with a cable. From the center of the span was suspended to the ground a two-inch manila rope.

"Now," said Bartow, "once every day you're going to pull yourself up and down that rope by your hands until you tire. I'm going to tie knots

Brereton C. Jones.

in it at one-foot intervals, then later I'm going to take them out so your grip alone will take you up and down."

In short order, Brerry developed unusual strength and endurance for a youngster. Making the high school football team was easy, and he played so well that he was offered 27 athletic scholarships. He chose the University of Virginia, where he starred.

After graduating, Brerry entered politics back in West Virginia. He was never defeated when he opted for a public office. He served two terms in the West Virginia Legislature, was a minority leader in the second, then discontinued his political career although no one had announced against him from either party for a third term. When he stated he was not running, the field became crowded.

Libby and Brerry have enjoyed a very happy and successful partnership in the Thoroughbred business. Their Airdrie Stud occupies 2,500 acres of choice land in Woodford County, Kentucky.

A Bottom-Line Guy

I sat ringside at Keeneland on November 6, 1989, and saw Gene Klein disperse 114 of his horses for $29,623,000. A short time after the dispersal, the former owner of the San Diego Chargers professional football team died of a heart attack.

In seven short years, Klein had a significant impact on the sport. He received three Eclipse Awards as an owner, and horses he owned wholly or in part won seven Breeders' Cup races. He raced Kentucky Derby (G1) winner Winning Colors and Preakness Stakes (G1) victor Tank's Prospect as well as the 1986 Horse of the Year, Lady's Secret.

Klein, in my judgment, was a bottom-line guy. He had to be. Starting from scratch, with no equity, he became a multimillionaire, always entering a field when business was down, then selling out at a

Eugene Klein.

profit. His business record read like that of a cold, calculating entrepreneur.

It was my guess that he figured his horses were worth more in November of 1989 than they would ever be in the future, and that he would stop the expense and take the money and run. For the last seven years, he had been quoted in the press and had stated on television how much he loved his horses and the game, which he termed "the best of any sport."

What puzzled me about all of this was that, if he did love his horses, why did he not retain his three favorites—Lady's Secret, Winning Colors, and Open Mind? I do not think doing this would have depressed the prices of the others, since they were such all high-quality bloodstock.

The Odds Are Improving

What were your chances of buying a Horse of the Year at auction over the last 60 years? Slim, to be sure, but the chances improved greatly in the late 1980s. Only six went through the ring. John Henry sold for $1,100 as a yearling,

Sunday Silence taking the 1989 Kentucky Derby under Pat Valenzuela.

$2,200 as a two-year-old; Seattle Slew, $17,500 as a yearling; Spectacular Bid, $37,000 as a yearling; Conquistador Cielo, $150,000 as a yearling; and Alysheba, $500,000 as a yearling.

Sunday Silence, 1989's Horse of the Year, went through the ring twice. Stone Farm's Arthur Hancock III thought he was doing a favor for the breeder, Oak Cliff Thoroughbreds, Ltd. of Tom Tatham, when he bid the colt in at $17,000 as a yearling. Hancock ended up with the horse, and he bid him in for $32,000 when Sunday Silence failed to fetch his reserve price at a California two-year-olds in training sale in 1988. Hancock sold a half-interest for $25,000 to trainer Charlie Whittingham, who in turn sold half of his interest to Dr. Ernest Gaillard for $25,000.

The horse that nobody wanted was, in the end, a piece of good horse trading by Hancock and his partners. He whipped Easy Goer in the $3-million Breeders' Cup Classic (G1) at Gulfstream Park, and Japanese horseman Zenya Yoshida purchased a quarter-interest in the Halo colt for $2,250,000 in March, 1990. Sunday Silence was retired in August of that year with earnings of $4,968,554, and the following month Yoshida bought out his partners and sent Sunday Silence to Japan.

A Very Big Horse

Biggest Thoroughbred horse I ever saw was Blind Poet, bred and owned by Dr. Charlie Hagyard and trained by Tom B. Young. That was back in the 1930s. He stood more than 18 hands and weighed in excess of 1,500 pounds. Nearly everyone who saw him said he would never get to the races. He did, however, for nine starts, one win, and $425. The most outstanding big one I have ever seen is Best Turn, who stood 17.2 hands and won $270,339. He sired the winners of more than $5-million, including champion Davona Dale and Cox's Ridge, a top sire.

A Tour With Some 'Faults'

Some people flew into Lexington to inspect a horse I owned. They had approved his racing record, pedigree, and price. They were to buy him if he passed their physical inspection. They allowed themselves, as I suggested, enough time to see the stallions at Claiborne, Gainesway, and Spendthrift, the greatest combined assemblage of stallions in the history of the breed.

As has often been the case, they turned down my horse because of a minor fault. He toed out slightly. I did not contradict their judgment or discuss the horse's "fault" in any way, and we immediately started our tour.

Seeing many things wrong in the conformation of the great racehorses and sires they inspected, they excused themselves at the last farm for a "short conference." One, looking very sheepish, turned to me: "We haven't much time left. Can we hurry back to your office? We've decided to buy your horse."

In my many years in this business, I have seen few great horses—other than Secretariat—whose conformation I could not fault. In judging young horses for racing or breeding, the bottom line is not finding the faults but in properly evaluating them. It is a key ingredient in breeding, buying, and selling.

Chapter 9
The Senor and Other Masters of the Turf

Horatio Luro's contributions to the Thoroughbred sport and to its lore are inestimable. Everyone, it seems, has their favorite story about the Senor. And, no one has given his friends more laughs than the inimitable Senor. He is in the Hall of Fame, and he was only the fourth trainer to be the honored guest of the Thoroughbred Club of America at its annual testimonial dinner. Sunny Jim Fitzsimmons, Max Hirsch, and Preston Burch preceded him. Please allow me to tell you some of my favorite stories about my good friend, and about three other masters of the Turf whom I have come to know in my years of tradin'.

Ever the Romantic

Horatio Alger Luro was born February 27, 1901, into wealth and social position in Buenos Aires. His father, Adolphe, was a founder and president of the Jockey Club of Argentina and also served as president of that country's breeders association. Early on, the young Luro, a third-generation horseman, was required to spend as much time as possible at the distant family farm to learn about horses, which he did well. But, as he grew into his teens, he acquired another fascination—girls.

When the father of a teen-age girl observed that her courtship with Horatio was getting more serious than he desired—"too hot to handle," as Luro later described it—he whisked her off to school in France. The elder

Luro, unaware of his son's intentions, acceded to Horatio's suggestion that a holiday in France would broaden his son's knowledge of racing. Horatio followed the young woman to France, but the romance that had blossomed in Argentina faded shortly thereafter. Horatio, however, was not exactly heartbroken. "Never saw so many beautiful girls in my life," he later told me.

When Horatio did not return as scheduled, his father began to receive reports that his son was playing the races at day and the dancing girls in the cabarets at night. Adolphe Luro immediately cut off his son's allowance, stranding Horatio in Paris, where he sold Chrysler automobiles until he could hitch a ride back to Argentina on a freighter.

Horatio Luro, in 1937.

A subdued Luro worked his way back into his father's good graces. He attended the University Veterinary Schools of Buenos Aires for three years, settled down as much as his hot Latin blood, good looks, and charm would allow, and managed his father's stables until the 1930s. It was then that he started bringing Argentine horses to the U.S. to sell, and acted as agent for Americans who traveled to Buenos Aires to buy.

In about 1936, the Senor came to the U.S. to stay. He soon met Charlie Whittingham, and together they "hustled"—Luro's word—the small tracks of the West Coast from Agua Caliente to Portland with moderate success before Whittingham enlisted in the Marines after Pearl Harbor.

By 1942, Luro had worked his way into New York. There, he persuaded one of his owners, Princess Audrey Djordjaze, to become an equal partner in claiming *Princequillo for $2,500. Over the next two years, *Princequillo was to become the best distance horse in America as well as Luro's first American stakes winner. Owners with top horses rushed to him—Arnold Hanger, John Ryan, Josephine Bryce (Mill River Stable), Liz Whitney, and Herman Delman. Whittingham came out of the service to be his assistant trainer. He was made; the rest is racing history. Charlie stayed with him until the mid-

Charlie Whittingham.

1950s. Whittingham, a Hall of Fame member himself, always said: "If I'm a success, I owe it all to Horatio. He taught me."

The Senor enjoyed all aspects of the game, and that included cashing a bet. One day at Keeneland after saddling *Skin Tonic, Horatio asked me to join him in watching the race. As the horses approached the starting gate and the odds on her were still something like 20-to-1, he handed me five $100 bills to bet on her to win, which I did. After she stumbled at the start, and was ten lengths behind the field, he slumped in his chair as though the wind had been knocked out of him. But Jimmy Nichols rode a very heady race, took his time in recovering from the disadvantage, and got up to win by a neck. Now upright in his chair, Horatio smiled and said: "Even a squirrel lays away a few acorns for the winter."

A Parisian at Heart

Senor Luro's favorite destination is Paris, and his second most favorite port of call is the Riviera. Horatio prides himself on knowing his way around in Paris, but there was good testimony that he got lost at least once, when he had taken Dr. Alex Harthill there to help him inspect a racing prospect. Driving a rental car back from Longchamp, Horatio missed a turnoff. After an unusually long time had elapsed, Alex inquired: "Senor, are we lost?" Pointing with his finger toward his brain and then toward the Eiffel Tower, Luro replied: "That's my landmark, I know where we are. We'll be back at the hotel in ten minutes."

After another 20 minutes had passed, Alex asked the same question and got the same gesture and answer. When still another 20 minutes had passed and Dr. Harthill had viewed the Eiffel Tower from the east, west, and south, he asked the Senor to pull over to the curb, saying: "I want to buy some fruit at that stand." Horatio did so, but Alex went immediately to a cab parked in front of them. "Now follow that cab and we will be at the hotel in ten minutes," Harthill commented upon his return. "I've just subsidized the driver to guide us there."

Not one to be outdone, the Senor came back: "Alex, are you not enjoying this wonderful sightseeing tour I'm giving you of wonderful Gay Paree?" He did, however, follow the cab to the hotel.

A Lover, Not a Fighter

Horatio was before the stewards at Saratoga one August morning for thoroughly shaking Eddie Belmonte down to his knees upon dismounting from a horse he had not ridden to orders. The verbal exchange between the two had been translated for the judges by other Spanish-speaking riders who had heard it.

Failing to make his case, Luro stated as his last defense: "Gentlemen, I'm a lover, not a fighter." "Thirty days," replied the presiding judge. "Good," the Senor concluded. "I'm off to the Riviera for a good vacation and to get away from this pollen that's causing my hay fever." (Liz Whitney once told the Senor: "Stay out of the hay and you won't get it.")

The trips to France and the Riviera became annual pilgrimages. When Northern Dancer was still an unraced two-year-old in 1963, owner E. P. Taylor read that the colt had had a very fast workout and asked assistant trainer "Peaches" Fleming: "When are you going to run him?" Peaches noted that the Senor planned to do so immediately upon his return from France. "I'm paying the bills," Taylor instructed, "so start him in the next maiden two-year-old race that comes up." Peaches did. Northern Dancer won by 6 3/4 lengths.

They Control More Than Money

One balmy August evening in the late 1940s, as I stood outside the sales ring at Saratoga awaiting Horatio's return, a disconsolate "El Gran Senor" emerged from inside, grimacing and shaking his head. "Damn women—they have too much money. I just got outbid by one of them again. I need yearlings, young horses. I have plenty of good, older ones," he said.

In reply, I said: "Don't you know, Senor, that women control 70% of the wealth in this country? They either inherit it from their families or have it left to them by their husbands, who work themselves to death at an early age in making it." "Yes, I know that," he rejoined. "Not only do they control 70% of the wealth—but also 100% of the sex!"

At that stage of the game, Horatio was about 48 and looked 35, a strikingly tall, handsome, graceful man with an infectious sense of humor and an unparalleled personality. Women went for him in a big way, and he for them.

Already behind him were raging flings with Lana Turner and Honeychile Wilder, as well as other stars of the stage and screen, not to mention the most beautiful woman I have ever seen in racing, Liz Whitney.

But never was Horatio a late nighter, and never did he let his social life interfere with the training of his horses, of which he was the master of the most minute detail. An example: In his stable office, he kept a scale for weighing exercise boys with their tack, which sometimes included weight pads, before serious workouts. This enabled him to make a more accurate assessment of their trials and to foil the clockers, which he enjoyed doing, and get big mutuel payoffs.

Early on in this country, the Senor got himself typecast as a trainer of distance horses through his success first with *Princequillo, and then with *Iceberg II, *Talon, *Miss Grillo, and *Rico Monte, each of whom he purchased in South America for less than $50,000 for his clients. Few good, young prospects came his way other than How, Decidedly, One for All, Go Marching, and, of course, Northern Dancer. Arnold Hanger, who had his greatest racing success with *Iceberg II and *Rico Monte, invariably sent his young horses to Max Hirsch.

Horatio did not get One for All until he had failed to win for another trainer, and he developed him into a first-class stakes winner. He took How, who started her career at age two against low-priced claimers, and developed her into a top-class filly. Later in the fall at age two, How equaled the six-furlong track record at Belmont. The next year, in 1951, she won the 1 3/8-mile Coaching Club American Oaks, beating the year's champion three-year-old filly, Kiss Me Kate.

The Fling With Liz

Mary Elizabeth Whitney, who had a torrid and tempestuous love affair with the Senor, was an unforgettable person. In the 1940s, it was not unusual for her to arrive on the Saratoga backstretch at dawn in high heels, a beautiful evening gown, a full-length mink coat, and loads of jewelry after an all-night party.

During the height of their romance in the 1940s, Liz got behind on her training bills and ignored Horatio's statements, whereupon the Senor ran one of her horses for a claiming price at which he was sure the horse would be haltered. From the proceeds, as her authorized agent, he withdrew sufficient funds from her racing account to square up the indebtedness. When she complained, he explained: "Money business comes before monkey business." That ended the love affair, with Liz swearing she would get back at him one day—and she did.

It was not until 1958 that Liz slipped up on Horatio's "blind side" and got it done. She persuaded Luro to take into his stable an unraced *Windy City II colt, named Restless Wind, that she had bought at Saratoga the previous year for $10,000.

Luro found the colt to be a quick sort with a lot of ability and pointed him for the two-year-old stakes. He responded by winning the National Stallion Stakes (males) on June 16 at Belmont, then the Tremont Stakes at old Jamaica by seven lengths on July 9. Luro used Monmouth Park's Sapling Stakes, in which Restless Wind finished an unpunished third on July 26, as a prep for the first rich juvenile race of the year, the Arlington Futurity on August 2 at Arlington Park. It was then that Liz pulled the blind switch on Horatio. She transferred the horses to Charlie Whittingham and told the Senor that he was now Restless Wind's former trainer. This put Charlie and Horatio in an embarrassing and uncomfortable situation, but it did not bother Restless Wind. He won the Arlington Futurity by three-quarters of a length and collected first money of $100,475.

Horatio sued Liz for the 10% trainer's commission from the Futurity, but his case was damaged by the testimony of S. T. Greene Jr., who said the "trainer of record" customarily received the bonus. The court ruled against Luro. At a dinner party hosted by Leslie Combs II a few weeks later, a newcomer to racing asked the Senor: "What do you think of my trainer, Mr. Greene?" Horatio paused to give accent to his answer, then firmly stated: "I'll not go into detail. Suffice it to say, the name perfectly describes the man."

The Senor Settles Down

Horatio's womanizing came to a halt in 1950 when he met Frances Weinman, who was socially prominent in Atlanta and Miami and who was a generous contributor of her time and money to civic and charitable causes in both areas. Additionally, she had an attractive teenage daughter, Cary, who was winning blue ribbons with American Saddlebreds in important national shows. Horatio and Frances were married the next year.

Frances was born in Nicholasville, Kentucky. Her father, Bill, made a fortune in the early 1900s by buying mules in Kentucky and selling them to Georgia planters, then parlaying the profits into real estate investments in and around Atlanta. No one enjoyed Horatio's humor more than Frances. "Johnny," he once told me in her presence, "you just don't know the comfort of being married to a woman who is going to be very, very rich some day." A few years later, when I offered my condolences to Frances and Horatio after the passing of her father, she thanked me, and the Senor remarked: "And, Johnny, I've been so patient."

Frances and Horatio.

One night, Frances had to place a difficult phone call for her husband. Fatigued mentally and physically when he returned to their seaside cottage at Atlantic City, New Jersey, Horatio asked her to phone Mrs. Frank Turner and tell her that her filly, Nautigal, eight lengths in front on the turf course in Atlantic City Race Course's stretch, spooked at an up-flying bird, jumped the hedge, and dove into the infield lake, where she drowned. After the incident, Horatio remarked to a fellow trainer: "How do you tell an owner that her horse drowned?"

"I'm not up to it," he told Frances that night. "I'm going for a walk along the beach and try to cool myself out." About a half-hour later, when Horatio had not yet returned, Cary asked her mother: "You don't suppose Horatio drowned, too, do you?"

I don't think Luro ever lost an owner he did not want to have leave his stable, yet I never heard of his firing one. Although he would diplomatically refrain from naming his favorite, he always gave me the impression it was True Davis, of South Saint Joseph, Missouri, and Washington, D.C. True never had but one or two horses at a time with him—and seldom one of the "Saturday" variety—and he patronized the Senor more years than any other owner. "He is a sporting gentleman, Johnny," Luro once told me. "It is always a pleasure for me to pick up the phone to call him, whether the horse won or lost, and always pleasant to have a call from him."

Murdering the Idiom

The Senor may have mastered French in his youth, but his English was another matter—even after a half century. When Horatio first came to the

United States, he relished in adding slang expressions to his repertoire. Having met the top rider Johnny Adams and separately hearing the line, "I didn't know him from Adam," he understood it to be "Adams." Ever since he first used it and got a laugh, it has been: "I didn't know him from Adams." The same for "pass the buck." For 50 years, it has been "pass the bucket."

Back in the early 1950s, Luro had in his string a young horse who had won only one race, but the Senor thought he had the potential to win a stakes race toward the end of the Hialeah Park meeting in late February. He told racing secretary Charlie McLennan that he would appreciate having an allowance race for non-winners of two or three races, going short, in the next condition book, and, in the following book, one going long. Well, Charlie got it backwards.

Luro trained champion Northern Dancer and *Iceberg II.

When the first race was written "long," the Senor screamed, but he pointed the horse for it and won. When the next book came out and Horatio saw the race was slated as a sprint, he raced to McLennan's office. "Charlie," he exclaimed, "what do you think my horse is, an accordion?"

Better Than He Looks

No one has a better eye for a racehorse than Charlie Whittingham, but on one occasion it did not work for him. One afternoon back in the late 1940s, when he was Horatio's invaluable assistant, the Senor notified Charlie that in an hour or so two horses were arriving at the stable from Argentina. "The racehorse is to go into the empty stall, and just tie the lead pony to the tree until I can find a stall for him," Luro instructed.

Upon his return, Horatio nearly exploded when he found the lead pony neatly groomed, bandaged, and lying down in a deeply bedded stall. *Talon, a near-champ in South America, was tied to the tree. Through the years, Charlie has taken a lot of good-natured ribbing about this. But, in his defense, the lead pony was a very good-looking horse, while *Talon was mule-headed, angular, raw-boned, and homely, the worst-looking good racehorse I have ever seen. *Talon was one of Luro's best imports from his native land, however. In two years of racing, he won the Santa Anita Handicap, four other major distance stakes, and $270,575, which was big dough in those days.

A Cow Barn for *Princequillo

Under Luro's training, *Princequillo was to win five major distance stakes in New York, and at stud under Bull Hancock's management, he was to become the leading sire in two successive years and was the leading broodmare sire eight times over a span of 11 years. Not at all bad for a horse who had been claimed for $2,500 from Tony Pelleteri, the president of Fair Grounds Race-

**Princequillo, with Eddie Arcaro up.*

track before the outbreak of World War II. With the war came travel restrictions, and the Senor was in Miami, with little chance of getting to New York. "Ah," he said gleefully, "I ship to New Orleans. They're running."

Upon his arrival at the stable gate, he informed the stall man that he had the top stakes horse *Princequillo with him. The stall man, being no fool, quickly telephoned Pelleteri, whose reply was relayed to Horatio: "No stalls for Luro and particularly not for *Princequillo." As a result, *Princequillo spent that night in a nearby cow barn.

Senor Luro picked up the story: "I hustle around and learn the old Bradley barn was under lease, and I make a deal with lessee to sublet me stalls. Pelleteri can't say anything about me stabling in that barn and using the track because of the way the lease was written. I move *Princequillo into the Bradley barn and train over the track. I outsmart Pelleteri again!"

Clocking the Pimlico Cup

The Senor and his attention to detail even outsmarted Ben Jones in the 2 1/2-mile Pimlico Cup Handicap in 1946. Horatio had the entry of *Rico Monte and *Miss Grillo. Jones had Pot o' Luck. The Senor, having thoroughly studied the pace of previous runnings of the marathon, drew up a time schedule he wanted his entry to maintain throughout the race. He hired four clockers to help his riders execute it.

The morning of the race, Luro reviewed his game plan with the clockers and his jockeys, giving the timers green and red bandannas as well as the time schedules, and assigning them their positions (a quarter-mile apart) for the 2 1/2 laps of the track. "The green flag of a clocker means to gradually increase pace, a red flag carefully slow your pace," Horatio instructed the riders, "and if everybody follows orders we run one-two." Which they did. *Rico Monte won by eight lengths, with *Miss Grillo second, and Pot o' Luck third. *Miss Grillo returned to win the Pimlico Cup in 1947 and 1948.

He Owned the Spa

In 1947, the Senor astounded the Turf world when he won six stakes at Saratoga with five horses. With *Rico Monte, he won the Saratoga Handicap and the Whitney Stakes; *Miss Grillo, the Diana Handicap; *Pujante, the American Legion Handicap; *Talon, the Saratoga Cup; and Peace of Mind, the Albany Stakes. The first four horses had been imported from South America by Luro. I helped him to acquire the last, Peace of Mind, a two-year-old filly.

At Hialeah Park, in early February of 1947, I told Horatio I was going to Santa Anita Park for the first phase of Louis B. Mayer's dispersal. "I have plenty of older horses," he said to me, "but if you see a well-bred, good-looking two-year-old filly, ring me up." I did. On the afternoon of February 27, just a few hours before the sale, I phoned him: "Senor, I've found only one I really like. She's by *Beau Pere out *Rosary II, a mare bred by Laudy

Lawrence. Her name is Peace of Mind."

"Ahhhhhh," Horatio replied gleefully, "I know the family. Go up to $50,000 or a little bit more to get her, and call me back, even if it's in the middle of the night if you do." At about 2 a.m., I awakened Luro with good news. "We got her for $37,000." "Good," he replied. "Charge her to Jo Bryce, Mill River Stable, and have her shipped to me here at Hialeah. Thank you so very much. I feel very lucky with her already."

No Time for Dreaming

Early one morning in 1966, upon arriving at Belmont Park, Luro was approached by his van driver, who asked if the Senor was still planning on sending *Grey Dawn II down to Delaware Park for the Brandywine Turf Handicap. Looking up toward the sky as if he were checking for rain, Luro expressed his doubts. A nearby employee, hearing this, exclaimed to the Senor: "Oh, Mr. Luro, please run him. I dreamed last night he won it off by himself." More than a bit perturbed, Luro yelled: "You are fired! You were my night watchman. You don't sleep and dream when you are supposed to be watching my horses."

He Followed the Wrong Van

Once, Luro enlisted a visitor from Argentina to drive his car from Belmont to Saratoga, noting that he was driving Frances up the following day in her car. The friend was a bit hesitant because he knew neither the route nor the language. "No problem," said the Senor. "You just follow that big horse van of Charley Ebert's. It's going direct from Belmont to Saratoga. Call me when you get there."

The call came, but not from Saratoga. "I'm in Atlantic City," the excited visitor gasped in Spanish. "There were two Ebert vans, and they got switched going across the George Washington Bridge. I followed the wrong one."

Under the Elms With Sunny Jim

My fondest memories of Saratoga are my visits with "Sunny Jim" Fitzsimmons. On a bench under a huge elm tree in the paddock, he held court each afternoon to say hello to old friends and dispense wisdom and advice to breeders, owners, trainers, journalists, and race fans who sought it.

Sunny Jim retired as a trainer in 1963, and passed on three years later at age 91. He was active in our game first as a jockey and then as a trainer for 78 years, which must be a record.

Mr. Fitz, who was the first trainer to be the honored guest at the Thoroughbred Club of America's annual testimonial dinner, never lost an owner except by death. He trained for three generations of the Phipps family over 37 years, from 1926 until 1963. Since then, the Phippses have had six trainers, with only one of them leaving them because of death (Eddie Neloy in 1970). Sunny Jim was a tough act to follow.

He also trained the Belair Stud horses for William Woodward Sr. and Jr., and he had a few other owners.

Sunny Jim Fitzsimmons.

Here is a brief recital of his record: 1) Trainer of 155 stakes winners who won 470 stakes. 2) One of two trainers to have two Triple Crown winners (Gallant Fox and Omaha). He also trained Kentucky Derby winner Johnstown. 3) Trainer of the winners of more than 50 stakes at distances beyond ten furlongs. 4) Trainer of four Horses of the Year: Gallant Fox, Granville, Nashua, and Bold Ruler. 5) Trainer of two horses who became the world's leading money winner (Gallant Fox and Nashua).

Compassion for the Underdog

Mr. Fitz was compassionate for the underdog, those who were down on their luck and needed a leg up, and he was an easy touch for money. After Bobby Permane had convalesced from a broken back sustained in a fall at the peak of a fine riding career, he was reluctant to return to the saddle. Mr. Fitz encouraged him to come to his stable each morning and gallop some "easy" horses. In a short time, Bobby recovered his nerve and coordination, was back riding the old gent's horses in races, and resumed his career.

For youngsters who had no horse experience but aspired to become exercise riders, he provided many of them with a chance to learn on his horses, and a few of them became jockeys.

A Mediocre Jockey

Sunny Jim was the easiest trainer ever for a jockey to please. Never once was he known to complain about a rider's mistakes. And when a jock would apologize for his misjudgments and confess that he gave the race away, the old gent would cool him out by saying: "On my best day as a jockey, I couldn't have ridden him as well."

For ten years before he turned to training, Mr. Fitz tried to make it as a jockey. "I was mediocre at best," he once told me. "I'll never forget riding at Guttenberg when the track held racing at night under lights before the turn of the century. I hadn't had a winner in some time and needed one very badly to keep going. I got on a horse that had some speed, I put him right on the lead and was racing him along easily, when I thought I heard a horse coming to me going down the backstretch.

"I looked back quickly and I saw one. I got into my horse and rode as hard as I could the rest of the way. When I pulled up, I learned that I had won by ten lengths. I'd been trying to outrun my shadow."

He'd Gladly Trade Nashua

Mr. Fitz always maintained a great sense of humor, although he was constantly in severe pain from an arthritic back that caused him progressively to bend over more and more when he stood or walked. "My height was five-nine," he once joked. "Now it's five-four."

Al Robertson, Nashua's groom and later assistant trainer to Sunny Jim, told me about how, after the fatal shooting of William Woodward Jr. by his wife in the fall of 1955, he had remained with the colt. "I took Nashua to Claiborne Farm and stayed with him there until we found out who owned him. Then I took him on back to Mr. Fitz at Hialeah Park," Robertson said. "Upon arrival at Hialeah, there were a lot of photographers there to photograph Mr. Fitz and Nashua. One of them asked Mr. Fitz to get closer to the horse's head and to stand up straight. Mr. Fitz replied: 'Son, if I could straighten up, I'd give you Nashua.'"

'I Got a Trainer Here'

I was with Sunny Jim one morning back in the 1940s at Hialeah, when he returned to his stable with a set of horses. A youngster on a big, sulking son of Gallant Fox was told to stay on the horse because he was going out again in the next set. The rider, apparently thinking Mr. Fitz was getting forgetful,

Nashua, groom Al Robertson, and Sunny Jim.

replied the horse had just worked five-eighths of a mile. "Hey, Brian," the old gent called to his foreman, Brian Sweeney. "Get me an exercise boy. I got a trainer here." The horse worked another five furlongs, and the horse extended himself the second time.

A Legend in His Time

So indelible is he in my memory that it seems only yesterday that Hirsch Jacobs, one of the finest gentlemen and greatest horsemen who ever graced the American Turf, died on February 13, 1970. Hirsch was a legend in his time, and he remains a legend with those who knew him and those who have read about him. Arnold Kirkpatrick, who wrote his obituary in the February 21, 1970, issue of *The Thoroughbred Record*, was correct when he wrote that,

Hirsch Jacobs.

"for as long as people gather to talk about great men in racing, the name of Hirsch Jacobs will be at the top of the conversation." He was among the first 12 trainers to be inducted into the National Museum of Racing's Hall of Fame in Saratoga Springs, New York, joining Ben Jones and Sunny Jim in 1958.

I first gained Hirsch's friendship in 1942, after he had been the nation's leading trainer in races won for seven of the eight previous years. And I spent as much time with him as he or I could allow thereafter—at his stable in the mornings, in his box during racing, and frequently at his home in Forest Hills, New York, as the luncheon or dinner guest of him and his lovely wife, Ethel. He usually visited me at my office when he came to Lexington, and when he would walk in, business was over until his departure. What I wanted to learn from Hirsch was how to train horses, but he invariably changed the subject to something on which he apparently thought I had a bit of expertise—bloodlines, pedigrees, sire lines, female families. This, I think, was part of his genius. He diplomatically kept conversation on matters on which he did not consider himself an expert at the time. I never heard him discuss training with anyone.

I was always impressed by his infallible memory, his ever-alert mind and eye, and his unrelenting attention to the most minute detail. He could get to the bottom of a situation better and quicker than anyone I have ever known.

Hirsch was no instant success as a trainer. He came into racing with Charlie Ferraro, and they hustled together, racing pigeons and cheap horses. "One time in Canada," said younger brother Eugene Jacobs, "they went completely busted and Aunt Florence had to wire them $100 to get home."

In 1928 at Oriental Park in Havana, Cuba, Hirsch and Charlie again were doing little good when brothers Isidor and Phil Bieber, both very opinion-

Ethel D. Jacobs, Hirsch Jacobs, Patrice Jacobs Wolfson, and Eugene Jacobs.

ated and argumentative, had a big falling out (they did not speak to each other in the next 20 years) and split their B. B. Stable. "Let me have that young red-headed trainer," Isidor said, in asking for Hirsch. "I'll give him a piece of my action." Thus was formed the Bieber-Jacobs Stable that was destined to breed and race champions until Hirsch's death.

Never were there two such dissimilar partners on the Turf. Isidor, who was known as "Beebe," was a loud, swashbuckling, high-stakes gambler (horses, boxing, elections) and keeper of Broadway beauties. Hirsch was a quiet, conservative, family-type man who never smoked, cursed, drank an intoxicant, or bet $2 on a horse in his life. Yet, there seemed to be some underlying, undefinable kindred spirit between the two men.

Back in New York, Hirsch and Beebe started claiming, often with one not knowing what horse the other was taking. Hirsch went for the horses he thought he could improve. Beebe, always in touch with bookmakers, reached for those involved in betting coups.

For $1,000 in 1936, Hirsch bought the sore-legged steeplechaser Action, then aged seven. He put Action back on the flat and won 11 races—seven in a row, including three major New York stakes—that year.

The Bieber-Jacobs horses ran in the names of Ethel, daughter Patrice (subsequently Mrs. Louis Wolfson), and the latter's nephew, Jerome Fendrick. Only two outside people ever had horses in the stable, Henry Salsbury, who boarded the partnership's breeding stock at his farm in

Maryland, and Damon Runyon, whose Angelic became Hirsch's first stakes winner in early 1934.

By 1933, Hirsch became the nation's leading trainer in terms of races won. In ten of the next 11 years, he retained that title. And he won most of those races where they are hardest to win—in New York—with horses he claimed, bought, or bred in partnership with Beebe.

No one was his equal at improving horses. My friends Charlie Whittingham and Allen Jerkens are in a distant dead heat for second. I always wanted to know what abilities set apart this man, who was never seen reading a *Daily Racing Form*, never used a pair of binoculars, and never arrived at his barn until 7 in the morning.

Sure, he changed horses' training routines, stable handling, feeding, and shoeing, from racing on the inside to the outside, from running up front to coming from behind, from short to long and vice versa. All good trainers do that. But Hirsch Jacobs did it better. No one seems to know why, not even brother Gene, who was his foreman during those record-breaking years.

Ralph Theroux, who worked for Hirsch in his first six years on the track, recalled for me that he never saw Jacobs dressed "other than like a businessman, neatly pressed suit with tie in place, even during training hours . . . and each afternoon when he viewed his horses, he looked at them not from outside their doorways but went inside the stall of each."

Claiming Stymie

One day at Belmont Park in 1943, Hirsch sent word for his trusted groom, Joe Jones. He was claiming a chestnut colt that had struck his fancy and told Jones "to hurry over here with a halter and shank." That was how Joe became the caretaker of Stymie, who was claimed that day for $1,500 and was to earn $918,485 in his 130 starts for the Bieber-Jacobs stable. Hirsch had a hunch that Stymie, making his first start at two for Max Hirsch, would make a good distance horse, and he most certainly was right. Until Citation came along, Stymie was the richest horse of all time.

Years later, I asked Hirsch if he had ever ribbed Max about Stymie. He replied, jokingly: "Son, you never carry rope into the house of a family that's recently lost a member by hanging."

Upon Stymie's retirement, Joe told his boss he hated to part with him. "Don't worry," replied Jacobs, "the first top colt he sires I'm going to name after you, and you'll rub him." The best get of Stymie, Joe Jones, won 34 races and $423,567.

A Change in Direction

Stymie's success, along with Hirsch's genius, enabled the Bieber-Jacobs partnership to change its breeding program from one that was numerically strong but weak in quality. One Sunday afternoon in 1943, while driving from Forest Hills out to Bailey Farm at Old Westbury, where Jacobs kept his lay-ups, Hirsch asked me: "Why aren't Beebe and I breeding better horses?" He asked the question in a manner that suggested he knew the reason but not the solution. I replied that there was nothing wrong with breeding in Maryland. "But you are breeding to your own stallions, which are not getting New York horses, even in your hands. Get your mares to Kentucky; we have so many top stallions there. Remember what Federico Tesio said: 'Any man who breeds exclusively to his own stallions is doomed to failure.'"

Isidor Bieber.

"But we can't get to the good stallions in Kentucky," Hirsch replied. "You all have sort of a closed corporation down there." I insisted he was wrong. "There isn't a stallion manager there who wouldn't be delighted to have foals by his stallion trained by you," I said.

After mulling it over for a bit, Hirsch said: "Okay, we'll try it for a couple of years. I'm going to send Beebe back to Kentucky with you. Get us a good farm for boarding about five mares and bookings to the best stallions for a couple of years. Beebe will sign any necessary contracts."

It worked. For the first time, Charlie Kenney took in outside mares as boarders at Coldstream Farm and provided bookings to *Heliopolis. Margaret Glass, at Calumet, gladly allocated services to Sun Again and Bull Lea. Up to that time, the Bieber-Jacobs Stable had not bred a stakes winner. From the first year of breeding in Kentucky came the good winner Our John Wm. In the second year came Palestinian, a winner of $296,525 and sire of another good Bieber-Jacobs runner named Promised Land, himself a winner of $541,707.

A few years later, when Henry Knight bought Coldstream Farm and all of its horses, the Bieber-Jacobs breeding operation in Kentucky was moved to Dr. Charles E. Hagyard's farm. From there, stakes winners continued to come in such numbers that Bieber-Jacobs became the leading breeders for four consecutive years, 1964 through 1967. In a somewhat unprecedented action, the partnership staked farm manager Edgar Blanton each year for his good work.

The record might have been even better had Beebe not gone on a selling spree of their prized broodmares in 1947—a spree that Hirsch stopped in the nick of time.

Isidor Bieber was an action man. He could not wait from the time of the closing of racing in New York in the fall until the opening of racing in Miami. So he took his play to Maryland, which had a longer season. In his last trip there, he had an unfortunate accident. I shall never forget a scrawled letter I received from him from Baltimore. "Dear Clarksy," he wrote (Beebe always had his own pet names for people). "Here I am in the hospital. Some guy pushed me as I walked out of a restaurant, and I cracked my skull when I stumbled and fell to the sidewalk. Hope I'm able to see you in Miami."

Thereafter, obviously affected by the mishap, Beebe lost interest in racing and concerned himself with giving speeches to anyone who would listen on current events, the nation's economy, foreign policy, and the hazards of smoking.

One afternoon, Beebe walked into Hirsch's box with a special edition of the New York *Journal-American* about unidentified flying objects that had been observed throughout the country that day. "The world's coming to an

Stymie, the $1,500 claim.

end," he shouted to Hirsch, "we're selling out. Coming into the track I sold our three best mares to Major Albert Warner." Jacobs took it calmly, commenting only: "What are we going to do with the money?" But, within 24 hours, Hirsch had an agreement in writing granting him sole authority to transact the business of the partnership.

Names for His Causes

The names of Bieber's horses reflected his viewpoints on a whole host of issues. He smoked until tobacco became a national health issue, and he noted his changing view on the subject with such names as Shedon't Smoke, Burnt Throat, Puffaway Sister, and Set An Example. If someone lit up while in his box, he would invite that person to desist or leave the box. If someone lit up in an adjoining box, he would continually cough to drop a hint.

His views on rebuilding Germany after World War II were reflected in the names Nothirdchance (and her son, Hail to Reason), Letritebedone, and Remember History. When the Soviets launched their attack on Germany, Beebe came with the names Russian Ally, Russian Valor, and Russian Action. He turned against them, however, when they wanted to divide Germany, naming Champion Liar for Josef Stalin.

Honest Bread was named to protest bakers who processed with "too much yeast, not enough flour." Oilomacy and Fight Inflation revealed his thoughts on foreign and domestic policy. Hirsch shared Beebe's views on these topics. He once bought a yearling colt (*Indian Hemp—*Soft Lights II) named Nose Candy. But, upon learning that the name was slang for cocaine, he promptly changed it to Indian Buck.

An Eye for *La Troienne

In early 1948, again while discussing breeding, Hirsch asked me if he had been far wrong in predicting some years earlier that *La Troienne would become a foundation mare. I agreed wholeheartedly. She was then 22, had just produced her 14th foal, nine of them daughters, and through three of them she was already the grandam of the champion three-year-old filly of the preceding three years, including Busher, the 1945 Horse of the Year.

"I'm going to get my hands on every filly possible tracing in the female line to *La Troienne," he said. I think he only found two, No Fiddling and Searching, granddaughters of *La Troienne who were both out of Big Hurry.

Jacobs claimed No Fiddling for $7,500 as a three-year-old at Saratoga that year. He was unable to break her maiden and retired her to stud. Had No

Fiddling not traced to *La Troienne, Jacobs would have shucked her as a broodmare. It was not until her eighth foal, Straight Deal, that he got what he was waiting for. Hirsch raced her six years, developed her into a champion handicap mare, and in 99 starts she earned $733,020, the second-largest amount ever won by a female up to that time.

The Purchase of Searching

I was with Hirsch the day he bought Searching at Belmont on May 27, 1955. After saddling Patricia Lynch in the fifth race, Jacobs returned to the box to tell Beebe and me: "I finally have been able to buy Searching. We get her right after this race for $15,000. Ogden Phipps told me as I was leaving the

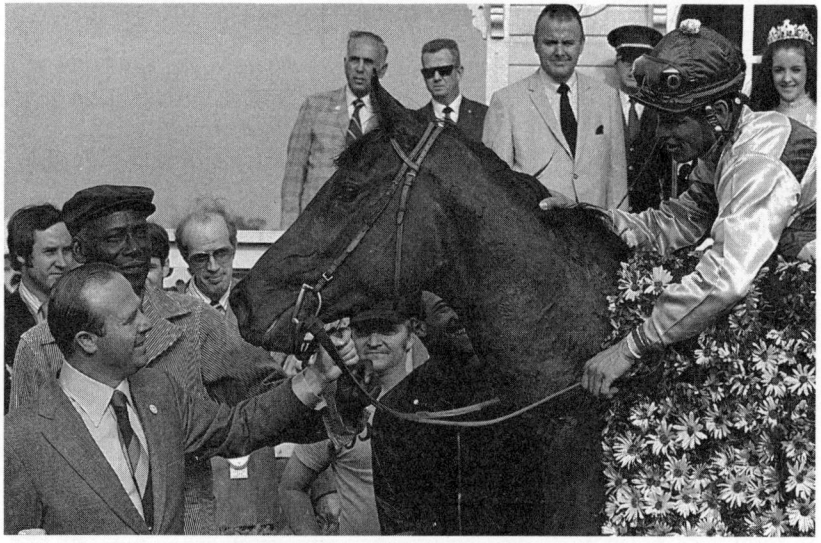

Personality after winning the 1970 Preakness.

paddock I could have her for that, and I agreed." Hirsch said he saw no great racing potential in Searching. "I've wanted her only because she's out of Big Hurry, who is out of *La Troienne," he stated. "She's a little, bitty, narrow thing, but the blood is there."

Up to that date, Searching had raced 20 times without winning, although she was second on six occasions. That day, she was second again. But exactly a week later over the same track, Hirsch stretched her out to a mile, and she led every step of the way to win by 3 1/2 lengths. By year's end, she had won 11 more races, including the Vagrancy Handicap and Gallorette Stakes.

For the next three years, through age six, Searching was to continue winning major stakes each year in New York and elsewhere, retiring from racing with 25 wins and $327,381. The long, hard grind of five years of racing and 89 starts did not diminish the breeding qualities of the honest little mare.

In her first year in the stud, Searching produced perhaps her best foal, Affectionately, winner of 28 races and $546,659 in 52 starts over four years of racing, including three divisional championships. Affectionately's rigorous campaigning did not affect her breeding qualities, either. Her first foal was Personality, 1970's champion three-year-old colt and Horse of the Year in the Thoroughbred Racing Associations poll.

Searching's second foal was the top stakes-winning filly Admiring ($184,581) and her third was Priceless Gem ($209,267), one of the few fillies to beat the colts in the Futurity Stakes at Belmont. (Buckpasser was second.) When Priceless Gem went to stud, she produced Allez France, who at one time was the leading money-winning mare of all time, with earnings of $1,380,565. Horse of the Year in France and four-time champion there, Allez France had been sold privately as a weanling to Daniel Wildenstein.

The Origins of Hail to Reason

Behind Hail to Reason, the partnership's champion two-year-old colt in 1960, lies a conversation I had with the wizard trainer and breeder that I shall never forget. Hirsch walked up to me at Hialeah one afternoon in January of 1947 and inquired:, "Young man, why weren't you at the paddock sales this morning? I bought a good broodmare prospect by *Sir Gallahad III for $10,000, Galla Colors." Astonished, I protested quickly: "Why? She's a bum. She hasn't raced, nor her two sisters before her. Why do you think Eddie Moore culled her? Why do you think you got a daughter of the leading broodmare sire of the last four years for only $4,500?" And I rattled on and on until Jacobs could get in his word: "She's got three great sires close up, *Sir Gallahad III, *St. Germans, and Man o' War, and that's half of her pedigree."

I could not have been more wrong. Jacobs did not try to race her. He sent her straight to Kentucky, had her bred to Blue Swords, and got 1951 Acorn Stakes winner Nothirdchance, the dam of Hail to Reason.

Sadly, Jacobs and Bieber, partners for 42 years, were not around in 1970 to see their horses go on to victory in two of the three races they most aspired to win—the Triple Crown contests. Johnny Jacobs succeeded his father as trainer and won the Preakness Stakes (G1) with Personality and the Belmont Stakes (G1) with High Echelon. In ill health and grief-stricken over the death

Champion juvenile Hail to Reason winning the World's Playground Stakes.

of his longtime friend, Beebe had gone into a nursing home, where he died in 1974, just five weeks before one of the best horses they ever bred, Allez France, won the Prix de l'Arc de Triomphe (Fr-G1).

Max Hirsch's Accomplishments

Max Hirsch died on April 3, 1969—at age 88—and he went out a winner, just eight hours after Heartland, whom he trained, won the feature race at Aqueduct. I knew Max rather well for the last 30 years of his life, and I felt privileged to be considered his friend. No one was ever more loyal to friends, or received loyalty to the same degree from them.

Max was born in Fredericksburg, Texas, on July 30, 1880. At age ten, he ran away from home to become an exercise boy at the Texas bush tracks and fairs, and at 14 he started riding races there. The Morrises, who had a ranch in Texas, brought him East as their jockey a year or so later. Max never thought much of his career as a jockey, although he did win 123 races from 1,117 mounts against the best of his day, in the era of Tod Sloan, "Snapper" Garrison, and Fred Taral.

Unable to continue to make the weights, Max turned to training at age 20, and by 1907 he had saddled his first stakes winner, Beauclere, in the Washington Cup at Bennings, near the nation's capital. His first truly great horse was Grey Lag, whom he bought privately as a yearling from John E. Madden in 1919.

"He was by Star Shoot," said Max, who intended to keep the horse for himself. "Harry Sinclair, one of the biggest bettors of his time, came to me one day and told me he needed a winner; the books were knocking his brains out. I told him I had Grey Lag in the next day in the Champagne Stakes and he could get even on him. He did, then after the race he asked me to price him. I told him it was $60,000, a lot of money in those days, hoping he wouldn't buy him. He didn't blink an eye—bought him." After the sale, Grey Lag was trained by Sam Hildreth.

Max used superlatives sparingly, but he always contended: "Grey Lag was the best horse I ever trained, or maybe anybody else." He also gave high marks to Sarazen and Assault. He bought Sarazen as a two-year-old from Colonel Phil T. Chinn for one of his customers, as he did another of his good ones, Roman Soldier. Assault was bred by and raced for King Ranch.

Max was a very unusual person. He attracted people of all

Max Hirsch.

Max Hirsch during his riding days.

Hirsch called Grey Lag the best horse he ever trained.

classes and walks of life. He measured them well and, although polite and gracious to all, was highly selective about those with whom he established a bond. The man who had run away from home at age ten and had no formal education had a boundless amount of "street" sense that enabled him to educate himself to the point where he was excellent company for anyone fortunate to be in his presence.

He was very self-assured and firm in his opinions, yet he never tried to force them on anyone. He only gave counsel when asked—and he was probably the most consulted trainer in New York. He hewed to the highest code of ethics in business and in life. To be a close friend of Max Hirsch was to be somebody.

Max's owners believed in him. He welcomed their input in decision-making and made owning racehorses fun for them. Can you imagine any owner allowing his trainer to use an apprentice rider on his colt in the Kentucky Derby? Morton Schwartz and Bob Kleberg both did at Max's behest. Ira Hanford won with Bold Venture in 1936, and Bill Boland (then only 17) with Middleground in 1950.

Max believed in bringing new riders into the game. He once stated: "I advocate a rule requiring each trainer to have an apprentice boy before he can get a license each year."

Chapter 10
Life Is A Gamble

Clarence Darrow, the famous lawyer, once said in defense of a client charged with gambling: "All business involves a large element of gambling. One buys something in order to sell again at a profit with no certainty that such will be the case. Practically all one's life is a gamble. In fact, if the speculative element were removed, there would be little left to live for. That is life."

It most certainly is life on the racetrack. Where else is bad luck—even for a fraction of a second—so crucial to the outcome? The fraction of a second that Man o' War was blocked in the 1919 Sanford Stakes and Native Dancer was roughed in the 1953 Kentucky Derby caused each of them to go down to their only defeat. Gambling—on the outcome of a race, on the outcome of a mating—is an integral part of the game. Let me tell you a few stories.

Cooled by the Ice

At one time, bookmaking on horse racing was a big business. It was rampant until Senator Estes Kefauver brought the biggies before his congressional committee in the 1950s and scared many of them out of business. The books were able to operate because so many influential politicians, public officials, and law enforcement agents accepted bribes, which were popularly known as "ice." The ice kept things cool for the books. It was considered as much a business expense as labor, rent, and telephone service.

Quite a number of our major, "respected" tracks maintained special accounts with bookies who dumped money into the mutuels when they wanted

185

to lay off bets that they considered too hot to handle. Without this play, some of these tracks would have gone under. With the crackdown instituted by Kefauver, those practices were banished forever. Today, racing is the cleanest and best-regulated of sports and, with its ever-constant vigilance, will remain so.

A Big Operator

The biggest operator from the 1930s into the 1950s was Frank Erickson. At his office in New Jersey, he had on most days as many as 36 telephones in operation for taking bets from throughout this country, Canada, and even overseas. He became a multimillionaire and, when Kefauver put on the heat, he retired. Seldom, if ever, did he send any "come back" to the tracks. Nor did he attempt to fix jockeys or trainers. The spread that he got by the take on the mutuels, combined with his tremendous volume of business, was good enough for him. He averaged out nicely.

For special high rollers who wanted to go racing but did not want to depress their odds with huge, last-minute bets at the track, Erickson would dispatch a special agent to accompany them. The players never had to inform the representative how much they wanted to wager or how they wanted it allocated between win, place, or show until they had observed the closing odds and the horses were in the gate.

I have been reliably informed by one old-time bookmaker that never before or since has a bookmaker operated on the scope of Frank Erickson. "On many days," he recalled, "Frank would handle more money than most tracks."

A Very Slow Pace

One of my favorite bookmaker stories concerned the fellow who was going to flimflam a bookie in a race with a five-horse field. The favorite was 1-to-10. Only two others seemed to have a semblance of a chance, and he bet heavily on them "around" the favorite. At post time, he gleefully told the bookie: "I own that 1-to-10 shot, and he ain't gonna get nothing!" "It's gonna be a damn slow race," replied the bookmaker, "because I own the two you bet on, and they ain't gonna get nothing, either."

In my early days in racing, I was amused by those who had a compulsive desire to past-post or "turn around" the bookies—and continually tried. For the most part, they lived in rented apartments or houses and were behind on one or more car payments. On the other hand, the bookmakers lived in expensive homes that they owned, ate in the best restaurants, and drove Cadillacs.

From Bookie to Breeder

One of my favorite bookmakers before the "heat" was the late Joe Metz. He had a rather successful bar and eating place in Newport, Kentucky, run by people whom he could trust, while he raced a small string of horses as an owner-trainer at Midwest tracks. Best of them was Gov. Chandler (named after Happy), with whom he won the 1938 Illinois Derby. I met him a year later, between college semesters, at the old Detroit Fairgrounds, where I toiled as a scribe for the *Daily Racing Form*. We developed a friendship that lasted until his death.

It was said that Joe would run outside the track just before it was time to saddle his horse, telephone his joint in Newport to learn how much play was on his horse, and then make up his mind if it were a "go" or "no" day. Joe always denied that to me, and I believed him. I never knew him to lie to me.

In the 1940s, the Thoroughbred Racing Associations and its investigating arm, the Thoroughbred Racing Protective Bureau, were organized. Joe had to go underground—get a program owner and trainer. He used bad judgment in his selection of an owner, a waitress in his bar and grill. When a TRPB agent called on her and asked her to answer how a waitress working mostly for tips could afford a string of racehorses, Joe quickly got out of racing, sold his Newport establishment, and took up breeding Thoroughbreds.

Joe Metz.

Joe's selection of a partner at the outset of his breeding operation was more judicious. He selected a former president of the Thoroughbred Club of America, a director of the Breeders' Sales Company, and a deacon in his church—a man above reproach by all standards. Joe leased a farm, and their mutually owned horses were kept on both farms.

The respected partner panicked a bit one evening in a phone call to Joe. "Ralph Lowe (later owner of *Gallant Man and other good ones) has an agent coming tomorrow to my farm to buy yearlings privately," he lamented, "but he doesn't like you and won't set foot on your farm to inspect those you have there that we own together." "That's no problem," Joe replied immediately, "I'll have them at your farm at six tomorrow morning—and you show and sell them like they're yours." The ploy worked.

Another slight problem caused the partnership to be terminated. The Breeders' Sales Company had a hard-and-fast policy that any consignor who gave or accepted a commission that constituted a conflict of interest would be permanently barred from selling with the company. Metz was set up. He accepted a $250 check one fall from a "fink" who turned Joe in to the company. The partner, still serving as director, was present at the next board meeting when the "evidence" was presented. He asked and received assurance from the board that they would not act on the matter until he could discuss it with Joe.

Metz exploded. "There's not a damn thing on the 'for' line of that check. Had there been, I wouldn't have deposited it. That check was payment to me for a bet the 'fink' lost to me on a Kentucky football game, and I have three witnesses to prove it. If the sales company makes any ruling on the matter, or embarrasses me in any way, I'll take them to court, get damages, and break up their cooperative." Needless to say, the matter was quickly dropped, and the partnership was dissolved at the next sale of the Breeders' Sales Company.

From that time on, Joe operated alone. He bought the L. R. Cooke farm on Shannon Run Road, stood Crafty Admiral and Royal Note there, raised very good horses—and made a lot of money. His consignments were always welcomed by the Breeders' Sales Company and later by Keeneland when the track took over the sales operation.

An Anonymous Benefactor

Lexington's bookmakers were, on average, pretty decent people—big givers to the church and to charities. I shall never forget my first year as a worker for the Community Chest, forerunner of the United Fund. I was given pledge cards with names of persons I was to contact; collectively, they had given something like $1,500 the previous year. When it looked like I was not going to obtain my quota, I called on the town's biggest book and told him my plight. Before I had finished my tale of woe, he shoved $2,000 in cash into my hand, saying: "Give it anonymously or in your own name—not mine!"

The Raid on the Lexington Club

On Saturday afternoon, October 9, 1948, one of the most humorous police actions in the long and glorious history of the city of Lexington occurred: The weekly poker game at the Lexington Club in the Phoenix Hotel was raided.

Fred Wachs, then the iron-fisted publisher of Lexington's *Herald* and *Leader* newspapers, pretty much set policy for the club—as he did for nearly every other local activity that interested him. If you wanted to get anything "done" in matters pertaining to Central Kentucky, it was extremely helpful if you first discussed your idea or plan with him and received his "blessing."

I must say I always found him to be fair, particularly in the seven years I handled Keeneland's public relations. But, in general, he had a reputation for making undue threats, meddling in matters that were none of his business, and "crucifying" those who opposed him in his monopoly press.

Earlier in October of 1948, he had summoned Detective Frank "Gum Shoe" Gravitt to his office and said he wanted all handbooks closed immediately for one week "to teach them they can't operate so openly. They've got to be discreet." Gravitt, smarting that the newspaper publisher was giving orders to the police, replied that he would think over the matter.

Gum Shoe did nothing about the books, but he laid secret plans for a raid of the poker game at the Lexington Club, whose members were the wealthiest and most influential men of the community. "Why is it right for them to gamble," he asked an assistant, "and wrong for some poor stiff to try to get lucky in a handbook?"

When that Saturday morning's combined edition of the *Herald* and *Leader* severely criticized the Lexington police for not enforcing gambling laws and noted that the handbooks were operating openly throughout the city, Gum Shoe struck the poker game at the Lexington Club. There, he arrested about a dozen of its most prominent members, all of whom gave fictitious names. When he questioned Burgess Carey, Gravitt remarked: "Okay, Burgess, what alias do you want to use?" Much to their surprise, the poker players were given citations that contained both their real names and their aliases.

Fred, knowing Gum Shoe to be fearless and highly intelligent, had a faint suspicion that he would react accordingly to the editorial, so he remained home that afternoon to listen to a radio broadcast of the Kentucky-Georgia football game from Athens. But he did not get in a lot of listening.

One by one, each of the poker players telephoned him, pleading, begging, and cajoling him to keep the police report out of his newspapers. "Hell no," Fred told each of them, including one sitting on the grand jury, "names make news. I'm going to page-one it. It'll be our best story of the year."

The case of the Lexington Club poker players was thrown out of court because no search warrant had been obtained, which Gum Shoe had failed to do by design, well knowing that there would be no suits for false arrest from such prominent citizens who would not want any more publicity. After all, he only wanted to prove the Lexington police treated rich and poor alike—and get Fred Wachs off his back.

Betting and Brawling

From what I have read in old periodicals and books on racing, the game's roughest and toughest brawler of all time was Ed Corrigan, owner, trainer, breeder, track operator, and gambler for stakes of the highest order. He dealt in excesses in all these pursuits.

His first good runner was Modesty, winner of the American Derby and the Kentucky Oaks in 1884. His next top one was Riley, with whom he won the 1890 Kentucky Derby and many other first-class stakes. He had other good ones following Modesty and Riley, but not enough to sustain his racing and breeding operation of 100 horses, which were sold at public auction at Lexington in 1908.

"Big Ed" made millions betting on horses he knew to be superior to their opposition, but he lost those millions on a reverse psychology—building new tracks to run against established tracks. His City Park, in New Orleans, lost out to Fair Grounds. Ingleside Park, in San Francisco, went under to the older Bay District track. Hawthorne, in Chicago, could not compete with Washington Park.

A Most Suspicious Bag

I got to know Paul Kelly at Hialeah in the early 1950s. We rode together on our lead ponies nearly every day, he in a Western saddle to which was attached a long, rolled-up rope, the type used for roping cattle. I never saw him use it, nor had any other racetrackers who had been around him for years. It was sort of a mystery, and Paul was a mystery of sorts in other ways—how he won bets, for example.

Paul was a pleasant, friendly fellow, yet very reticent. He would not talk about his or other people's business; he would converse only on other subjects. I never met anyone who knew so accurately when his horse would win. Paul came into racing at a time when purses were so low that the only way to make it was to win bets. Those who did not failed to survive. I was told he was the nemesis of bookmakers. He had busted so many of them, the only way he could get down was through the pari-mutuels. To throw off his foreman and stable help, he would give one of them $500 to bet for him on a "no go," but he would always "stake" them when he won a bet.

Paul trained for Jimmy Norris, a big sports gambler (boxing, baseball, hockey, you name it). Before that, his main man was Sam "Golf Bag" Hunt, a suspected mobster. Sam got the nickname by walking down a street in Chicago's Loop, a golf bag over his shoulder, shortly after another suspected mobster had been machine-gunned in his place of business on the same street. The police stopped Sam, looked into the golf bag, and found a machine gun—no golf clubs, balls, or tees. Despite this evidence, the prosecuting attorney was never able to tie Hunt to the crime.

An Action Man

One of the most colorful players and skillful trainers the Turf has ever known was Robert A. Smith, who acquired the nickname of "Whistling Bob" when he came on the New York tracks at age 12 as a stable lad for the elder August Belmont in the early 1880s. Colonel Phil Chinn, for whom he trained at times, introduced me to him at Belmont Park in the late 1930s, a few years before Whistling Bob's death in 1942.

"There, young man," the colonel noted as we meandered on, "you have met the greatest money destroyer of all time, and I'm no piker at that game. He's an 'action' man. Can't pass up a bet on a race or a prizefight. He's always been a top trainer, made big money, but he blows it as fast as he gets his mitts on it."

Whistling Bob left the Belmont stable in 1887 and went out on his own as a trainer at age 18. That year,

"Whistling Bob" Smith.

he hustled enough money to buy his first horse, a swayback colt from the yearling sales at Sheepshead Bay. Whistling Bob's $210 colt, Tenny, was to become one of the greatest runners of his day (earnings of $87,025) and was immortalized in a painting by Edward Troye.

Cavalcade, winner of the 1934 Kentucky Derby.

Good horses and good owners were ever on their way to Smith, and among his patrons were Walter M. Jeffords, James Cox Brady, Audley Farm, Jefferson Livingston, and Isabel Dodge Sloane. For Mrs. Sloane, he bought Cavalcade for $1,200 at the Saratoga yearling sales and trained him to win the 1934 Kentucky and American Derbys. Cavalcade retired with earnings of $127,165.

Mrs. Sloane's Brookmeade Stable was loaded with stakes horses that year—High Quest (Preakness Stakes; Cavalcade was second), Good Goods, Time Clock, Psychic Bid, Special Agent, and Good Harvest. With total earnings of $251,138, her stable rose to the top of the owners' list in 1934. It was, however, just "another" year for her trainer. Although Whistling Bob drew a handsome salary plus 10% of those earnings, he ended the year "tapped out." He had to back any of his horses who he thought had "a chance." He often said: "I just can't let them run naked."

In 1925, James Cox Brady entered the Thoroughbred game. He bought Dixiana Farm; hired the person considered the best adviser, Chris Fitzgerald; the best farm manager, Howard Oots; and the finest trainer, Whistling Bob Smith. The next year, he called a meeting of his three key men at Dixiana and told them he was more than pleased with the manner in which they had organized his Thoroughbred operation. To show his appreciation, he was giving each of them a block of stock in Chrysler Corporation or the cash equivalent. He stated he had great faith in the growth potential of Chrysler stock.

Fitzgerald and Oots, knowing Brady to be a financial genius, immediately accepted the stock and thanked their benefactor for the advice to hold it. Whistling Bob, true to form, took the equivalent in cash. "I'll run mine up in the betting ring," he noted. The adviser and the farm manager retired years later as millionaires off their Chrysler stock. Whistling Bob was "tapped out" again in a few months.

In the late 1930s, failing health and heart attacks restricted Smith's training, but he somehow came up with enough "scratch" to stay in "action," although it was on a much smaller scale. On one occasion, as he was hurrying to the paddock to gather some intelligence for the next race, down went Whistling Bob with another heart seizure. J. P. "Sammy" Smith, another colorful racetrack character, saw him fall, told a security guard to call an ambulance, and hurried to his friend's side. "Sammy," Bob whispered as he gasped for air, "there are three twenties in my right pocket. Bet 'em across the board for me on Max Hirsch's horse if he likes him. He's a price."

Finally, in December of 1942, the "big one" felled Whistling Bob. Sammy rode in the ambulance with him to the hospital. "What are his chances?" Sammy asked the examining physician. The doctor, thinking the old man was in a coma, replied, "only one chance in ten."

Hearing this, Whistling Bob barely opened his eyes and gasped: "Doc, I'll take those odds for the ten that's in the right pocket of my pants." The physician, to soothe his patient, quietly said to him: "Okay, you're on," the dearest words ever to an "action man," regardless of whether he was destined to win or lose. A few moments later, Whistling Bob passed on, serene in the knowledge that he was "down." The game had lost another colorful racetracker who enriched our lives and the lore of racing.

The Train Ruined This Bet

W. J. "Rusty" Marlman, a trainer who wintered at Hialeah Park in the 1960s, was telling his tale of woe outside the racing secretary's office one afternoon.

"I let this guy from the beach bet on my horse in the last race yesterday, the one that paid $58, but to beat the crowd he leaves before cashing. I can't find him anywhere. I phone him up, and he tells me he'll meet me at the stable gate before today's first race. I'm there looking down Palm Avenue and here he comes flying, trying to beat that switch engine at the railroad crossing. He doesn't.

"I run down there. His car is all smashed in, and he's dead as a doornail. I try to tell the cops he's got my mutuel tickets and to get 'em off him and give 'em to me. They tell me to beat it before they lock me up. There went my fifty-six hundred. Damned if I don't have the worst luck!"

A Heavy Plunger

Back in the late 1950s, a track detective came to Marje Everett at Arlington Park with what he thought was an alarming report. "There's a valet in the jocks' room who's betting $14,000 a day on the races here. You got to get him out of there."

Marje asked if he was placing the bets with bookmakers or through the mutuel windows. "Through the windows. That's how I found out about him," he said. "I've checked with the mutuel clerks. That is how I learned the amount of his betting, and his name—Tex Sutton."

Much to his astonishment, Marje told the security agent: "Leave him alone so long as he's putting the money through the windows." Tex long since has learned you can beat a race but not the races. He developed a large and successful domestic air transportation business for horses.

Tex Sutton.

The Vet Knew the Field

John Gaver once called Dr. William H. "Bud" Wright at about ten on a Saturday morning, very much disturbed about one of Greentree's best horses who was to run in a stakes that afternoon. Pointing to a slight filling on one of the horse's legs, John said: "Guess I better scratch him, shouldn't I?"

However, after examining the area and stating that it was of no consequence, Dr. Wright advised: "Run him—and I think he'll win." As Bud got back into his station wagon, Gaver yelled: "Since when did you become a handicapper?" "Tell you later," Bud replied. The Greentree horse won.

The next morning, when Dr. Wright stopped by the Greentree barn and found the filling completely gone, Gaver asked: "What did you know that I didn't?" Bud said: "I'd been treating four of the toughest horses in the race, and not one of them was as sound as your horse. But I couldn't ethically tell you that."

The Bookie Was a Cop

Sandy Hook was a delightful Irishman and completely uninhibited. He freely expressed every thought or emotion that entered his mind—joy, anger, hate, humor, love, whatever. I never knew a horse or man to challenge him. And he was never cruel to either. He commanded respect.

That was why Calumet Farm trainer Frank Kearns put him to rubbing Bull Lea, who was a pretty tough customer. His biting, kicking, and pawing would intimidate other grooms, but not Sandy. They had a mutual respect.

My favorite story about Sandy concerns a situation that occurred when he was rubbing horses in New York. Buddy Raines had shipped in from New Jersey a filly who had fully extended another filly, who was cared for by Sandy. "Watch and tell me when that filly runs back," Sandy, who could not read, asked his foreman. "I'm gonna bet on her if it's here or down in Jersey."

Ten days later, he was told she was back in, and he was directed to a bookmaker outside the track. "Want to bet ten dollars across the board on Buddy Raines's filly in the fourth," Sandy told the bookie. "Don't know her name, you just look her up." The clerk found her name, took Sandy's money, gave him his ticket—and then issued him a citation for illegal gambling. Those were the days of Mayor Fiorello La Guardia's cleanup of vice and illegal gambling in New York, and he had plainclothes cops clerking in the books.

At his trial, the judge imposed a fine on Sandy. "Ain't paying it," replied Sandy. "You owe me $75.60. When you bet a book, especially one run by a cop, you expect to get paid. So I want my payoff, and if you don't pay me I'm walking out."

Sandy's statement caused virtual pandemonium in the courtroom, and by the time the judge had restored order, Sandy had quietly walked out right before the astonished judge and bailiff. Several times, a police squad car called at his stable at Belmont, but each time it was spotted in time to hide Sandy in the loft while the officers were told he had "jumped town."

A Falsified Scratch

Racing, like any other business, has its share of slickers and con men, people who subsist by their wits rather than gainful employment. Here is a ploy that worked once for one of them. A trainer was reading the *Daily Racing Form* one morning and commented: "If that horse wasn't in the first race, my horse would win at a big price. I'd not only bet him, but I'd wheel him in the double." A slicker, overhearing the conversation and deciding he would help the man with his plight, scratched the problem horse by forging the signature of his trainer. The trainer, very sure of his horse, did not think to check the scratches, and it was not until the program came out—and too late to do anything about it—that he learned his horse had been withdrawn. He did, however, create a ruckus.

Track security officers questioned those who cashed in on the deal, but each insisted he had handicapped the race himself. The culprit was never detected.

Taking a Short Cut

Bobby Dotter.

For his lead pony, owner-trainer Bobby Dotter always had a Thoroughbred who could run as fast as his trainees. He won many a bet from unsuspecting trainers who thought they were better mounted. One morning back in the 1960s, Dotter and George Baker were on the backside of the Aiken track waiting for their sets of horses to pull up. "George," said Bobby, "when our horses get pulled up, I'll race you for two hundred bucks from here to the finish line." To Bobby's great joy, George agreed. At the appointed time, when they both broke off, George quickly checked his pony, jumped the inside rail, and headed at full speed across the infield toward the finish pole, where he again jumped the rail and halted.

About 20 seconds later, when Bobby had pulled up and galloped back to Baker, George said: "Bobby, give me two hundred. I beat you an eighth of a mile." Noting good-naturedly he had been "had," Dotter dug down in his pocket and handed over two "Franklins" to George.

'Goofy Gerald' Cashes In

He was known only as "Goofy Gerald," a misnomer if there ever was one. His hustle stood the test of time, some 20 years to my personal knowledge, at the New York and Miami tracks. Everything he took in was pure profit; he had no overhead. He passed out overnights, sheets listing the following racing day's entries, which he got for free from the racing secretary's office.

Gerald, unknowingly or by design, looked absolutely pathetic. He was a small, roundish man with a reddish-hued, weatherbeaten face, tattered clothes, and faded suspenders, never evenly adjusted, that were forever slipping off his round shoulders.

An hour before first post each racing day, Gerald would arrive at his station, just inside the gate through which owners and trainers passed when coming from and going to the horsemen's parking lot. His transportation was a battered old bicycle with worn-out tires that he methodically secured to any nearby iron fixture with a large padlock and heavy chain. Besides his frayed clothing, the bike appeared as his only other earthly possession.

Few passed Goofy Gerald without taking an overnight and leaving a gratuity. To each person who accepted his offering, whether or not there was a drop, he would politely say: "Good luck." Early on, owners and trainers, superstitious lot that they are, associated good fortune with tipping Gerald and seldom passed him by. On one occasion, one who had two odds-on favorites beaten by bad racing luck told me: "I'll never pass up 'old Goof' again."

After the second race each day, Gerald would carefully check the security of his bike, then disappear into the crowd, only to return to his station after the feature race, when the exodus of horsemen would begin. He was again in business.

I often used Gerald's gate as a meeting place. Once while awaiting a horseman, I noticed a passerby had given Goof a Canadian quarter. "He stiffed you, Gerald. That's not a U.S. coin," I observed. "I know," he replied. Then, with a wink of an eye, he continued: "Don't worry, I shall use it. It shall be passed on."

Once, outside the racing secretary's office at Belmont, I asked an assemblage of jock agents (they know more about what is going on in racing than any other one group) some questions about Gerald. What's his daily take? The consensus: "About 75 skins a day." Where does he sleep? "At the nearest Salvation Army post or YMCA." What does he do with his money? "He's a diehard horse player."

One day, when Goof appeared at the secretary's office to pick up his stack of overnights, he asked Jack Campbell for permission to place a large glass jar on the front counter. A sign attached to it with rubber bands displayed this scrawled message: "gerald is going home. am leaving racetrack for good. thanks for any help." The permission was granted.

Campbell, the most generous man that ever set foot on a racetrack, opened his wallet and started cramming ones, fives, and tens into the jar, priming it well. Nearly every horseman who entered the secretary's office that day contributed. After the last race, Goof collected the jar—and its contents!

But Gerald's reappearance before the first race the next day to pick up overnights nearly was his undoing. "What are you doing here?" Campbell thundered. To which Goof replied: "Mr. Campbell, who ever heard of a guy quitting the racetrack with $185 in his kick?"

"Okay," said Campbell, restraining a grin, "from now on you're going to be allowed only one hustle, and that's with the overnights. Now get out of here." When Gerald departed, Campbell broke into laughter as he turned to Francis Dunne: "I'm glad I'm not the only one who got suckered into Gerald's swindle," he said.

After that it was the same old hustle for Goofy Gerald. His take was off for a few days while his *bon voyage* contributors cooled out, but they all did come around again.

The Burial Fund

Another old hustle on the racetracks, before the advent of the Horsemen's Benevolent and Protective Association, was the "burial fund." Generous givers that they are, horsemen were easy marks. There was one case where the "deceased" merely stayed off the job a couple of days and split the "fund" with the solicitor.

"Sunny Jim" Fitzsimmons, a real soft touch, was "had" so many times he finally was compelled to suggest: "Have the funeral director bill me directly for a hundred. The last time I handed out to bury one of our brethren, he claimed a horse off me the next day."

Betting Came First

Randy Sechrest died in 1982, only eight days after the death of Bold Bidder, the best horse he ever trained. Randy saw talent in the colt and persuaded Paul Falkenstein to put up the $45,000 purchase price for Bold Bidder, beaten 55 lengths in the 1965 Belmont. He assured Paul he would get him sound, and indeed he did. In his first stakes start for them, Bold Bidder took the Jerome Handicap at odds of 81-to-1, and before the end of the year he had

Trainer Randy Sechrest with Bold Bidder.

won a couple more major stakes and was ranked as the eighth-best three-year-old male of 1965.

John Gaines saw in the son of Bold Ruler a lot more good racing days and a bright future at stud. He purchased him for $600,000, subject to veterinary examination, and dispatched Dr. Arnold G. Pessin.

Randy was a compulsive horse player. He had to have action every day. When Arnold arrived at Aqueduct just before the last race one day in the fall of 1965, he remarked to Randy: "Let's hurry over to Belmont so I can examine that horse. I've got a short time to catch a plane back to Lexington."

"Wait a few minutes, I got to bet on the last race," Randy replied.

Not averse to betting on a "good thing," Arnold pulled out two "Franklins," and suggested: "Let's both bet and leave; we don't have to watch the race."

"Can't do it that fast. First, I got to read the past performances, then handicap the race, then we can bet, and then we can go."

"First time I ever heard of a $600,000 deal being held up by the handicapping of eight starters in a $5,000 claiming race," laughed Arnold, who at that time did not know Randy well.

Randy was a kind, charitable soul, liked by everybody on the racetrack. A recovering alcoholic, there was one thing that always got his immediate attention—a phone call from Alcoholics Anonymous to go to the aid of a brother who had fallen off the wagon. Once, Randy tried to break the spell of the mutuel windows. He bought and started operating a motel in California. But that experience was short-lived. He was soon back at the track.

Beating the Crowd

Joe Palmer once wrote that the "true test" of placing judges "is the ability to throw up the finish of the last race and beat the crowd out of the track." Efforts by officials and other track employees to "beat the crowd" have been the basis for many a humorous yarn.

One wet winter at New Orleans, when Jack Campbell was racing secretary and handicapper at Fair Grounds, he was having trouble filling the entries because of muddy tracks. On an occasion when the only horse possibly available to complete the field for the next day's feature was on the starter's schooling list, Campbell called in the starter and told him: "Let me have that horse. I need him badly. Take him off the list so I can use him tomorrow."

The starter refused, and Campbell told him: "I have it on pretty good information this horse is on your list because of a personality clash you've had with his trainer. I, too, can play this game."

The last race on each racing card that winter had customarily been at a mile or slightly longer, placing the start in front of the grandstand or clubhouse. Immediately after the field was dispatched, the starter and his assistants would dash to the nearby horsemen's parking lot, jump into their cars, and beat the crowd—with ease.

To foster a spirit of cooperation in the starter, Campbell scheduled the last event at six furlongs for the next five days, forcing the starting crew to walk or run from the backside to their parked cars. Seldom did the starter and his crew beat the crowd.

I shall never forget in the early days of Keeneland when the operator of the photo-finish camera averted a disturbance, in large part because he was holding a live mutuel ticket that was about to be invalidated by placing judges trying to beat the crowd. In their haste, they had posted the wrong order of finish, then bolted for the parking lot. Immediately, the camera operator rushed to the stewards' booth. "Please," he begged, "don't make the finish official until I bring you the picture of it. They've got the second and third horses switched."

The stewards immediately flashed the "inquiry" sign on the tote board and telephoned the placing judges' stand. No answer. By the time the camera operator returned with the picture that vindicated his observation, a steward had posted the correct order of finish. The "official" sign followed—as did some stern admonishments to the placing judges the next morning.

Chapter 11
Around the Circuits

At all times during racing's long history, the racetracks have been populated by an amazing variety of colorful characters. Unfortunately, some of their stories have been lost over the years. I remember some of them, and I have been told about others who lived before I actively became involved in training and tradin'.

One of the more colorful figures from around the turn of the century was William C. Daly, who was the first person to make a specialty of developing jockeys. Daly, who was widely known as "Father Bill," instructed all of his jockeys: "Go to the front and stay there until you're out of horse." Thus came about the expression, not much used anymore, for being on the lead in a race—"on the Bill Daly."

Father Bill's school at old Sheepshead Bay in Brooklyn was very successful, and he attained a bit of wealth from it. Graduates of his school were some of the outstanding riders of that era: Jimmy McLaughlin, Edward "Snapper" Garrison, Winnie O'Connor, and Danny Maher. In those days, Daly was selling jockey contracts for as much as $10,000 apiece.

Often, he would have as many as a dozen or so youngsters, most between the ages of 12 and 14, all of them bound to him by "adoption" or "legal contract." Runaway kids were welcomed into his school if he thought they would not grow too heavy to ride. Discipline was tough. The kids worked from dawn to dusk, grooming horses and performing other stable chores when not riding. They were fed and sheltered at the Daly stable. Those who got out of line—more specifically his "line"—he thrashed with a rawhide whip, which kept him in constant trouble with child abuse organizations and the police. Daly was a tough taskmaster, but he did develop more top riders than any other man of his day.

A runaway pupil, with severe whip cuts up and down both bare legs, once appeared at the Coney Island police station, appealing for his "freedom."

"How old are you?" asked the desk sergeant.

"Sixteen," replied the youth.

"When will you be 14?" the officer continued.

"Just as soon as you get my adoption papers away from Mr. Daly!"

"Father Bill" Daly.

Fooling the Humane Official

Father Bill Daly practiced borderline cruelty not only on the pupils of his jockey school but also on any sore-legged horse in his possession. His treatment was, alternately, icing and steaming a sore leg to stimulate circulation and remove soreness. The Society for the Prevention of Cruelty to Animals, a frequent visitor to his stable, finally thought it had "caught him in the act."

The horse, standing in a tub, seemed in intense pain from the near-boiling water. Father Bill increased the temperature by adding more hot water, just as the enforcement agent arrived and announced: "This time I've got you, Mr. Daly."

"That's not hot," the old man answered. "Watch me put my foot and leg in that tub," which he did. The agent walked away dumbfounded, little knowing that the leg Father Bill had plunged into the hot tub was made of wood, a false one that he had had made years before following an amputation.

Older Than He Looked

Back in the 1920s, truant officers frequently raided the old Kentucky Association track in Lexington to pick up youngsters not in school. One spotted Howard "Squeaky" Stearns, who had a youthful appearance at age 25, and asked trainer Danny Stewart why he was not in school. "Take off your hat," Danny instructed Squeaky. Startled to find him completely bald, the truant officer blurted: "Well, I'll be damned!" Squeaky had lost all his hair due to a high fever associated with a childhood sickness.

They Had To Be Tough

The Thoroughbred must have been mighty tough and strong before the turn of the century. In an 1892 interview with a New Orleans newspaper, James Rowe, the foremost trainer of his day, described how he trained horses. Here are a few of his quotes:

Edward "Snapper" Garrison.

"Just as soon as we got them (unbroken yearlings) off the cars I would have a bridle put on and a boy put up, and usually they were so tired they couldn't raise much of a fuss... and (they'd) give in.

"If they were broken in the middle of July, a good time to try them is the latter part of October. I always tried them thoroughly as yearlings. . . . I usually tried them two or three times at three furlongs, and after that I breezed them along for a half (mile) two or three times. If the first trial didn't satisfy me, I'd give them a rest of a day or two and try them again.

"The best trial I ever had (from a yearling) was 36 seconds (for three furlongs).... She carried 122 pounds.

"It is better for their shins to 'buck' while they are yearlings; they get sore sooner or later anyhow, and it is just as well to get all the little troubles and hinderances one can over before racing begins.

"A hardy horse can race twice a week without doing himself any harm. . . . It is an odd fact two-year-olds require more work and will stand more hard racing than an older horse."

These training procedures, just the exact opposite of those of our leading trainers today, give further credence to the point that it is impossible to compare horses of different eras.

James Rowe Sr.

Matt Winn Could Have It

Gone are the days of the tough old stewards who were The Law. Recalcitrant horsemen called before them seldom got a hearing. In most cases, they only appeared before the judges to learn what their penalty was, and often the ruling was handed down in an abusive, insulting manner. Those rulings stuck.

In those rugged days, there were few, if any, appeals of rulings to racing commissioners or the courts. Those old-time judges knew nothing of due process, or they chose to ignore it. Frequently, they exceeded the power vested in them by the rules of racing, and their questioning of suspects often went into matters not germane to the issue.

Initial rulings against offenders were not harsh, but for repetitions of misconduct, they were severe, to put it mildly. In those days, racing jurisdictions did not have reciprocal agreements honoring each other's rulings. Often, the presiding steward would tell a jock: "Pack your tack; we're giving you the meeting," or "You're through here—and don't come to ride at any other track where any of us is serving." Trainers were told: "By tomorrow night, you and all your horses will be off the grounds."

Once, when one comical jock was told he had been "given the meeting," he retorted: "I'm giving it back to Colonel Matt Winn. He ain't doing no good with it, so I know I can't."

A Steward From the Old School

The only "old time" steward I knew was Sam Nuckols, uncle of Alfred and Charlie. He had mellowed by the time we first met in the late 1940s and became friends, but he still could needle. Jocks' agents were his favorite prey. I was visiting with Sam one morning in the stewards' office at Tropical Park when one came in to get his license application approved. The judge asked me to stay. In answer to the judge's various questions, the agent noted his own weight was 280 pounds, his jock's 95; he drove a current-model Cadillac, the jock a three-year-old Ford.

Sam Nuckols.

Putting his initials and okay on the application, Judge Nuckols observed: "This doesn't make sense to me. I can't see how a 95-pound boy, who drives an outdated Ford, can support a 280-pound man with a brand new Cadillac. Don't let me catch you touting!"

The next one in to see the judge was a woman with her application for a groom's license. After reading it and initialing his okay, he freely gave her his thoughts on women working on the backstretch and admonished her: "Above all, you must be chaste in your conduct there." She snatched the license from his hand and, as she stalked out of the office, turned to him and said sarcastically: "Who do you think you've been addressing, your wife?" Judge Nuckols just grinned.

I asked the judge what was the best alibi he had had from a jock for a form reversal. "Had a good one last summer up at Narragansett," he chuckled. "He said he'd like to refer me to the Bible, in the New Testament, Book of Matthew, chapter 19, verse 30. It says: 'The first shall be last and the last shall be first.'

"I told him I was going to give him more time to read the Bible and less time to read the odds board—60 days. That night, I checked the Gideon Bible in my hotel room. By golly, he had the right citation and quoted it correctly."

The judge was working the Centennial Park meet near Denver in 1952. Stephen Strang, of Meeker, Colorado, invited him out to his nearby ranch one Sunday afternoon, feeling the old gent was a bit lonely and could use some hospitality on his day off. Offered some very old bourbon, the native Kentuckian coyly replied: "Haven't touched it in years, but I'll be a good guest and just have a taste."

Interspersing racing stories between sips, the judge singlehandedly consumed the whole fifth, "but left the house cold sober so far as his speech and coordination were concerned. We enjoyed him immensely," said Strang. Judge Nuckols never bet on a horse once he started officiating, but he was a shark at cards or dice. Many who took him on, thinking they had an edge because he was drinking, were stripped bare.

He Knew His Isaiah

Back in his boyhood during the 1930s, Charlie Nuckols knew a lot more about racing than about his Bible lessons in Sunday School. One Sunday, when the teacher asked what had happened to Isaiah, Charlie quickly replied: "Ma'am, he finished second in the feature race yesterday at Latonia." Isaiah was quite a nice stakes horse, bred and raced by James W. Parrish of Midway, Kentucky.

This Gelding Had Been Roaming—But Where?

The Thoroughbred Club of America paid tribute to Charlie Nuckols as its honored guest at the 1987 testimonial dinner. Needless to say, he is the complete horseman, but he is also a role model for anyone entering or participating in our business. In his private life, he exemplifies the highest standard of conduct.

Charlie and I have been friends for more than 50 years, and during that time we have been partners on some horses and have done a lot of buying and selling and tradin' with each other. Not one of those transactions had to be put into writing.

Little or nothing has been written about it, but Charlie served as a steward at River Downs in Cincinnati in the late 1940s to broaden his knowledge of racing. One day when he had the morning duty, a young man who had been trailering his horses onto the track for workouts asked permission to run an unraced six-year-old gelding. Of obscure breeding, the gelding had been electrifying the clockers with five-eighths in around :58. The horse was a bay without markings and without a tattoo. His teeth indicated he was six. He matched his certificate of registration.

Charlie Nuckols.

"Where's this horse been all this time?" asked Charlie, who had heard the horror stories of ringers whose markings had been painted on or off—even the entire coat color changed—to fit another horse's description.

"Well," replied the young owner-trainer, who had been licensed before, "when we weaned him from his mother, we cut him, then turned him back out on the range. Weren't able to catch him until last fall." Charlie asked the young man to come back the next morning, and meanwhile he would do some checking. He wanted to give the young man a fair shake.

From Lillian Brennan at the Jockey Club, he learned that the gelding had not been registered until he was a late yearling (when he was supposed to be running the range), and from me he learned that his sire had about a half-dozen foals to race and no winners. From about 15 foals out of the first two dams, only eight had raced, with no winners. The next morning, Charlie gave the aspiring young horseman the bad news. The horsewas never returned to the track for a morning workout the rest of the meeting.

The next spring while Charlie was in my office on other business, he said: "While I'm here, look up and see if that horse I called you about from River Downs ever raced." Quickly I checked the chart book index for the previous year. The gelding had not raced. "You mean," Charlie laughed, "under that name!"

Well, Something Should Be Fixed

Not every racing official is as knowledgeable as Charlie. I shall never forget what one racing commissioner told the late, great Turf commentator, Joe Palmer, when he was asked what the political appointee thought about the "breakage"—the difference between the actual odds payout and the rounded payout that is posted on the tote board. In most cases now, the payouts are rounded to the next lower 20 cents. Mathematically, a wager might pay out $4.75, but the payment will be $4.60. The whole concept, however, was lost on the commissioner. "If someone breaks something," he replied, "I think he certainly should be punished if he doesn't immediately pay for it."

The Poor Horse Got Knocked Off

Keene Daingerfield, the dean of American stewards, recalled one other absurdity committed by a racing commissioner. A trainer was appealing his suspension in a "hop" case, and his employees testified that the horse was closely guarded before the race in question.

One commissioner was cross-examining an old groom about his whereabouts during the afternoon of the race. "I was rubbing only one horse at the time. When I came back from the betting ring, I picked out his stall, filled up his water bucket, give him some more hay, grained him, then knocked him off (in the argot of the racetrack, brushed or ragged him), then left for the night."

"What?" exclaimed the benighted commissioner. "You knocked him off—you killed the poor creature!"

An Official Ahead of His Time

If there ever was a racing official "before his time," it was Marshall Cassidy. He died in 1968, at age 76, when a truck jumped the median of a New York highway and crashed head-on into the car he was driving. Kent Hollingsworth wrote this about him: "A man of honesty, strong will, and vision, he looked for the right of things, and was unwilling to compromise for what he thought was less than right."

He had power, more than any person I have ever known in racing. It was given to him without limit by the many tracks where he served as a starter and steward, in Mexico, Canada, and the U.S., and by the Jockey Club as its

Marshall Cassidy.

H. Guy Bedwell.

executive secretary. But he used this power judiciously and with compassion.

Back in the 1940s, a horseman displeased by a suspension Cassidy handed him remarked that he was the "czar" of racing and ruled by "Marshall law." Those witty terms caught on and were often repeated by others who did not like the way he handled matters that pertained to them.

Eddie Arcaro thought differently. Once, Cassidy gave him an entire year off for rough riding. Arcaro was grateful for it. "The idle year gave me time to do a lot of thinking. I learned how to control my temper," he said.

An illustration of Cassidy's compassion was his request in 1938 that the Jockey Club reinstate the trainer's license of H. Guy Bedwell, who had been ruled off for life in 1920, one year after he had won the Triple Crown with Sir Barton, a maiden going into the Kentucky Derby. Bedwell had been the nation's leading trainer by races won in six successive years, 1912-'17. "Eighteen years is a long time," Cassidy said. The Jockey Club acquiesced.

I experienced some of Cassidy's compassion personally. In the winter of 1955-'56, I was training a small string of racehorses and playing polo in Camden, South Carolina. That spring, I found I had four two-year-olds that "could run." They needed to go to New York to be raced and eventually to be sold. I could get stalls in

New York (Mrs. Marion duPont Scott invited me to use her private barn), but getting a license for my head exercise boy, whom I shall refer to only as Art, posed a problem.

I telephoned Cassidy, whom I had known since 1939, and told him I needed very badly to bring Art along, but feared he would not be licensed in New York. I explained that Art had been convicted of a minor crime but had served only three months and was out on probation. His answer came quickly: "If you trust him, I do. Bring him along." (The foray was successful as two of the fillies, Dotty Bishop and Jane Gess, ran third and sixth in the Rosedale Stakes.)

Cassidy, in his 60 years in racing, served in nearly every capacity—from hot-walker, to groom, to blacksmith, to exercise boy, to jockey, to trainer, to starter, to racing secretary, to patrol judge, to steward, to executive secretary of the Jockey Club. He was honored by the Horsemen's Benevolent and Protective Association at its 1955 national convention "for his great contribution to the sport of racing." His other contributions to our game have been many. I will try to list those I remember:

- Cassidy helped to develop the present-day, portable starting gate with stalls supported from overhead steel structures, enabling quicker and safer starts.
- He invented the photo finish, first with one camera on the outside, then with two cameras—one inside and one outside—and finally with one camera on the outside with a mirror on the finish pole to give both views.
- The electric timer was invented by Cassidy.
- He invented the movie patrol.
- Cassidy was the first steward to allow the press and media to view the films as the stewards viewed them before making a decision.
- He introduced the saliva test, first for the winner, then for the winner and the horse that finished second, and later for random checks of other starters or a specific starter.
- Pre-race veterinary examinations to certify that all starters were sound for racing were first introduced by Cassidy.
- He introduced the photographing of night-eyes of horses for identification purposes.
- The practice of rotating officials so all would be thoroughly experienced with the duties of each other was introduced into racing by Cassidy.
- He started the Jockey Club school for officials, whereby the inexperienced could get on-the-job training and others attended the refresher courses.
- Cassidy initiated the Jockey Club Round Table Conference, held each August at Saratoga, whereby people in the U.S. and other countries can exchange views on matters pertaining to racing and breeding.

- Blood-typing to verify parentage of Thoroughbreds was introduced by Cassidy.
- He instituted the recording of equipment worn by starters in each race and also the type of shoes worn.
- He was the first to send the registrar of the Jockey Club to forums held throughout the country, and dispatched employees of the Registration Department into the field.

Recalling in the later years of his life his experience in our game, Marshall Cassidy wrote: "Because certain innovations in racing are credited to me, I rather welcome the opportunity of explaining why I do not deserve special acclaim.

"Every effort of mine that was successful has been rewarded to a thousand times over in my satisfaction that I was contributing to the welfare or improvement of the sport I love. Perhaps, now that life is nearly over, I can be extremely happy in boasting that I never accepted a cent for any project I introduced. My life has been letter-perfect for me, and I would not change a single thing if I had it to do over again."

Francis Dunne.

Cassidy was not one dimensional. He excelled in his hobbies, also. He participated as a prizefighter, performed as a skilled, daredevil motorcyclist, rode broncs in a rodeo, flew planes well enough to obtain a commercial pilot's license, and was certified as a deep-sea diver.

I never found him to be a "hail fellow well met" or full of jokes and laughter, although I never knew him well enough to make a judgment that he did not have a lighter side. He surely had one, because he was a close friend of Francis Dunne, one of the greatest humorists of the Turf in my time. Like Hal Price Headley, Cassidy appeared always to have his brain engaged on matters other than social. Francis did love to tease him.

Once Francis rang him up on his private line at the Jockey Club. When Cassidy answered, Dunne said in a disguised voice: "I'd like to speak to jockey Arcaro."

Cassidy's answer: "He's not here. You may reach him at the track."

Dunne: "Well, let me speak to jockey Atkinson."

Cassidy: "No, he's not here either. I think he's at the track, also."
Dunne: "Well, let me speak to any jockey there."
Cassidy: "There are no jockeys here."
Dunne: "This is the Jockey Club isn't it?"
Cassidy: "Yes it is."
Dunne: "Well, if you call yourself the Jockey Club and have no jockeys there, are you using a phony name as a front for a bookie joint?"

A Quick Answer Would Be Appreciated

Cassidy's school for racing officials was an invaluable contribution to the sport. Even people who already were serving in an official capacity came to New York to get instruction and practical training from bottom to top. After graduation, the former students sometimes would call Cassidy when they were confronting a sticky situation. One of the most serious, yet humorous, calls came from Myron Davis when he was presiding steward at Suffolk.

After he listened carefully to the details for a possible disqualification of the unofficial winner of a race, Marshall told Myron: "Let me think about it a few minutes and I'll phone you right back—you have a tough decision to make."

"That'll be too late," replied Myron. "The crowd is booing, screaming, and throwing things. The other two stewards and I have to do something now."

That's Quite a Rock

FBI Director J. Edgar Hoover had a great love for horse racing. The Maryland tracks would hold his table in the clubhouse until the fourth race each day on the chance that he would get out of the office for a few hours. The same was true at Del Mar when he was there on vacation.

Hoover knew and liked racetrackers of the Runyon type, and they thronged to him. He seldom went for their tips; he just liked the stories they told. Fred "Snoz" Krieger and Yancey Christmas were two of his favorites.

One day, Swifty Morgan, sporting a huge diamond ring, sat down at his table and Hoover, who collected diamonds, remarked: "Swifty, that's a nice ring; give you five hundred for it." Nonplussed, Swifty paused for a moment, then exclaimed: "Why, Director, you more than anybody in the world would know the reward alone for this rock is three times that amount."

J. Edgar Hoover and his FBI assistant Clyde Tolson at the races.

A Badly Needed Rest

The stewards at Keystone called in a trainer for an explanation of an astounding form reversal after the four-week-long strike there in early 1982. "Didn't do nothing with him during the strike, not knowing when it would end," the trainer stated. "Guess the rest got him strong and fresh. Maybe I've been training and racing him too hard. After three years I think I've finally got the key to the old horse."

But the 'Hop' Was Okay

In the "good old days" when anything went and the crime was getting caught, "hopping" horses was not unusual. Some it helped, some it did not. Jack Keene, one of my early mentors, once told me: "There was nothing wrong with it. It merely made a cheating horse honest."

I once read where a trainer was called on the carpet by the stewards to explain a form reversal of one of his horses. "That's easy," he was quoted as saying. "I ran him on the 'hop' yesterday." The stewards conferred for a few moments, then the presiding judge told him: "We've discussed this matter. We're not going to fine or suspend you, but you keep him on it. We don't want any more form reversals on him."

Caveat Emptor

> *I bought this horse off morning works,*
> *I liked his black-type style,*
> *His moves were timed 'round thirty-six,*
> *And they were at a mile.*
> *But now that I am training him,*
> *And the check has cleared the bank,*
> *I find him sore from head to toe,*
> *That seller I'll not thank.*
> *I've found a way that I can sell,*
> *Of that I'm resolute,*
> *This horse will work in thirty-six,*
> *He's going back on Bute.*

Beating the Clockers

One of the delights of most trainers—myself included—was "beating the clockers." It is a challenge, more of a game than gainful. It has to be done before daylight or in a fog when the starting point of the workout is not visible. Two stopwatches are required.

When the horse leaves the stable, the trainer starts both watches at the same time, hands one to the pony boy or girl, and instructs that the watch must be stopped at the instant the horse passes the pole designated for the start of the workout. The trainer stops his watch immediately when the horse passes the pole that ends the workout.

Later, and generally back at the stable, the trainer collects the other watch, then calculates the difference in time on the two watches; the variation is the exact time of the work. To his utter joy, especially if the time is good, the trainer is the only one with any knowledge of it.

The above method was used only for distances less than six furlongs. At six furlongs, I would do the timing by myself. On a fast polo pony, I would gallop alongside the work horse to the three-quarters pole, start my watch at the break, then wheel my pony around and gallop the wrong way back to the finish line and stop the watch there. It was easily done. All my polo ponies could easily get me back to the finish line in time to complete my private clocking of the workout.

Another ploy is working "look-alikes." In the spring of 1961, I shipped from Aiken into Keeneland, and among my horses was the fastest two-year-old I had ever trained, Jetting Home. Unnamed at the time and identified only by his age, sex, color, he had run in the Aiken Trials, and Kilmoray (later to win the Toboggan Handicap and $250,134), the fastest youngster there, was life and death to beat him by a whisker. Starter Bill Simpson insisted he would have to okay him from the gate before I started him at the meet.

A bit annoyed, I did, but I took to the starting gate three other chestnut colts virtually like Jetting Home in markings and conformation. I gave the names of each to Bill and requested that he okay all at the same time. They all broke perfectly, but Jetting Home distanced them, working the half-mile from the gate in :46. After pulling up on the backside, they regrouped, and I grabbed Ole Roscoe's left rein and led him beside my pony, giving him special attention.

Scotty Poole, then the *Daily Racing Form* clocker, was at the exit gap to meet me. "What's the name of that colt you're leading?" he asked, wrongly assuming that I would be leading the colt who had worked the best. "Ole Roscoe," I replied gleefully. "He's a runner," Scotty replied. "I got him in :46."

Later that morning, I phoned Jetting Home's owner, Jimmy Stone, and told him: "Get your betting money together. Jetting Home worked out of the gate this morning in :46. He'll start in the next maiden allowance race." Jimmy, who only bet big money on his own horses, was at Keeneland for the colt's racing debut. I do not know how much he bet, but I well remember that Jetting Home opened at 25-to-1 and ended up paying only $13.80 to win. The next morning Scotty was furious.

"You lied to me," he steamed. "No," I replied, "you asked me the name of the colt I was leading. He was, indeed, Ole Roscoe. You asked the wrong question. You falsely assumed I was leading the best one."

The Yellow Sweater Incident

Racetracks and racing commissions have long since passed rules whereby the name of the horse and the distance of the workout must be reported correctly; it is a very important safeguard for the wagering public. One of the milestones on the progression to this regulation was the "yellow sweater incident" on the West Coast many years ago.

Back in 1952, West Coast trainer Ross Brinson had a two-year-old he had been hiding, and he wanted to get one more good work into him before the gelding made his first start at Hollywood Park. Monte Parke was the trainer for John D. Hertz, whose exercise riders always wore bright yellow sweaters. Monte either loaned Ross one of the sweaters or one of his riders for the workout. The time turned in by Ross's two-year-old was exceedingly fast, but it was credited to Two Bit Hug, a Hertz horse, in the *Daily Racing Form* workout tab.

Ross's runner, named La Bull, had no published workouts and was 15-to-1 in the morning line. After he won off by three lengths at 6-to-1 odds, Jack MacKenzie, then general manager of Hollywood Park, ordered a complete investigation, which uncovered the "yellow sweater incident." It became a *cause celebre*. The stewards called both Monte and Ross on the carpet, and suggested lengthy suspensions and heavy fines were in order for both because of their "conspiracy."

Hertz was in Europe at the time and was informed of the incident by Vic Heerman, his stable and farm agent. More one to seek out an argument than avoid one, Hertz fired back to Heerman: "Tell Jack and the stewards to do what they want, but they better be right." That stopped any notion of fining or suspending either trainer. No rule had been violated.

MacKenzie stewed over the matter for days. Shortly thereafter, the California Horse Racing Board issued an order that a trainer was obligated to inform an official at the gap of the correct name of his horse, the distance the horse was to work, and that this information was to be relayed immediately to the clockers. Anyone willfully violating the rule, or falsely identifying a horse, was subject to summary suspension.

In reacting to the new rule, Jimmy Jones, who had a large contingent of Calumet Farm horses there and brought them on the track in sets of eight or ten, complained: "How can a man train horses that way? I know generally when I come on the track what I plan to do with a horse, but I never make a final decision until after I observe them. Did Jack MacKenzie ever train a horse?"

Midnighting a Horse

Bill Shoemaker and Dr. Alex Harthill have been friends for many years. On one occasion when it was going on 10 o'clock at a formal dinner party, Harthill said to Shoe: "Let's get out of here. I've got to daylight a horse at five tomorrow before the clockers get out."

"Let's stay another couple of hours and midnight him. There's a full moon tonight," Shoe suggested.

"Now, silly boy, who am I going to get on him at midnight?" asked the good doctor.

"You're looking at him," returned the great jockey.

As Shoe exited the track with his mount breathing deeply after a three-eighths blowout, he observed an old man on wobbly legs stop and stare. "Damned if I'm going to that bar again. They put something in my drinks that's affecting my mind and my sight," the man said. "I'm seeing jockey Bill Shoemaker dressed like a head waiter riding a racehorse in the middle of the night."

At a gabfest about the good old days, one ex-jock observed: "Fixed races didn't work then, just like now. Something always goes wrong." Another old rider once told me that in his long career he had ridden in 21 races whose finish had been prearranged by jockey conspiracies that he had masterminded. "Not one of the sonofabitches have worked," he laughed. I have committed a "meter murder" about one of that old jock's attempts at race fixing.

The Race That Came Unfixed

We thought we had the race all fixed,
The contenders all locked up.
Only the longshot was runnin' free,
And he was to fill our cup.
On him we had bet a giant wad,
The time was going to be slow,
The stewards would ask about the race,
But how were they to know.
But now that the race is over,
We're all in a terrible state,
The bum we bet our money on,
Collapsed when he left the gate.

Keeping the Faith

Rusty Marlman, a colorful old trainer, was bragging about an old jockey who "always kept the faith."

"I told him in the paddock this was 'no' day," he related, "and under no condition was he to hit the board. Well, the old horse got running with him turning for home. He steers him to the rail behind a wall of horses, but the bum in front of him bolts, carries the horses alongside him out, and my horse pulls the jock to the lead. Just as I start to sweat, the old rider stood straight up in his stirrups and made the most beautiful swan dive I've ever seen—right into the infield. I'll tell you, that old jock had class."

The 'Rollers' Meant No Go

"Rollers" were shoes that were rounded at the toes to prevent a horse from getting hold of the track on "no" day. They were used in the days of racing when anything went. Now, shoe checks are made on every starter, and shoe boards at many tracks indicate how each runner is shod.

Best story I ever heard about "rollers" concerned John Whitlow. Back in World War I days, Whitlow had a pretty honest horse named Westy Hogan who could really perform on "go" day. He won stakes at two, three, and four from 1916 to 1918. The only way to get ahead then was by cashing a bet—and it was often done by participating in the winnings of a well-touted third party.

If the bet was made at the track, a sizable wager paid off at short odds. "Cincinnati Rosie" booked more money on Kentucky racing than the tracks did themselves. Rosie would hold the money on a horse he did not like, or join it and lay it off to other unsuspecting bookmakers. On one particular occasion, Whitlow's partner in a Westy Hogan coup came to the stable a half-hour before the race. He said he could not get down, not even with Cincinnati Rosie. Immediately, John picked up a rasp and started toward Westy's stall. "What you gonna do?" inquired the confederate. "Roll his shoes, of course," replied Whitlow.

"Don't do that," the bettor bleated. "I did get down with Rosie for a grand." After thoroughly cursing and physically threatening the doublecrossing slicker, Whitlow regained his composure, took Westy to the race, and saw him win easily at good odds.

A Talent for Managing People

Preston Burch, asked to name the prime requisite of a top trainer, replied that the person must be "a good manager." What kind of a manager, he was asked. "A manager of people. You manage to get yourself rich owners who will buy you good racing stock. Horses make trainers, trainers do not make horses," Burch said.

Salesmanship Counts, Too

Personal salesmanship is never to be underrated in trainers. Those who can talk get good jobs and good horses to train, and thus they climb the ladder of success. This is known in our trade as "training the owner." Those who cannot have to make it alone on sheer ability.

Dr. Alex Harthill once was asked by the owner of a large West Coast stable to recommend two young trainers who he thought were "comers." Alex named two, and they were flown to California for job interviews with the stable owner. When Alex encountered the first to return, he asked: "How did you make out?"

"Didn't get the job," the young trainer responded. "The other guy did—he *out-talked* me."

Down to Food and Water

The owner of a private racing stable related to me how his trainer was slurring his words and making very little sense when the owner called one night to get a report on his horses. He told the trainer to give up either the bottle or the horses. In their next conversation, the owner asked his reluctantly sober trainer how he was doing. "Not very good. You got me down to living off food and water."

An Education in Jumping

In 1940, while attending the dispersal sale of Willis Sharpe Kilmer's horses at his Court Manor farm in Virginia, I observed Thomas Hitchcock, one of the leading steeplechase trainers of that era, buying weanlings. Knowing he would not race them until they were four- or five-year-olds, I asked Humphrey Finney why Hitchcock was buying such young horses.

"He starts 'em jumping at an early age," Finney said. "He will turn them out on his large farm near Aiken, South Carolina, and their only access to grain or water is by jumping a series of small jumps. When they've had their fill, they jump their way back out of the pasture. As they grow older, he raises the height of the jumps. Jumping will become second nature to them. That's why you see so few of Hitchcock's steeplechasers fall."

The Strain of Training

The life of a successful trainer is not an easy one, particularly for one with a large public stable. You are running one in the afternoon at Aqueduct, another that night at the Meadowlands, and you must be back at the barn at 5:30 the next morning. You're shipping, by van or air. Then there is the telephone. The owners must be kept informed, told how each horse is training, and called before and after each race.

Even several decades ago, the trainer's life was no bed of roses. The physical and mental demands to attain and sustain success were nearly unbearable. I imagine this caused R. H. "Red" McDaniel to take his own life in his mid-'40s.

Red came on the racetrack at age 15. He became a jockey, but never made a mark in that facet of the game. Switching to training, he experienced many dry years until things started picking up for him in California in the late 1940s. Red's day ran something like this. Up at five each morning, seven days a week. From six until 11 a.m., he trained his string of horses. Before he went back to the track at 1 p.m., he grabbed some lunch between phone calls to and from owners.

During racing hours, he observed others' horses for possible future claiming and saddled his own. After the races, he would check the

Red McDaniel.

horses again at his stable and attend to other details. Back at his residence or motel by 6 p.m., the next three hours were devoted to dinner and more phone calls to owners. He was lucky to get to bed by 10 p.m., which left only seven hours before it all began again.

But Red was dedicated to the job, and in 1950 he was the nation's leading trainer in races won with 156 victories, and he retained that title for the next four years. In 1953, he saddled 211 winners, becoming the first trainer to saddle more than 200 winners in a single season. In May, 1955, after having saddled Aptos, he did not return to his stable. He drove instead to the middle of the Golden Gate Bridge, parked his car, walked to the railing, and plunged to his death.

At the time of his death, Red was training 30 horses for 18 different owners. He obviously could not cope with the demands he made of himself to achieve success.

He Was Able to Walk Away

One of the few trainers who have walked away from the job while still on top was Bill Winfrey. He left in the fall of 1965, he said, "to enjoy life, to spend more time with my family, and to take them on a trip around the world. Money or pseudo-fame aren't everything." In the stalls of the Phipps stable when he took his parting were four champions: Buckpasser, Bold Lad, Castle Forbes, and Queen Empress. Before taking over the Phipps job, he had trained champions Native Dancer, Bed o' Roses, and Next Move for Alfred G. Vanderbilt. At the time of his retirement, only one modern-day trainer had developed more champions, Ben Jones, with nine. Bill told me decades later that he never regretted getting out of the "pressure cooker."

He Forgot His Breakfast

Woody Stephens freely discusses his "ulcers" and his "pressures" as a trainer in his book, *Guess I'm Lucky*. Not mentioned was an amusing recollection I have of him. I had shipped to Belmont in April of 1956 with some two-year-olds "to run and sell and sell and run (home)" as best I could. While I was having breakfast in the track kitchen, Woody joined me at my table. Until 1954, when his owner Royce Martin had died, Woody had always had a private job or a public stable with one principal owner. Before Martin, he had trained for Herb Woolf and Jule Fink. When we sat down for breakfast, Woody's public stable had 22 horses and 11 different owners.

"Let me give you some advice," Woody cautioned. "If you ever decide to train a public stable, school your owners. Don't let them bother you, particularly with needless phone calls. My owners are well-trained. They don't disturb me."

While our conversation flowed, the waiter had taken his order and placed the check in front of his place. When the waiter returned, both Woody and the check were gone. "What happened to Stephens?" he asked. I replied: "Look toward the cash register." There stood Woody, paying his check and picking his teeth with a toothpick. He may have "schooled" his owners, but he was still feeling the heat. The next year, he was back in a private job, training for Captain Harry F. Guggenheim.

'Ain't That Hell'

Back around the turn of the century, Green B. Morris was a leading owner-trainer. He was, in fact, the nation's leading owner in 1902 with purses totaling $98,350. But that distinction did not mean that Morris was lettered, or even literate. He was neither. Once, he loaded one of his stakes horses in a boxcar and shipped him from Sheepshead Bay in Brooklyn out to Washington Park near Chicago. He instructed his foreman to telegraph him the result immediately after the race.

The telegraph arrived, and Morris took it up to the gap and opened it before several horsemen. Pretending he had read it, he passed it among them, saying: "Ain't that hell!" They all agreed: "It sure is." Not until he went to see his lawyer later in the day did he learn that his horse had won.

They Were Very Well Matched

Among nearly 200 recorded match races going back to 1822, some have had very close finishes: Eternal by a head over Billy Kelly in 1918; Zev by a nose

Chris Evert ran away from Miss Musket in their match race at Hollywood Park.

over In Memoriam in 1923; Alsab by a nose over Whirlaway in 1942; Convenience by a head over Typecast in 1972.

One of the most interesting match races was the 1935 contest between Myrtlewood and Clang, both three-year-olds. They raced at even weights of 110 pounds even though Myrtlewood was a filly and Clang was a gelding. Myrtlewood beat Clang by a nose at Hawthorne Race Course on September 25. Clang then beat her by a nose at River Downs (at that time Coney Island) on October 12.

One of the most amusing match races was run at Rockingham Park in 1946 over 1 1/8 miles between Dinner Party and Float Me. With a six-length lead at the three-eighths pole, Float Me jumped the inner rail and fell with jockey Jimmy Martin.

The two biggest pots for match races were offered at Hollywood Park. The first was in 1972. The track put up $50,000, and owners Leonard Lavin (Convenience) and Westerly Stud (Typecast) added $100,000 each. The horses carried level weights of 120 pounds over the 1 1/8-mile distance. Convenience won by a head, winner take all. Typecast was later voted an Eclipse Award as the best older filly or mare of 1972.

The second race came two years later over 1 1/4 miles for three-year-old fillies at level weights of 121. Carl Rosen kicked in $100,000 for Chris Evert and Aaron Jones put up $100,000 for Miss Musket. The track added $150,000, winner take all. Chris Evert won by 50 lengths.

Rumors About Doc Harthill

Ever since I established a lifelong friendship with Dr. Alex Harthill in 1948, vicious rumors have abounded that he could "give a horse something" to make him win. The best answer I have found to counter that rumor is: "If that be true, why does he not win more races with his own horses?"

Taming the Bully of Keeneland

Young Pat Devereaux was the "bully of Keeneland" in the 1960s. His uncle by the same name was a professional boxer of local prominence before him, but young Pat's career in the ring was somewhat less successful. He turned to training the horses bred by his father, Tom. He developed a pretty good one in Royal Harmony, who won 22 stakes.

One hot July afternoon at River Downs, after one of his horses had disappointed him, he decked the first two people he encountered, Danny Terrell and Doug Davis, for no apparent reason. The same year during the fall meet at Keeneland, Windy Miss was squealing and jumping as Willard Proctor, astride his pony, led her off the track after a morning gallop. At the same time, Pat had a couple of two-year-olds going on the track. "Why don't you take that gray bitch down to the little track and teach her some manners," yelled Pat.

Springing from the saddle as he had in the days when he helped out on his family's Texas ranch, Proctor hollered as he landed on his feet: "I'm going to teach you," then flattened Pat with one mighty blow to the jaw. Kicking dirt and sand into Pat's face, the ex-cowboy continued: "Now, if you want another lesson, just get up." Devereaux did not. Proctor then returned to the filly and the pony, both of whom had been perfectly still as though they were watching their master's performance.

Willard Proctor.

A Champion Brawler

Perhaps the biggest racetrack brawler of all time was Edward Corrigan, otherwise known as "Big Ed." In 1887, according to accounts in *The Thoroughbred Record*, he had "thoroughly insulted" the stewards at Washington Park. It noted that "instead of ruling him off as they were justified in doing, they merely asked for an apology, which he refused to make."

The following year, at West Side Park near Chicago, a track in which he had become a managing partner, Big Ed took offense at a complaint by an owner, Samuel Lavis. The Louisville *Courier-Journal* reported that Corrigan, "raising a loaded cane, brought it down full force on the head (of Lavis), cutting through a stiff hat and laying the skull bare. Mr. Corrigan has been the fear of all who have been brought in contact with him. A few days ago he struck a track employee, fracturing his jaw."

Corrigan's ire naturally extended to the press. After a Kansas City *Times* writer, Thomas Mosier, had displeased him, the newspaper reported that upon their next meeting, "Corrigan, who is a tall, heavy man, struck him a fearful blow ... felling him to the ground, then kicked him several times. Five

"Big Ed" Corrigan.

minutes later, thinking Corrigan had cooled off, Mosier got back on his feet, only to be assaulted again in the same manner."

When Dr. Morrison Munford, editor of the newspaper, took up the matter on the editorial page, Big Ed called upon him at his office. Result: "Munford's injuries consist of two scalp wounds, several cuts, and bruises," the *Times* reported.

Colonel Matt Winn, in the wonderful biography written by Frank Menke, recalled his days as manager of Hawthorne for Corrigan. "Ed Corrigan was a fiery, dynamic Irishman. If he liked you, he'd knock 20 men to please you. If he didn't, he'd knock you down 20 times just to keep in practice."

Colonel Phil Chinn, a longtime pal of Corrigan's, once told me how Big Ed handled a threatened strike of the bartenders at Hawthorne. He invited the strike committee to his office. "When the four negotiators arrived," Chinn recalled, "quick as a cat he hit each a stunning blow, then returned to them one at a time with his knockout punch. With all four out cold on his office floor, he walked out of his office to announce to those awaiting the result of the meeting there would be no strike—and there wasn't one."

Chapter 12
Clients and Other Owners

Contrary to popular myth, bloodstock agents do have friends. And, if they are any good at all, they have clients. I was particularly fortunate in my years of tradin' to have clients who also were very close friends. As I said quite a while ago, I considered my association with Hal Price Headley to be a treasure.

Some clients were merely clients, of course. John D. Hertz and I were very close for seven years, but we split after I refused to be "owned." But other clients, such as Dr. Eslie Asbury and Jimmy Stone, were close friends and associates throughout their lifetimes. I will start with "As," whom I knew from my earliest days as a Turf writer.

A Renaissance Man

Dr. Eslie Asbury died suddenly on Sunday, September 4, 1988, in Cincinnati, Ohio. He was just two months shy of his 93rd birthday. "As" was a leading physician and an excellent golfer. Up to the day of his death, he could shoot his age. Although rather small in size, As had so much athletic talent that he played semi-pro baseball, basketball, and football in his younger years.

In addition to his daily golf games, he could also hold his own with the best at bridge and poker. He smoked about three cigars a day, and downed about the same number of Bourbon toddies each evening before bedtime. He disdained wasting time. When "rained out," he wrote excellent books that

Dr. Eslie Asbury.

sold well, and he donated the profits to charity. He also frequently contributed papers to the Cincinnati Historical Society, the Filson Club, the Literary Club, and the Kentucky Historical Society—organizations which, he noted, "have tolerated my talks and papers for more than 50 years." He was an excellent speaker, greatly in demand, and never spoke from notes.

Although he had the greatest vocabulary I have ever known, As wrote and spoke in common words and phrases that a seventh-grade student could understand. He once wrote that a person he did not admire "uses big words to cover his ignorance." Once, after we had listened to a breeder bragging about his horses, As turned to me, grinning, and said: "He doesn't suffer from the hypocrisy of modesty!" On the low standing of education in Kentucky, he quoted Mark Twain: "God first made idiots. That was for practice. Then he made School Boards."

Investing Wisely for the Future

Both As and his wife Mary were physicians who worked hard and saved their money, invested in bonds, and thus avoided the ravages of the 1929 Wall Street crash. In the early 1930s, they bought, at a very low price, the first of several tracts of land that were to become Forest Retreat Farm near Carlisle, Kentucky, not far from the log cabin where As was born. Its primary attractions to them were the beautiful undulating terrain and immense woodlands, as well as its rich soil. Its abundance of briar bushes, fallen fences, dilapidated buildings, and dirt roads could be dealt with later. And were.

My first visit to Forest Retreat was in the mid-1930s with Colonel Phil T. Chinn, renowned as much for his wit as his superior horsemanship. Observing the steep hills, the colonel remarked: "Well, Dr. Asbury, I don't think you'll have a drainage problem here." A few years before his death in 1962, Colonel Chinn made his last visit to Forest Retreat and found it to be one of the most beautiful farms anywhere. Dr. Asbury recalls that visit in his book, *Horse Sense and Humor in Kentucky*: "Colonel Chinn, with julep in hand, looking against the forgiving rays of a setting sun, said: 'It is unforgettable to see such beauty. Wouldn't it be hell, sir, to die and leave it.'"

Mary and As entertained many prominent horsepeople from overseas at Forest Retreat and in turn were guests in their countries. Lord Derby was very much taken by Revoked, one of the best horses they raised at the farm, and was amazed that he had been developed on such hilly terrain. Another guest, Jacob "Jakey" Astor, a very successful English owner and breeder, told the Asburys about a speech made by his mother, Lady Astor, who was a bitter enemy of wine and whisky. After she had stated, "Rather than have a drop of alcohol pass my lips, I would rather commit adultery," a drunk in the crowd yelled back: "Who wouldn't?"

Forest Retreat is a Kentucky landmark.

At his Newmarket training yard, Captain Cecil Boyd-Rochford was showing Dr. Asbury some X rays of his stable jockey's fractured lower leg and saying that, as a result, his yard had not had as good of a season as he had anticipated. "He's been laid up for six months," the captain complained, "and it's been bloody hard for me, you know."

The Mystery of the Genes

As was an expert geneticist, but he was hard-pressed to explain how a $700 Alsab, a $1,100 John Henry, or a T. V. Lark (raised in his owner's backyard) could become great horses. In fact, he never pretended to have any hard knowledge about it. He did state, however, that "some people rise above their forebears. This does not repeal the laws of genetics. They spring from families with latent superior genes, previously untested."

Standing Behind the Product

In 1944, Max Hirsch bought one of As's yearlings (at the high price of about $40,000) at the Keeneland July sales, but he noticed a wind impairment when he watched the colt at Arnold Hanger's farm the following day. Max immediately called As, who insisted the colt be returned to him. Max agreed, making his second big mistake in two years. (The year before, he had lost Stymie to Hirsch Jacobs.)

Revoked, returned to breeder Eslie Asbury from a yearling sale because of suspicion of wind trouble, won the Washington Park Futurity while racing for Asbury.

The colt, Revoked, won the Washington Park Futurity the following year for the good doctor, then became a good stallion for him and Hal Price Headley. Max continued to bid on Asbury yearlings and bought a number of them.

I have never known a horseman to stand behind his products more than Dr. Asbury. In 1952, when the bidding was rather low and slow on a smallish gray colt by *Alibhai he had sent into the Keeneland sales ring, Andy Crevolin—who had not inspected the colt—threw in a bid of $12,000 and got him. After inspecting the colt, Andy complained: "I must have been standing in a hole when I bid on that colt. Why, he isn't any bigger than a greyhound dog."

Dr. Asbury then made a big mistake. He offered not only to take the colt back, but also to give Crevolin $3,000 for his "trouble." Had he only agreed to void the sale, the colt probably would have been returned, but the $3,000 premium from such a knowledgeable horseman convinced Andy he had a bargain.

The little gray colt, later named Determine, won the 1954 Kentucky Derby, sired 1962 Kentucky Derby winner Decidedly as well as 19 other stakes winners, and became a very good broodmare sire.

Determine won the 1954 Kentucky Derby and later sired Derby winner Decidedly.

The Deaths Were Unpremeditated

I have never "bought" the story that some mares, after the pain and suffering of delivery, intentionally kill their foals. I have always attributed these losses to unattended foalings. The mare steps or rolls on the youngster, and most vets seem to agree with me—and so did As, to his great benefit.

Back in the spring of 1953, Dr. Asbury told me he "could use another summer-sales type of mare" if ever I ran across one. Shortly after the doctor had placed his order, an agitated Joe Metz came storming into my office. "You know that mare Egretta you got me to buy out of the Jerry McCarthy sale?" Joe remarked loudly. "Well, I didn't steal her for $5,000. Two of those foals listed in her produce record are dead. They told me over at the farm where she boarded she killed them. Get rid of that horse for me."

As fate would have it, I was shortly to leave for Forest Retreat Farm to look at the yearlings and have supper with As and Mary. After we had devoured the thinly sliced old ham and the vegetables that Mary had picked that day from her garden, I posed the question: "Do some mares deliberately kill their foals immediately after delivery?" Both said they doubted the stories of killer mares. "We've certainly never had such a case at Forest Retreat," As said.

"Well, folks, if you discount the story that comes with her, I've got your 'summer sales' mare for $6,000, $500 of which will go to 'little Johnny' as commission and the rest to Joe Metz." Then I told them about Egretta, a six-year-old stakes-winning mare from a good female line. Without saying a word, As left the patio and almost instantly returned with a check made out to Joe Metz for $6,000 as "payment in full for Egretta." He handed me the check and said: "Buy her."

Shortly after returning home, the phone rang. It was Joe, calling to reiterate that I should get busy and sell the mare, "even if I have to take a loss." I replied she was sold for $6,000 to Forest Retreat. "You don't lose; you make $500 and I make $500. I'll give you the check tomorrow morning. The mare will be picked up in the afternoon." I guess Joe, then relaxed, went on to bed—and had pleasant dreams. He had made money on what he thought was a bad buy.

For Forest Retreat over the next 16 years, Egretta produced 12 foals, nine of which were sold as yearlings at Keeneland for a total of $222,500, and four of which were sold privately. She was retired from breeding at age 24 and, As noted, "she never presented us with a problem."

When Forest Retreat sold their first foal from Egretta (Asgard, for $45,000), Joe remarked: "I'd like to get my hands on the bum that put that bad story on me."

He Was Hard on a Horse

Shortly before his death, As recalled for me that he had treated William Howard Taft, the Cincinnatian who had been President of the United States from 1909 to 1913. His White House physician constantly admonished Taft, who weighed in at 365 pounds, about his voracious appetite and his disdain for exercise. Once, while on vacation out West, Taft telegraphed his doctor: "Rode a horse 25 miles today. Feel great." The doctor immediately wired back: "How does the horse feel?"

As, who was Taft's Cincinnati physician, said he had to coerce his patient into playing golf to get any exercise into him. "His belly protruded so much he had to bend over to a 90-degree angle to hit the ball. Had the lowest swing I ever saw."

Dr. Mary Knight Asbury died in 1986 and was buried in the family cemetery, a short distance from the main farm residence. Dr. Eslie Asbury joined her there. On September 8, 1988, members of the Asbury family and close friends attended a memorial service at the cemetery. It was not a mournful or tearful affair. It was a happy, humorous event that evoked many laughs, just as Mary and As would have liked. Presiding was Dr. Gordon Steward, and eulogists were longtime friend and former governor A. B. "Happy" Chandler, and Bob Newman, husband of the oldest Asbury grandchild, Mary.

Newman recalled driving As, then 92, to Berea College to receive the Berea College President's Medal. En route, he jokingly asked the good doctor if he expected to be doing the same things in another ten years. "Yes," he replied, nonchalantly. "How're you going to arrange that?" Newman continued. "Get me a younger chauffeur," As said. Goodbye, old friend. We will miss you.

The Saga of John D. Hertz

So often when I read the name of Count Fleet or Prince John, I recall the seven wonderful years that I was retained as consultant by their breeder, John D. Hertz, who died in 1961 at age 82.

I am reasonably certain that he won the Horatio Alger Award, but if he did not, he certainly deserved it. At age five, he was brought from his native Austria to live with relatives in Chicago, where he was to make his fortune. A kindly, soft-spoken person—except when he lost his temper and reverted to the antics required for survival in his youth—he loved to recall his life's experiences and those of others with whom he was close.

Not knowing a word of English, he was taught by his relatives to say, "Buy a paper," and given money to buy newspapers to resell on a Chicago street corner. The distributor took him in. "I was yelling 'buy a paper, buy a paper,' to everyone that passed," he recalled, "but couldn't sell a one. I looked across the street and another kid

John D. Hertz.

had about sold out. I started crying, still saying 'buy a paper, buy a paper,' when some nice man came over to me, gave me $3, and told me in German: 'Son, someone has been very cruel to you. They've sold you the morning newspaper. Take this and buy afternoon papers and you'll be all right." Hertz made the second effort that was so characteristic of him, obtained his updated product, and was sold out in short order.

Self-educated—there was no time for school because he had to work—he moved onward and upward as he scaled the ladder of life and business at a furious pace: racetrack valet (when he first got interested in racing and vowed he would own horses some day), manager of prizefighters, fight reporter for a newspaper, and so on.

Having learned a bit about repairing autos as a mechanic's helper, he made a decision that was to propel him to immense wealth. He bought an old black auto, painted "taxi" on the front and back and both sides, and went into business for himself. He was doing only moderately well until he lucked upon a passenger who gave him perhaps the best advice he ever received in his life.

"I'm head of the art department at the University of Chicago," began the passenger, "and we've just completed a study of the most visible color at a distance for the State of Illinois. It's yellow. In the near future, all the state's traffic signs will have yellow backgrounds. Why don't you paint this cab yellow? If you hadn't been parked so I could read your sign, I'd never have known this was a cab."

"I'll do that tonight," replied Hertz, "and I'm going to put a sign on the top facing forward, yellow background, black letters, 'yellow cab,' so people can see me two blocks away. I can cruise around, be hailed down at any point. Won't have to wait for fares at cab stands."

The first day out in his yellow cab, Hertz did 20 times as much business. The Yellow Cab Company—for many years an American institution—was born.

As revenue increased, more used cars were bought and more drivers (mostly ex-fighters, because collecting the fare was not always easy in those days) were hired. In time, Hertz had the biggest and best fleet of cabs in the "Windy City"—and later the United States.

When Hertz had developed his company to its fullest potential, he sold out to the giant automaker whose best single customer he had become, General Motors. With so many millions to invest, Hertz left Chicago permanently and moved to the financial capital of the world, New York City.

Buying Reigh Count

Hertz once told me the story of how he came to buy Reigh Count. He said he was watching a two-year-old race at Saratoga in 1927. Reigh Count was on the lead, trying his best and not wanting to give up, but he was becoming leg weary. As another colt came up to pass him, Reigh Count opened his mouth wide and tried to bite him as he passed.

Hertz bought eventual Kentucky Derby winner Reigh Count as a two-year-old after the colt tried to savage another horse in a race.

"Frank Hackett was sitting beside me," Hertz recalled, "and I said: 'Go buy that colt for me, regardless what he costs,' before they reached the finish. After the finish, Frank said that '$10,000 ought to get him,' and I told him to give that or more, just get that colt for me."

Willis Sharpe Kilmer, his breeder, sold the *Sunreigh colt to Hertz immediately after the race for $10,000. Under Charles "Chick" Lang, the colt won the 1928 Kentucky Derby and became champion three-year-old that year. He later sired Count Fleet, Hertz's second Derby winner. "I judged that colt on what I had seen in young prizefighters I had managed," Hertz concluded. "The ones that tried to go on when there was nothing within them to do it ultimately make top fighters."

'Stuck' With a Good One

Before Hertz started sending his yearlings to auction, he offered them for sale privately. In 1941, he got "stuck" with a colt he had priced at $4,500. Excellent judges, including Max Hirsch, turned him down for various reasons: "too light in the body," "too weak," "too leggy," "not enough bone." The unwanted colt was 1943 Triple Crown winner Count Fleet.

Pensioned after a very successful career at stud, Count Fleet lived on to a ripe old age, dying on December 3, 1973, less than a month before he would have turned 34.

Count Fleet, winner of the 1943 Triple Crown.

The Reluctant Retainer

I really did not want the Hertz retainer. He had a history of turning against his closest friends—Albert Lasker and Warren Wright, to name just two. It extended to the trainers of his Kentucky Derby winners, Bert Michell (Reigh Count) and Don Cameron (Count Fleet). I was warned the time would come when Hertz would try to "buy" me—lock, stock, and barrel. John Hertz, like other successful businessmen, liked to "own" people.

I tried to price myself out of the job, thinking of the misery that would come with it, so I told him it would be $10,000 a year. "That's a lot money for a young man who hasn't yet turned 28, but you got a deal," Hertz said. "You'll make me that on the sale of one yearling a year."

Each year for the next five years our sales were up. No longer was Hertz embarrassed by his yearling sales. Each year, the $10,000 stipend was followed by another "grand" as a Christmas present. Working for him was a pleasure up through 1952, the year we got our highest price ever at Keeneland, $40,000 for a Count Fleet—Obedient colt, and another record for us at the CTBA sale at Santa Anita Park, $15,500 for a Count Speed—Cosmopolite filly. They were sold to customers I had recruited, Riley Allison and Bill Prestridge, owners of the Saxon Stable.

In early April, 1953, the "takeover" move came. Shortly after I had arrived at his farm in Paris, Kentucky, and we had chatted briefly about other matters, Hertz tightened up and his face stiffened when he changed subjects. "I am changing our deal," he told me. "I am going to pay you $100,000 a year to run my horse affairs, or more if you require it, but you will give up your horse agency, your retainerships, and work only for me. You may breed and race a few horses, but, if you take a partner, it will have to be me. Take it or leave it."

Startled and "shocked to my socks," I could not believe the words "take it or leave it" had come from a man who had been so reasonable in discussing problems in his horse business, who had been so fatherly, so generous, who had sent me up to Leahy Clinic in Boston, Massachusetts, for a checkup at his expense to be assured I was in good health, and who let me breed mares to Count Fleet.

I stood up, looked him squarely in the eyes, thanked him for letting me advance myself in the business by working for him, but said I was going to leave it.

He frowned at me for the first time, then he continued: "Then get me Joe Thomas. He works for you; you taught him the horse business. He'll do what you tell him to do." I replied that I would neither encourage nor discourage Joe, but I would insist that he discuss the job with Hertz. Joe did, and he declined the post. Two years later, Joe went with E. P. Taylor, for whom he did a tremendous job.

Hertz never spoke to me again, would not even look me in the eye. I was later told by people who had known him for many more years: "You don't say 'no' to John Hertz if he has his heart set on something." I value those years, however, and I looked upon him as more of a father figure than a client. In addition, he taught me an important lesson, not to give in to greed. I stood by my longtime clients, and they always have stood by me.

A Demanding Mogul

Louis B. Mayer was a dynamic participant in both racing and breeding. He ran his Thoroughbred operation much as he did the motion picture industry, "with an iron hand." If he wanted something, he generally got it, with money or with clout. He had a string of advisers, and he played each against the other—to their great irritation—when making a decision.

"Don't tell him something can't be done," Dan Midkiff once told me. "If you do that, even after you have worked on the problem for days or weeks, he'll pick up the phone and get it done in 30 minutes." Back in 1940, Dan told Mayer that *Beau Pere, the leading sire in Australia, was not for sale. By the time L. B. got through throwing dollars over the phone at the horse's owner, he had bought him. "See," he turned to Dan, "you guys don't know what you're doing. If the horse wasn't for sale, how'd I buy him? Now you get him to California."

Dan tried tirelessly for days, but shipping space was unavailable. "Oh, me," said Dan. "When I go into his office with this, he'll make a damned fool out of me."

"Gimme the numbers of the companies you've called," Mayer told Midkiff, "and when I get through talking to the president

Louis B. Mayer.

Busher in 1945, when she won Horse of the Year honors, with trainer George Odom, right, and Washington Park executive director Benjamin Lindheimer holding the filly.

of one of them, you get on the phone and give him the details." Dan was right. "Mr. Mayer bombarded the man with threats, words, and money, then motioned for me to pick up the extension, and I heard the shipper say: 'Sir, I'll be glad to ship you a boatload of horses today.'"

Mayer wanted a top New York trainer. His advisers told him no one was available; the good ones would not move to California. "We'll see," L. B. replied. In a week's time, he had hired George Odom, Maje's father.

The movie mogul was told by Odom in March, 1945, that he would like to have Busher in the racing stable, "but Colonel Bradley won't sell her; she won five of her seven starts last year, including the Matron and Selima Stakes as well as the Adirondack Handicap." Mayer replied he knew Bradley and would call him personally. "I'll get her for you." And he did, for $50,000.

That year, in Mayer's silks and trained by Odom, Busher was the champion three-year-old filly, champion three-year-old of either sex, and Horse of the Year. Before retiring, she became the leading distaff earner ($334,035) of all time.

"Now what are we going to do about *Alibhai, put him to stud?" Mayer asked his advisers after he had pretty much made up his mind. They agreed he was well bred and had shown top speed in workouts before bowing a tendon. But, because he had never raced and his class had not been determined, it was inadvisable to breed him—sell him or give him away. L. B. replied: "I'll lease him, and if he starts siring runners, I'll take him back." Before *Alibhai died in 1960, he had sired 54 stakes winners from 395 foals, 13.7%.

Mayer loved being defiant. He told me that he once received two early-morning phone calls from Saratoga. "The first one was from Tony Pelleteri, the next from Mervyn LeRoy. Both said I'd better stop that crazy Dan Midkiff from buying for me. The previous night, he bought a curby-hocked colt by *Blenheim II for $3,500, just a fraction of the sire's stud fee. He's such a bad looker and so weakly bred on his dam's side. I told both of them Dan knew what he's doing, he's still thumbs up with me. I'll win the Santa Anita Handicap with that horse."

That was how Thumbs Up got his name. He won the 1945 Santa Anita Handicap, won or placed in 17 other stakes, and earned $249,290.

Mayer once taught Lloyd's of London how to pay off an insurance claim. The firm contended their vets recommended a waiting period to determine if Your Host's fractured leg could be stabilized to enable him to serve at stud. "He's on three legs now," L. B. boomed over the phone. "You pay my claim, and you take him and stand him at stud. MGM is paying you millions of dollars a year for insurance, and if you don't pay off on Your Host, I'll cancel every one of those policies." Lloyd's was prudent. It did as Mayer suggested.

Lloyd's sold Your Host to a New Jersey syndicate. Allaire duPont sent Maid of Flight to him, and the result was Kelso, winner of nearly $2-million and five-time Horse of the Year.

He Thrived on Chaos

Like many before him, Walter P. Chrysler Jr. was a man of great inherited wealth who tried to buy his way into racing and breeding, and failed. An even greater disappointment, he once confided to me, was his not being invited to become a member of the Jockey Club.

Walter never worked a day in his life, except when he served in the Navy in World War II. His mother told him early on, he also related to me: "Walter, I do not want you to work. Your father has provided well for you. I want you to enjoy life to the fullest." That he tried to do, but he derived little or no pleasure from it.

Walter was not a snob, yet he had few loyal friends. He did not know how to make friends and keep them. He would do the craziest things to get attention, and this alienated many of the better-respected people in our game.

Chrysler came into the business in the late 1930s, bought the best of yearlings, broodmares, and led the syndicate that imported the great English racehorse *Bahram as a sire. It looked like he was going places. He hired the very capable Bill Finnegan as head trainer.

Without advice, he had done this on his own. Also, without advice, he bought about 1,000 acres of the poorest land near Warrenton, Virginia, improved it lavishly with brightly colored barns, white fences, and paved roadways. He named it North Wales Stud. Dr. William Caslick left his veterinary practice in Paris, Kentucky, to run the horse department.

Walter Chrysler Jr.

Instead of allowing his general manager to hire a foreman to run each department, he chose to do that himself, giving each a title and allowing each to confer with him directly—if and when they could find him. He was nearly always away.

I first met Walter in 1941, shortly after I had opened my office as a sales agent and consultant. I sold him Dinner Date, one of the top fillies of 1938, when she won the Matron and Spinaway Stakes. We became friends immediately and dined together whenever our paths crossed—in Lexington, Warrenton, New York, or Miami.

By 1945, North Wales was in total confusion, something I honestly believe Walter relished, for it gave him an opportunity to interview people to replace "department heads" who had walked away from their "positions" in utter disgust. He loved to interview people.

Late that year, Walter requested that I come to North Wales and evaluate his operation. "Stay a couple of weeks or as long as it takes," he said. "I'm naming you general manager so you can be in full charge and find out exactly what's going on." I accepted, much to my later regret. Dr. Caslick had resigned and returned to his practice in Paris. He had been succeeded by Dr. William O. Reed, who had completed his internship under Dr. Ed Caslick at Claiborne.

When I phoned Bill Reed, with whom I had established a friendship while he was in Kentucky, and told him the purpose of my coming to North Wales, he replied: "You're in for the shock of your life." No truer words were ever spoken.

I found the grooms—who were taking care of only about half the number of horses that should be assigned to them—arriving late for work and leaving early, and stealing feed. The maintenance crew members each had a key to the gasoline tank, and about twice as much fuel as was needed for the farm machinery and vehicles was being used. More than twice the amount of feed the chickens could possibly consume, according to the county agent, was being purchased for the poultry department. And, worst of all, the "department heads" were backstabbing each other in their phone calls to Chrysler.

I reported all of this to Walter by telephone, then in writing, including the opinion that the farm would "never grow the pasture needed to raise good racehorses," and suggested solutions for the personnel problems. He quickly paid my rather hefty fee. Along with the check came a note. "Johnny: Deeply appreciate your report. I'll immediately implement the corrections needed, and I'll need your counsel in the future." But he did nothing. He loved confusion.

There were only two good men at North Wales, Bill Reed and Howard Gentry. Bill left the next year to set up a lucrative practice in New York. Howard went down to Chris Chenery's Meadow Farm at Doswell, Virginia, where he raised the champions Secretariat, Riva Ridge (two Kentucky Derby winners in a row), Hill Prince, First Landing, and Cicada.

In 1947, I was at Saratoga to help sell a consignment of North Wales yearlings. Two nights before the youngsters were to be sold, I was sitting at ringside with him when Walter started buying yearlings. Amazed, I said: "Walter, Walter, don't do that. You're giving the impression that we'll be offering our culls." He smiled, said nothing, and continued bidding. (The North Wales yearlings did not bring anything near their value.)

The same evening, Alex Mackay-Smith came to Walter and invited him to join a Virginia syndicate to buy *Piping Rock—already the sire of the good stakes filly Pipette—who was being offered at the dispersal sale of William H. LaBoyteaux, who had died. "Not interested," Walter said. "You should have come to me first." When Alex departed in a rather disappointed manner, Chrysler turned to me and said: "Don't need him, not even one share. I have better stallions." I considered the matter closed.

But at the LaBoyteaux sale, the opening bid for *Piping Rock was made by Walter P. Chrysler Jr.; a bidding battle ensued between him and Isabel Dodge Sloane, who was representing the syndicate of Virginia breeders. Mrs. Sloane, after going beyond the syndicate's maximum price and seeing the stallion knocked down to Chrysler for $81,500, raised herself up out of her seat to her full height. Pointing her finger and raising her voice to a shout, she stunned the audience with her fury: "Okay, junior, you got him, and now you can stick him up your a—!"

Chrysler grinned and turned to me. "What do you think?" he asked. My reply was: "I wouldn't count on any of those syndicate members breeding to him, or to any of your other stallions." About a week later, Walter phoned and said he heard I had Pot o' Luck for sale for $75,000 and that he wanted to buy him. I replied, "No, Walter, I don't want you to have him. He's a vicious horse. You can't confine him to a stall. He's got to be kept in a paddock with a run-in shed for shelter and feeding. That's why Calumet sold him to me for $25,000, a horse that's won seven top stakes and been second in the Kentucky Derby." Walter prevailed.

Three years later, Walter phoned. "You were right for the first time in your life," he said. "Pot o' Luck has badly injured another man. Get rid of him. I don't care what you get for him." "Okay," I said. "But keep him turned out; don't let him be put into a stall. You'll have to get his disposition sweet again in order for me to sell him."

Luck prevailed. In less than a month, I got an order out of France for a horse fitting his exact description: "Proven distance runner, winner of major stakes, placed in at least one classic, good American pedigree, Fair Play sire line preferred, 16 hands, price limit $150,000." I explained the horse's disposition to the agent for Ralph Beaver Straussburger and how he should be handled. No problem. The sale quickly closed at $150,000 and Walter P. Chrysler Jr. made a profit on a horse for the first time.

In the late 1950s, Walter gradually lost interest, sold all his horses, and then disposed of the farm. He cast them out of his life as would a rich child who tires of an expensive toy.

He Was the Marrying Kind

I first met Russell Firestone Jr. in the 1940s, when he came to the Keeneland sales as a youngster with his father. Our friendship was bonded in the 1950s and 1960s, when he was in both racing and polo.

The senior Firestone, one of my earliest business associates, was so conservative in spending money for yearlings that his best friends ribbed him about his frugality. Once, when he went over $10,000 to get a colt at

Russell Firestone.

Keeneland, Arnold Hanger advised: "Careful how you open your wallet. We don't want moths flying all over this sales arena."

Russell Jr. was just the opposite. He was a spender of the highest order. He went for polo teams, racing stables, airplanes, jewelry, horse farms, heavy equipment, and the most expensive of all, wives—six in all.

The elder Firestone died at an early age in 1951, leaving his horses to his widow Dorothy (later Mrs. John Galbreath), who retained me to conduct appraisals for estate taxes. Among the horses was the mare, Miss Zibby, carrying the *Heliopolis colt Summer Tan, second best to Nashua in the 1952 foal crop and destined to earn $542,796 and to sire 20 stakes winners. It was indeed sad that a wonderful sportsman did not live to see his best horse on the racetrack.

Russ was running a Firestone Tire and Rubber Company store (founded by his grandfather, Harvey S. Firestone) and playing polo in Texas at the time of his father's death. I never did learn the manner in which his inheritance came to him, but I understand it came from a trust managed by conservative trustees with wide discretionary powers. Apparently, they were pretty liberal with him the first dozen years.

He put together a polo team—Del Carroll, Ray Harrington, Billy Mayer, and himself—that won the U.S. Open Championship in 1959 in two overtime periods. Russ, at two goals, carried his own weight, enough so his national handicap was raised to three goals the next year. That placed him among the top 10% of registered players nationwide. Though polo can be dangerous, he had no fear.

Russ bought a twin-engine, 12-passenger plane, hired a private pilot on a year-round basis, then learned how to fly it himself. Most of the time I was aboard the pilot was back in the cabin with his guests performing the duties of a steward, serving drinks and snacks. The greatest problem presented by the plane was finding a use for it.

Del helped Russ to select yearlings at the sales and to buy made horses at the track. With Del doing the training, the racing part of his fast-lane life carried itself for a few years. His best horse during that period was 1963 Bay Shore Stakes winner Jet Traffic. But after a divorce from his second wife, Linda, and his marriage to Mary Alice, a Palm Beach socialite who was Burt Lancaster's ex-girlfriend, the trustees apparently slowed down the money supply.

Russ and Del made a pact. Carroll was made authorized agent, which empowered him to withdraw funds from the Firestone racetrack account as payment toward training bills. This worked out well until the balance reached zero. Shortly thereafter, a Firestone filly won. Two days later, when the filly's post-race test had cleared and the funds were eligible to be withdrawn, Del wrote out a transfer of the purse from Russell's account to his, only to be told by the horsemen's bookkeeper: "Mr. Firestone went out this morning and withdrew all the money in the account."

Del, in a fury, that night, phoned me: "That dirty little rascal beat me to the bookkeeper," he said. "I begged him to stop payment on the check, but he said he couldn't do that, that it was Mr. Firestone's account." Del swore he would get even, somehow.

A short while thereafter, Russ phoned me: "I'm shipping you Tellahward," he said. "She's through racing. Sell her for breeding the best you can, take out your expenses and commission, and send me your check for the balance." That was easily done; in fact, it was accomplished in about a week. She was a good-looker, well-bred, and stakes placed. Thomas Mellon Evans was then getting into the business and paid me better than a fair price for her.

Not being able to locate Firestone—he was constantly on the go and it was during the off season for polo—I mailed the check to Del. About two months later a call came from Firestone. "Johnny, what about Tellahward?" he asked. "Have you sold her?" My reply was: "Sold her immediately to Tom Evans for $30,000. Couldn't reach you, so I took out my commission, made out a check payable to you for $27,000, and mailed it to Del, thinking you'd be in Chicago in a day or so to see your horses."

A short pause followed. Then, in a soft, low voice, drifting off into a murmur, he said: "You sent the check to Del.... You sent the check to Del. See you before long. Thanks a lot." The canceled check was located in a matter of minutes, and the endorsement showed it had been deposited into the Firestone account at the racetrack.

The marriage to Mary Alice took place on Long Island, where Russell was playing polo one fall in the 1960s. Mary Alice had set her eyes on a very large diamond ring, and Russ had to buy it for her to prove his love. Otherwise, there was not going to be a wedding. Jack Cartasella, the polo announcer, handled the wedding details, including the purchase of the ring, booking of the parson, serving as best man—and selling Firestone's best pony, Little Mac, to Pete Bostwick for half his value in case extra money should be needed.

Russell did one thing himself, perhaps the smartest ever in his life. He had the ring appraised and insured—in his name! The newlyweds were off on their honeymoon, and Russell wanted all his friends to meet his beautiful bride. One of their first stops was Lexington, for a dinner at my house one evening. Upon my introduction to her, Mary Alice poked the big gemstone nearly into my face. "See what Russy bought me," she said. "Don't you think it sets me apart from the other girls?" "Your looks alone do that for you," I replied. It was true. No starlet in Hollywood was more beautiful.

Mary Alice seemed to have an obsession about the ring. During dinner and in the living room as we chatted late into the evening, she continuously fondled it and stroked it as though it was her first-born child. "Johnny, help me talk Russy into letting me own the fillies and him the colts," she said. "The first one I'm going to name 'Gotrocks.'"

I announced that breakfast would be at 8 a.m. if either wanted to watch the workouts and morning activity at Keeneland. Russ, a notorious late sleeper, did not make it, but Mary Alice did, bounding into the kitchen on the dot, hair full length, snug leather jacket, tight-fitting jeans, jodhpur boots—and her big diamond ring.

The ring was like "Mary's little lamb." Wherever Mary Alice went, the ring went, too. A year or so later in Chicago, when she stopped at a traffic signal, two thugs joined her, removed the ring, and departed from her car with it before the signal turned green. The robbery made Chicago newspaper headlines, as did the divorce action later in the Palm Beach-area papers. When the ring was not recovered in the time specified in the insurance policy, Russ Firestone was paid the proceeds. Mary Alice, I understand, did not receive much in the divorce settlement.

Russ's fourth wife, Myrna, wanted to live on a Kentucky farm, so Russ bought a 40-acre tract of land at the northwest corner of Versailles and Rice Roads, just a half-mile west of Keeneland's entrance. Some time after the marriage ended, the main residence became the home of the Thoroughbred Club of America.

Russell's next union was with a Lexington beauty, Jane. She had been born and raised in the city, and also lived there during her first marriage. She very much wanted to live on a farm, and the couple found the one of their dreams, a 150-acre tract bordered by Harrodsburg, Military, and Keene Roads. It was an excellent real estate investment because of its location. Lexington was growing in that direction.

In my mind, that marriage, Russell's fifth, was going to last, because each had so much to do. Jane busied herself with remodeling the old residence and surrounding buildings and Russ with operating his bulldozers (which he learned how to use after an hour's instruction), burying dead trees, correcting contours of the land, and building a training track.

That work done, the marriage was over, the farm was sold, and within a few years, the property was sold again for a huge profit for commercial and residential development.

Rex Ellsworth Enters the Business

Rex Ellsworth first came to Lexington from Safford, Arizona, in 1933 in a rented Ford truck with $600 in cash in his pocket. He arrived only ten minutes before the start of an auction at the old Lexington Sales Paddocks on the Paris Pike. It took him six days to get back to Safford with the six mares and two weanlings that had cost him $600. Upon his arrival, he was displeased to learn that his cargo refused to be herded by cattle ponies onto the range where they would reside. "We had to lead every one of them there," he later recalled.

In less than 30 years, Rex Cooper Ellsworth was to be one of the few to breed five $500,000 winners—Swaps, Candy Spots, Prove It, Olden Times, and Terrang. All five of those horses were trained by Mesh Tenney, who should be credited for the success of the Ellsworth racing operation. In 1962 and 1963, he was America's leading owner and breeder. Over three decades, he had parlayed his original $600 into an estimated net worth of $12.5-million in land and horses. In 1963, he owned approximately 400 Thoroughbreds and 1,100 square miles of land. Six years before, he had sold Horse of the Year Swaps to Mr. and Mrs. John Galbreath for $2-million, the then-record price for a Thoroughbred. Two years

Rex Ellsworth.

later, John Gaines was to syndicate Olden Times, Candy Spots, and Prove It for a combined $3.6-million.

Rex noted he sold Swaps "out of necessity," vaguely paraphrasing Colonel Phil T. Chinn's humorous remarks about badly needing to generate some money. "I've always operated under pressure of money problems. I've been fighting in a business in which people have a lot of money."

Ellsworth added that he had fewer than ten mares who did not have the blood of his sire *Khaled that were good enough for Swaps. It is my gut feeling, knowing the courage and optimism of Rex, the latter was his reason for parting with Swaps.

It was not until the early 1940s that Rex got himself established—and recognized. Silver Cord, whom he had purchased for $1,250 in 1933, and Arigotal, out of one of the six mares he had bought on his first trip to Lexington, were siring useful moneymakers for him—both on the track and at the sales. Through his friend of rodeo days, Ray Bell, Rex swapped cattle to Louis B. Mayer for services to *Beau Pere, and from those breedings got a number of good ones, including U Time, the best two-year-old filly at the 1946 Hollywood Park meeting.

Swaps, bred and raced by Ellsworth, trained by Mesh Tenney, and ridden by Bill Shoemaker.

Horsemen thought the Arizona "cowboy" to be crazy for turning down Mayer's $100,000 offer for U Time. They underestimated his financial worth as well as his borrowing power. The rejection of the Mayer offer strengthened his posture with the bankers, and Rex immediately went off to Ireland to try to buy *Nasrullah, who previously had been purchased by Joe McGrath for $76,000 and whose first foals were then yearlings.

"They didn't want to talk 'sale' to me," Rex recalled later. "It was my impression they thought I didn't have enough money." In time, a syndicate headed by Bull Hancock purchased *Nasrullah for $372,000 and imported him.

There was, however, one person who had a horse for Rex. Prince Aly Khan offered the Aga Khan's three-year-old *Khaled. But Aly, known as the "richest slicker" in the world, did not want the horse led from his stall, fearing that Rex would detect he was a "roarer." When Ellsworth punched *Khaled in the belly, the horse grunted as roarers do, and that issue was settled. The $160,000 price posed a problem, as did the fact the horse was booked for 1947. Rex liked the horse so much he returned to the U.S., borrowed the $15,000 he was short, bought him, and then did not take delivery until *Khaled had served the mares booked to him for the 1947 season. Rex, from

*Khaled, sire of Swaps and 60 other stakes winners.

his vast experience with horses, knew the paralysis that causes roaring was not hereditary—contrary to the belief of European horsemen.

U Time, Rex's first good one, did not produce well for him, but her full sister, Feather Time, did. Two of her daughters by *Khaled, Time to Khal and Candy Dish, produced Prove It and Candy Spots. Iron Reward, by *Beau Pere, could not even place for Rex in eight starts. But, bred to *Khaled, she produced Swaps and two other stakes winners and was named Broodmare of the Year in 1955. And a daughter of Iron Reward, Track Medal, produced four stakes winners and was voted Broodmare of the Year in 1962. Rex's blending of *Khaled and *Beau Pere blood worked phenomenally well.

I should report one of the observations he made during his glorious heyday with so many top-class and valuable horses. It is indicative of his deep thinking. Noting that he did not think much of buying insurance, he stated: "Insurance is a money-making business. The companies are putting up tall buildings; they finance industry. Because that business appears so good, I self-insure."

She Loved Her Horses

Elizabeth Arden remains one of my most unforgettable persons. I served as her consultant on Thoroughbred matters for four years preceding her death in October of 1966. I never had a client more appreciative of my feelings—or my work.

This was not so with jockeys, trainers, and farm managers. She fired them upon the slightest whim. One trainer was hired one morning and sacked four hours later! Trainer Monte Parke was told to stop chewing tobacco or be dismissed.

I knew going in that the utmost diplomacy would be required. I knew never to tell her that she was wrong, or that she could not or should not do something about which she had nearly decided. I would tell her that her thoughts had considerable merit, but that, before making a final decision, we should consider alternatives, which I would then offer. She generally did the right thing.

In 1963, a tax year for her Thoroughbred activities, she waited until the 11th hour to decide whether to deduct her losses that year and pay tax on the losses claimed the previous four years, or sell off horses she wanted to keep to show a profit in one of five years and thus fulfill the IRS's presumption that she was operating her horse enterprise as a business. She was inclined to pay the tax. "I like my horses more than I care for the money the tax will cost me," she told me.

"What would you do if you were in my position?" she asked. My answer was that she should consider how paying that tax would affect an industry that she loved so much and that had given her so much joy. "Oh, I know," she replied, "the IRS wants to 'hobby' all of us in the horse business. If I give in with the amount of tax I'd pay, that would just 'steam them up' to go after other wealthy horse owners, many of whom may be friends of mine."

She meditated a few moments, then said: "Johnny, I don't want to set a bad example for people in racing with IRS. You know my anticipated losses for this year and you know all my horses. Let's make a list of what we can sell to make my tax year."

Elizabeth Arden.

In a short interim (I had done my homework before this meeting), I had written a "sacrifice" price alongside each of the racehorses, broodmares, yearlings, and weanlings, then asked her to check the ones with which she would part. Though she appeared in great mental anguish as she checked, she did give me a list to sell with sufficient value to make her tax year.

"I hate to give up Gun Bow and Gun Boat, but I'm keeping Get Around," she sighed. Get Around that year had won the Withers and Choice Stakes and was second in the Hollywood and Jersey Derbys, as well as the Blue Grass Stakes.

In 24 hours, I had sold Gun Bow and Gun Boat to trainer Eddie Neloy for a new client, Harry Albert, for $150,000, but the going was slow from that November day until Monday morning, December 30, the last banking day of the year, when I appeared in the main offices of Elizabeth Arden, Inc., with checks that barely put us over our goal.

The next year, when Gun Bow was in an intense battle for Horse of the Year honors with Kelso, whom he beat in the Woodward Stakes and Brooklyn Handicap while running up season earnings of $580,100, Miss Arden never showed a sign of regret. She instead rooted for him. And, when he was syndicated a year later, she bought one share in him for more than she got for all of him.

Miss Arden loved her horses, good or bad, with a passion that defied understanding. That is, with the exception of those who would bite when she offered sugar from her hand. They were soon separated from her Maine Chance Stable. The same was true of a trainer who would speak disparagingly of her horses—or her Eight Hour Cream, which she insisted had to be used on the horses.

In 1945, when the rider was thrown up aboard her Beaugay for the Arlington Lassie Stakes, her only instructions were: "Don't hit my baby!" He did not have to; Beaugay won in a breeze and went on to be champion juvenile filly.

Miss Arden lost 22 select two-year-olds in a devastating fire at Arlington Park in the first week of May, 1946. She took it in stride, noting: "Fate has a way of equating things." Jet Pilot, then two, avoided the tragedy because he had accompanied stablemates Lord Boswell and Knockdown to Churchill Downs, where he broke his maiden on Derby Day. A few races later, the

Jet Pilot won the 1947 Kentucky Derby for Arden's Maine Chance Farm.

other two ran as favorites, 1.10-to-1, but could finish no better than fourth and fifth in Assault's Derby. Jet Pilot came back the next year and did a bit better in the Derby. He led every step of the way.

In 1956, when she had too many yearlings to fit into Maine Chance Stable, she offered a number of them at the Saratoga sales. A very, very successful buyer herself at yearling auctions, she felt the buyers "don't appreciate a nice colt when they see one." Her colt by Jet Jewel was then in the ring. She bid him in for $3,500, which caused considerable consternation. "She's crazy," said one oldtime horseman, "she thinks all of hers are great." This one was. The following year, as Jewel's Reward, he was champion two-year-old colt in one poll and had earnings that season of $349,642.

Our game has known few like Elizabeth Nightingale Arden, thrice married to men whose terms as her husbands were as short as the tenures of most of her trainers. During her 30 years in this business, by conservative count she had as many as 35 trainers. She hired instantly, and she fired instantly. If you went to work for her, it was prudent not to buy a house or enter into a long-term lease on one. In fact, it was also wise not to unpack completely. Ike Mourar served many times as her interim trainer because, although he did not have the highest ability, he was honest and kind "to my babies," as she referred to her horses.

"Silent Tom" Smith, of Seabiscuit fame, trained for Elizabeth four different times, the only one to serve more than one term. After getting to know Tom through Phil Chinn, I asked him why she ever fired him. "After all," I noted, "you trained her only Kentucky Derby winner, Jet Pilot, in 1947."

"She wanted me to argue with her about her horses," he grinned, "and I just wouldn't. I'd just stare at her and say nothing. That would make her boil over and she'd fire me. She'd send to the stable many jars of her health or cosmetic products, particularly Eight Hour Cream, and I'd use them as she directed. They didn't do the horses any good, but they didn't do any harm, either, so I used them to make her happy. The reason the other trainers weren't hired back was she learned from her stool pigeon in the stable they threw her products into the manure pit."

Henry Clark's Little Fib

Very early one morning at Belmont Park, Henry Clark was at the trainer's stand to watch a Christiana Stables runner whom he had shipped up from Delaware for a stakes race. A woman emerged from a chauffeur-driven Cadillac, ascended the steps, and asked him: "Sir, are you a trainer?" Henry knew that she was Elizabeth Arden and answered softly: "No, ma'am, I'm not. I'm just here watching the horses."

"Oh," the cosmetics queen continued, "I was so in hopes you were. I'm in need of one. I just relieved mine of his duties five minutes ago, and I must immediately hire a dependable one to take over my horses." At that time, Henry was well into his long tenure as head trainer of the Christiana horses.

No Sitting Around

Once when Miss Arden arrived at her Belmont stable at "doing up" time and found two grooms sitting down, she approached them and stated quietly: "Both of you are fired." One retorted: "Oh, no, Miss Arden, you can't fire me, I'm just visiting, I work for Max Hirsch." Not to be contradicted, she replied: "Well, I'll have Mr. Hirsch fire you—you should be working. I'll tell him." She did, and Max sacked him.

The Fink on the Farm

One of Miss Arden's idiosyncrasies was the feeling that she needed a secret informer to keep her apprised of any irregularities or contraventions of her orders in her racing stable. She had a dandy in a young man whose nickname was Chico. Each succeeding Main Chance trainer had to agree to retain Chico as a groom. Chico was remunerated quite handsomely on the side for those services.

Once, Miss Arden transferred Chico to her Maine Chance Farm at Lexington for the same purposes. Upon his arrival, the young stoolie announced to the farm manager, Jim Lockwood: "I take care of only three horses, just like in the racing stable," so Jim acceded to his wishes. When the other farm workers complained, Jim asked and got their forbearance. Jim did know how to handle Miss Arden.

When asked by her how things were going upon her arrival a few days later, Jim sheepishly noted there was a "labor problem. Chico has convinced the other grooms they shouldn't have to care for nine horses, only three." That did it. Miss Arden immediately sent Chico back to her stable in New York.

A Change of Breeds

John Gaines raised Standardbreds on Gainesway Farm for himself and his father with considerable success. Classical Way, the 1980 trotter of the year and one of the best trotting mares of all time, was raised there for Clarence Gaines. John put together the first syndication of a Standardbred stallion when he was 28. Having been associated with trotters and pacers in some form since I was just a kid, I have known John most of his life.

In 1962, John walked into my office and announced: "I'm now in the Thoroughbred business. I've got shares in Nashua and *Turn-to. Now let's get some mares." We did. But I did not last long. Keen student that he is, in a year's time John could analyze racing records and pedigrees as well as I—and how to find and buy what he wanted!

He was successful from the very beginning. In 1962, he purchased the mare Cosmah privately from Gene Mori for $55,000. She was in foal to Swaps and had a *Ribot colt at her side. John immediately resold the *Ribot colt, eventual stakes winner and stakes sire Maribeau, for $23,000 to Tony Imbesi. He sold Cosmah's colt by Swaps, eventual stakes winner Fathers Image, as a yearling to John Olin for $75,000. Cosmah later would be voted Broodmare of the Year. Early on, John also bought stakes winner Sofarsogood, from which he bred the stakes winner Burd Alane.

John R. Gaines.

Also in his first year, John privately bought the stakes winner Oil Royalty for $60,000 from Elmendorf Farm. Before he retired her, Oil Royalty won $336,598, most of it for him. He also had the shares in Nashua and *Turn-to, foals by whom he sold for fantastic prices.

Signing On With the Captain

In Saratoga's paddock one August afternoon in 1947, Captain Harry Guggenheim asked me to join him in his box to discuss a business matter. "For several years I have been trying to get Joe Estes to do some consulting work for me on my breeding program. But each time I've asked him, he tells me to get you," Guggenheim said. "He says you know how to research, buy your own horses off of it, and make money. Eslie Asbury told me Estes

Capt. Harry F. Guggenheim.

considers outside work a conflict of interest with editorship of *The Blood-Horse*, and he also suggested you. So here we are."

The captain at the time had 12 mares, the best of which was Good Morning, and two very bad stallions, War Dog and *The Sultan. He acknowledged that, in the 13 years he had been racing and breeding, he had not accomplished much. I signed on to do the matings and a minor amount of consulting on purchases. My retainer fee was $2,000 a year plus a small fraction of the stable earnings.

For 17 years, I made all the matings and not one was changed. I was consulted on the purchase of Dark Star as a yearling for $6,500 and recommended it. He gave the captain a Kentucky Derby win in 1953, and in so doing the *Royal Gem II colt handed Native Dancer his only defeat. I would like to claim credit for the purchase of *Turn-to as a yearling for $20,000, but he made that decision completely on his own. I purchased only one broodmare for him in the 17 years I worked for him, Azalea, in foal to Roman, for $15,000. She was carrying his stakes winner Nile Lily, the grandam of Riverman, who was sold as a weanling in his dispersal sale of 1969 for $41,000 to Alec Head.

In 1964, when the Guggenheim program had grown so large I could no longer do an efficient job part time, we parted on the best of terms, and remained good friends up until his death at age 80. I was ably replaced on a full-time basis by Humphrey Finney.

At Saratoga in 1960, in accepting a plaque for being the leading owner of 1959 in money won, he stated: "I could not accept this honor without sharing it with my trainer Woody Stephens, my jockey Manuel Ycaza, and a young man down in Kentucky named John H. Clark, who helped me breed these horses."

Woody Stephens and Guggenheim on opening day at Belmont in October of 1962.

A Favorite Client

Jimmy Stone, for whom I worked as a consultant on Thoroughbreds since back in the late 1950s, is my all-time favorite client. If one of his horses runs badly, he telephones the trainer and "cools" him out. The same goes when deals that I have advised go wrong.

"Stoney," as many of his friends address him, was born to wealth and social position in New York in 1925, but he never used those benefits to gain the stature he achieved in big business. He was a self-made man, a risk-taker, a seven-day workaholic. He considers a five-minute telephone conversation during work hours to be an eternity.

Entering the United States Marines as an enlisted man in 1943 during World War II, Stone attained the rank of first lieutenant before being mustered out in 1946. My favorite story about Jimmy was told to me by the late Robert Lehman, senior partner in Lehman Brothers, who was a close friend of Jimmy's father. "I'd known and liked Jimmy since he was a tiny youngster. World War II was just over and Jimmy had served with distinction with the

Marines, I knew he had studied geology at Texas A & M, so I asked him to come into our oil department.

"Jimmy accepted, and he showed such ability that one day I called him into my office and told him we were sending him at company expense to study advanced geology at Texas A&M. He agreed and went, but when he returned he came into my office and said, 'I want to thank you with all my heart for helping me make up my mind as to exactly what I want to do—to go into the oil business on my own. I want you to release me. I want to set up my office in Cincinnati. I'll pay you back, or work out, what it cost Lehman Brothers to send me to Texas.'

"I'll do it for two reasons," Lehman recalled saying. "First, I like you personally and admire your ambition, and, secondly, Lehman needs an oil representative in Cincinnati. Go on out there and set up your business. Lehman will be your first client."

James H. Stone.

In Cincinnati, Jimmy formed Stone Oil Company. He also met and married his charming and brilliant wife, Lib Asbury, daughter of Drs. Eslie and Mary Asbury, and that, of course, led him into Thoroughbreds.

By the 1970s, Stone Oil was so successful that it was partners with such companies as Exxon, Shell, Sun Oil, Continental Oil, and the Dow Chemical Company in drilling activities. By 1990, Stone had offices in Cincinnati; Houston, Texas; Tulsa, Oklahoma; Lafayette, Louisiana; and New Orleans, where he resided. He was the largest individual shareholder of a Fortune 500 company, an underwriting member of Lloyd's of London, a director of the Los Angeles Rams of the National Football League, and the Hibernia National Bank of New Orleans.

In addition, James Hiram Stone was a director of the New Orleans Opera Association and a trustee of the New Orleans Museum of Art, the New Orleans Symphony, and Tulane Medical Center. In real estate, he was the principal partner in Place St. Charles, a 55-story office building in New Orleans, and Riverstone, an office building and park in Lafayette.

Back in the 1950s, when we were discussing the Thoroughbred business, I told him that making money in breeding and racing had about the same odds for success as drilling for oil. "I hear you," he remarked, nodding his head. "So let's keep our operation small, numerically and dollar-wise, so we don't create a yearly 'nut' so big we can't show a gain once in five years on racing earnings and sales and be hobbied by the Internal Revenue Service."

It was agreed we would breed a few mares and buy two or three yearlings each year. Also, we would buy and sell stallion shares, the best investment in the business if done prudently.

Well, Jimmy has never failed the test of the IRS, although to show a profit one year he had to sell eventual graded stakes winner Young Bob, a colt he had bred, for $32,000 at the Keeneland July yearling sale. Olden was the hardest to give up. We bought her for $25,000 as a yearling at Saratoga, and she won the Bewitch Stakes at Keeneland and the Debutante Stakes at Churchill Downs on Derby Day in 1976. Pretty nice to win a race on Derby Day—but a stakes! We sold Olden to Will Farish for $125,000 after she was through racing.

On his own, Stoney bought Pittsburgh as a yearling for $27,000 at Saratoga in 1976 and sent him to France to trainer John Fellows, for whom he won and was placed in a Group 2 race. I sold the Roberto colt to a Colombian breeder as a stud prospect for $50,000.

Flagship, Pirogue, and Capital Punishment, purchased by Stone as yearlings for $5,000, $27,000, and $15,000, respectively, each placed in stakes and proved bargain buys. Stoney made the best bargain himself. In 1972, he purchased a share in Naskra for $3,000 and used the season or sold it for seven years. I sold the share to Verne Winchell in 1979 for $100,000.

Stoney had remarkable success in England, where he goes once each year to meet with other underwriting members of Lloyd's and to take in a bit of racing. Several of his horses there were trained by Henry Cecil.

His biggest thrill in racing came there on October 1, 1981, when his Cajun, firmly backed by him at 20-to-1, won Newmarket's William Hill Middle Park Stakes (Eng-G1), one of the richest races of the year in England. That win and a second in the Richmond Stakes (Eng-G2) placed Cajun among the top 11 juveniles on the English Free Handicap. Cajun, purchased by Stone for the equivalent of $60,000 as a yearling, was retired to stud in Ireland and subsequently was moved to Japan.

Also in 1981, Ardross, whom he owned in a partnership, won Group 1 stakes in England and France, and was weighted as champion stayer in those two countries' free handicaps.

The following season, Cajun was again a group winner, and Ardross had six more group wins, and finished second, beaten a head, in the Trusthouse Forte Prix de l'Arc de Triomphe (Fr-G1). The Arc was Ardross's last race.

Again, he topped the French Free Handicap for stayers. He retired to stud as the 19th leading European earner of all time ($760,819), and as a champion in England, Ireland, and France.

As his oil and other enterprises began to take more and more of his time, Stoney asked me if I would assume power of attorney on all matters pertaining to his Thoroughbreds. "The paperwork is killing me—taking out licenses in every state in which I race, transferring certificates of registration, making stakes entries. You can do that for me." When the papers arrived, I was shocked by the broad powers Jimmy had given me. I could buy or sell any horse without consulting him—do anything "I might do or could do if personally present." I immediately rang him up.

"Jimmy, I don't need all this power," I said. He replied: "My lawyer didn't think so either, said he wouldn't give that much to his own brother, but I trust you and want you to be able to manage the whole show if it becomes necessary." Well, we never had any problems with that 2 1/2-page document. Stoney and I have done a great deal of trading between ourselves, each making money on every deal.

In 1976, I bought for him a share in Sham for $95,000, and each year sold the service for $20,000. The same year, I purchased for him the yearling filly Auld for $31,000, telling him her residual value, if she won just one race, would be $25,000. At the end of her three-year-old year, after she had won a maiden race, we agreed to offer her for sale at $30,000. There were no takers, not even a counteroffer of $25,000.

I suggested to Jimmy: "You've generated $60,000 in the sales of services to Sham. I'll give you $25,000 for Auld if you'll sell me the Sham share for $90,000, the going price right now for a Sham. I'll breed Auld to Sham." He was elated.

In the breeding season of 1979, Auld got in foal with two covers. Brownell Combs gave me $80,000 for the Sham share, and thus my investment in Auld was now $35,000. In the November sale at Keeneland, much to my amazement, she brought $180,000. I immediately telephoned Stoney and, grand guy that he is, he was as happy as I.

In 1976, I bought two shares in Olden Times for $26,000. When I told Jimmy about it, he asked if I would mind if he gave me a profit for them. I told him the horse was 18 years old, a high-risk gamble, and he could have them at my cost. "No, I insist you make a profit. I'll give you $30,000." The deal was made.

In three years of breeding for Stoney, at ages 19, 20, and 21, Olden Times generated more than $100,000 in net revenue to him. "I don't want to stretch my luck too far. Sell the shares as best you can," he told me. I replied: "I'll take them for $10,000." Another deal was made, the best ever in my life.

Although he was 22 when I started selling the seasons, Olden Times was coming on as a leading broodmare sire. This created a demand for his services. In 1982, he was second-leading broodmare sire (to Prince John), leading sire of two-year-olds, and sire of champion juvenile colt Roving Boy. Pretty good for a 24-year-old stallion.

The stud fee went up to $50,000 in 1983. In 1984, when Olden Times was serving his last season at stud at the age of 26, I sold one share to Richard Winn of Welcome Farm in Pottstown, Pennsylvania, for $50,000. He got his mare in foal, as I did with the mare I sent to Olden Times. My $10,000 investment in Olden Times netted me well over $325,000. It has been profitable and a pleasure to work for James H. Stone.

A Tireless Worker

The word "tireless" aptly describes Albert G. Clay. Ted Bassett, board chairman of Keeneland, said of him: "If you ask Albert to do something, consider it done."

As of 1990, Albert was secretary of the American Horse Council, a position he has held since its formation in 1969. He was chairman of the University of Kentucky Equine Research Foundation, for which he had raised millions of dollars in donations, and he was a member of his regional Boy Scouts of America executive committee.

For 20 consecutive years, he served on the Board of Trustees of the University of Kentucky, most of them as chairman or vice chairman, and for this service he received an honorary doctoral degree.

In 1969, when legislation very adverse to the industry was before Congress,

Albert Clay.

Warner Jones Jr. and A. B. "Bull" Hancock Jr. persuaded Albert to become a member of the Thoroughbred Breeders of Kentucky and help unite the organization with other similar groups throughout the United States in the formation of the American Horse Council. The AHC was formed to promote and protect all horse breeds on a national level. Its offices are in Washington, D. C. Albert "got it done" in a few short months, and he has remained a vital part of the AHC.

The AHC represents some 17 breeds involving 5.2-million horses and approximately one-million horsemen. Congress pays attention to such numbers, as do the multitude of regulatory bodies of the federal government.

R. Richards Rolapp, president of the AHC, told me: "Albert has the unique ability to understand the important issues affecting the horse business and to relate those issues to government policy.... He is content to work behind the scenes and let others be in the spotlight."

Nick Nicholson, director of the Jockey Club, recalled his work with Albert when he was with the Kentucky Thoroughbred Owners and Breeders Association. "I worked with him on every major horse issue during those days. When the going got tough and I'd look around to see who was still in there fighting with me, Albert would always be there. He never wanted credit for a job well done. He was only interested in results," Nicholson said.

Despite his enormous contributions to the industry, Clay is not as well known as he might be. He prefers to maintain a low profile in racing and sales, keeping only a few mares, all of whom are of high quality, and most of which are owned in partnership with son John. Their produce are sold by son Robert's Three Chimneys Farm as yearlings. An occasional filly is held back for racing and breeding. From this small group have come about ten stakes winners.

Kamar, whom he owned in partnership with Warner Jones and son Robert, sold in foal to Danzig for $2.6-million as a part of Jones's Hermitage Farm dispersal at the 1987 Keeneland November breeding stock sale. Her Slew o' Gold yearling filly had sold for $575,000 in the July sales at Keeneland that year, with Robert Clay buying out his partners. The filly Gorgeous has since earned more than $1-million.

Albert, though he was breeding a few run-of-the-mill runners, never gave serious thought to making a substantial investment in the business until he was called upon to help guide its destiny. He felt he should make a larger investment if he were to speak for the industry. His first major purchase for a broodmare prospect was the Northern Dancer filly, Aladancer, who won a division of Aqueduct's Firenze Handicap for him in 1971.

I have never had a better partner than Albert Clay. We made money on every horse we ever owned together, largely because he worked as hard as I did in their reselling. One day in October of 1977, while he was in my office to discuss an unrelated matter, I mentioned to Albert that I had just received a phone call from an out-of-state owner offering me a young, well-bred, stakes-winning son of Northern Dancer for $100,000. I noted he was worth considerably more than that for resale, but I said I was hesitating in buying him because I had never put that much money in a stallion prospect. "If my taking half of him will help you," Albert said, "go ahead and buy him for us—I'd like to be a partner with you in a horse." Within three weeks we resold the horse to Japanese interests for $250,000.

After that, we bought two very well-bred fillies off the track. When we were unable to resell them for what I considered their true worth, Albert bought my half out at a handsome profit to me and put them in his broodmare band.

In the spring of 1978, again in my office on unrelated business, Albert inquired if I had any mares. "I need just one," he said. I replied: "Just one, but she's not good enough for you. She's Royal Ermine, age 17, and due to foal shortly to Olden Times. I want $25,000 for her." After reading her pedigree, he said: "I'll take her."

The foal Royal Ermine was carrying, Olden Thoughts, brought him $45,000 at auction, and his full sister, Broadtail, got him $150,000 at a yearling sale the following year. Broadtail was a nice race filly, winning three races and placing second in stakes at Hollywood Park and Del Mar. Indeed, Albert has been a good partner, a good customer, and a good friend.

Chapter 13
Horsemen and Other Friends

In the many, many years that I owned racehorses, I knew several great trainers, including my dear friend the Senor, Horatio Luro. But I never had any great trainers for my horses. That is not to say that the trainers I employed were not talented. It was simply a case that they were not on the same level as Horatio or Allen Jerkens or Ben Jones. My program trainers were every bit as interesting and amusing as the great trainers, and perhaps even more so. I would like to tell you about a few of them and some other horsemen I have encountered in my years of tradin'.

'One Horse Ike'

Isaac Perlstein ran away from his Pittsburgh home at a very young age before the turn of the century. He had little or no formal education, but he did possess an abundant amount of common sense and integrity, as well as a humorous outlook on life and a deep feeling for his fellow man.

Ike caught on as an exercise boy—poor vision precluded a career as a jockey—and oldtimers have told me there was none better. In the 1940s when we became close friends—almost immediately—he was known as "One Horse Ike." He had never been able to sell himself as a trainer, and therefore all he had to train was some old critter he had bought for a pittance or on the cuff.

I "inherited" Ike from Al Jolson. Jolson liked to bet, and on one occasion Ike made a misjudgment on the ability of Al's horse. Ike found what he thought was the right spot, thought the horse could not lose, and Jolson told him he was wiring him $1,000 to bet. "I'll be on location that day," the star of stage and screen instructed. "You won't be able to reach me by phone, so get a telegram to me the morning of the race stating: 'Ship sails today.' I don't want to let those telegraph operators and their friends get in on our action. After the race, send me another wire on how we made out."

Ike did as he was told, sent the "ship sails today" message, but as

Ike Perlstein.

with many "sure things," bad luck prevailed. The horse was knocked to its knees at the start, losing the jockey. Ike's wire after the race was, "Ship sunk, no survivors."

Jolson used Ike for a leg man but refused to buy him horses. I changed that. I kept him in horses until failing health prevented him from keeping up with the rigid routine of a trainer. And we did very well together.

In October, 1952, when I was handling public relations for Keeneland, I could not get up to New York for the Correction Handicap, a race we had set our hearts and hopes on for Quiz Song. The fall meet at Keeneland was in progress, but Ike managed well. The filly I had claimed earlier in the year for $15,000 won the Correction over a large and classy field, including the next year's handicap female champion, Sickle's Image, on October 13, 1952, at old Jamaica, paying $42.30, bringing great joy to a relatively unknown owner and trainer as well as apprentice jockey Willie Lester.

I have owned a few stakes horses, including 1954 Arkansas Derby runner-up Winning Count, whom I bought at auction from C. V. Whitney for $800 as a two-year-old. But I have never had or expect to have another Quiz Song. Ike also got five wins, nearly all in a row, with Mabe Cee, plus a couple of stakes placings at Garden State Park. And he had others for me that helped me get a foothold in the business.

Ike had but one failing. It is what I have always called the "New York trainer syndrome"—the reluctance or refusal to ship elsewhere when their horses were not competitive in the Big Apple. Once, when everything was going out and nothing coming in, I directed Ike to take my horses to Suffolk Downs and get them all sold or claimed. When he refused—the only time he said no to me in his life—I shipped them to Red Ness, who got the job done.

Shortly thereafter when I had to be at Belmont, George Widener, then the track's president, said to me: "Come on, Johnny, get Ike a horse or two. He seems so sad. He's lost without something to train." I told him I would try. Moments later, Tommy Trotter told me Jack Campbell would like to see me at my convenience.

"Do me a favor," said the great racing secretary and handicapper, "and get Ike a couple of horses. I'll find him the stalls." I knew Ike's friends were legion, but I was astonished, though pleased, that two eminent members of racing's establishment would go to the front for him. Needless to say, I had bought two horses for Ike before I left New York—and we were in business together again.

Once I asked Ike to name for me the people he felt to be the most important in U.S. racing. In a few moments, he reeled off a dozen or more, all of them New Yorkers, of course. His list included Hirsch Jacobs, Jack Campbell, Hollie Hughes, "Mr. Fitz" (James Fitzsimmons), Bert Mulholland, George Widener, Sammy Smith, George Poole, Jimmy Kilroe, and Francis Dunne. When I asked him why he deemed them important, he said: "They treat me like a friend."

Ike was a horseplayer, but he was not compulsive. He could pass up a race. I never in my life knew him to ask a trainer if he liked his horse, but many times I have heard trainers such as Max Hirsch tell him to bet on his horse. Seldom was he ever completely busted, but on occasion he would get an advance from me for "walking around" money or a car payment. He always squared up.

Once Ike hit it very big at Gulfstream. At around 3 p.m. one afternoon I received a "collect, emergency call from Mr. Perlstein," which I accepted immediately. "Collect" was the usual, but not the "emergency." With grave trepidation, I asked: "Ike, are you in trouble?" "Hell, no, I just cashed an exotic ticket. I got more than forty-five hundred clams in my pocket—I need to send you some for safekeeping."

Although Ike was 35 years my senior, I instructed him in the manner of a father to a son: "Listen, Ike, Dixie McKinley is down there and coming home tomorrow. Give four grand to Dixie and he'll give it to me. Every time you need $500 phone me and I'll send it."

Ike insisted he should keep more—he was on a lucky streak and could run it up. He did as I suggested, however. But eight phone calls and eight weeks later he had zeroed out his safekeeping account with me. I am still amused about the "collect" part of Ike's call.

Ike's Poor Vision

Ike had terribly bad vision. The lenses of his glasses were exceedingly thick, and about as far as he could see was the odds board, which was all right with him. When he started training for me, I bought him a pair of binoculars, but his reports to me on my horses' races never squared with the racing charts or movies I would later see. Riding with him in his car when he was driving was a terrifying experience—lane switching in heavy traffic, running stop signs, and the like. But, oddly enough, I never knew him to be involved in an accident or get a traffic ticket.

Ike's thick glasses, his sagging clothes, his observations on racing, the Broadway crowd, marriage, and other matters made him, indeed, unique. He was truly a Damon Runyon character. Once after having a good day at the races and dining at Lindy's, Ike and his pal Moe Gallop, who also wore thick glasses and had less vision, came out of the restaurant and started across Broadway, only to walk into the side of a passing street car. To the screams of bystanders, the conductor stopped the car so suddenly it almost jumped the tracks.

As Ike started scrambling to his feet, Moe, always eager for a quick, unearned buck, yelled to him: "Get back down and hold your back and holler from pain, we'll get ten grand apiece from the insurance company for this."

Ike replied: "I don't get money that way. And, besides, I got to be at the track tomorrow. I think I can win the double." Ike was a man of integrity.

One night in 1970, Isaac Perlstein returned from dinner with his newspaper, said goodnight to the landlady of the house in which he roomed in Elmont, New York, and retired to bed. By morning, another credit to our game had passed on.

The Firing Squad

A trainer "between jobs" stopped by the office to inquire if I knew of any openings. I told him of one. "Nope," he replied, "I'm not interested. That outfit has changed trainers so many times the last few years it has become known as the firing squad. The four partners in that stable have an agreement that, if one becomes dissatisfied with the trainer, he's got to go."

He Could Tell Some Whoppers

"Lyin' Harry" Smith was another Runyon type of character—had every kind of hustle known on the racetrack, the least successful of which was touting.

"Lyin' Harry" Smith.

The nickname came to him not by speaking untruths, but by his telling of humorous tall stories. Some of his stories were partially true, with figments of his imagination added.

I'm pretty sure the year was 1969. I was joking one afternoon with Doug Davis, Jake Lowenstein, and Henry Forrest outside the racing secretary's office at Churchill Downs, when my trainer-away-from-home, Lyin' Harry, joined us, a bridle in his hand. "Well, boss, we're out of business again," he said. "They just claimed our last horse. Guess I'll have to get me a jock's book until you send me some more horses."

"Got any prospects?"

"No," he replied as he started another of his big lies, "but I'm gonna try to get hold of that two-headed jock that came to me earlier in the meeting and wanted me to take his book. I got his name and number over at the tack room."

"A two-headed jock!" Doug and I virtually yelled in unison. "Now come on, Lyin' Smitty," Jake chimed in. "Yes," Lyin' Harry returned in the low voice he used when he was fabricating at his best, "his neck forks out of his shoulders, and he can turn either head in any direction. He can look back over his right shoulder with the right and do the same thing with his left, all at the same time. He's got 360-degree vision available to him at all times, never changing his balance on a horse.

"Some of these trainers complaining about jocks looking back on the wrong side and letting a horse slip by 'em on the other sure could use him. Then, too, a trainer has another advantage in using him, three heads are better than one in planning race strategy or discussing what happened in a race."

"What's his name and where's he from?" I inquired, again playing straight man for my prevaricating trainer. "Best I recall at the moment, it's McAndrew McAndrew and he's from Walla Walla, Washington. As I was talking to him, I was on the backside looking at the grandstand. I decided if ever I took his book, I'd nickname him 'Twin Towers.' " Smitty always referred to Churchill Downs's twin spires as the twin towers.

"Does he bet the races?" Doug asked with a grin, egging Smitty on. "Only the daily double," Lyin' Harry answered. Alex Harthill, who had arrived just about the time Smitty started his story, put in: "Has this freak got any other road game?" Lyin' Harry, still holding a straight face, said: "Yes, and he said he could make big bucks if he worked at it, but he don't like the game. He's a tennis umpire."

Jake said that, in his long years in the business, he had already heard too much double talk from jockeys. "I don't think I could stand any in quadruple."

By this time, a goodly crowd of horsemen, curious about what was keeping us hardened racetrackers spellbound and laughing, had moved into our group. Since Lyin' Harry, fresh out of horses, had no "doing up" time that afternoon, I asked him to stay on and relate a story he had told me about his barnstorming the West one summer, match-racing at catch weights at unregulated tracks.

That type of racing has been going on in this country since the 1600s and was still very much in vogue. There are "no holds" barred—batteries, hop, you name it. Many of the country's leading riders graduated from that bush racing—Earl Sande, Ivan Parke, Cash Asmussen, and Eddie Delahoussaye. Jimmy Nichols won more than 200 races at the bush tracks before being licensed as an apprentice at the age of 19. If a child was unable to stay on the horse's back, he was tied on with rope or strapped on.

Now, Lyin' Harry picks up his yarn: "I had this ten-year-old horse who knew as much about racing as I did, but age and his bad legs had caught up with him and he couldn't hit the board around here (meaning River Downs, Beulah Park, and Ellis Park), so I give a hundred dollars for an old rickety trailer and headed west with him, taking along my fighting rooster.

"I set out for Oklahoma. My Ford pickup, much older than the horse, would overheat and I'd have to stop every 30 or 40 miles, let it cool off, then fill the radiator with water. If I paid to have it fixed, I wasn't gonna have no money to bet. Finally, I got there and found the place they raced. Everybody wanted to match me—I was fresh meat.

"The first guy that came over wanted to match me even, and I said: 'No, I gotta get 5-to-1 for my $100.' They kept coming by and coming by. At last I got faded, and the sheriff was the stake holder. I called the sheriff to one side and told him what I was going to do and that he better get down on my horse, too. He did. Then I knew I wasn't gonna get beat up or have my horse hurt.

"The guy I bet came back and said: 'Where's your rider?' I said: 'What do you care, it's catch weights, ain't it?' He said yes. I said my rider is having lunch, soon as he's through I'll run you. The rooster was in the back of the pickup, pecking away at a pan of yellow cracked corn. 'Meet you at the start in ten minutes,' I told him.

"I put the fighting spurs on the rooster, put a surcingle on my old horse, tied the rooster on top of his back, and led him to the post. The guy I bet screamed bloody murder, said he thought he'd already been had every way possible, but this was a new one. I reminded him he had agreed to catch weights.

"When the starter hollered go and my old horse broke like lightning, the rooster started flapping his wings and digging in with his sharp spurs. It wasn't even a contest. When my old horse hit the finish line, he knew it, pulled himself up, and started grazing. I told you he was smart. The rooster quieted down as soon as he stopped. I fetched them, collected from the sheriff the $600, and got out of town in a hurry, looking for another bush track. I was through there.

"I soon was able to trade for a reliable truck, and I pulled this off at every bush track I could find in Oklahoma, Texas, and Louisiana. When I ran out of tracks, I came back with enough scratch to get back into racing at River Downs, Beulah, and Ellis again."

A Cure for Stall Walkers

Lyin' Harry had a goat that would settle down any stall-walking, weaving filly. He would never sell him, only rented him out. But every time the goat's stall mate would win, Harry would raise the rent, and before long the filly would be claimed. "Finally got put out of business," he told me. "Mince Johns had some kind of a bad weaving filly, and that damned old filly got my goat to weaving, and I could never break him of the habit."

Father-and-Son Touts

Lyin' Harry was level-weighted with Elizabeth Taylor and Mickey Rooney in a marital handicap; he made eight starts. I asked him how he got rid of them. "Drop 'em down cheap and let somebody else claim 'em. Your friend, Mose Lowenstein, took one, to his regret. The best of 'em was Louise—she was the dam of Li'l Jimmy."

In eight marriages, Lyin' Harry always carefully selected a "working wife" just to be sure there was bread on the table. He invariably came home tapped out every night. Little Jimmy was a story in himself. Although racetracks in those days did not admit children, by age 12 Jimmy could tout the gruffest, most inaccessible horse players that ever came through a turnstile. Who could turn down a kid with shoes half-untied, tattered clothes, and a big smile? He always "knew" a good thing and wanted to get down $2 across the board. He missed more often than he hit, but he was ever on the prowl during the afternoons, mostly for elderly horseplayers.

I inherited Lyin' Harry from Calumet Farm. He galloped Bewitch for Calumet and he was one of the best of exercise men. But touting was his real game and he needed more credentials than just being an exercise boy—he wanted those of a trainer. That was where I came in, since there was hardly any room to get that kind of a title with Calumet. A couple of pretty fair trainers by the names of Ben A. Jones and Jimmy Jones were the trainers of record.

Smitty would take horses that I could not sell to the smaller tracks and run them at the bottom claiming prices until they were claimed or sold off on his "story" that Clark was a very poor trainer and there was a chance to improve the horse. Others that Lyin' Harry handled for me were well-bred fillies who could not break their maidens because they lacked speed or class or were such bad eaters they were lucky to have strength to gallop once around. These were sent to Harry at tracks like Dade Park or Beulah, the lowest level of competition. Once they won, they were immediately returned to my farm where they were fattened and put in order as broodmare prospects.

"This last one you sent me is a doozy," trainer Harry informed me in a collect call from Beulah one fall day. "Oats look to her like they're footballs. She actually turns her tail and craps in her feedtub. But I think I've found a way to make her eat." He then explained to me that some horses have the same incurable habits as some very wealthy people: "They're kleptomaniacs.

"The partitions between stalls at this old leaky-roofed track have big cracks. The other day, instead of eating her own hay, I catched her stealing from another of your stumble bums in the next stall through a crack in the boards. I knocked off the top half of the plank and hung her hay rack and feedtub over in his stall and she now has a vote-ratious appetite." I assume he meant "voracious."

Trouble With the Bottle

I have known quite a number of boozers who became successful trainers, but not one of them was able to sustain his success for very long. Their ever-increasing dependence on the bottle robbed them of their mental and physical faculties, as well as their health, and the pitiful souls had to be cared for as invalids until they died, usually at an early age.

The first one I knew was Tom B. Young, son of Colonel Milton Young, one of the leading breeders around the turn of the century. Fresh out of Notre Dame during the Knute Rockne years—a roommate of Don Miller, right halfback of the "Four Horsemen"—Tom was an instant success as a trainer.

With the filly Fiji, he won the 1934 Latonia Derby, Latonia Oaks, and Kentucky Oaks.

He had one of the largest public stables at the old Kentucky Association track. But, by the time Keeneland opened in 1936, it was down to a dozen horses because most of his owners had left him because of his boozing ways. Ten years later, he was finished, an invalid. Only Dr. Charlie Hagyard stayed the course with him as an owner.

Better Than Most When They Are Sober

The most successful boozing trainer I have known was Vester "Tennessee" Wright. When he came on the racetrack, Harold Sherman hired him as a groom. Sherman was so impressed with Wright's dedication and horse sense that in a year's time he had elevated him to stable foreman. Harold could not remember the name Vester, called him "Tennessee" instead, and the nickname stuck. Sherman was then training for Perne L. Grissom. When the latter's brother, T. Alie Grissom, got into the game, Harold recommended Tennessee as his trainer, but warned Alie: "He drinks."

"Tennessee" Wright.

"If he can do the job, that's all I care about," replied Alie. And what a job he did for Grissom. Four times in six years, he was America's leading trainer in races won—1956, '57, '59, and '61—and he was third in the other two years of that span. During that period, Wright never drew a sober breath. He was imbibing mornings, afternoons, and nights.

A friend of Alie's, new in racing, telephoned him one night from New Orleans in a disturbed state. "You better get down here right away," he said. "Your trainer is drinking." Alie broke out in laughter. He replied: "Watch him close. If he stops drinking, call me and I'll be down there on the next plane. He can see and discern more through bloodshot eyes than most trainers with crystal-clear vision."

In the 1950s, with Tennessee calling the shots, Alie engaged in claiming wars with two of the top haltermen of the day, W. H. Bishop and Marion Van Berg, and he remained friendly with both during the process. Both battles ended with a mutual truce, but the peace accord with Bishop had to be renewed when he later broke it by claiming one of Alie's horses. Tennessee phoned Grissom at the farm in Lexington immediately and reported the matter. "Take every horse Bishop runs tomorrow," instructed Alie, which Wright did, and he got some very nice horses. One of them, *Shoerullah, was to win stakes for Grissom before the year ended. Bishop never claimed another horse from Grissom.

T. Alie Grissom.

Alie once told me: "Few trainers can do two things as well as mine: develop young horses from scratch and improve on claimed horses. Hirsch Jacobs and Allen Jerkens are two, and I guess I should add Willie Molter."

Getting the Line on Roman Line

Wright never had any top stock to work with, but he did win the 1953 Florida Derby with Money Broker, and in 1962 he was second in the Kentucky Derby and third in the Preakness Stakes with Grissom's Roman Line. Tennessee knew early on that Roman Line was a good one.

I was sitting on a little Thoroughbred I was making into a polo pony near the gap at Keeneland one morning in early April of 1961 when Tennessee started yelling: "Clarky, Clarky, catch that colt of mine. He's about to kill himself. The damned outrider missed him."

He pointed to a riderless horse running full tilt, zigzagging from the inside rail to the outside rail, barely missing horses and riders. The colt, while schooling, had burst through the starting gate, dropped his exercise boy, and knocked his blinkers askew, which left him nearly blinded and in a panic.

When I returned with the colt, now calm with his blinkers removed, the relieved Wright laughingly said to me: "Why don't you run that sonofabitch you're on instead of those skates you've been running at the meeting?" Then he quietly told me: "This is the best colt I've been near in my life. His name is Roman Line. Bet on him the second time I run him. I'll give him a race the first time." I've never been much of a bettor but, because of this information from such an outstanding trainer, I had to go to the windows. Roman Line won his second start, and I got a good return on my $500 investment.

Tennessee and I had been friends since he first came on the racetrack, but catching Roman Line brought us closer together, enabling me to ask him questions I would not have otherwise.

One was why did he have his jockeys pull up immediately after the finish line? I thought that this allowed his horses to form a bad habit, and they would soon start easing themselves up before the finish. "You're wrong," he said. "I don't want them to run a foot more than the race calls for. I don't think it makes sense to let them continue on until they run themselves down over on the backside. I want to conserve that energy they spend going an extra quarter of a mile."

Up and Over

Wright was a very likable guy, had no enemies, and many friends, many of whom also were his drinking buddies. As time wore on in the 1960s, his daily consumption increased until it started sapping his training skills and memory. I shall never forget an amusing incident in the paddock at Churchill Downs when I was saddling a horse in the next stall. When paddock judge Charlie Gormley hollered: "Riders up," Wright threw jockey Bobby Baird up with such force he cleared the horse. Looking up and finding the saddle empty, he asked the groom: "Where's Bobby?"

"Over here on the ground rubbing his shoulder," was the reply.

Jim Grissom, Alie's son, recalls another amusing incident about Tennessee. Jim and his wife, Mary, stood up for jockey John Sellers and his bride at their marriage ceremony, conducted by a Catholic priest who was an avid horse player and a pal of most of the jockeys, trainers, and owners at the Detroit tracks. Johnny was then doing most of the riding for the Grissom stable. The 30 minutes that elapsed from the time he arrived and the completion of the ceremony had challenged Wright's thirst.

The ritual over, the priest invited the small group over to his parsonage for a celebration commemorating the event. Everyone immediately started following the priest. Tennessee walked up to him and said: "Father, I can't come along unless your wife fixes me a quick bourbon and water as soon as we get there."

In the middle 1960s, when alcoholism had taken such a hold on Wright that he no longer could function properly, Alie hospitalized him for detoxification. But, when Alie visited on the second day, Tennessee was drunker than the day before. The owner also found two pints of whiskey hidden under the mattress of his bed.

This ended the Grissom-Wright partnership. Tennessee immediately went to work for Frank J. Carlin, and one of his first claims was T. Bird, a consistent winner while he was with the Grissom stable. Inwardly, this hurt Alie badly, but outwardly he was philosophical about it. It was like a son turning against his father.

Tennessee finally lost to the bottle. His heavy drinking over a long period of time deteriorated his health to the point he became pitifully and hopelessly ill and died at the age of 52.

In his prime, Wright was not only a great horseman, but also an excellent judge of grooms who had the talent and dedication to become fine trainers. Three that came up under him and made it are Dewey Smith, Gordon Potter, and John Meaux, all of whom later trained for T. Alie Grissom.

A Humorous Horseman

Phil Chinn is the most colorful character I have known in more than 60 years in the game, but he wins only by a photo finish over Doug Davis Jr., whose "attributes," if they can be condensed, were horsemanship, hard work, sense of humor, fiscal irresponsibility, charity, unguarded respect for truth (he would lie a little), undying loyalty to friends and employees, love of nature, and joy of living.

Doug came to Lexington in his 20s from Texas, where he sold used cars and insurance, to manage High Hope Farm for his ailing father, a wit himself and a hard taskmaster. One day after the elder Davis had read his son the riot act over a very serious oversight, Doug asked: "Well, Dad, haven't you ever made so much as one mistake?" To which his father replied, gesturing with a pointed finger: "You!" They both laughed.

With the passing of the senior Davis, his widow Helen asked young Doug to take over High Hope and operate it in partnership with her. That he did, and in a big way, never being one to do things in small measure. He built a training track, new barns, new paddocks, and black-topped every road—and

Doug Davis Jr.

filled the farm to capacity with horses owned to a large degree by people who were slow pay.

Doug had about as little respect for an account receivable as an account payable, much to the chagrin of the farm's auditor, Helen Fortune, and his stepmother, both of whom after two years of "everything going out, nothing coming in" insisted Davis slow down long enough for a business meeting. A few days before, the two Helens had gone over the office records.

The auditor explained to Doug: "We've got about $100,000 in payables and $200,000 in receivables, and the office records show that you've never sent out an account rendered statement on any of these unpaid bills; you apparently just send one bill and if it isn't paid you do nothing about it. Please try to collect what is owed the farm." Stepmother Helen nodded in silent agreement.

"Uh, uh, well, well," Doug stuttered, "those people who haven't paid are friends of mine. I don't want to insult them by sending more than one statement. Tell you what I'll do. Every time one of them wins a race I'll phone 'em and congratulate 'em and hint at their bill. You write them."

Auditor Helen did. She collected the bills and paid what the farm owed in less than a month. Under the auditor's watchful eye, the farm made money. After the death of Doug's stepmother, Doug had accumulated enough to buy his own farm.

He indulged himself with only two luxuries, one of which was a passion for western clothing. He owned 75 pairs of custom-made boots and 60 cowboy hats. He also spent two weeks deer hunting each fall.

Doug, Hal Price Headley, and Hirsch Jacobs were the only horsemen I have ever known who could make a living by racing and selling the horses they bred. For a span of about 20 years, Doug was a leading trainer at Keeneland, Churchill, Oaklawn, and Delaware Park at the same time that he was running the farm. He bred his share of stakes winners, but most of his homebreds were bred for speed, had little pedigree, and were in claiming races for prices below their value.

Jack Rosenthal was constantly claiming from him. Doug once told Jack: "Your men will run out of money before I run out of horses." One morning as he was leading a group of ten two-year-olds onto the track at Churchill, he caught Clarence Breedlove observing only their legs. Doug hollered to him: "Say, Breedlove, these horses have heads and necks and bodies, too." Clarence was a frequent claimant of Doug's young horses.

Well-Timed Scratches

Even then, Doug seemed to dodge the bullet often when he ran his horses in Kentucky. By happenstance, his horses would be late scratches when claims were in for them. The matter was brought up in a Horsemen's Benevolent and Protective Association meeting by an aggrieved trainer who said he had failed to get four of Doug's horses because of late scratches and wanted an investigation. He insisted Doug was in cahoots with one of the stewards.

"That steward," he charged, "holds the white envelope up against a light, and if I've got a claim for one of Doug's horses, he notifies him, and the horse is scratched."

Being a pal of Doug and "that steward," I suggested he insert a black or opaque card inside the envelope to prevent it from being read. Henceforth he did, and before the end of the meeting he had claimed three cripples from Davis.

Removing His Expertise

Once while he was saddling a horse in the Keeneland paddock, I asked Doug why he was carrying a pair of shoe pullers in his back pocket. "I've finally got this horse shod so he doesn't hit behind," he explained. "If he's claimed, I keep the shoes, and they only get the horse." The horse won, Davis pulled the shoes, and the claimant, Jimmy Cowden, complained to the steward to no avail.

Speaking Up for Hoss

Doug Davis could talk a good line, even if not everything he said was true. One of his most eloquent speeches was before the stewards at Oaklawn Park when his friend, Hoss Inman, was called on the carpet for what Davis thought they might deem a serious rules infraction. He had received permission to appear as a character witness. Billy Sunday could not have been more convincing.

"Now, gentlemen," began Davis, "the matter before you today is minor to you and Mr. Inman, but it is very major to a 14-year-old girl back in Lamar, Colorado. She is Jamie Inman, his daughter. Now let me tell you about Jamie. Jamie is an honor student at Lamar High School; in fact, she's never made less than an 'A' in any subject since she started in school in the first grade. She is president of her 4-H Club, the youngest ever to hold that position, and last year at the Colorado State Fair she exhibited the champion calf, which she bred, groomed, prepped, and showed herself.

"I personally know Jamie. She's a highly intelligent, sensitive, shy girl who is extremely self-motivated," said Davis. "She's exactly what you would expect in a daughter of Hoss and Virginia Inman, who have always worked hard and lived by the Golden Rule, believing in God and our country and never taking advantage of their fellow man in spite of having started their lives under impoverished conditions.

"Now, where you gentlemen come in is the ruling you do or do not make in this matter before you today," he continued. "If you make an adverse one it most assuredly will tear out the heart of Jamie. She reads everything in the *Daily Racing Form,* and she will not miss the ruling if you make one. Please in your deliberations, reflect on the integrity and honesty of Hoss Inman, his unblemished record in racing, and think of Jamie." The stewards dismissed the Inman case for lack of evidence.

All that Doug said was true, except Jamie was never an "A" student (her mind was too much on horses and cattle), was never president of her 4-H Club, never exhibited at the Colorado State Fair, and was not exactly shy and sensitive. A real tomboy, she could whip any male her age and weight and do more on a horse's back than any of them.

Only 2% Was Mental

Once when Doug Davis was doing a slow burn over the way a jock had disobeyed his riding orders and blown the race, the jock's agent was quick to the scene, begging: "Doug, listen to me, don't get upset. He's just temperamental." To which Doug replied: "Yes, I've just figured him out. He's 98% temper, 2% mental."

On another occasion Doug had backed a jock into the wall as he was giving him a thorough tongue-lashing. When the rider rebelled and called him a dirty name, Doug let go with what he thought was a right to the jaw. The jock ducked and the blow landed forcefully against the wall, leaving Doug with a broken hand. Later, with his hand in a cast, he told me, laughingly: "From now on, I'm going to do what I do best—talk!"

No Harthill in the Tank

In his off hours, Doug was forever developing new hobbies. One year at Hot Springs, it was motorcycling and, after he thought he had mastered the skill of racing, he challenged another trainer-cyclist, Dick Vance, to a race. After they had agreed to the size of the wager, the time, distance, and place, Dick laughed and said: "And one more condition. Your close pal, Alex Harthill, can't fuel up your machine!"

He Went Out a Winner

Doug's greatest training feat was in the last days of his life. On August 27, 1976, a Friday, he was at his stable at Delaware Park at five in the morning, supervising the training of his large string and shipping out two of his charges to run in stakes at Atlantic City. Returning to Delaware in the afternoon, he saddled Bunny Grey to win the eighth race, then drove 85 miles to the Atlantic City track. That night, he won the Northfield Stakes with Do the Bump.

Arriving back at his Delaware motel early on Saturday morning, he got in only a few hours of sleep before starting his training chores at 5 a.m. That night, he was back in Atlantic City to saddle Dancers Countess for a victory in the Matchmaker Stakes (G1). Back in Delaware in the early hours of Sunday, he again only had a few hours of sleep before it was training time again. That morning's chores completed, Doug then flew back to Lexington to check things out at the farm and join friends at dinner to celebrate his back-to-back stakes wins.

Doug always thought sleep and rest were a waste of time. For the better part of his 58 years, he had gone at this pace without encountering any warning signs of the toll it was taking on his health. Never had a checkup. That Sunday night, he retired to his own bed at the farm, never to awaken. A coronary did him in. Thus he was lost to all of us who knew and loved him as one of the dearest guys our industry has ever known.

Trained to the Minute

Abe Hewitt was a friend and admirer of Federico Tesio, the most successful horseman of all time in Italy—and perhaps the world. Tesio was a master of detail and timing, as were Horatio Luro and Ben Jones. On one occasion, Abe asked Tesio in the saddling paddock whether his horse was "fit and ready."

Tesio replied: "If this race were run 30 minutes earlier, he'd have been overtrained. He would be undertrained if it were to be run 30 minutes later."

Some Help for His Golf Game

Oleg Dubassoff was a lean, tall, slightly hunched trainer who for many years wintered his New York string in Aiken. To those he did not know well or who pushed a little too fast for his friendship, he was cool—even insulting at times. Once he accepted you, though, he was a good friend who would tell stories about himself that were quite humorous. Dr. William H. "Bud" Wright was perhaps his most trusted friend and confidant.

Oleg, then in his 70s, talked and moved slowly. No longer did the White Russian have the early turn of foot that enabled him to escape the purge of the gentry class when the Communists took over the country. Dubassoff was lucky again when he became the trainer for such owners as Lazy F. Ranch and John W. Schiff, retaining them until his retirement.

Oleg Dubassoff.

No longer agile, Oleg asked Dr. Wright to buy him a horse for going to and from the track with his horses, "one that will only walk, not shy and jump around and act silly." The perfect horse was found, and Oleg was pleased with him until the blacksmith, who came to shoe him, pointed out that he was foundered. A proud perfectionist, Oleg immediately told his foreman, named "Do Right," to sell or give the horse away.

When the first prospective customer asked if the horse was gentle, Do Right guaranteed that "for sure," then added: "Gentle, my sakes alive. Why, he's so gentle even the boss can ride him." As soon as the horse was loaded on a trailer and gone, Dubassoff bounded out of the stable office, where he had been doing some bookwork, and bee-lined for his foreman. "Now don't you ever say anything like that again, Do Right. I'll have you know I am an honor graduate of the Spanish School of Riding," he said. Oleg often did live in yesteryears.

Oleg never came to our afternoon polo practice games or our Sunday matches, as did John Gaver, Mack Miller, Mike Freeman, Barry Ryan, Joe Kramer, and other Aiken trainers. This rather burned polo nuts like Pete Bostwick and John Clark. The Aiken winter horsemen were then a close-knit bunch and made some effort to support each other's favorite sport. But Oleg played golf every afternoon.

When we would hear Oleg had a bad round the previous day, Pete and I would delight in needling him about his game. Once, when Dubassoff had entered himself in a tournament and grew more nervous by the day as it approached, he turned to his good friend, Dr. Wright, for advice. "Take a quarter teaspoon each day of that tranquilizer powder I gave you to put in the feed of that stall-walking filly about an hour before you practice. It won't hurt you. Find out your level of tolerance and adjust your dosage accordingly," Bud advised.

The next morning, Oleg reported to the good doctor: "It worked. Had the best round yesterday ever in my life. I've got the dosage down pat. I'm ready for that tournament."

The next Sunday afternoon while making his rounds, Dr. Wright stopped by the Dubassoff stable to learn how Oleg had done in the tournament. "He's late. He ain't got here yet. Something must have happened to him," reported Do Right. A bit alarmed, Dr. Wright went into the stable office and phoned the club. He was told: "Mr. Dubassoff didn't finish. He went to sleep on the bench at the third tee and didn't wake up until the tournament was over. Bobby Knowles took him back to the Green Boundary Club (where he lived) and put him to bed. Nothing's wrong. He's just sleepy. He'll be okay tomorrow."

Trainer's Lament

I'm not allowed to train the horse,
The way that I know best.
I'm not allowed to pick the race,
My judgment fails his test.
I'm not allowed to choose the jock,
That he does with zest.
But if the damned horse runs bad,
My ignorance he'll attest!

Owner's Lament

*Now I am in the Sport of Kings,
I bought myself a hoss,
I worked for others all my life,
I thought, at last, I'm boss.
But trainers think a different way,
Your input they'll not take,
They send you bills quite regularly,
Reports they do forsake.
They call collect if your horse wins,
They're very up, not down,
But if the critter's up the track,
They're nowhere to be found.*

He Had Influential Friends

J. P. "Sammy" Smith, one of the most entertaining and delightful wits of racing, trained few horses of renown with the exception of Miss Merriment. Sammy was the friend and confidant of giants of industry, people of high station in government, the elite of high society, and chieftains of the underworld who came racing. He also was the friend of hot-walkers, grooms, trainers, and owners. No one, to my knowledge, ever had a broader spectrum of friends.

He possessed what are perhaps the two most respected attributes in life, particularly on the racetrack—style and class. Everyone seemed to want his friendship, which he extended generously to those he felt were worthy of it. He possessed a great compassion for the underdog.

On days when they would be at Belmont or Aqueduct, neither John Hertz nor Harry Guggenheim would feel their day quite complete if Sammy did not drop by the box and let them in on the latest, which was never anything of significance but was most assuredly humorous.

In the late fall of 1948, Arnold Hanger, one of my early benefactors, decided I should go immediately to Italy "to buy the very best older horse available." That year the great Italian horse Tenerani (later to sire *Ribot) had invaded England to beat the European champion, Marcel Boussac's Arbar, in the Goodwood Cup. Nearco, ten years before, had swept the boards in Italy and France, was retired undefeated, and sold for a record price to Martin Benson, former managing director of the London bookmaking firm. He subsequently was leading sire in England. "The time is right, there's a general strike on in Italy, and the money exchange is something like 200 lire to our dollar," Hanger noted. I was on my way.

Upon my arrival in New York I called on Captain Guggenheim, hoping he would have time to discuss 1949 matings for his mares. He kindly made time for me, and after we had reviewed what I had on my mind, he asked: "What are you doing in New York?" I told him, adding I was flying out that night. Pausing with a bit of anguish, he spoke guardedly: "Johnny, there's a great deal of turmoil in Italy right now. There's a general strike on. Even if you're able to buy horses, you may not be able to get them out." I insisted I would take my chances.

J. P. "Sammy" Smith.

"Very well," he said, "but wait until I give you a letter to Jimmy Dunn, our ambassador there. He was my executive assistant when I was ambassador to Cuba." That done, I departed to catch the last few races before plane time.

The first person I encountered upon arrival at the track was Sammy Smith. "Where are you going?" he asked, pointing to my travel bag. I told him of my mission. "You know anybody over there?" I replied I did not, but I had a letter from Captain Guggenheim asking the ambassador there to render me assistance if I needed it. "Hell," exclaimed Sam, "I can do better than that. You wait right here." Sammy grabbed an overnight, turned it over, and wrote a message. He then walked into Jack Campbell's office, opened a drawer, and took from it a large and a small envelope. He addressed the smaller envelope, inserted his note, sealed it, and then placed it in the larger envelope, which he also sealed. "If you have any problems," he said, "put your return address and telephone number on the letter inside, mail it at the general post office in Rome, and within a few hours help will be on the way."

Fortunately, when I went to Federico Regoli's stable in Milan, I immediately made a good friend. He not only counseled and advised me, but also acted as my guide to the famous stables in Naples, Pisa, and Rome, as well as in Milan. Such hospitality I had never known before, nor have I since. I was able to inspect Tenerani, Trevisana, all the great horses in training in the stable of Federico Tesio, who raised Regoli and after whom my new friend had been named.

We then phoned various owners of horses I thought suitable. None was for sale. Tesio remarked he still regretted selling Nearco. I returned to the U.S. empty-handed.

In flying back across the Atlantic, curiosity got the better of me. I had to open Sammy's letter. It was addressed to Charles Luciano, P.O. Box, Rome, Italy. The message read, "Dear Charlie, Johnny Clark is my friend. If he needs your help, please favor me by giving it to him. Best, Sammy."

This Charles Luciano was the same man who headed one of the strongest and most feared Mafia families in the U.S. before being deported. "Lucky" Luciano and "Charlie Lucky" were his nicknames. Yes, Sammy had a broad spectrum of friends.

Success Came Early

Not many trainers win their first major stakes race before their 25th birthday, but Willard C. "Mike" Freeman did in 1954 when he saddled Parnassus to win the Bougainvillea Turf Handicap in track-record time at Hialeah Park in February of 1954. Mike, a steeplechase jockey, had learned from trainer W. Burling Cocks in Pennsylvania after World War II.

John S. Phipps had sent the War Admiral colt to Mike in New England as a maiden three-year-old in 1953, and by year's end he had won six races and placed in two stakes. Then it was off to Hialeah with Parnassus and a couple of other ordinary horses.

It was that winter when Freeman and I first became friends, and he agreed to take some horses back to New England to race for me. At Lincoln Downs on March 29, 1954, he won with my horse Represent.

Mike Freeman.

With his training talent, it was just a matter of time before New York beckoned, and Mike accepted the call. That was the end of 1955, a year neither he nor I will ever forget because of a horse named Pogo Lotti. I had been unable to get him near the money, and his form was horrid. Mike agreed to take him, try to win a race with him, and sell him. In his first start there, "Pogo" won and paid $94.40, with no one in the stable betting but the groom, who packed up and left as soon as the horse was cooled out and put away. A short while later, Mike sold Pogo Lotti, who went on to win two more cheap races.

In New York, Mike has done well. His best horse was the two-time champion mare, Shuvee, who won the 1969 New York filly triple crown and was elected to the National Museum of Racing's Hall of Fame in 1975.

Upon his departure from New England, Mike recommended I send the horses I wanted raced and sold there to his assistant, William "Red" Ness. I followed his advice, and we did well. Red won the 1957 Narragansett Park Nursery Stakes for me with Chalk Talk.

Doubling the Stall Allotment

Reggie Cornell was a trainer who could cope with unusual situations. Back in the 1940s, the California tracks agreed they would allot no more than 20 stalls to one trainer. Reggie had 40 horses. At the first track that put the rule into force, Tanforan, Cornell called in a gang of carpenters upon his arrival with his 40 runners and, in quick order, had each of his 20 stalls divided in half to accommodate his entire string. Needless to say, he was leading trainer at the meet.

And It Was His Work Day

There are some trainers who follow the same routine with all their horses. Work one day, walk the next, gallop the next two, then work again. I have known several of these trainers, and I clearly recall an incident involving one of them.

He would write out his schedule a month ahead of time. Upon arriving at the track early one morning, he opened his training book and started reading it as he walked from his car to his stable. Before he was able to say good morning to his foreman, the latter exclaimed: "Boss, that new man you hired yesterday, when he went in that gray colt's stall to muck out this morning, he spooked the colt and the colt flipped over backwards and broke his neck. He's down there dead in his stall."

"You don't say," replied the trainer, still looking down at his training book. "And, my gawd, this was his work day!"

Keeping His Horses Happy

I shall never forget when Billy Reynolds took me to lunch at the Louisville Country Club one Sunday in the summer of 1948 to meet a young friend of his. "Johnny," Billy said, "I want you to meet Dr. Alex Harthill, a young veterinarian just starting his practice. I think he'll make it."

That turned out to be quite an understatement. In my opinion, and I'm sure I'm with the majority of horsemen on this, Alex is the best racetrack veterinarian in the business.

Alex is a third-generation veterinarian. Oddly, neither he, his father, nor his grandfather has ever had a partner or an associate. He graduated from the Veterinary College of Ohio State University in 1948 and immediately caught the attention of Ben and Jimmy Jones.

Dr. Alex Harthill.

From that day on, he was the veterinarian of choice of the Joneses as they completely dominated racing for a decade with Calumet Farm runners. One of his first patients was Citation. Other great trainers followed by having him attend to their best horses: John Gaver, Frank Whiteley, Tennessee Wright, Horatio Luro, Charlie Whittingham, Marion Van Berg, and his son, Jack.

Alex and I have been close friends since he came out of veterinary school, and for 42 years I have heard the false rumors that he has had "something that wouldn't show" which would make horses run faster and gamer. Were that so, why then would he not win more races with his own horses?

His only advice to me has been, "Keep your horses healthy and happy, and run them where they belong." Early on, in the 1940s, Preston Burch, one of the most respected trainers of that era and one always helpful to youngsters seeking his counsel, told me very much the same thing: "Seek the best company for yourself and the worst for your horses."

Alex and I always did the latter, but we did not do the former. Among our mutual friends was Morris "Mushie" Wexler, whose wire service furnished bookmakers their information until United States Senator Kefauver's investigation put them all out of business.

Alex got nailed by the press for such associations. I escaped, I guess, because I was a member of the Fourth Estate.

Over a period of time, some members of the press have taken rumors and innuendo and reported them as truth, or taken Alex's quotes and turned them around to mean the opposite of what he said. This has caused him to be overly cautious and turn away some good reporters.

A cause of Harthill's problems with the media may have come from a few disgruntled veterinarians. Alex's practice is not local—it is all over the United States, and about ten times a year it is in England, Ireland, and France. No practitioner is overjoyed when the "big horse" in a stable he serves gets in trouble and he is bypassed when the trainer or owner flies in Dr. Harthill to take over the case. There is a little professional jealousy in all of us, regardless of our profession.

On Call at a Moment's Notice

Alex does not let himself get tied down making routine calls at clients' stables daily. He keeps himself free to leave instantly for out-of-town emergencies. When Whittingham phoned on the Sunday before the Preakness Stakes (G1) and told him Sunday Silence had bruised his hoof, he replied, "I'll be at Pimlico tomorrow with my horseshoer, 'Little Joe' Carroll."

The bruised area was opened sufficiently to allow drainage, a bar shoe was nailed on to guard against pressure, and Sunday Silence missed only two days of training. Little Joe and Dr. Harthill were back again the day of the race. The shoe was not removed, but the bar was filed off, and Sunday Silence won the Preakness by a nose over Easy Goer.

"The media blew it all out of proportion that I was barred from the backstretch of Belmont while Sunday Silence was there for the Belmont Stakes (G1)," Alex recalled, "but I was never told that directly by Charlie or anyone from the New York Racing Association. I was plenty teed-off. Charlie insisted I at least come up and watch the race. He said, 'I want you here just in case he should get injured or injure himself in the race. He's become pretty valuable property, you know.'"

That was in June, 1989. In September of that year, he got a call from Mack Miller at Belmont. Alex recalls the conversation.

"Mack said, 'Dr. Harthill, I want you to come up here and fire the shins of Red Ransom. I think he's the best horse I've ever trained.' I replied that the press said I was barred from the backstretch in June. How could I be welcome in September? 'Don't pay any attention to what you've heard or read, just come on,' Mack said. 'I'll leave word at the gate you're coming. Everything will be all right.' In a few days I flew up and did the job, was treated courteously by track security. The press had to know I was there. Not a word was printed. Such hypocrisy."

Chapter 14
Jockeys I've Known

It was indeed a joy to see Bill Shoemaker riding in near his best form at age 58 as he approached his retirement in February, 1990, after 41 years in the saddle. The perfect gentleman, he has been a role model for other jockeys—not only on but off the tracks as well. When Eddie Arcaro retired in March of 1962, at age 46, "The Master" was asked who would succeed him as the nation's best rider. He replied: "No doubt in my mind at all about it, Bill Shoemaker." Hearing of the compliment, Shoe told an interviewer: "How nice to hear that come from the best rider I've ever seen or ever expect to see." Then he added with a grin: "It was so nice of him to retire and get out my way."

Five years later, in 1967, when Bill was at the top of his game, he was asked if there were any younger riders he could name who he expected to some day share the top with him. "One," he replied. "Laffit Pincay." Arcaro to Shoemaker to Pincay. They were masters of the saddle, and it has been my great pleasure to know many jockeys during my years of training and tradin'.

'Riding a Racehorse Is an Art'

Tod Sloan, the greatest rider in the U.S., England, or France around the turn of the century, turned in to the New York *Herald* in the summer of 1897 a signed article that was published. His remarks on race riding are as applicable today as they were then.

Tod Sloan.

"Riding a racehorse is an art, and I feel that I learn more about it every time I have a mount. . . . A horse is more intelligent and observant than most people give him credit for being, and remembers kindness or abuse longer than a good many men.

"Instead of attempting to rule him (a horse), I try to act with him, and he generally appreciates the consideration shown him. I found early in my career that fighting a horse is an uphill game.

"(At the start) I bend forward over the horse's withers and take a short hold on the reins, having them run through my half-closed hands, which are together and resting on the horse's neck.

"I never go out on the lead. I let some other horse set the pace and, incidentally, break the wind for me. ... No matter what direction the wind is blowing, there is always some resistance, because the horse goes much faster than it does, and therefore I make myself as harmless as possible, and the other starters as useful as possible.... The closer you can be behind a horse or several horses in a long, distance race the better it is for you. I generally pull out at the right time and very few pockets are worked on me.

"... Whip lashing and arm work are absolutely useless. If he (the horse) is game and has been properly ridden he will keep trying, and spectacular work again is unnecessary. I believe he (the horse) appreciates victory and deplores defeat."

The foregoing illustrates to a great degree what we saw in the riding style of Bill Shoemaker. Sloan, unlike Shoe, was a flamboyant person. He smoked "foot long" cigars, was a dapper dresser, and often dressed in formal attire for dining at the foremost restaurants of New York, London, and Paris. He also was a high roller: rich today, busted tomorrow.

A dispatch to *The Thoroughbred Record* in 1902 from Paris noted: "He had to give up an ambitious plan to establish an automobile manufactory in the United States. At the end of May, Sloan had lost $500,000 in Turf speculation. ... With June, his fortunes changed, and he has now not only recouped himself, but has amassed a fortune in addition.... He was a heavy winner on Kizil-Kourgan in the Grand Prix de Paris (beating the great Sceptre), having, it is said, cleared $180,000."

Aside from his Grand Prix victory, Sloan's most pleasing win was the 1900 Sheepshead Bay Futurity with William C. Whitney's Ballyhoo Bey. Whitney sent him $5,000 in travel money to come from England for the one race. James R. Keene, an arch rival of Whitney on Wall Street and on the Turf, entered three to assure himself of beating Whitney. Jockeys Harry Spencer, Winnie O'Connor, and Milton Henry kept Sloan pocketed most of the way on the Keene horses. But, when one of them tired in the stretch, Sloan shot Ballyhoo Bey through the opening to win by daylight. For the great ride—and the thrill of beating Keene under the circumstances—Whitney rewarded Sloan with an additional $10,000 from the winning purse of $33,580.

Todhunter Sloan was never apprenticed or under written contract to a stable in his entire riding career. His agreements were always verbal and, it is said, he kept his word. He died at age 60 in 1933 in Los Angeles, California.

Few Were Old and Bold

When I first came into this game in the 1930s, there were plenty of old jockeys, but very few old, bold riders. In fact, there were very few old jocks still riding. They had either lost their nerve or their battle with the scales by becoming so heavy that they could not reduce enough even to ride at five pounds overweight. There were many "bug" boys taking their place.

Then, riding was even more hazardous than it is today. There was no movie patrol. The stalls of the starting gates had no front doors, and there were never enough members of a starter's crew to handle the bad actors. Instant starts were a rarity, delays were commonplace, and ragged starts often caused falls that injured both riders and horses. The riders who threw care to the wind and dashed away after the bell, whether or not they had clearance, were called "good gate jocks."

Those who anticipated the starter's ringing of the bell and broke before it rang "beat the gate." They were hailed for their keen sense of judgment, much to the resentment of the starter, who generally got even by "leaving them" in a future start when their mounts were not standing properly. The rest of the race was everybody for "hisself," and only the most flagrant foul was detected by the patrol judges and the stewards.

Overweight riders reduced by wearing a rubber suit, several layers of clothing, and jogging two or three miles in the mornings, which left them fatigued and without the strength to perform at their best in the afternoons.

Others would dress similarly and ride around in automobiles with the heater on at full force—even in the heat of the summer.

The safest place to be during a race was on the lead or in a position where it would be nearly impossible to get shut off. A cardinal sin was letting an oncoming horse and rider get through on the rail. Jockeys had an established "pecking order." They knew who and who not to take on with their unfair riding tactics, and were well aware of the ones who would pay them back in the future.

Then, there were the daredevil apprentice riders out to make a name for themselves, but many of them were unable to control their mounts. Some were not even 16, the minimum age, and had gotten their licenses through falsified birth certificates. One was the great rider Jackie Westrope, and more recently "Cowboy" Jack Kaenel used a birth certificate that had undergone some minor alteration, such as changing the year.

Of course, the rough riding did not occur in every race. Still, I shudder to think how aggressive Angel Cordero Jr. and Manuel Ycaza would have been if they had been riding in those days. Not until the movie patrol came along in the early 1940s were the stewards able to bring safety to race riding. The documentary evidence they obtained from the films made rulings stick that would have been difficult to prove previously.

From the turn of the century up through the 1930s, there were owners and trainers who turned a profit by taking a youngster under contract, developing him into a rider, and then selling his contract. The agreements generally ran for five years and stipulated very low wages. They were particularly valuable if the youngster developed early and could ride with the five-pound apprentice allowance for a goodly number of the months from the date of his first winner. The contract holder paid no jockey fees, only $1 per mount to the valet. And the same went for others who were allowed or persuaded to use the young rider's services.

It was important for the young rider not to break his maiden until he had become reasonably proficient, so that he could make the best use of his one-year term with the "bug."

I shall never forget the day in 1938 when I was covering the meeting at Thistledown for *Daily Racing Form*. The best rider on the grounds was Haden Dupuy, under contract to his uncle, Maderis Dupuy. He was the best even though he had not yet ridden a winner. Maderis was putting him on "no chance" horses, long shots, and it was amazing that he was finishing second, third, and fourth on them.

On this particular afternoon, a long shot closed with a terrific rush, made the lead about 70 yards out with Haden standing up and pulling with all his might, and finally succeeding in slowing him down enough to finish second. Presiding steward Joe Murphy, expecting this to happen sometime, had

Haden in the stand within minutes. Young Haden's explanation was: "My uncle is not ready for me to break my maiden yet." The stern old judge replied: "Have your uncle in my office tomorrow morning at 9 o'clock."

The Tow Job

Bobby Dotter, a former rider and subsequently a successful trainer, once told me about some of the goings-on before the advent of the movie patrol. "We were going 1 1/8 miles at the old Jamaica track," Bobby began, "and nobody seemed to want the lead, so I just let my horse gallop on to the lead around the first turn.

"As we straightened away into the backstretch, this apprentice came driving up on the outside of me. I switched my reins and whip to my left hand and with my right took a firm hold of the kid's saddlecloth, knowing well the stewards and patrol judge's view was obstructed. Going into the last turn, I turned loose, yelled to the kid, 'Thanks for the tow job.' My horse opened up a quick lead, not having had to exert himself up to that point, and was fresh to take on the horses coming from behind. We won easily."

Bobby Dotter.

"What happened when you and the kid got back to the jock's room?" I asked. "Oh, nothing. He was just 16, weighed about 90 pounds, and I was older and doing '14'," Bobby replied. "I did go over to him and told him he'd learned a lesson and next time it happened to ease his horse back until the other rider had to let go."

Once, Bobby was on the other end of the tow. "Going down the backstretch at Arlington Park one afternoon," he said, "I felt my horse was not striding out right behind. I looked back and this jock had a hold of my saddlecloth getting a free tow job. I whacked him a good one with my whip and went on about my business. Another time, I caught one hanging on to my horse's tail."

Getting Through on the Outside

In 1938 and 1939, while out of college those summers, I worked with the *Daily Racing Form* crews at various Midwest tracks, first as "call taker" and later as "trackman", which meant I called the charts and wrote the footnotes. At the 1939 meet at Latonia, Earl Pool—in his 60s, bald, and toothless—was still hanging on as a rider. The courage was gone, however, and he always took the overland route. One morning after reading a chart, Pool noted that I had written he "came through on the outside." He raced to the press box and said: "Johnny, don't do this to me. I'm trying to make a living." I apologized, and told him: "It won't happen again. That was sick humor on my part."

Earl had been a fine jockey in earlier years. In fact, he was riding in the Kentucky Derby before I was born. His first start was in 1915, and he rode in seven more through 1929. His best finish was a third with John Finn in 1922.

Willie Pool, a former jockey himself, was then Earl's agent and often loafed in the press box during the afternoon. Borrowing my binoculars on one occasion to watch the horses come onto the track, he yelled gleefully: "Brother's not wearing his false teeth, he thinks he has a shot. I'm off to the mutuel window." He left with a rush, a trail of Turf writers behind him.

George South on 1945 champion three-year-old colt Fighting Step.

Too Wide To Be Squeezed

Back in the 1930s and early '40s, one of the leading riders around the Kentucky and Midwest tracks was George South, best known as Myrtlewood's jockey. Georgie was so short and fat that his stomach almost touched the pommel of his saddle as he paraded to the post. On one occasion when he charged between horses in the stretch, the other two riders threw their bodies into Georgie. South, dropping his reins and using both hands, pushed both horses off stride, then resumed riding to win by plenty of daylight. The foul claims by both riders were disallowed, with one steward noting jokingly: "Georgie's too fat and soft to be squeezed like that."

A Handy Guy Like Sande

Earl Sande at the time he returned to riding, in 1953.

Through the 1920s and into the 1930s, Earl Sande was the toast of the Turf—and of Broadway. Damon Runyon immortalized the jockey with a poem he hastily wrote in the press box after Sande had brought Flying Ebony home the winner of the 1925 Kentucky Derby. It went, in part, "Maybe there'll be another, heady and game. Maybe we'll find his brother, at driving them horses through. Maybe—but, say, I doubt it, never his like again—Never a handy guy like Sande, bootin' them babies in." Two years earlier, he had ridden Zev to victory in the Derby. In 1930, he rode Gallant Fox to a sweep of the Triple Crown.

Sande treated money like it was his enemy—he got rid of it. Soon after he had retired from racing and had blown what little money he saved, he sang at the Stork Club and on radio. An introduction at the Stork Club to Maxwell Howard, a paper tycoon out of Dayton, Ohio, enabled him to return to racing as a trainer. He had a meteoric rise in this facet of the business.

In 1936, with Howard's money, Earl was able to buy what were thought to be two culls from his old friend and patron, Joseph E. Widener. It was beginner's luck, and it did not last long. In 1937, Fencing won the inaugural Blue Grass Stakes, beating Colonel E. R. Bradley's prerace favorites for the Kentucky Derby, Billionaire and Brooklyn. In 1938, Stagehand, not yet a three-year-old by the calendar, won both the Santa Anita Derby and the Santa

Stagehand, with Jack Westrope up, and trainer Earl Sande.

Anita Handicap in the space of a week. (No other three-year-old has won the Big 'Cap.)

Sande was again making big money—strangely, more than he could spend. He was second-leading money-winning trainer in 1938. Maxwell Howard died in 1944, and in his will did the worst thing possible to Earl. He left his trainer Stagehand and Sceneshifter, and Sande set out "to prove" them as stallions. He soon lost both of them and died still owing keep bills on them. Friends tried to prop Sande back up as a trainer. Jock Whitney was one, and Clifford Mooers was another. Earl failed miserably for both. Again he left the racetrack.

Earl made a futile attempt to return to the saddle a month before he turned 55, in 1953. His best friends cringed. He no longer was the strong, quick-witted, fearless man, the complete master of all the skills of that ancient art. In his first nine mounts, his best finish was a second, beaten a head. I was there for his tenth and last. It was October 14 at old Jamaica.

Trainer T. F. White had given Earl the mount on 12-to-1 shot Miss Weesie. Arcaro was aboard the 4-to-5 favorite, Will Be There. The latter alternated on the lead with Piedmont Lass until deep stretch, when Earl and Miss Weesie ran them both down to win by a half-length. If ever there was a boat race, that was one, but nobody cared. The crowd gave a thunderous ovation; even the stewards cheered. Earl immediately announced his retirement. He went out a winner.

Years later, I asked Eddie if he had "orchestrated" that race. "Hell, naw," he replied with a wink, "us jocks rode bad—we were watching Sande. And if we did, what's wrong with giving an 'easy out' to an old guy who's done so much for our profession?" Earl Sande died penniless in a nursing home at age 69 on August 18, 1968.

The Careers of Ted Atkinson

No jockey or racing official has ever been held in higher esteem by his peers in my lifetime than Ted Atkinson, and no one ever worked so hard with such determination to get a hold on the first rung of the ladder he was to climb to success.

Let us pick up his story in the summer of 1939. Ted had won his first race the year before at Beulah Park on Musical Jack, a cheap claimer. Ted's contract holder, Bill Ashbridge, did not see much future for his bug boy, so he sold the contract to Warren Wright of Calumet Farm for a paltry $1,300.

Ted Atkinson.

When Calumet bought the contract, Ted thought he was finally going to get some mounts with a big outfit that would allow him the opportunity to prove his skill and get the recognition he so badly yearned for as a jockey. Little did he know it, but he had "jumped from the frying pan into the fire."

Wright put together a second division, the worst bunch of culls I have ever seen carry the colors of a major racing outfit, hired as its trainer Jack Hodgins, and dispatched them to Randall Park, across the road from Thistledown, near Cleveland, Ohio. Ted was sent along to do the riding. In the draft was the highest-priced sales yearling Wright ever bought—and the worst bum. Ironically, he had named him Temulac, Calumet spelled backwards. That year, 1939, he earned a grand total of $150.

Head trainer Frank Kearns, a pal of mine, laughed to me: "I'll not worry about any of those horses embarrassing me by improving. Jack Hodgins will never get my job."

(Kearns was quite cocky at the time, having won the Widener Handicap in March with Bull Lea. By fall, when the first division had not done so well, he was fired and replaced by Ben A. Jones.)

When the second division started failing immediately in its attack on Randall, Jack Hodgins did exactly what most untalented trainers do—blame it on the rider. Wright was furious, but agreed to let him use jocks of his choice. He did, but the results were the same. Ted was in a Catch-22 situation, if not worse. If Calumet had a horse in a race, he could not ride another in the same race because of the contract conflict. On top of that, Jack was knocking him to other trainers. Ted did win five in a row on Heartease, an appropriate name for a winner that helped keep his spirits and hopes up.

I covered the Randall meet for the *Daily Racing Form* that summer, and met Ted through his future wife, Martha Shank, whom I knew through Lexington relatives. Ted was lodging in a rooming house across the road from her home. Martha's father was the mayor of the township of North Randall. It was quite obvious Ted and Martha were infatuated with each other. The three of us spent many pleasant evenings and Sundays together.

I must say, honestly, I never thought Ted would succeed as a jockey. Not because of his ability as a rider, but because time was passing him by. He was going on 23, had very few wins, and no connections to get on competitive horses that would allow him to demonstrate his abilities. On the other hand, I saw in him great determination—a person of the highest character, industry, intelligence, and education, and who possessed a thirst for knowledge.

Going to Randall was a professional failure, but, in another way, his greatest success. It led to his marriage to Martha. Ted bought out his contract from Warren Wright, went on to the New England tracks, kept in touch with Martha through letters, phone calls, and short visits, and the next year he returned to Randall for their wedding. While on their honeymoon, they drove to Calumet to pay off the final installment on the $1,300 that it cost him to buy his contract.

It was not until the summer of 1941, at age 25, that Ted won his first stakes race. Trainer Walter Carter took Sam Riddle's War Relic up to Suffolk Downs for the Massachusetts Handicap. Ted was the only jock around with any ability who could also do the weight—102 pounds. War Relic won easily. The race then was one of the richest in the country, $50,000-added.

Two months later, War Relic was shipped back to New England for the Narragansett Special. Also returning were other New York stakes horses and their top riders, including Calumet's eventual champion three-year-old Whirlaway. Ted had to ride a heady race to win. Both colts were three but War Relic was carrying only 11 pounds less than Whirlaway. Atkinson's game plan was to grab the lead early, set as slow a pace as possible, and have a fresh horse when the Calumet colt challenged in the stretch. It worked.

War Relic led every step of the way; Whirlaway was last until he made his stretch run and moved alongside the leader in the late stages, at which time Ted galloped merrily away by 4 1/2 lengths to win "easily," according to the race chart. Whirlaway saved second by only a length over Equifox.

It was strictly a jockey victory. Ted had made it. The next year, 1942, Atkinson moved to New York to ply his trade. The rest is history, but here are some interesting facts:

In his 16 years of riding in New York, he was the leader there 11 times. He was the nation's leading rider in 1944 and 1946, both times in money earned by his mounts and in races won. In 22 years as a jockey, he "got days" only five times and received just five fines, totaling $250, none of which he appealed.

Ted has always been a no-nonsense type of guy who hewed to the highest standards of conduct in his public and private life. Friendly and polite, yes, but hail fellow well met, no.

A Stand-In for Martha

One winter during the Hialeah season, Ted and Martha started receiving threatening calls from an extortionist at their Miami Springs, Florida, home. The demand was that they appear in person at a specified place and time to drop off in a box $20,000 in $100 bills. Otherwise, they would suffer bodily harm. Ted strung the guy along, saying he needed time to get the loot together. He told the extortionist to call back in a couple of days and give directions.

Ted immediately notified the FBI, and two of their agents were at the Atkinson house in 30 minutes. "I don't mind appearing, but you'll have to provide another 'Martha,' " he said. "I don't want to chance my wife being

Handicap Triple Crown winner Tom Fool and Ted Atkinson.

hurt if something goes wrong." The agents agreed that could be done, and by the next day they had produced another FBI agent who was such a look-alike that she could have been Martha's twin sister.

The trap set, Ted and the other "Martha" promptly delivered a box—stuffed with heavy paper and neatly sealed—to a telephone booth in Hallandale at the exact time designated by the extortionist. Then, they slowly departed. When the extortionist moved in shortly thereafter and picked up the package, the FBI took him into custody.

The Back Improved in a Hurry

As contract rider for Greentree Stable over 11 consecutive years, Atkinson had ridden Tom Fool, 1953's Horse of the Year, in all his races. Off a few days because of a chronic back problem that troubled him in his later years of riding, Ted told trainer John Gaver he was afraid he would not be able to ride Tom Fool in his race the following week. John sort of grinned and meditated.

Later in the afternoon, when John saw Eddie Arcaro, he asked: "Eddie, do you want to do more for Ted's back than his doctors?" "Hell, yes," Arcaro replied. "Come out tomorrow morning and work Tom Fool," Gaver said. Arcaro did, clocking the fastest mile worked that year at Belmont Park. The next morning, Ted was back at Greentree Stable.

I once asked him to name the best jockey of his riding era. "Arcaro, by far, and second-best was George Woolf," he stated. The best trainer? "Preston Burch. Never saw him run a horse that wasn't in top physical condition; never saw one of his horses beat off. Marvelous gentleman, too." Second-best trainer? "I'd say, without question, Allen Jerkens."

Slashing With a Glancing Blow

While riding in New York, Ted was known as the "Slasher" for his use of the whip, but I never saw a whip mark on any of his mounts. "I don't know," he said. "I did take a full swing, but I only brushed as it hit."

The Position Was Taken

Jockeys tell me that riding instructions are pretty standard, that more than half of the riders in a race will have the same orders: "Lay just off the pace and save ground if possible." After one race at Keeneland, a young trainer was overheard as he read the riot act to his jockey. "I told you to lay second or third. Why in hell didn't you do that?"

Reply: "Couldn't, boss, those positions were occupied."

A Mirror Was His Best Friend

The most conceited jockey I ever encountered was Joe Culmone. When asked by an interviewer to name the best rider he had ever seen, Culmone replied: "You're looking at him!" This brought the following response from a top jockey of the same era who asked that his name be withheld: "Joe's only regret in life was he couldn't sit in the clubhouse and watch himself ride."

He Wanted the Attention

Andy LoTurco.

I never bought the story that Andy LoTurco was a "crooked jockey" or believed his wild behavior in the saddle was for anything other than attracting attention. Andy came into Thoroughbred racing out of Brooklyn, New York, in 1935, a kid with a lot of riding ability, nerve, and laughter. He was well-liked by nearly everybody on the track—including those he had disenfranchised at some time or other. If you had a temperamental horse others feared, it was said: "Get LoTurco, he'll ride him."

LoTurco simply could not resist the temptation to shut off another rider, carry one out, or grab him by his knee, elbow, or saddlecloth when those opportunities presented themselves. He once wrenched the shoulder and nearly unloaded a jockey who was passing him with greater speed than pleased him.

While Keene Daingerfield was serving in the Army in World War II, his foreman, Dick Mitchell, was trying to hold the stable together for his return. Among the horses was a very, very fast stakes filly named Jo Agnes. On LoTurco's one and only opportunity to ride the filly, he gunned her out of the gate, then lost contact with the rest of the field until the quarter pole, at which point the others all passed her.

"How am I going to explain your ride to the boss?" Mitchell asked. "Tell 'im I made a side bet with Arnold Kirkland I'd beat him to the quarter pole, and I did," Andy said, and walked away to the jockey's room. "But," Mitchell shouted, loud enough to be heard all around, "Kirkland's mount was left at the gate."

Another of Daingerfield's experiences with the jockey was at Keeneland, where LoTurco once rode a five-year-old maiden named Good Son, who was owned by Lexington banker Ollie Randolph. After the horse was life and death to win—and at bountiful odds—Andy asked trainer Daingerfield at the weighing-in point, and within earshot of the clerk of the scales, Charlie Gormley: "Did you see me knock Steve Brooks's foot out of his stirrup at the sixteenth pole?"

"No, I didn't," Daingerfield diplomatically replied. Later, Keene told me: "I didn't see it, the stewards obviously didn't, so I put that down as another of LoTurco's boastful lies."

Andy's jockey career spanned 18 years, during which he was suspended 33 times for rough or careless riding and fined 11 times for other infractions. Over each infraction, the stewards of America's tracks heard LoTurco put up the most soulful pleas that ever came before their boards—often punctuating them with tears. Real tears, mind you. His remorse had no bounds.

If a board would not license him, LoTurco's next ploy was to take a pauper's oath and beg carfare to get "to the next town," where he thought his chances might be better. On one occasion, it has been said, the stewards divided the cost of carfare among themselves.

LoTurco may still hold the record for the most suspensions per winning rides—one for every 21 wins. In 1952, officials in Florida tired of LoTurco's incorrigibility and gave him an "indefinite" suspension. (Joe Bollero finally got him reinstated as a hot-walker.)

Whatever chance LoTurco had of riding again was obliterated at Keeneland in August of 1958. The track was dark, of course, and the Southern Governors Conference was convening in Lexington. The track's management invited them out to the track for an afternoon of some fine food and drink and to see the safeguards that racing had in place to insure its integrity. The governors accepted, and with them arrived members of their staffs, friends, and some freeloaders.

Caterer Joe Wolken was up to the occasion. Kent Hollingsworth wrote that, besides all the booze, Wolken rolled out about "25 yards of roast beef, ham, chicken, shrimp, and incidentals." It was a festive occasion, a good time being had by all. Then came the *piece de resistance*—the horses and the race. The horsemen were delighted to put on the race. It was unofficial. That gave each trainer an opportunity to take his "bes holt," and there is no thrill like that for a horseman. Horses ran under the wrong names and so did the jockeys, who looked more like 140-pound exercise boys.

J. B. Faulconer, then head of publicity, explained the history of the Thoroughbred and gave some background on such jobs as a track vet, blacksmith, and paddock judge. Spencer Drayton, racing's head cop, described the Thoroughbred Racing Protective Bureau's elaborate system for detecting ringers and the post-race drug tests. Listeners were given the impression that the game was as pure as Ivory soap with its checks and double checks.

My younger brother, Charlie, telephoned me that Jimmy S. Jones wanted to borrow him and my best polo pony to lead Palm Beach to the post for the race. "No ordinary lead pony will be able to take him there," he was told. I said to use Pink Fox, a gelding that never failed to move another horse off the ball for me. The next time I talked to Charlie, he told me, "I'm a pretty good horse wrangler and Pink Fox is the strongest horse I've ever had between my legs, but we came near not making it. Roughest trip I ever had. Jimmy's horse was hopped out of his head."

"How did he run?" I asked.

"He won by the length of the stretch. Andy LoTurco couldn't get him pulled up."

"Andy LoTurco!" I screamed. "There'll be some hell over this!"

Jones had entered "Law Man," to be ridden by "Strother Griffin." In the paddock before the race, Andy had explained his license problem to Governor Frank Clement of Tennessee, the "owner" of "Law Man," and had extracted the promise that he would get him reinstated if "Law Man" won. The ringer with the phony name and ruled off jock galloped home an easy winner, much to the elation of Clement. Drayton, racing's head cop, had failed to recognize the notorious Andrew LoTurco! Needless to say, the politician's promise was not kept.

A year later, in the September issue of *Confidential*, Andy was identified as the author of an article entitled: "I Was a Crooked Jockey," and headlines over it stated: "The crooked jockey who took 13 governors for a ride," and "It was a demonstration of 'clean' racing—but who got the horse-laugh?"

Conn McCreary.

An 'Atlas' in Silks

I first met Conn McCreary back in the mid-1930s at Keeneland, where he had just gotten on with Steve Judge, then the trainer for Royce Martin. He

Count Turf and Conn McCreary after the 1951 Kentucky Derby.

had hitchhiked into Lexington with empty pockets and all of his earthly belongings in a suitcase you could have lifted with a forefinger. More importantly, he brought with him the physique, the will to sacrifice, and the burning desire to become a jockey.

Conn only stood about four foot six inches, or less, but he had the build of a miniature "Atlas," a big plus for a youngster who appeared fully mature physically and mentally. He was to ride throughout his brilliant career at around 102 pounds. Judge started Conn off as a jockey, and Woody Stephens polished him. But Conn figured out the mastery of the saddle more on his own than from the counsel of others.

Conn was quiet and patient, both in and out of the saddle. It was his concept that if a horse had any "run" in him, the best place to use it was the homestretch. Only when he wanted to spring a surprise would you find him on the early lead—and then you would generally see him "suckering" the other riders into following a false pace.

Early on, Conn earned the reputation of being the best "come from behind" rider in the business. If Ben Jones, Horatio Luro, or John Gaver had a horse they wanted rated off the pace, you could bet they would get McCreary. Hirsch Jacobs used him regularly on Stymie.

No trainer with a heart problem ever rode him. "Why does he do this to me?" John Gaver once exclaimed to me during the running of a stakes. "There's only a quarter-mile left, he's still last and hasn't moved yet." Suddenly, the Greentree colorbearer came alive and started passing tiring horses two and three at a time, getting up to win by a half-length. A few strides after the wire, he had ten lengths on the field. Conn had no peers in timing a stretch run.

Top trainers respected McCreary's judgment of the horses he rode for them. Never one to make gratuitous remarks, Conn appraised well when asked. Only twice that I know of did he offer unsolicited advice. It was accepted in both cases and resulted in his two wins in the Kentucky Derby.

In April of 1944, Conn was at Pimlico riding the Calumet horses trained by Ben and Jimmy Jones. As of April 12, when Conn rode Pensive in the Rowe Memorial Handicap, the three-year-old colt had not won a stakes. Fifteen minutes later, he had. McCreary-style, he came from behind and won by a head, with Porter's Cap second. Three days later, with only two days between races and again in with older horses, Pensive was second in the Bowie Handicap, beaten three lengths by Tola Rose.

After each race, Conn told the Joneses: "You all should be thinking about the Kentucky Derby with this horse. He's improving with every race. The colts this year aren't much, it's going to be a bad Derby." Ben and Jimmy both respected McCreary's judgment, and said they would "think about it." A day or two later, Ben told Conn: "I've thought it over. Pensive is going to run back here on the 29th in the Chesapeake. He still needs some seasoning. He likes Pimlico. We'll be ready for them when they come up here for the Preakness." McCreary grinned: "You're the boss, I'm with you."

Immediately after Pensive had lost by a nose to Gramps Image in the Chesapeake, Conn jumped down off him at the unsaddling and exclaimed to Ben: "It's my fault. This horse should have won. I moved too late. The longer the race, the better the colt likes it. I hope you'll still consider the Derby. It's next Saturday and the favorite is Stir Up; think about it."

The next morning Ben told Jimmy: "We're going to the Derby. If the favorite is a son of Stimulus, we got a good shot. The Stimuluses I've seen like five furlongs better than seven. We're going to try them. We got a distance colt and a come-from-behind rider." In the 1944 Derby, Conn did not let Pensive "see daylight" until well into the stretch. He then went to work on him and had him 4 1/2 lengths in front at the finish.

In the spring of 1951, owner Jack Amiel and McCreary, close friends, agreed that year's Derby was coming up weak (so weak that 20 horses started). Of that group, Count Turf was hardly the standout. He had had only one allowance win in ten starts that year and had won only one stakes (the Dover at Delaware Park) at two. His fifth-place finish in the Wood Memorial Stakes did not inspire much confidence, but Conn suggested: "Come on, Jack, let's go. It's going to be a big party. Everybody is going."

"Are you going with us?" Jack asked trainer Sol Rutchick, who replied: "Hell, no. You two can make fools of yourselves, not me. I'll send the foreman (Slim Sulley) down with Count Turf." McCreary kept Count Turf off the pace the first half-mile, then gradually let him pick up horses, but not until he hit the homestretch did he put him in overdrive. Count Turf won by four. Sol took a lot of ribbing over missing his Derby victory, but to his dying day never relented, saying: "The Derby makes fools out of owners, trainers, and jockeys. Jack and Conn got lucky."

Eddie Arcaro.

His Intention Was Mayhem

One of the most severe rulings of modern-day racing, next to banishment, was the one-year suspension Marshall Cassidy handed jockey Eddie Arcaro back in 1942. At Aqueduct in the Cowdin Stakes, Arcaro was riding Occupation, but he was virtually wiped out at the start by Breezing Home, who had Venancio "Vince" Nodarse in the saddle. It took a quarter-mile of the 6 1/2-furlong event for Arcaro to catch Nodarse, and he repeatedly bashed Occupation into the side of Breezing Home, nearly putting the Cuban-born rider and his mount into the infield.

Arcaro's intentions could not have been much clearer, but the stewards asked if he was trying to foul Nodarse. "Was it deliberate? Hell, yes!" Arcaro said. "I tried to kill the son of a bitch."

'The Master' Was Right on Target

Joe Palmer once observed that Eddie "seldom hung an opponent on the fence without the justification that he either wanted to win or the guy had done something to him yesterday." In reporting on Arcaro's book, *I Ride To Win*, Joe also noted that the title should have been extended with, *And To Hell With the Place and Show*.

A rather amusing incident occurred once that earned Eddie a $50 fine. The Master thought he was the winner in the closing stages of a race when the rider on a fast closer passed him, then raised and turned his rear end directly toward Eddie's face as he passed by. With the same force that he could knock a horse offstride, Arcaro struck the perfect target with such a devastating blow that the rider was unable to sit down to undress after the race. In the shower, the offender had an awesome welt a foot-and-a-half long.

Mistakes in Two Big Ones

Airdrie Stud owner Brereton C. "Brerry" Jones once asked me: "Did you ever see Arcaro make a mistake in a big race?" My reply was that the two most memorable were Jet Pilot's and Middleground's Derbys. Jet Pilot took the lead right out of the gate in the 1947 Derby, set a false pace under the beautiful rating of Eric Guerin (his best ride ever), and was ready for Eddie's late challenge with Phalanx. Arcaro, terribly overconfident, was in last place for the first half-mile or more, then gradually closed ground. He figured Jet Pilot would back up to him, but he did not. Guerin beat Arcaro by a head.

In Middleground's Derby in 1950, Eddie tried to get through the pack on Hill Prince—few Derby riders "accommodate" you with racing room in the big race—and had to bull his way through in close quarters, then was forced to check when pacesetter Your Host stopped in front of him. When he got clear, it was too late to catch the flying Middleground. Hill Prince finished second, beaten a little over a length. If Hill Prince circles the field, he wins easily.

I shall never forget the chewing that Mike Barry gave Arcaro for these two rides when he was publishing the late, lamented *Kentucky Irish American*.

The Wrong Brother Shows Up

A friend of mine was a bit chagrined once when the "wrong brother" showed up in the paddock to ride his horse. When he entered his horse, he failed to specify which of the brothers was to have the mount. That reminds me of when Joe and Sammy Renick were riding in New York during the 1940s. Both were good riders, but Sammy was the better. I was standing with the late Sammy Smith, quite a wit, when an out-of-town trainer asked him: "Which of these two Renicks is the best rider?" "Don't make no difference," Smith said dryly. "Whichever you ride, you'll wish you rode the other."

Jimmy Nichols Changes Careers

Jimmy Nichols.

Jimmy Nichols, a very capable jockey and a good friend, became a steward at Fair Grounds in 1980 and served there through the decade. He did take a bit of a break after the track's 1987-'88 season, though, to gallop Risen Star before his victories in the Preakness Stakes (G1) and the Belmont Stakes (G1). The Secretariat colt was trained and partly owned by Louie Roussel III, who was then Fair Grounds's president.

Jimmy was born on a ranch near Las Cruces, New Mexico, which his father managed for some landholders. He cannot remember his first time on a horse, but he does recall he started riding races at unregulated tracks in the Southwest at age six. That was 1933, and he continued riding at the bush tracks for 13 years until he was licensed for the first time at a recognized track, at Pleasanton, California.

Horsemen there were amazed to see such a finished rider with "the bug," not knowing that he had some 200 wins in the bushes. Every jock is entitled to ride as an apprentice, but the weight allowance did not do him much good because he was already fully grown. Jimmy's weight would deny him many mounts then and in future years.

Jimmy rode for four years at the major California tracks before his wanderlust brought him East in 1950 with his wife, Ronnie, whom he had married in 1948 at Del Mar. He rode for ten years in New York with moderate success. In 1960, he started following the New Orleans-Hot Springs-Kentucky-Chicago circuit, and before his retirement at age 52 in 1978 he rode with some frequency at Delaware Park and Meadowlands.

Never a glamour rider, Jimmy always did his job in a conscientious, workmanlike manner. He never promoted himself well, nor did his agents. Still, good horsemen used him, horsemen such as Ben and Jimmy Jones, "Sunny Jim" Fitzsimmons, Doug Davis, Horatio Luro, Gene Jacobs, and Fred Hooper (for whom he won two stakes on Susan's Girl).

In his 33 years of riding on recognized tracks, Nichols encountered only 32 adverse stewards' rulings, less than one a year. So few misjudgments over such a long period indicates that he was a pretty clean rider, especially because he never refused to ride the most skittish two-year-old or the worst rogue. They were largely responsible for the rulings—and his injuries.

It was primarily Nichols's courage, his propensity for going through a narrow opening or weaving through the field, that caused many of us to talk Jimmy into retiring. He simply would not go around if there was a chance to get through. I told him once: "You've got to change your strategy or hang up your tack. You've been broken up too many times. Now that you're past 50, you'll not heal so quickly."

His riding injuries included broken legs, arms, collarbones, ribs—and three "broken backs." I witnessed one of his worst wrecks. It was in the 1963 Arlington-Washington Futurity. Jimmy was up on Amastar, on whom he had won consecutively the Lafayette, Bashford Manor, and Arch Ward Stakes. Coming out of the inside stall, Jimmy put Amastar on the lead immediately. After leaving the chute for the main track, Amastar crashed through the inner rail, with both rider and horse landing in the infield.

I hastened to the track's emergency room. "Don't worry, Clarky," Jimmy remarked to me, his weather-beaten face twisted with great pain, "I'm not hurt bad, just shook up." The "shook up" turned out to be three broken ribs, a punctured lung, three fractured vertebrae, and two crushed discs. Jimmy never wanted his friends to worry. In another six months, he was back doing the thing he enjoyed most in life—race riding—and with the same style and intensity.

Now, That's a Drastic Wish

Donnie Brumfield, who went from jockey to racing official in the late 1980s at the Kentucky tracks, was a leading rider at Keeneland and Churchill Downs for many years. But, one day, he was administered a thorough tongue-lashing by a novice female trainer immediately after her horse had not run to her expectations.

As she wound down her diatribe, she screamed: "I wish I'd never put you on this filly.... I wish I'd never even heard of you."

"Anything else you wish, ma'am?" Donnie interjected when she briefly paused to take a breath. "Yes," she exclaimed, "I wish I were your widow!"

He Was His Own Man

After a long apprenticeship as a racing official at the Southern California tracks, Hall of Fame jockey Bill Hartack became a state steward at the major Illinois racetracks in the late 1980s.

Bill has always been his "own man" since he started his sensational jockey career back in the early 1950s around the "leaky roof" tracks of West Virginia and Maryland. Utterly lacking in diplomacy, he always spoke and did exactly as he felt, never sparing anyone's feelings. But I do think I saw him mellowing in the latter years of his riding career here in the states.

Chick Lang, the greatest peacemaker in racing, handled his book as Bill gained national recognition. Chick could "cool out" trainers and owners better than any other jocks' agent I have ever known. They parted as the best of friends at the height of Bill's career. Once during his prime, Bill fired

Bill Hartack.

another of his agents and booked his own mounts, something I have never known any other top rider to do. During that period, he still rode a high percentage of winners; he booked himself on good, live mounts that were placed where they belonged.

But Bill had two big things going for him—unquestioned integrity and complete mastery of his profession. I always rode Hartack whenever I could get him. I ignored his sullen manner, his scowling face, and his sharp tongue. I wanted a job done, and could he do it! I know he won for me numerous races I did not deserve by capitalizing on the mistakes of other jocks and riding the hair off my horses.

To list all of the riding accomplishments of William Hartack would take too much space, so I will just offer his record in the best-known race in the world, the Kentucky Derby. Bill won it five times, a record he shares with Arcaro. But Eddie rode in 21 Derbys, second only to Bill Shoemaker, who won with four of his 26 Derby mounts. Hartack had only 12 appearances in the Derby, between 1956 and 1974.

One Way to Stop a Horse

Eddie Delahoussaye.

Eddie Delahoussaye started riding at the age of 11, weighing only 60 pounds, in the unlicensed bush tracks of his native Louisiana. Those courses, laid out in an open field, had no inner or outer rails. At one time in the 1980s, when I was discussing with him this preliminary training, I asked him how he got a horse pulled up after a race. "That was easy," he replied. "You rode until you spotted a barn or a pond, then headed him at it, and he'd pull himself up."

Leave the Meter, Please

Jacinto Vasquez had a remarkably fine career as a reinsman—winning the Kentucky Derby (G1) with Foolish Pleasure and Genuine Risk. When he made his way from Panama to the United States in 1960, he arrived "skeletonrigged," as Phil Chinn would say when his pockets were empty. He complained to Dr. Alex Harthill that he badly needed "wheels," so the friendly veterinarian negotiated the purchase of a battered old junk taxicab for $400. The dealer offered to remove the outdated meter, but Jacinto insisted it remain, principally because it still worked. "That will pay for the gas," Vasquez said.

Always a Hard Worker

Bill Shoemaker won the first race of his career aboard Shafter V. on April 20, 1949, when he was 17. He was not what you would describe as an overnight wonder. Sure, he was a lightweight kid with natural riding ability, but he had been galloping horses on the racetrack for a year and a half, and before that on a horse farm for two years. At the farm, he also mucked stalls, groomed, drove tractors, and even helped with fence repair and hay baling.

Bill Shoemaker.

Unlike most jockeys nowadays, he came up the hard way.

"To be good at anything you have to like it," said Jimmy Jones. "He stayed around so long because he liked being a jockey. I never thought he stayed on for the money or glory, as do so many stars in racing or other sports, and I never heard or read of anyone suggesting it."

Shoe—who launched a new career as a trainer in 1990 and had his first stakes victory within months—was no stranger on the backside in the mornings during his riding days. He was often out in the mornings even when he did not have horses to work. While other jocks left immediately after doing such a chore, he was there because he liked the morning activity. I know of trainers who consulted him on those occasions about decisions they were considering on changes of equipment, spacing of workouts and races, going from dirt to grass, or vice versa.

One leading rider told me: "Bill is one hell of an analyst. By the way he rides, sometimes it seems he knew my riding orders before I was given them. He is a master at getting a contender on the inside of him if he doesn't like it there, or the outside if that be the case. And he does it cleanly and neatly. If a rider is in close quarters and in danger, he'll make room for him if it's possible—even to the extent of sacrificing his own chances in the race."

The guy on top in any business seldom ever wins a popularity contest with his fellow tradesmen—that is a fact of life. His peers, however, elected Bill president of the Jockeys' Guild in 1975, and reelected him to the post each year until his retirement.

'Shoemaker's Law'

I first met Shoe in the summer of 1949, when he was an apprentice. He was then 18, and I was 30. I was in California at the time representing the interests of John D. Hertz, for whom I was doing consulting work. It was through a statement he made then that I judged him to be a very mature thinker. I called his statement "Shoemaker's Law."

Bill Shoemaker and Harry Silbert.

I was in the paddock with T. D. "Pinkie" Grimes, who had trained and sold a horse for me, when we were approached by Harry Silbert, Shoe's agent. A few days earlier, Shoe had finished second in the rich Sunset Handicap aboard Natural. Silbert was insisting that Pinkie persuade Natural's owner to "stake" Shoe 10% of the second money. Pinkie said the owner was adamant. "He doesn't believe an apprentice deserves it— he's lucky to get a mount in a $50,000 stakes," he said.

Silbert was still in a lather when Shoe joined us and said: "Forget it, Harry. If you lose your head, your ass is sure to follow." Thereafter, that bit of barnyard wisdom was "Shoemaker's Law."

Another time that Shoe's "cool" paid off was in 1973 in his dealings with Mary Bradley. He had won seven major stakes for her on *Cougar II, including the Century Handicap (G1) on May 5, 1973, but she had disapproved of his ride in the Hollywood Invitational Handicap (G1) on May 27, in which *Cougar II finished third. She had asked Charlie Whittingham not to use him for the June 24 Hollywood Gold Cup (G1). Shoe picked up the mount on Kennedy Road as a result and won the Gold Cup, with *Cougar II finishing third. Bill was back on *Cougar II in his next start, the Sunset Handicap (G1) on July 23, and won it for an overjoyed Mary Bradley. William Shoemaker has never burned bridges behind him.

A Man of Great Patience

I asked Shoe's wife Cindy if she could name any particular things that set Bill apart from other great riders. "I can think of two," she replied. "The first is patience—the patience to wait in a race for the most opportune time to move, the patience to wait until he was fully recovered from an injury before he returned to riding . . . and then his ability to deal rationally with his 'highs' and 'lows.' He never let himself get carried away with either."

I asked Bill what was his greatest challenge right now as a trainer. "Getting good older horses and well-bred young ones of good conformation," he said. "Most of the owners with them are happy with their present trainers. I'll have to bide my time, develop a clientele of my own. It won't happen overnight."

"How did you make out on your written trainer's test?" I asked.

"Boy, was it tough. I knew they shouldn't and wouldn't give me an easy one because I was William Shoemaker. While on my 'Farewell Tour' I read and reread every book with information on which I thought the questions would be based. I could almost recite the rules of racing backwards! Then I invited over to the house a very smart young trainer, a vet, and a retired steward to fire questions at me. They each thought I was ready. If I hadn't prepped, I'd have flunked. When they told me I scored 100, I couldn't have been prouder if I'd just won the Triple Crown."

He Remained With the Horse

On occasions, Shoe has had to cool out a trainer who strayed out of line. An irate trainer once asked him why he had not gone to the lead at the head of the stretch as instructed. Bill replied: "I didn't want to leave the horse."

His Enemy Was Father Time

As his retirement neared, I asked Bill what had given him the greatest satisfaction in a career that had footprints in six decades. "I'm going to surprise you," he replied. "It is not a particular race I rode or the race-winning and money-earning records I set. It's the fact that today, at age 58, I can ride as well as ever in my life. Can't do it as often, but with enough rest in between, I can do it. Also, that great trainers like Charlie Whittingham acknowledge the fact by using me on their best horses. My only enemy has been Father Time."

Riding greats Bill Shoemaker, Johnny Longden, and Eddie Arcaro.

A Prank on Arcaro

Bill, Eddie Arcaro, and Alex Harthill have been close friends for many, many years. Riding along Brownsboro Road in Louisville with Alex at noon one day en route to the veterinarian's home, Bill pointed to a motel on the left and asked: "Is that the motel you've booked Eddie into?" Arcaro was arriving that night for the Derby.

"Yep," Harthill noted. "He told me to get him away from the Derby crowd. He's tired of being pestered for his autograph, asked who'll win the big race, and all that crap. The manager's a friend of mine, and I've registered him under another name."

"Turn the car around, Doc, and go back there. I want to talk to the manager."

Bill gave the motel keeper a "Franklin," then explained his plan. He and Alex were picking up Eddie at nine that evening at the airport, and about five minutes before they would arrive at the motel, Alex would phone the motel manager from his car to turn on the electric sign out front, which would read: "Welcome Eddie Arcaro," and then he would turn it off when they arrived in the lobby.

"When Alex turned north off the Watterson Expressway and Eddie saw his name emblazoned on the sign," Shoe recalled, "he gave us a worse cursing than he did Vince Nodarse when he shut him off at the start of the 1942 Cowdin Stakes. He called me a 'hundred-pound' idiot and Alex a 'quack' vet. When we explained the prank, he started laughing and telling stories, and we were back having fun like we always did."

Photo Credits

Below is a list of photographers whose photos appear in this book. Following the name of the subject of the photo is the page number on which it appears and the name of the photographer.

CHAPTER 1—Pocket Ruler, 8, J. C. "Skeets" Meadors; John H. Clark, 13, George Featherston.

CHAPTER 2—Colonel Phil T. Chinn, 15, George Featherston; Colonel Jack Chinn, 16, Keeneland Library; Pancho Villa and Matt Winn, 19, Photography, Inc.; Colonel Phil T. Chinn, 24, George Featherston.

CHAPTER 3—James R. Keene, 28, New York Racing Association; Hal Price Headley, 35, J. C. "Skeets" Meadors; Keeneland's entrance post, 42, Chris Maguire; Brownie Leach, 44, Louisville *Courier-Journal*; W. T. Bishop, 47, Chris Maguire.

CHAPTER 4—John Madden, 51, Keeneland-Cook; Preston Madden with Bel Sheba, 53, Chris Maguire; Colonel E. R. Bradley, 54, Bert & Richard Morgan; William Woodward Sr., 61, Bert & Richard Morgan; *Nasrullah, 63, J. C. "Skeets" Meadors; Leslie Combs II, 66, George Featherston; Nashua with William Woodward Jr., 68, Belmont Park.

CHAPTER 5—Herbert M. Woolf, 75, Arlington Park; Bull Lea, 77, *The Thoroughbred Record*; Lawrin with Ben Jones, 78, Keeneland-Cook; Warren Wright Sr., 79, Bert & Richard Morgan; Jimmy Jones with Citation, 80, Bert & Richard Morgan; Ben A. Jones with Whirlaway, 81, Bert & Richard Morgan; Armed, 82, Washington Park; Bewitch, 83, Washington Park; Coaltown, 85, Gulfstream Park.

CHAPTER 6—E. Gay Drake, 88, Murray White; John Stanley, 93, Bert & Richard Morgan; Willie Lee Nutter, 95, Murray White; Joe Palmer, 101, Mack Hughes; Joe Estes, 103, *The Thoroughbred Record*; Clem McCarthy, 104, Keeneland-Morgan; Red Smith, 105, New York *Times*.

CHAPTER 7—August Belmont I, 111, Keeneland-Cook; August Belmont II, 111, New York Racing Association; Upset defeating Man o' War, 112, Keeneland-Cook; Man o' War with Sam Riddle and Louis Feustel, 113, Bert & Richard Morgan; Sam Riddle, 115,

321

Keeneland-Cook; Exterminator, 117, Caufield & Shook; Sun Beau with Willis Sharpe Kilmer, 118, Keeneland-Cook; Exterminator with Peanuts, 120, New York Racing Association; Nellie Morse, 121, Keeneland-Cook; Seabiscuit defeating War Admiral, 122, Keeneland-Cook; Alsab with Al Sabath and Sarge Swenke, 127, Belmont Park; Northern Dancer, 129, Kinetic Corporation; John Henry, 131, Arlington Park.

CHAPTER 8—Abram S. Hewitt, 133, Conway Studios; Sanders D. Bruce, 135, DeWeese painting, from the collection of the National Museum of Racing and Hall of Fame; Robert Aitcheson Alexander, 135, Jean Lacretelle painting, courtesy of James Alexander; Jack Van Berg, 139, Brant Gamma; Ethel Mars, 140, Keeneland-Cook; Gallahadion, 141, Caufield & Shook; Henry H. Knight, 143, Columbus *Dispatch*; Liz Whitney Tippett, 146, Bert & Richard Morgan; John Galbreath, 147, George Featherston; George Blackwell, 151, Chris Maguire; John Finney, 152, Bill Straus; Monty Roberts, 153, Mari Carlos; Eugene Klein, 156, Shigeki Kikkawa; Sunday Silence, 157, Suzie Oldham.

CHAPTER 9—Horatio Luro, 161, Bert & Richard Morgan; Charlie Whittingham, 162, New York Racing Association; Frances and Horatio Luro, 166, Bert & Richard Morgan; Horatio Luro, 167, Laurel Race Course; *Princequillo, 168, Bert & Richard Morgan; "Sunny Jim" Fitzsimmons, 171, J. C. "Skeets" Meadors; Nashua with Al Robertson and "Sunny Jim" Fitzsimmons, 173, Bert & Richard Morgan; Hirsch Jacobs, 174, Bert & Richard Morgan; Ethel D., Hirsch, and Eugene Jacobs and Patrice Jacobs Wolfson, 175, New York Racing Association; Isidor Bieber, 177, New York Racing Association; Stymie, 178, Bert & Richard Morgan; Hail to Reason, 182, Turfotos; Max Hirsch, 183, New York Racing Association; Grey Lag, 184, Keeneland-Cook.

CHAPTER 10—"Whistling Bob" Smith, 191, Keeneland-Cook; Cavalcade, 192, Bert & Richard Morgan; Tex Sutton, 194, George Featherston; Bobby Dotter, 196, Allen Ludwick.

CHAPTER 11—"Father Bill" Daly, 203, Keeneland-Cook; Edward "Snapper" Garrison, 204, Keeneland Library; James Rowe Sr., 205, Keeneland-Cook; Sam Nuckols, 206, Carroll Photo Service; Marshall Cassidy, 210, Beidler-Viken; H. Guy Bedwell, 210, Keeneland-Cook; Francis Dunne, 212, New York Racing

Photo Credits **323**

Association; J. Edgar Hoover, 214, Henry Miller; Red McDaniel, 221, Miller's Photo Service; Chris Evert, 223, Hollywood Park; Willard Proctor, 225, Four Footed Fotos; "Big Ed" Corrigan, 226, Keeneland-Cook.

CHAPTER 12—Dr. Eslie Asbury, 228, George Featherston; Revoked, 230, Washington Park; Determine, 231, J. C. "Skeets" Meadors; John D. Hertz, 233, Blackstone Studios; Reigh Count, 235, Keeneland-Cook; Count Fleet, 236, Caufield & Shook; Louis B. Mayer, 238, Carroll Photo Service; Busher with George Odom and Benjamin Lindheimer, 239, Washington Park; Russell Firestone, 244, Bert & Richard Morgan; Rex Ellsworth, 247, Henry Miller; Swaps, 248, Jim Raftery Turfotos; Jet Pilot, 252, Bert & Richard Morgan; John R. Gaines, 255, Fara Bushnell; Capt. Harry F. Guggenheim, 256, George Featherston; Woody Stephens and Harry Guggenheim, 257, New York Racing Association; Albert Clay, 261, Suzie Oldham.

CHAPTER 13—Doug Davis Jr., 276, George Featherston; Oleg T. Dubassoff, 280, Delaware Park; J. P. "Sammy" Smith, 283, Bert & Richard Morgan; Mike Freeman, 284, Delaware Park; Dr. Alex Harthill, 286, Donna Membrino.

CHAPTER 14—Tod Sloan, 290, Pimlico Race Course; Bobby Dotter, 293, Keeneland-Morgan; George South, 294, Bert & Richard Morgan; Earl Sande, 295, Bert & Richard Morgan; Stagehand with Jack Westrope and Earl Sande, 296, Santa Anita; Ted Atkinson, 297, Bert & Richard Morgan; Tom Fool with Ted Atkinson, 300, Bert & Richard Morgan; Andy LoTurco, 302, Bert & Richard Morgan; Count Turf with Conn McCreary, 305, Caufield & Shook; Eddie Arcaro, 307, Bert & Richard Morgan; Jimmy Nichols, 309, George Featherston; Bill Hartack, 311, George Featherston; Eddie Delahoussaye, 312, Shigeki Kikkawa; Bill Shoemaker, 313, Four Footed Fotos; Bill Shoemaker and Harry Silbert, 314, Four Footed Fotos; Bill Shoemaker, Johnny Longden, and Eddie Arcaro, 316, Santa Anita.

Index

The designation "p" after the page number indicates that a picture of the person or horse can be found on that page.

A

Action—175
Adams, Johnny—167
Admiring—181
Affectionately—181
Aga Khan—63, 249
Aiken Mile training track—39
Airdrie Stud—156
Aladancer—262
Albert, Harry—251
Alexander, A. J.—50, 67
Alexander, Robert A.—135p
*Alibhai—133, 239
Alice Blue Gown—33
Alleged—153
Allez France—181, 182
Allison, Riley—237
Almahmoud—144
Almahurst—143
Alsab—125, 126p, 127p, 224
Alydar—41
Aly Khan, Prince—249
Alysheba—52, 158
Amastar—310
*Ambiorix—61
American Horse Council—13, 261
American Stud Book—134
American Thoroughbred Breeders Association—40
Amiel, Jack—307
Anderson, W. T. "Fatty"—15, 31
Angelic—176
Arbar—282
Arcaro, Eddie—85, 210, 289, 301, 307p, 308, 316p
Arden, Elizabeth—7, 62, 67, 68, 122, 250, 251p, 253, 254
Ardross—259
Arigotal—248
Armageddon—127
Armed—80, 81, 82p, 85
Asbury, Dr. Eslie—5, 14, 87, 133, 227, 228p, 230, 231, 232, 255, 258

Asbury, Dr. Mary Knight—228, 232, 258
Asgard—232
Ashbridge, Bill—297
Asmussen, Cash—269
Assault—21, 183
Astor, Jacob "Jakey"—229
Astor, Lady—229
Atkinson, Martha Shank—298, 299
Atkinson, Ted—4, 297p, 299, 300p
Audley Farm—192
Augustus, Betty (Mrs. John Knight)—144
Auld—260
Azalea—256
*Azucar—89

B

*Bahram—241
Baird, Bobby—274
Baker, George—196
Baker, Smith—98
Baker, Walter—2
Balding, Ivor—133
Ballot—102
Ballyhoo Bey—291
Banquet Bell—147
Barry, Mike—308
Barton Stud—63
Bassett, James E. "Ted"—33, 261
Battle, H. H. "Pete"—45
Beard, Clarkson—42
Beard, Major Louie—35, 38, 39p, 43, 47, 58
Beauclere—183
Beaugay—62, 68, 252
*Beau Pere—238, 248
Bed o' Roses—222
Bedwell, H. Guy—210p
Bee Mac—56
Belair Farm—65
Bell, Ray—248
Belmont, August I—109, 111p, 191

325

Belmont, Major August II—111p, 112, 115
Belmonte, Eddie—163
Bel Sheba—53p
Benson, Martin—282
Berryman, Charlie—30
Best Turn—158
Bewitch—72, 74, 80, 83p, 271
Bieber, Isidor—174, 177p, 178, 179
Bieber, Phil—174
Bieber-Jacobs Stable—175, 176, 177
Bierman, Carroll—126
Big Hurry—58, 179, 180
Billionaire—295
Billy Kelly—223
Bimelech—40, 54, 58, 59p, 141
Bishop, W. H.—139, 273
Bishop, William T.—40, 42, 47p
Black Gold—77
Black Servant—57
Black Toney—55, 57
Blackwell, George—151p
Blanton, Edgar—178
*Blenheim II—133
blind mares—26
Blind Poet—158
Blue Delight—41, 145
Blue Larkspur—40, 54, 57, 58, 145
Blue Swords—181
Boland, Bill—184
Bold Bidder—64, 199p
Bold Commander—64
Bold Lad—222
Bold 'n Determined—151
Bold Ruler—61, 64, 171
Bold Venture—184
Bollero, Joe—303
Bostwick, Pete—39, 246, 281
Boussac, Marcel—82, 145
Boyd-Rochford, Captain Cecil—229
Bradley, Colonel Edward R.—40, 53, 54p, 55, 56, 58, 71, 146, 239, 295
Bradley, Mary—314
Brady, James Cox—192
Breeders and Owners Association—136
Breeders' Sales Company—35
Breedlove, Clarence—277

Breezing Home—307
Bric a Bac—56
Brinson, Ross—217
British Bloodstock Agency—63, 151
Broadbent, Martha—49
Broadtail—263
Brokers Tip—53
Brooklyn—295
Brooks, Steve—83, 302
Broomshot—93
Brown, "Pinky"—74, 80
Brown, Sidney—45
Brown, Tom—9
Brownstown Stud—63
Bruce, Colonel Sanders D.—135p
Brumfield, Don—310
Bryan, A. P.—44
Bryce, Josephine—161, 170
Bryson, G. Ray—21
Bubbley—41
Bubbling Over—56, 57
Buckner, John—110p
Buckpasser—57, 222
*Bull Dog—134
Bull Lea—77p, 81, 145, 178, 195, 298
Bunny Grey—279
Burch, Preston—160, 219, 286, 301
Burd Alane—255
Burgoo King—53, 56
Burton, Hobert—42
Busanda—57
Busher—56, 179, 239p
Businesslike—57
Busy K.—38

C

Cajun—259
Calumet Farm—10, 11, 41, 50, 70, 79, 122, 145, 178, 195, 297
Camden, Senator Johnson N.—3, 25
Cameron, Don—237
Campbell, Jack—6, 85, 198, 200, 266
Campbell, Ralph—108
Candy Dish—250
Candy Spots—247, 250

Can't Wait—94
Cap and Bells—28
Capital Punishment—259
Caracolero—151
Carey, Burgess—189
*Carlaris—15, 31
Carlin, Frank J.—275
Carroll, Del—244
Carroll, Joe—287
Carter, President Jimmy—154
Carter, Walter—298
Case Ace—142
Caslick, Dr. William—241
Cassidy, Marshall—209, 210p, 307
Castle Forbes—222
Castleton Farm—27, 143
Cavalcade—192p
Cecil, Henry—259
Cella, Charles—48
Celt—60
Centre College—17
Certificate of Registration—8
Chalk Talk—4, 285
Champion Liar—179
Chance Shot—33
Chandler, A. B. "Happy"—232
Charles, William E. "Fats"—91p
Chateaugay—147
Chenery, Christopher—242
Chicleight—41, 133
Chinn, Colonel Jack—16p, 23
Chinn, Colonel Phil T.—3, 14-26, 15p, 24p, 28, 30, 51, 87, 88, 104, 122, 144, 154, 183, 191, 226, 228, 248, 275
Chris Evert—89, 223p
Christmas, Yancey—213
Chrysler, Walter P. Jr.—240, 241p
Churchill, Winston—136
Cicada—242
"Cincinnati Rosie"—219
Citation—70, 80p, 83, 286
Claiborne Farm—60
Clang—128, 224
Clark, Charlie—303
Clark, Henry—253
Clark, John H.—2p, 4p, 5p, 13p, 43, 256, 281
Clark, Mrs. F. Ambrose—39
Clark, Robert Sterling—138

Clay, Albert G.—13, 261p
Clay, Catesby—109
Clay, Everett—105
Clay, John—262
Clay, Nancy—60
Clay, Robert—262
Clement, Frank—304
Coaltown—74, 82, 85p, 86
Cocks, W. Burling—284
Coe, William R.—56
Cold Heart—4
Coldstream Farm—143, 177, 178
Coldstream Stud—31
Colin—28
Collins, Martha Layne—49
Combs, Brownell II—66, 260
Combs, Leslie II—12, 65, 66p, 67, 68, 77
Commando—28
Conquistador Cielo—158
Constantine, Eugene—67
Convenience—224
Cordero, Angel Jr.—292
Cornell, Reggie—285
Cornish Prince—64
Corrigan, Edward "Big Ed"—190, 225, 226p
Corum, Bill—104
Cosmah—144, 255
Cosman, Mosey—55
Cosmic Bomb—143
*Cougar II—314
Count Fleet—233, 235, 236p
Count Turf—305p, 307
*Court Martial—61, 134
Cowden, Jimmy—277
Cox's Ridge—158
Crafty Admiral—188
Crevolin, Andy—230
Crimson Satan—150
Cromwell, Tom—30, 34, 40
Crusader—114
Culmone, Joe—301
Cyclotron—148

D

Dade, A. B.—29
Dade Park—29
Daingerfield, Elizabeth—114

Daingerfield, Major Foxhall A.—27, 29
Daingerfield, Keene—28, 209, 302
Daly, Marcus—52
Daly, William C. "Father Bill"—202, 203p
Dancers Countess—279
Danzig—262
Dark Star—256
Darrow, Clarence—185
Davidson, Dr. Art—148
Davis, Doug Jr.—224, 268, 275, 276p, 277, 278, 279, 310
Davis, Helen—275
Davis, Myron—213
Davis, True—166
Davona Dale—158
Decidedly—164, 231
Delahoussaye, Eddie—269, 312p
Delhi—28
Delman, Herman—161
Denemark, Emil—67
Determine—231p
Devereaux, Pat—224
Devereaux, Tom—224
Devine, Chris J.—67
DiMauro, Steve—4
Dinner Date—241
Dinner Party—224
Dixiana Farm—193
Djordjaze, Princess Audrey—161
Dodson, Doug—83
Doherty, Lou—46, 68, 149
Domino—28, 29
Do the Bump—279
Dotter, Bobby—196p, 293p
Double Jay—61, 93
Drake, E. Gay—88p
Drayton, Spencer—303
Drymon, Ira—147
Dubassoff, Oleg—280p
Dunne, Francis—198, 212p, 266
duPont, Allaire—240
Dupuy, Haden—292
Dupuy, Maderis—292
Durazna—145

E

Easy Goer—58, 158
Edgar, Patrick—134
Edwards, Jim—6, 7
Egretta—231, 232
Eleanor C.—31
Ellerslie Stud—60
Ellsworth, Rex—247p
Enslow, Dorothy—66
*Epinard—133
Equifox—299
Equipoise—40
Erickson, Frank—186
Estes, Joe—3, 5, 47, 102, 103p, 133, 255
Eternal—223
Evans, Thomas Mellon—245
Everett, Marje—194
Exterminator—114, 116, 117p, 120p, 143

F

Fair Grounds—54
Fair Play—56, 111
Falkenstein, Paul—199
Fallon, Harold—37
Farish, Will—259
Fasig-Tipton Company—36
Fathers Image—255
Faulconer, J. B.—303
Faultless—79
Feather Time—250
Fellows, John—145, 259
Fencing—295
Fendrick, Jerome—175
Ferraro, Charlie—174
Feustel, Louis—112, 113p
Field, Bryan—115
Fight Inflation—179
Fighting Lady—127
Fighting Step—294p
Fiji—272
Fink, Jule—222
Finnegan, Bill—241
Finney, Humphrey—36, 138, 220, 256
Finney, John—152p
Fireman's Fund Insurance Companies—9
Firestone, Russell Jr.—243, 244p
Firm Policy—41
First Landing—242

Fisher, H. C. "Bud"—121
Fitzgerald, Chris—193
Fitzsimmons, James "Sunny Jim"—
  123, 160, 170-172, 171p, 173p,
  198, 266, 310
Flag Is Up Farm—152
Flagship—259
Fleet Nasrullah—64
Fleming, "Peaches"—163
Float Me—224
Flying Ebony—50, 295
Forego—128
Forest Retreat Farm—228, 229p
Forever Yours—140, 143
*Forli—92
Forrest, Henry—268
Fortune, Helen—276
Forward Pass—41, 145
Free America—83
Freeman, Willard C. "Mike"—281,
  284p
Furlong, "Uncle Johnny"—106

G

Gaillard, Dr. Ernest—158
Gaines, Clarence—254
Gaines, John R.—12, 152,
  199, 248, 254, 255p
Gainesway Farm—254
Galbreath, John—147p, 247
Galbreath, Mrs. John (Dorothy
  Firestone)—244, 247
Galla Colors—181
Gallahadion—59, 141p
Gallant Fox—171, 295
*Gallant Man—188
Gallonia—62
Gallop, Moe—267
Garr, Junior—108
Garrison, Edward "Snapper"—182,
  202, 204p
gate schooling—11
Gaver, John—194, 281, 286, 301,
  306
Gentry, Howard—242
Gentry, Olin—56, 57p, 58,
  144, 145, 147
Gentry, Raymond—102
Gentry, Tom—154, 155

Get Around—251
Gilbert, Johnny—39
Gilpin, Kenneth—36
Glass, Margaret—178
Gluck, Maxwell—68
Globemaster—145
Go Marching—164
Good Goods—192
Good Harvest—192
Good Morning—256
Goose, Roscoe—69
Gordon, Alec—121, 138
Gorgeous—262
Gormley, Charlie—274, 302
Gov. Chandler—187
Graham, Frank—105
Grand Slam—33, 34
Granville—171
Gravitt, Frank "Gum Shoe"—189
Grayson, Admiral Cary—76
Greely, William C.—33
Green River Jockey Club—29
Greene, S. T. Jr.—165
Greentree Stable—194, 300
Greentree Stud—40, 58
*Grey Dawn II—170
Grey Lag—183, 184p
Greyhound—11, 144
Griffin, Jack—103
Grimes, T. D. "Pinky"—22, 314
Grissom, Jim—274
Grissom, Perne L.—272
Grissom, T. Alie—272, 273p, 275
Grover B.—31
Guerin, Eric—308
Guggenheim, Captain Harry F.—5,
  12, 64, 127, 223, 255, 256p, 257p,
  282, 283
Gummo—64
Gun Boat—251
Gun Bow—251

H

Haggin, Louis Lee II—33, 45
Hagyard, Dr. Charles E.—
  110, 158, 178, 272
Hail to Reason—149, 179, 181,
  182p
Halcyon—93

Hall, Crawford—153
Hamburg—52
Hamburg Place—50
Hancock, A. B. "Bull" Jr.—5, 12, 61p, 64, 168, 249, 262
Hancock, A. B. Sr.—36, 40, 60p, 62, 132, 133, 140
Hancock, Arthur III—158
Hancock, Captain Richard J.—60
Hancock, Seth—62
Hanford, Carl—130
Hanford, Ira—184
Hanger, W. Arnold—3, 21, 128, 161, 164, 230, 244, 282
Hanson, John—7
Hardin, Taylor—146
Harrington, Ray—244
Hartack, Bill—129p, 311p
Harthill, Dr. Alex—130, 162, 217, 220, 224, 269, 279. 286-288, 286p, 312, 316
Haste—33
Hasty Road—148
Hay, Timmy—30
Head, Alec—256
Headley, Duval—36, 37p, 38
Headley, Hal Price—30, 33, 35p, 36, 37, 38, 40, 42, 43, 45, 47, 103, 132, 227, 230, 276
Healy, Jim—39
Heartease—298
Heartland—182
Heerman, Vic—217
*Heliopolis—133, 144, 177
Helis, William G.—143
Henbit—151
Henry, Milton—291
Henry T. Adios—150
*Herbager—61
Hernandez, Butsey—72
Hernando Building—3
Hertz, John D.—5, 33, 64, 149, 217, 227, 233-238, 233p, 282, 314
Hervey, John—116
Hewitt, Abram—133, 279
Hialeah—54
Hibbert, Bob—92
High Echelon—181
High Hope Farm—275
High Quest—192

Hildreth, Sam—33, 183
Hill Gail—74, 80, 84
Hill Prince—242, 308
Hindoo—67
Hirsch, Max—15, 21, 128, 160, 164, 176, 182, 183p, 230, 236, 254
Hitchcock, Thomas—220
Hodgins, Jack—298
Hollingsworth, Kent—209, 303
Honest Bread—179
Hook, Sandy—195
Hoop, Jr.—62
Hooper, Fred—62, 310
Hoover, J. Edgar—213, 214p
How—164
Howard, Charles S.—58, 116, 123
Howard, Maxwell—295
Huff, Orville—152
Hug Again—100
Hughes, Hollie—266
Hunt, Sam "Golf Bag"—191
Hurley, Bill—58

I

*Iceberg II—164
Idle Hour Farm—40, 54
Imbesi, Tony—255
Inman, Hoss—277
Inman, Jamie—278
Inman, Virginia—278
In Memoriam—224
Insco—76, 132
Inscoelda—70
Inscolassie—76
Iron Reward—250
Irvana—145
Irwin, C. B. "Cowboy"—123

J

Jackson, President Andrew—154
Jackson, Buck—34
Jackson, Caroline—34
Jacobs, Ethel D.—175p
Jacobs, Eugene—174, 175p, 310
Jacobs, Hirsch D.—149, 173-181, 174p, 175p, 230, 266, 273, 276, 306
Jacobs, Johnny—181

Janss, Eddie—93
Jean Valjean—32
Jeanne Bowdre—33
Jeffords, Walter M.—192
Jerkens, Allen—176, 273, 301
Jerome, Jenny—136
Jersey Act—136
Jet Jewel—253
Jet Pilot—69, 122, 252p, 308
Jet Traffic—245
Jetting Home—216
Jewel's Reward—253
Jo Agnes—302
Jockey Club, the—135
John Henry—130, 131p, 157
Johnson, Albert—56
Johnstone, David—149
Johnstown—171
Jolson, Al—264
Jones, Aaron—224
Jones, B. A. "Ben"—59, 70-86, 71p, 78p, 81p, 169, 222, 271, 286, 298, 306, 310
Jones, Brereton C.—155p, 308
Jones, H. A. "Jimmy"—11, 70-86, 71p, 80p, 126, 217, 271, 286, 306, 310, 313
Jones, Jack G.—89
Jones, Jimmy S.—303
Jones, Joe—176
Jones Stock Farm—75
Jones, Warner L. Jr.—12, 62, 262
Judge, Steve—305

K

Kaenel, Jack—292
Kamar—262
Kane, Al—110
Kane, Ed—111
Kane, Elizabeth—111, 112
Kane, Frances—110
Kane, Kenneth—110
*Kayak II—124
Kearns, Frank—100, 195, 298
Keene, George Hamlet—32, 33
Keene, J. O. "Jack"—30p, 31, 32, 33, 34, 45, 120, 214
Keene, James R.—20, 27, 28p, 29, 30, 55, 60, 291
Keeneland Association—42

Keeneland post—42p
Keeneland Race Course—27, 32, 38, 40, 43, 45
Keenon, Rodman—14
Kefauver, Senator Estes—185, 287
Keith, Joseph P.—107
Kelly, Paul—190
Kelso—128, 130, 240
Kennedy, Joseph P.—54
Kennedy Road—314
Kenney, Charlie—34, 149, 177
Kentucky Association—42
Kercheval, Ralph—36
Kerler, George—2
Kerr, Bert—63
*Khaled—133, 248, 249p
*Kiev—33
Kilmer, Willis Sharpe—116, 118p, 220, 235
Kilmoray—216
Kilroe, Jimmy—266
Kingmaker—64
King Ranch—40, 58, 183
Kirkland, Arnold—302
Kirkpatrick, Arnold—173
Kleberg, Robert J.—58, 184
Klein, Eugene V.—156p
Knight, Dixie—143
Knight, Henry Hudson—95, 142, 143p, 178
Knight, John "Jack"—67
Knight, Mrs. John (Betty Augustus)—144
Knockdown—252
Kramer, Joe—281
Krieger, Fred "Snoz"—213
Kurtsinger, Charlie—124

L

LaBoyteaux, William H.—242
La Bull—217
Lady Broadcast—75
Lady's Secret—156
Lafayette Hotel—38, 106
La France—132
La Guardia, Mayor Fiorello—195
Lang, Charles "Chick"—235, 311
Lasker, Albert—237

*La Troienne—40, 146, 179, 180
La Venganza—120
Lavin, Leonard—224
Lavis, Samuel—225
Lawrence, Laudy—169
Lawrence, Margaret—76
Lawrin—70, 75, 76, 77, 78p
Lazerev, Michael—31
Lazy F. Ranch—280
Leach, Brownie—43, 44p, 102, 103
Lear, King—43
Lee, Dr. John—130
Lehman, Robert—257
LeRoy, Mervyn—240
Lester, Willie—265
Lewis, Major Hector P.—67
Lexington Association track—22
Lexington Rotary Club—44
Lindheimer, Benjamin—239p
Livingston, Jefferson—192
Llangollen Farm—40
Lloyd, Libby (Mrs. Brereton C. Jones)—155
Lockwood, Jim—254
Loftus, Johnny—113
Long, Huey—55
Longden, John—316p
Look, David M.—28
Look Out Jeep—69
Lord Boswell—252
Lord Derby—229
Lorillard, Pierre—52
LoTurco, Andy—302p
Lowe, Ralph—188
Lowenstein, Jake—268
Luciano, Charles—284
Lucille K.—75
Luro, Adolphe—160
Luro, Frances Weinman—165, 166p
Luro, Horatio—124, 129p, 160-170, 161p, 166p, 167p, 286, 306, 310

M

Mabe Cee—4, 265
Mackay-Smith, Alex—242
MacKenzie, Jack—217
Madden, John E.—21, 50, 51p, 52, 118, 183
Madden, Preston—52, 53p
Maher, Danny—202
*Mahmoud—133
Maid of Flight—240
Maine Chance Stable—252
Malacate—151
Manhasset Stable—40
Man o' War—56, 109, 110p, 112, 113p, 114, 115, 116, 149, 181
Maribeau—255
Marlman, W. J. "Rusty"—193, 218
Mars, Ethel V.—140p
Mars, Frank—140
Mars Shield—141
Marsch, John—41, 69, 145
Martin, Royce—222, 305
Martin, "Slow and Easy"—74
Mason, Horatio P.—3
Mayer, Billy—244
Mayer, Louis B.—133, 169, 238p, 248
McCann, Phil—106
McCarthy, Clem—3, 104p
McCarthy, Jerry—231
McCarthy, Sean—153
McCoy, Chase R.—52
McCoy, Jimmy "Goggles"—34
McCoy, Rush—76
McCreary, Conn—304p, 305p
McDaniel, Henry—116
McDaniel, R. H. "Red"—221p
McElligott, Dr. Gerald—63
McGarvey, Bob—140
McGinnis, Dr. J. R.—97
McGrath, Joe—63, 249
McKnight, June—154
McLaughlin, Jimmy—202
McLennan, Charlie—167
McMahon, Dick—10, 95, 100
McMillen, Freeman—80
Meadow Farm—242
Meaux, John—275
Mellwain, Robert W.—65
Menke, Frank—226
Menow—37
Metz, Joe—147, 187p, 231
Meuser, Mike—10
Michell, Bert—237
Middleground—184, 308
Midkiff, Dan—132, 238

Milam, J. Cal—116
Milky Way Farm—140, 143
Miller, Don—271
Miller, Eddie—43
Miller, Mack—281, 287
Mioland—141
*Miss Grillo—164, 169
Miss Merriment—39, 282
Miss Weesie—296
Miss Zibby—244
Mitchell, Dick—302
Modesty—190
Molter, Willie—273
Money Broker—273
Moody, Hunter—53
Mooers, Clifford—137, 138p, 148, 296
Moore, Edward S.—58, 181
Moreland, Bob—76
Morgan, Swifty—213
Mori, Gene—144, 255
Morning Lark—145
Morris, Green B.—223
Morrow, Governor Edwin P.—30
Mosier, Thomas—225
Mourar, Ike—253
Mr. Busher—56
Mr. Smith—32
Mulholland, Bert—266
Munford, Dr. Morrison—226
Murphy, Joe—292
Musical Jack—297
Myrtle Charm—69
Myrtlewood—39, 224, 295

N

Nail—145
Nashua—64, 67, 68p, 171, 172, 173p
Naskra—259
*Nasrullah—61, 63p, 133, 249
Natalma—128, 144
Native Dancer—222, 256
Natural—314
Nautigal—166
Navanod—75
Nearco—282
Nearctic—129
Nellie Flag—122

Nellie Morse—120, 121p
Neloy, Eddie—171, 251
Ness, William "Red"—4, 265, 285
Nevada Stock Farm—40
Never Bend—64
Newman, Bob—232
Next Move—222
Nichols, Jimmy—162, 269, 309p
Nicholson, Nick—262
Nijinsky II—61
Nile Lily—256
No Fiddling—179
No Strings—145
Nodarse, Venancio "Vince"—307
Norris, Jimmy—191
Northern Dancer—128, 129p, 144, 163, 164, 262, 263
*North Star III—57
North Wales Stud—241
No Strings—145
Nose Candy—179
Nothirdchance—179, 181
Nuckols, Charlie—62, 69, 207, 208p
Nuckols, Sam—206p
Nursery Stud—109
Nutter, Willie Lee—94, 95p

O

Oak Cliff Thoroughbreds, Ltd.—158
Oaklawn Park—42, 48
Occupation—307
O'Conner, Winnie—202, 291
Odom, George—239p
Oglebay, Crispin—5
Oil Royalty—255
Oilomacy—179
Old Hickory—14
Old Rockport—148
Old Rosebud—50
Olden—259
Olden Thoughts—263
Olden Times—247, 260, 263
Olin, John—255
*Olympic Zenith—143
Omaha—171
One for All—164
O'Neill, Paddy—114

Oots, Howard—193
Open Mind—157
Osmand—33
Our John Wm.—178
Our Mims—41

P

Palestinian—178
Palmer, Joe—3, 47, 101p, 200, 209, 308
Parke, Burley—69
Parke, Ivan—269
Parke, Monte—217, 250
Parnassus—284
Parrish, James W.—207
Partee, W. Cal—4
Partridge, John—73
Paul Jones—50
Payson, Mrs. Charles—40, 58
Peace of Mind—169
Peak, Judge Bart—48
Peanuts—120
Pelleteri, Tony—168, 240
Pennant—55
Pensive—306
Perlstein, Isaac—264, 265p, 267
Permane, Bobby—171
Personality—180p, 181
Pessin, Dr. Arnold G.—199
Peter Pan—28
Phalanx—308
*Pharamond II—132, 134
Phipps, John S.—284
Phipps, Ogden—40, 58, 180
Phipps, Ogden Mills "Dinny"—58
Piatt, Tom Carr—40, 132
Pincay, Laffit—289
Pipette—242
*Piping Rock—242
Pirogue—259
Pittsburgh—259
Pocket Ruler—7, 8p
Pogo Lotti—285
Pompey—56
Pool, Earl—294
Pool, Willie—294
Poole, George—266
Poole, Scotty—216
Post, Fred—39

Pot o' Luck—169, 243
Potter, Gordon—275
Preeminent—38
Prestridge, Bill—237
Price, Charles F.—19
Price, Judge Charles—90
Price, Ray—147
Priceless Gem—181
Prime, William A.—55
Primonetta—147
Prince John—233
*Princequillo—60, 61, 161, 164, 168p
Princess Turia—41, 145
Proctor, Willard—225p
Promised Land—178
Prove It—247, 250
Psychic Bid—192
*Pujante—169

Q

Queen Empress—222
Quiz Song—5, 6p, 265

R

Raceland—30
Raines, Buddy—195
Raise a Native—64
Raja Baba—64
Ramirez—151
Randolph, Ollie—302
Real Delight—41, 145
Reaping Reward—142
Red Ransom—288
Reed, Dr. William O.—242
Regoli, Federico—283
Reigh Count—234, 235p
Reineman, Helen—143
Reineman, Howard—143
Relaxing—58
Renick, Joe—309
Renick, Sammy—309
Restless Wind—165
Reuben, Allie—148
Revoked—46, 229, 230p
Reynolds, Billy—286
*Rico Monte—46, 164, 169
Riddle, Samuel D.—37, 41, 56, 112,

113p, 115p, 144, 149, 298
Riley—190
Ring, Gus—23
Rippey—143
*Rise 'n Shine—147
Risen Star—309
Risky Miss—75
Riva Ridge—242
Riverman—256
Roberts, Monty—152, 153p
Roberts, Pat—152
Robertson, Al—172, 173p
Robertson, Alf—142
Robertson, Corbin—151
Rodegap, John—22
Rolapp, R. Richards—262
Roman—141, 256
Roman Line—273
Roman Soldier—183
Rosen, Carl—224
Rosenthal, Jack—277
Round Table—61
Roussel, Louie III—309
Rowe, James "Jimmy" Sr.—33, 204, 205p
*Royal Charger—133
Royal Ermine—263
Royal Harmony—224
Royal Note—188
Royal Raiment—39
Rubin, Sam—131
Runyon, Damon—71, 176, 295
Rutchick, Sol—307
Ryan, Barry—281
Ryan, John—161

S

Sabath, Al—125, 127p
Sabiston, Jim—8
Sager, Colonel Floyd—64
Salaminia—41
Salmen, Peter W.—150
Salsbury, Henry—175
Sande, Earl—33, 269, 295p, 296p
Sangster, Robert—154
Saratoga yearling sale—35, 36
Sarazen—21, 183
Saxon Stable—237
Sceneshifter—296

Schiff, John W.—39, 280
Schwartz, Morton—184
Scott, Harrie B.—114
Seabiscuit—116, 122p, 125p
Searching—179, 180
Seattle Slew—158
Sechrest, Randy—199p
Secretariat—242
Self, Max—138
Sellers, John—274
Selznick, Myron—94
Seth—75
Shaffer, Charlie—31
Shafter V.—313
Sham—260
Shea, Ty—86
Shehan, Tom—78
Sherman, Harold—272
shipping—11
Shoemaker, Bill—217, 289, 290, 313-317, 313p, 314p, 316p
*Shoerullah—273
Shuvee—285
Sickle's Image—6, 265
Silbert, Harry—314p
Simpson, Bill—216
Silver Cord—248
Sinclair, Harry—183
Sir Archy—135
Sir Barton—50, 114, 210
*Sir Gallahad III—133, 134, 181
Sir Gaylord—61
Sir Ivor—61
*Skin Tonic—162
Sky Larking—142
Slew o' Gold—262
Sloan, Tod—182, 289, 290p
Sloane, Isabel Dodge—138, 192, 243
Smith, Dewey—275
Smith, J. P. "Sammy"—193, 266, 282, 283p, 309
Smith, "Lyin" Harry—267, 268p, 270
Smith, Red—105p
Smith, Robert A. "Whistling Bob"—191p
Smith, "Silent Tom"—122, 253
Snowden, Harold "Bubba" Jr.—131
Sofarsogood—255

Sotto Voce—4
South, George—294p, 295
Spectacular Bid—158
Spencer, Harry—291
Special Agent—192
Spendthrift—28, 67
Spendthrift Farm—66
Springside Farm—93
Stagehand—295, 296p
Stanley, John W.—92, 93p
Star Pilot—68
Stearns, Howard "Squeaky"—204
Stephens, Woody—222, 256, 257p, 305
Stevens, Herb—97
Stewart, Danny—75, 204
*St. Germans—181
Stimulus—306
Stir Up—306
Stone, Elizabeth Asbury—258
Stone, James H.—216, 227, 257, 258p
Stoner Creek Stud—149
Straight Deal—180
Strang, Stephen—207
Stymie—176, 178p, 230, 306
Sulley, Slim—307
Summer Tan—244
Summit—132
Sun Again—178
Sun Beau—118p
*Sun Briar—116
Sunday Silence—157p, 158, 287
Susan's Girl—310
Sutton, Tex—194p
Sutton, Walsh—111
Swaps—247, 248p, 250
Sweeney, Brian—173
Sweep—56
Swenke, Sarge—127p
Swigert, Daniel—66
Swinebroad, George—136p, 138
Swoon's Son—89

T

Taft, President William Howard—232
*Talon—164, 167, 169
Tank's Prospect—156
Taral, Fred—182
Tatham, Tom—158
Tax Reform Act of 1969—12
Taylor, E. P.—128, 129p, 144, 163, 238
T. Bird—275
Teddy's Comet—143
Tellahward—245
Temulac—298
Tenerani—282
Tenney, Mesh—247
Tenny—192
Terrang—247
Terrell, Danny—224
Terry, George—21
Tesio, Federico—177, 279
The Blood-Horse—40
*The Sultan—256
The Thoroughbred Record—29, 34
Theroux, Ralph—176
Thomas, Joe—101, 237
Thomas, Major Barak G.—29
Thompson, H. J. "Derby Dick"—71
Thoroughbred Breeders of Kentucky—12, 262
Thoroughbred Club of America—36, 40, 246
Thoroughbred Racing Associations—187
Thoroughbred Racing Protective Bureau—7, 187, 303
Three Chimneys Farm—262
Thumbs Up—240
Tige O'Myheart—79
Tiger—142
Time Clock—192
Time to Khal—250
Tippett, Elizabeth Whitney—146p, 161, 164
Tolson, Clyde—214p
Tom Fool—300p
Top Flight—40
Track Medal—250
Traffic Judge—137, 148
Tranter, Jim—36
Trapp, Juliette Combs—66, 69
Trinchera—75
Trotter, Tommy—266
Trovato, Joe—131
Troye, Edward—192

Turner, Lana—164
*Turn-to—256
T. V. Lark—52
Twenty Grand—40
Twilight Tear—81, 145
Two Bit Hug—217
Two Bob—41
Typecast—224

U

Unerring—75, 76, 79
U Time—248
United States Trotting Association—9
Upset—112p

V

Valdina Farm—143
Valdina Orphan—143
Valentine, Charles R.—96, 98, 99, 100
Van Berg, Jack—139p, 286
Van Berg, Marion—273, 286
Van Clief, Danny—144
Vance, Dick—279
Vanderbilt, Alfred G.—222
Vanderbilt, Mrs. W. K. III—21
Vasquez, Jacinto—312
Villa, Pancho—19p, 73
Vosburgh, Walter S.—102

W

Wachs, Fred B.—2, 189
Waggoner, W. T.—116
Waldron, Roy—141
Wall, Nick—38
Wallace, Tony—30, 31
Waltz—128
War Admiral—37, 56, 114, 115, 123
War Dog—256
War Minstrel—38
War Relic—114, 298
Warner, Major Albert—179
Waterford Park—6
Watkins, Griffin R.—76
Westerly Stud—224
Westrope, Jackie—292, 296p
Westrope, John—83

Wexler, Morris "Mushie"—287
What a Pleasure—64
Wheeler, Fish—25
Wheeler, Tex—125
Whirlaway—11, 70, 74, 80, 81p, 126, 224, 299
White Cross—41
White, T. F.—296
Whiteley, Frank—286
Whitlow, John—219
Whitney, Cornelius Vanderbilt—40, 144, 265
Whitney, Harry Payne—40, 55
Whitney, John Hay "Jock"—38, 40, 58, 296
Whitney, Liz—See Elizabeth Whitney Tippett
Whitney, Mrs. Payne—40
Whitney, William C.—291
Whittingham, Charlie—158, 161, 162p, 165, 167, 176, 286, 287, 315
Widener, George—266
Widener, Joseph E.—33, 54, 295
Wildenstein, Daniel—181
Wilder, Honeychile—164
Wilkerson, Walter "Fats"—89
Wilson, Bradley—29
Wilson, Lex—89
Windfields Farm—102, 128
Windy Miss—225
Winfrey, Bill—222
Wingfield, George—40
Winn, Colonel Matt—19p, 40, 205, 206, 226
Winning Colors—156
Winning Count—4, 265
With Regards—22
Wolfson, Mrs. Patrice Jacobs—175p
Wolken, Joe—303
Woodward, William Sr.—60, 61p, 64, 171
Woodward, William Jr.—67, 68p, 171, 172
Woolf, George—124, 126, 301
Woolf, Herbert M.—70, 75p, 76, 79, 132, 222
Woolford Farm—70, 75, 76
Woolworth, Norman—149
Worden, Tom—75

Wright, Dr. William H. "Bud"—
 194, 280
Wright, Vester "Tennessee"—272-
 275, 272p, 286
Wright, Mrs. Warren—95
Wright, Warren—11, 50, 145, 237,
 297
Wright, Warren Sr.—10, 79p, 80,
 81, 122
Wright, William M.—10

Y

Ycaza, Manuel—256, 292
Yellow Cab Company—234
Yoshida, Zenya—158
Young Bob—259
Young, Colonel Milton T.—139,
 271
Young, Tom B.—41, 139, 158, 271
Your Host—240, 308

Z

Zev—50, 223, 295
Zombrewer—10